AMERICAN
CULTURAL HISTORY
1607-1829

A FACSIMILE REPRODUCTION OF

LECTURES ON AMERICAN LITERATURE
(1829)

BY

SAMUEL LORENZO KNAPP

WITH AN INTRODUCTION AND INDEX
BY

RICHARD BEALE DAVIS

AND

BEN HARRIS McCLARY

University of Tennessee

GAINESVILLE, FLORIDA

SCHOLARS' FACSIMILES & REPRINTS

1961

SCHOLARS' FACSIMILES & REPRINTS
118 N.W. 26TH STREET
GAINESVILLE, FLORIDA, U.S.A.
HARRY R. WARFEL, GENERAL EDITOR

L.C. CATALOG CARD NUMBER: 60-6514

MANUFACTURED IN THE U.S.A.
LETTERPRESS BY J. N. ANZEL, INC.
PHOTOLITHOGRAPHY BY EDWARDS BROTHERS
BINDING BY UNIVERSAL-DIXIE BINDERY

INTRODUCTION

The *National Journal* of Washington, D. C., in its issue of December 19, 1828, carried a long proposal for publishing by subscription "A Course of Lectures on American Literature, with remarks on some passages of American History." The statement of aim and content was signed by the author of the proposed volume, Samuel Lorenzo Knapp. To disprove the frequent assertion of both foreigners and natives that there was no such thing as American literature, he planned a survey of the American past, including the days before the Revolution. Since he could not cover everything, he would attempt to give "a panoramic effect to the whole." For convenience's sake the two centuries of settlement would be divided into periods of fifty years each and the fourth part would include a history of the events which have made us a nation. Most particularly the book would be "the history of the American mind, and the productions of that mind." It would satisfy the strong desire of the rising generation "to know all things concerning their forefathers." Finally, the author hoped that after parents had read and criticized the book's contents, a revised edition might appear which would be suitable as a school textbook. In such terms was announced the first attempt at a full-length study of American cultural progress.

This modestly ambitious proposal was made by a lawyer and newspaper editor who was best known to his contemporaries as a public speaker. Born in Newburyport, Massachusetts, in 1783, he had graduated at Phillips Exeter and Dartmouth, studied law under Theophilus Parsons, and for some years from 1809 practiced his profession in his native town. He soon became the leading spread-eagle orator of his region. During 1812-1816 he served as colonel of a local militia regiment. Although it is not clear whether war or oratory kept him from making a success in the legal profession, in 1816 he was thrown into jail for debt. From that time on he wandered from one city to another as free-lance writer, newspaper or magazine editor, and sporadically practitioner of his original profession. From 1824 to 1826 he edited the *Boston Commercial Gazette* and for fourteen months from June 1825 the *Boston Monthly Magazine*. In 1827-1828 he was in Washington, D. C., as editor of the *National Journal*. By the end of 1828 he had removed to New York, where he again assumed the practice of law for a few years. He died in his native Massachusetts in 1838.

Knapp was always in demand as orator or lecturer. His 1810 oration at Newburyport on the Fourth of July is the earliest of the long series of speeches surviving in print. He gave the Phi Beta Kappa address at Dartmouth in 1824, one of the two Boston eulogies on Adams and Jefferson in 1826 (Daniel Webster gave the other), and the Forefathers' Day oration before the New England Society of New York in 1830, the last reprinted in this century. He addressed Masonic bodies, institutes and lyceums of all kinds, and patriotic assemblies.

As he often claimed, the written as well as the spoken word took time he should have devoted to the practice of his profession. A book appearing as early as 1802, when Knapp was a sophomore at Dartmouth, is usually ascribed to him. *The Letters of Shahcoolen, a Hindu Philosopher, Residing in Philadelphia*, a series of commentaries on American life including some feeble discussion of literature, shows little, however, of the qualities of his later writing. Several of his early patriotic speeches were published.[1] In 1818 he brought out, under the pseudonym of Ali Bey, *Extracts from a Journal of Travels in North America, Consisting of an Account of Boston and Its Vicinity*. In 1821 appeared the first of his long series of "lives," *Biographical Sketches of Eminent Lawyers, Statesmen, and Men of Letters*. Shorter studies of Lafayette, DeWitt Clinton, Aaron Burr, Andrew Jackson, and Timothy Dexter, among others, appeared between this time and 1838. Perhaps his most significant longer work after the *Lectures* of 1829 is *Sketches of Public Characters. Drawn from the Living and the Dead* (1830). In this he devotes considerable space to the "living" he deliberately failed to discuss in the *Lectures* of the year before, contemporaries such as Everett, Wirt, and Randolph among the orators; Percival, Bryant, Halleck, Mrs. Sigourney, and Mrs. Hale among the literati; and Dunlap, Vanderlyn (who did Knapp's portrait), Allston, and Weir among the painters.

(1)See bibliography in F. L. Pattee, "A Record of Forgotten Fame: Samuel Lorenzo Knapp," *Dartmouth Alumni Magazine*, XXIX (1936), 9, 72. This is the most extensive bibliography, though it is neither complete nor entirely accurate.

In 1832 appeared Knapp's *Advice on the Pursuits of Literature,*
the first practical textbook in literature, especially English, for
American school children.[2] In the Preface the author states that
he had not contemplated this work when he wrote the *Lectures
on American Literature,* a statement which may partially explain
his failure to bring out the revised *Lectures* in textbook format.
The content of the two books is for the most part, however,
quite different. In 1834 he anticipated Sarah J. Hale and Rufus
Griswold in *Female Biography, Containing Notices of Distinguished Women in Different Nations and Ages.* He was still
writing biographical sketches in 1838.

Knapp also published two volumes of insipid short tales and
a Revolutionary War romance, *Polish Chiefs* (1832). He is said
to have had a hand in *Miriam Coffin* (1834), the anonymous
and rather crude whaling novel to which Melville is indebted[3]
and the authorship of which is usually ascribed to Joseph C.
Hart. His literary fame was sufficient as early as 1826 for him
to have been awarded an LL. D. by a French university. Like
many another contemporary lawyer, he might in a different age
and clime have devoted all his effort to creative and critical
writing instead of attempting to earn a living in a profession for
which he held an affection but to which he was but indifferently
suited.

Such a man was the author of the present work. From what
has been noted above, it should be clear that Knapp was consistently a strong literary nationalist. The very first sentence of
Lecture I and the last of the final Lecture are among those
which afford strong evidence of his feeling. The reader will
observe that in the Dedication he strikes the note he continues
to sound throughout the book. This volume, he modestly states,
is but "the opening argument of junior counsel, in the great
cause instituted to establish the claims of the United States to
that intellectual, literary, and scientific eminence, which we
may say, she deserves to have, and ought to maintain." Then in
his Preface he suggests to school teachers that they inculcate
national pride in their pupils: "No people, who do not love themselves better than all others, can ever be prosperous and great.

(2)Pattee, pp. 7-9. The book went through several editions in Knapp's life-
time.
(3)See the unpublished sketch-review of Knapp by Thomas Brownell
Church, c. 1834, among Dartmouth College Manuscripts. For Melville's
indebtedness, see Perry Miller, *The Raven and the Whale* (New York
1956) pp. 64-67.

A sort of inferiority always hangs about him who unduly reverences another." Seeming to agree with Melville rather than with Poe as to the most efficacious means of producing a great American literature, he urges that his readers "Encourage the game, and the victors will come" (p. 189).

Literature is for Knapp a comprehensive term, embracing the written (and to some extent the spoken) word in many forms. Behind his concept is the usual mixture in his time of neoclassical, romantic-and-aesthetic, and Scottish-common-sense-and-rhetorical theory. But he seems to be considering its origins in what were to become peculiarly American terms when he points out in his Preface the "intimate connexion between thinking and acting, particularly among a free and an energetick people." He observes elsewhere (p. 31) that "A man's business, most assuredly, is with those about him, . . . for literature, in its proper sense, is the transcript of the head and heart of man." Therefore literature may be scientific, theological, historical, as well as belletristic. Its study affords "the best criterion, by which may be judged the principles and powers of a people, as well as their rank in the scale of civilization" (p. 29).

Thus it is clear that Knapp thinks of *literature* in much the same terms as did his contemporary and friend Noah Webster. In the 1828 *American Dictonary of the English Language* the latter defined *literature* as "learning; acquaintance with letters or books. *Literature* comprehends a knowledge of the ancient languages, denominated classical, history, grammar, rhetoric, logic, geography, &c. as well as of the sciences." He adds finally an illustrative use of the word: "A knowledge of the world and good breeding give luster to *literature*.'" All this seems implied or expressed in Knapp's book.

Characteristically the lawyer-orator-author emphasizes political writing. To him *The Federalist* is "foremost among American literary productions, whether we consider the subject, the matter, or style of the work, or its usefulness in explaining the views of those learned statesmen who achieved the second part of our independence" (p. 112). George Washington's addresses are of a high order. "The literature of nations may be seen, in some measure, in the style in which their laws are written, and by their state papers" (p. 113).

And it may be seen too in scientific treatises and in theological and philosophical speculation. For example, though Knapp admits that Jonathan Edwards' metaphysics has been largely discarded for the more recent theories of Reid and Stewart of the

Scottish school, he discusses the Puritan divine in considerable detail, concluding that "few ever equalled the author of the Freedom of the Will in strength and depth" (p. 83). Edwards and his like, he observes, laid the foundations of modern knowledge.

American legend, folklore, and aborigine expression interested him as part of the national mind. The ballad of Lovewell's Fight, the account of Pocahontas and Captain John Smith, the epic of Daniel Boone's career, he saw as facets of the American intellect. Peculiarly American idiom he calls attention to in several instances and points out the importance of philologists and lexicographers like Pickering and Noah Webster. He was greatly impressed by the invention of the Cherokee alphabet by Sequoyah, "the American Cadmus." The American Adam, with his dream of a new and better world, he sees more clearly, however, in the first settlers: "Every thing, in America, was to be begun, and every thing seemed to depend on themselves; with this happy difference, however, between us and those in paradise, for our safety and happiness were to depend upon eating freely of the tree of knowledge, which was forbidden to him who first sprang from the dust of the earth" (p. 37).

Satirists, poets, biographers receive attention. Oratory as one of the strongest emanations of the national mind naturally is considered in great detail, for Knapp knew it stood high in the esteem of his contemporaries. His personal predilection did not have to be considered.

In his consideration of American painters and their work Knapp extends his coverage from the literary to the artistic mind generally. The objective and data-filled discussion of Revolutionary military and naval figures seems less integrated with the earlier materials, though he asserts that it was brought in to round out his study and allow the reader to see "the energy of mind" his countrymen have displayed in heroic action. His passion for monuments as symbols of American and individual and group achievment, evidenced in his discussion of Washington's tomb in comparison with the magnificent funeral edifices of the Old World, is interesting particularly in its actual realization, or materialization, in the later Washington, Lincoln, and Jefferson memorials.

Knapp is at his best stylistically and analytically in such a passage as his summary of the state of the American mind one century after the first settlement (pp. 70-75), a comprehensive survey which bears modest comparison with Henry Adams' famous summary of the condition of the United States in 1800. Though his style here and elsewhere suggests occasionally the spread-eagle oratory for which he was best-known, it is quite subdued as compared with that of his earlier and later biographical sketches and printed orations. Apparently he consciously restrained himself. The part of Lecture IV he did not reprint in the book from an earlier newspaper version, clearly intended for oral presentation, was a soaring and bombastic peroration.

Only a few of the riches of this book have been touched upon. Something should be said of its specific background and of what it does not contain. Knapp had gathered his materials over a period of at least eight years and had during that period presented portions of them orally. For the *National Journal* prospectus mentions that individual lectures had been given at Dartmouth (the Phi Beta Kappa oration of 1824), at the West Point Military Academy, and in Washington, D. C. The *National Journal* for March 22, 1828, contains a lecture on the American origins of the word *caucus,* a detailed disquisition he apparently decided eventually to discard as too inconsequential for his panoramic view. But the very issue of the *National Journal* (December 19, 1828) containing the prospectus also includes most of Lecture IV and Note A of the Appendix (pp. 70-75, 289-291) without any difference in phraseology. Information he had accumulated from a variety of interesting sources for his 1821 *Biographical Sketches* he put to good use in his *Lectures.* Presumably he obtained his data on Joseph Dennie from Royall Tyler,[4] for example, and used it in both books. From private and public libraries he gathered much of his information.

Since his book was intended to present the American mind of the past to explain the American mind of the present and future, Knapp made little mention of living orators, poets, or painters. The reader will notice, however, that Irving receives a graceful tribute but that Cooper is ignored. Franklin receives relatively little space, and other Colonial writers such as Anne Bradstreet and Benjamin Tompson do not appear. Though Charles Brockden Brown is mentioned favorably, fiction generally is almost ignored. Knapp probably regarded it as lightly, despite the fact that he had written some, as did Jefferson or the New England clergy. Drama likewise is almost entirely neglected, probably because too little was known about it. Dunlap's first history of

(4)Letter of March 1, — 1820 — from J. T. Buckingham to Royall Tyler, in Manuscript Collections, Boston Public Library.

the American theater was still three years off. One should remember that Edward Taylor's poems, William Byrd's prose, and
William Bradford's *History* lay hidden in manuscript in Knapp's
day. Quite clearly he knew little of Southern writing, as he
himself acknowledges. At least two-thirds of his space is devoted to New England for the simple reasons that he already
knew it best and could find out most about it. But unlike the
later Barrett Wendell he seems to have thought of literature as
the product of an inclusive *national* mind.

In his "Proposals" for the *Lectures* Knapp asserted that the
work would be in one volume, octavo, containing four or five
hundred pages, on good paper, in boards, at $2.50 a copy to
subscribers. Though he adhered to the octavo format, the attractive volume bound in rose-colored cloth he brought out in
1829 had been drastically reduced in number of pages.

Knapp's publisher, Elam Bliss, was certainly sympathetic to
what the author was trying to do. Dr. Bliss, a Broadway publisher and bookseller, had sponsored several magazines and at
least two different annuals or gift-books. He was the friend and
patron of the New York poets Robert C. Sands and William Cullen
Bryant, and in 1825 he had brought out volumes of verse by
J. G. C. Brainard and James A. Hillhouse. In 1831 Bliss published
the famous "second edition" of Edgar Poe's *Poems,* including
Poe's first prose criticism, the well-known "Letter to Mr. ——,"
the addressee generally believed to have been Bliss himself. And
in 1832 he brought out the second collected edition of Bryant's
verse. Though not a major figure in the publishing world, Bliss
thus had a significant part in the promotion of American literary
genius.

Contemporary estimates of Knapp's *Lectures* differ widely.
One unpublished review by Thomas Brownell Church of Rhode
Island comments that Knapp had written "a *History of American
Literature,* which might, without sarcasm, be ranked among the
'Histories of Events which have never happened.' "5 A writer in
the Charleston, S. C., *Southern Review* (VII, 1831, 431-459)
employed it as a point of departure for an analysis of reasons
why Southerners do not contribute to a national literature, with
the implication that such a literature did not yet exist. The
whole review is as supercilious as Church's. But a friendly critic
in *The New-England Magazine* (I, 1831, 426) predicted that
"Long after the writings of the puny revilers of American genius
shall have supplied the grocer with wrappings, and the book

(5) – about 1834? – , Dartmouth College Manuscripts.

worm with food, the 'Lectures on American Literature' will have a place in the library of the American scholar, and minister to the instruction of youth." Though this prophecy was hardly literally fulfilled, Knapp's book deserves a place in the library of the American scholar. One who reads it will have a clearer understanding of the foreground of Emerson's Man Thinking.

RICHARD BEALE DAVIS
BEN HARRIS MCCLARY

The University of Tennessee
August, 1959

LECTURES

ON

AMERICAN LITERATURE,

WITH

REMARKS ON SOME PASSAGES

OF

AMERICAN HISTORY.

BY SAMUEL L. KNAPP.

" Nor rough, nor barren, are the winding ways
Of hoar antiquity, but strewn with flowers."

" Peace to the just man's memory,—let it grow
Greener with years, and blossom through the flight
Of ages ; let the mimick canvass show
His calm benevolent features ; let the light
Stream on his deeds of love, that shunn'd the sight
Of all but heaven, and in the book of fame
The glorious record of his virtues write,
And hold it up to men, and bid them claim
A palm like his, and catch from him the hallowed flame."

Bryant.

———————" The freshness of that past shall still
Sacred to memory's holiest musings be."

Sands.

STEREOTYPED BY JAMES CONNER.

PUBLISHED BY ELAM BLISS,
No. 107 Broadway.

1829.

Ludwig & Tolefree, Printers.

TO

WILLIAM AUSTIN SEELY, ESQ.

COUNSELLOR AT LAW.

My dear Sir,

To you, who, amid the cares of a full practice in a laborious and an all-absorbing profession, surrounded by clients and engaged in courts, have found time, by system and method, to collect the literature and science of every age, and to taste, most liberally, of their sweets, I respectfully dedicate this humble volume, in which I have attempted to describe, by a few faint sketches, and with some passing remarks, the literature, the talents, and the character of our ancestors. I have taken this liberty, because I was confident that you would favour the effort, whatever might be its success with the publick, as you understood the motives which called it forth; and for another reason, which is, that I know you are among the number who are anxious that we, as a people, should speak freely and justly of ourselves, and honestly strive to place our claims to national distinction on the broad basis of well authenticated historical facts; this would soon be accomplished, if all our able and enlightened scholars would come forward to aid the few who are toiling in the cause: yet, with a few exceptions, our pride has rather led us to make spirited retorts, than laborious researches, for an answer to those who question our literary and scientifick character:—The work I now present you and the publick, is only offered as the opening argument of junior counsel, in the great cause instituted to establish the claims of the United States to that intellectual, literary, and scientifick eminence, which we say, she deserves to have, and ought to maintain; and in this, I have attempted but little more than to state my points, name my authorities, and then have left the whole field for those abler advocates who may follow me. To be thought by you, and those like you, capable of judging, that I have opened the cause fairly, and made out a respectable brief to hand to others, will be sufficient praise for me; I will not, in these few lines, devoted to personal respect and friendship, enter far into my plans, or fully express my hopes; but leaving these for time to develop, or for your private ear, I will only add my sincere prayers that your life may be long, and continued as happy and prosperous as it has heretofore been, and that your generous exertions, of every kind, may at all times meet with a just measure of gratitude, the richest recompense a high mind can receive.

Your obliged friend and humble servant,

SAMUEL L. KNAPP.

November, 1829.

PREFACE.

Every book that is ushered into the world, is a mental experiment of the writer, to ascertain the taste, and to obtain the judgement of the community; and the author can only be certain of one thing, and that is, of his intentions in his publication. Of my intentions, I can only say, as, perhaps, I have a dozen times said in the course of my work, they were to exhibit to the rising generation something of the history of the thoughts and intellectual labours of our forefathers, as well as of their deeds. There is, however, an intimate connexion between thinking and acting, particularly among a free and an energetick people. My plan, when I commenced my researches, was an extensive one, and I gathered copious materials to carry it into effect. For several years past, I have had access to libraries rich in American literature; but when I sat down to work up the mass I had collected, the thought suggested itself to my mind, that no adequate compensation could ever be reasonably expected for my pains; and then the consciousness that I was in some measure trespassing upon my professional pursuits, went far to quench my zeal, and to chase away my visions of literary reputation. Still, I could not be persuaded to relinquish altogether my design, and I therefore set about abridging my outlines, dispensing with many of my remarks, and giving up numerous elaborate finishings I had promised myself to make in the course of my work. And another thought struck me most forcibly, that a heavy publication would not be readily within the reach of all classes of youth in our country; but that a single volume of common size, in a cheap edition, might find its way into some of our schools, and be of service in giving our children a wish to pursue the subject of our literary history, as they advanced in years and in knowledge. The instructors of our youth, when true to their trust, form a class in the community that I hold in respect and esteem, and they will pardon me for making a few remarks to them. Your calling is high, I had almost said holy. To your intelligence, patience, good temper, purity of life, and soundness of principles, parents look for the forming of healthy, vigorous minds, in their children. If you cannot create talents, you can do something better; you can guide the fiery, and wake up the dull; correct the mischievous, and encourage the timid. The temple of knowledge is committed to your care; the priesthood is a sacred one. Every inscription on the walls should be kept bright, that the dimmest eye may see, and the slowest comprehension may read and be taught to understand. Your task is great, and every member of the community, who is able to give you any assistance, should come to your aid in the great business of instruction. In this way much has been done:—much, however, remains to be done. The elements of learning have been simplified, and thousands of children have been beguiled along the pathway of knowledge, who never could have been driven onward. Geography has been made easy and fascinating, and the elements of natural philosophy very pleasant; and what was once difficult and harsh to young minds in many studies, has become attractive. History, both sacred and profane, has assumed new charms as it has been prepared for the school-room; I speak of the history of other countries, not of our own. We have very good histories—narrative, political, military, and constitutional; but I know none, as yet, that can be called literary—meaning by the term, a history of our literature, and of our literary men; and probably it will be a long time before we shall have such an one as we ought to have. Our Sismondis, D'Israelis, are yet to arise. You will struggle in vain to make American history well understood by your pupils, unless biographical sketches, anecdotes, and literary selections, are mingled with the mass of general facts. The heart must be affected, and the imagination seized, to make lasting impressions upon the memory.

One word to your pride:—you are aware that it has been said by foreigners, and often repeated, that there was no such thing as American literature; that it would be in vain for any one to seek for proofs of taste, mind, or information, worth possessing, in our early records; and some of our citizens, who have never examined these matters, have rested so quietly after these declarations, or so faintly denied them, that the bold asserters of these libels have gained confidence in tauntingly repeating them. The great epoch in our history —the revolution of 1775—seemed sufficient, alone, to many of the present generation, to give us, as a people, all the celebrity and rank, among the nations of the earth, we ought to aspire to, without taking the trouble to go back to the previous ages of heroick virtue and gigantick labours. Many of the present generation are willing to think that our ancestors were a pious and persevering race of men, who really did possess some strength of character, but, without further reflection, they are ready to allow that a few pages are "ample room and verge enough" to trace their character and their history together. I have ventured to think differently, and also to flatter myself, that, at the present day, it would not be a thankless task to attempt to delineate some of the prominent features of our ancestors in justification of my opinion. This errour can only be eradicated by your assistance, and that by instilling into the minds of our children, in your every-day lessons, correct information upon these subjects;—and while you lead your pupils through the paths of miscellaneous and classical literature—and, at the present day, even the humblest education partakes of much that is of a classical nature—be it your duty, also, to make them acquainted with the minutest portions of their country's history. No people, who do not love themselves better than all others, can ever be prosperous and great. A sort of inferiority always hangs about him who unduly reverences another. If "*know thyself*," be a sound maxim for individual consideration, "*think well of thyself*," should be a national one. Patriotism and greatness begin at the maternal bosom, are seen in the nursery and primary school, and quicken into life in every advancing stage of knowledge. Guardians of a nation's morals, framers of intellectual greatness, show to your charge, in proper lights, the varied talent of your country, in every age of her history; and inscribe her glories of mind, and heart, and deed, as with a sun-beam, upon their memories.

New-York, Nov. 1829.

CONTENTS.

A 2

LECTURE I.

" Words are things."

Mirabeau.

ALMOST every thing the people of the United States now possess, has grown from their own sagacity, industry, and perseverance. The little patrimony they had, has been multiplied ten thousand fold; for they have been blessed by a kind providence, in their basket and their store. Their institutions, if in some measure copied from those of other countries, have been modelled to suit the genius and habits of the people, and have been changed and enlarged to correspond with the growth of the nation. Their language alone is theirs by inheritance. They received it from their progenitors, and have kept it unpolluted and unchanged. It has been in different ages here a little modified, as in England, to be a more explicit medium of thought; and taste and euphony have, at times, made some exertions to drop one class of words and assume another; but they have destroyed none; and as occasion requires, those left out of fashionable use, for a season, have, after a while, been called up and restored to their former places in good company.

From the extension of commercial relations, and from the numerous conquests of the mother country, it would have been natural to expect that her language would have, in process of time, become somewhat a different one from that of her colonies in this country: but our commerce has followed hers so closely, and we have had so entirely the benefit of her mass of literature as soon as it was known to her own people, that the first adoption of a foreign word, or the slightest change in the use of one of her old stock, has been noticed on this side of the Atlantic; and we have wisely followed the public taste of the mother country, nor vainly thought that it would be wisdom to struggle for an independency in letters, as far as they regarded the use of our vernacular. This language was our birthright as Englishmen, and its preservation in its purity clearly shows how much we value it. The language that is addressed to the ear alone is soon changed or lost, but that which is addressed to the eye as well as the ear, is long preserved by a twofold impression upon the mind. The sight is more faithful than the ear, and preserves her knowledge longer; both are necessary to keep a

2

language alive in its purity. The study of the language of a people is one of the best methods of sounding the depths of their knowledge, and of measuring their advancement in arts and arms, and of ascertaining the nature of their general pursuits and habits; and perhaps it may not be going too far to say, that geographical positions may be known by the examination of a nation's vocabulary alone. The soft air of Italy and France has given, in a long succession of years, by natural causes, operating upon body and mind, and which might be easily analyzed, if we would take the pains to do it, a delicious sweetness to the tones of the human voice, a melody to the sounds of words, and a harmony in the construction of sentences, which the inhabitants of the colder regions of the north can never know among themselves. This principle is tested by the still softer and more musical notes of the West India creoles. With them almost every word is vitiated in pronunciation, and reduced to a sort of infantile imbecility, yet it is most musical. The English language has not with us, generally speaking, been deeply studied by those who use it, either for the common business of life, or by those who make it a vehicle of matters of high import in enlightening and directing their countrymen.

English etymology has not, until lately, been a part of a classical education. Our scholars have been content to take, and use, words as they found them, sanctioned by good writers, without much enquiry into their derivations, or primitive significations; nor is it my object to go further in these remarks than to show, that we have kept a constant watch over our mother tongue, and if we have sometimes, after great English models, laboured to sink many of the good old words of our language, and to supply their places by those formed from the Latin and Greek languages, yet that we were ready, from taste and judgement, to go back again, and take those discarded, home-bred words of strong meaning and peculiar fitness, whenever the established writers have led the way. Several modern scholars have shewn us the force, precision, and even beauty of our old English, and we hail this returning to the homestead as an unfailing sign of good judgement. I have thrown together a few observations upon our language, to induce the English scholar to examine the treasures he is in possession of, and to shew the reader, that if our fathers' style does not always suit the present taste, yet that they were masters of their vernacular, as well as deeply read in the learned languages. And this I shall do, not by pointing out particular passages, but by calling the attention of the reader to the general tenour of their works.

It is the belief of the learned, that all languages had a common origin; for there are words in all the languages they have examined, which bear relationship to each other. Sometimes the resemblance or kindred features are near and strong, at other times remote, but containing such resemblances as cannot be mistaken: and until some other account more satisfactory is given by some retrospective seer, I am willing to take the account given by Moses of the confusion of tongues, as sufficiently true to answer the phenomenon which has no other solution. I am a lover of words, for I do not believe that there can be much reasoning of a moral nature without them; and sure I am, that no man ever despised the science of words who understood it to any considerable extent. It may be true, that the mind may be so much engaged in the pursuit of various tongues as to enfeeble its force in more severe studies; but the literary world exhibits so few instances of this nature, that we need not fear the effects of a pretty liberal attention to the languages; certainly, a careful examination of our mother tongue will not be thought improper by those who object to the attention paid to the learned languages. The origin, the history, the sweetness, the copiousness, the force and majesty, and importance of the English language, are subjects worthy the attention of the English scholar in our country at the present day, when so many facilities are offered him for the study of it; such facilities, that one may learn more in six months upon this branch of knowledge now, than he could have done in ten years if he had commenced half a century ago.

The language of the ancient Britons, from the time they were first known to the Romans, was Teutonic, or Scythian. The people were rude and fierce, and their language had the same cast of character, as far as we know any thing about it. When Julius Cæsar first landed on the shores of Albion, the people exhibited the highest traits of courage, and met the polished armour of the skilful Roman soldiers in dauntless nakedness. From this time, which was before the christian era, until the conquest of Alaric, more than four centuries these rude people were instructed by the Romans in arts and arms. The sons of the native kings and chiefs were taught the philosophical and polished language of their conquerors; and this instruction was pursued and enforced as a mean of bringing the Britons to a state of quietude and obedience. During this time many of the Roman words had found their way into the native language, or at least those formed from the Latin were in use. This is more evident in the names of places, perhaps, than in any other class of words. Those Britons who acquired the Latin, wrote the native language in the Roman character, as we now write the Indian dialects, or different languages of the several tribes, in the same character at this day. If the Scythians brought letters with them from Asia, they had probably been lost; or if any relic of them was left, they were only used as a sort of a Cabala, as the fragments of some languages were by the Druids—such as by them were called Runic characters, something out of which to make a charm.

About the middle of the fifth century (449) the Saxons made their first invasion, of any importance, of the island of Britain. Soon after Hengist gained a foothold, Horsa followed; and Cedric and other invaders took the same course; but it was not until after a lapse of many years, that the island was conquered; and then, not from the strength of the invaders, but from the dissensions of the natives. This conquest was, however, a blessing; for, notwithstanding the Saxons were barbarous as well as the Britons, yet they were a fearless, roaming race of men, who had made more improvements in the arts of life than the ancient Britons, and their habits of thinking were more enlarged and approximated nearer to civilized life than those of the natives of the island. The laws and institutions of the Saxons were of a higher mental character than those of most other nations then about them on the continent; but the Saxons recieved a vast accession to their stock of knowledge, by the introduction of christianity into the island in 596, through the auspices of Pope Gregory, a most benevolent representative of Saint Peter. This father of the Church sent the learned and pious Augustin on a mission to Britain, who after many struggles succeeded in diffusing the doctrines of the gospel amongst them, and in inspiring a taste for learning, and the arts of industry, and social life. If not before, certainly at this time, the Saxon tongue became a written one, and was soon expanded and improved by the attentive study of it among those ecclesiastics, who wished to diffuse through it the knowledge of the scriptures, until then a sealed book to the Saxons, and then only partially opened.

About ninety years after the introduction of christianity into the island of Britain, Alfred the wise, of Northumbria, began his reign. He had passed his youthful days, when by the death of his brother he came to the throne of his father. His early years, and many of his riper ones, had been spent in study in the cloisters of Ireland, whose ecclesiastics were then more learned than all those on the continent, if we except a few in Italy. The Irish institutions of learning at this period furnished professors for those of France, Germany, and many other places. Alfred, when in possession of power, did not forget his taste for letters, but gathered about him as many learned men as he could obtain. Adhelm, a West-Saxon poet, wrote for his instruction and amusement "Flowers of the Bible," probably a sort of dramatic paraphrase on some portions of scripture; and also treated his royal patron with some touches of the philosophy of that age. The wise king bent his mind to improving his people and their language at the same time, and shone conspicuously as a firm supporter of Christianity and letters. He was the first to give a relish for these pursuits to his nobles, who had hitherto found no delight but in war, or the chase.

The improvement of the Saxon tongue was, generally speaking, constantly going on, although the knowledge of the Latin had greatly declined from the time of Alfred the wise, until the time of Alfred the great, who was born in eight hundred and forty-nine. This monarch fills a wider space in the Saxon history than all his predecessors, or those Saxon kings who came after him, although his grandson was quite as great a man as himself. Alfred was a pet child of his father, who took his son to Rome when he was quite young, and brought him to France also, when Athelwelph, the father, married Judith the daughter of Charles of France; but in all these journeyings the young Alfred had never learned to read. It was his fond step-dame who set about this task, and succeeded in laying the foundation of making him one of the greatest scholars of that age. He sought learned and good men from Ireland, France, and in his own country, and commencing with the poetry of his own language, which had taken fast hold of his affections when young, he pursued it, until he had exhausted all the ballads and legends which were written in Saxon, and then set about enlarging the narrow limits of the Saxon muses, by compositions of his own, which, in fact, surpassed in excellence all the poetry of his country, as he did his predecessors in civilization and knowledge. He was not content with this, but learned the Latin, Greek, and Hebrew, and assisted to bring the rich treasures of these repositories of wisdom into his own market for the supply of his own people, and the refinement of his own court. He was not a mere book-worm neither, for he was as ready to fight as to write; to enforce laws as to make them. He was no pedant, but the great instructor of his people, anticipating ages by the power of his understanding, and the reach of his genius. Institutions of learning arose under his fostering care. The son of Alfred, Edward the elder, was not a whit behind his father in his attention to the encouragement of learning, but having a regular education, there was no necessity for such efforts as were made by his father; and the infant institutions his father established were in a flourishing state. The son of Edward, Athelstan, was a more powerful Prince than his father or grandfather had been, and extended his intercourse with the world more widely. The monastic institutions which Alfred founded, Athelstan endowed, and gave them books collected from every country to which he had access. Whatever we may think of monasteries now, they were the protectors and preservers of all the learning of antiquity, and the faithful

B

trustees of all the knowledge committed to their care when they
were first created. Through several changes of fortune, now
smiled upon by Edward the Confessor, and then neglected by his
ambitious successors, learning flourished or declined in the more
public institutions until the invasion of William the conqueror; but
it was not often that contemplation was disturbed in the convent's
shades, for ages after his accession to the throne of England. Here,
indeed,

" The little, fat, round oily man of God,"

laughed, slept, or idled life away; " but these deep solitudes and
awful cells," contained men of true piety and profound learning;
and to whose industry and wisdom we are now indebted for much
of our present advancement in knowledge.

In 1066 William defeated Harold, and became king of England.
His triumph was so complete that a sudden revolution was made in
the information, taste, and pursuits of men in that island. It was
natural for him to think his Norman language, uncouth and rough
as it was, greatly superior to that of the Saxon, which he did not
understand. The Church and convent, and perhaps court records,
which had been kept in Latin, were now in many instances ordered
to be in Norman. The ballad makers who flocked round the conqueror sung his praises in the Norman measure and language, and
even the deeds of former kings, whose praises had for ages been
echoed in pure Saxon, were now sung in the rude rhymes of the
minstrels of the Conqueror: and such was the influence of the new
order of things, that in the course of half a century the pure Saxon
was no longer to be found in England; and a new language, the beginning of what is now our vernacular tongue, grew up there.
Ellis, a learned writer on these subjects, says this was effected in the
course of forty years after the conquest, and that this change in the
language of England was completely brought about in this time;
but we should be nearer the truth, I imagine, if we should allow
nearly a century for this transformation. The language was indeed
changed to the eye and the ear; but still a great proportion of all its
elements remained, and will forever remain, a strong proof that in
all the permanent improvements in civilization and knowledge, the
Saxons were greatly in advance of their conquerors. This change
assisted the advancement of knowledge; for language when advanced
towards perfection, is the most labour-saving machine that ever ingenuity attempted to invent. The scanty words found in a primitive language are inadequate to the conveyance of refined or extended thought. By these simple elements the nice shades of difference
in thought could be no more than indicated, not fully conveyed by

the words written; therefore much was left to the imagination of readers, which was supplied when language was only spoken, by the looks, gestures, and accents of the speaker; hence arose the superiority, in the early times, of eloquence over written compositions. The oral communication was then a better method of conveying ideas than the record, however fully exemplified by the scanty language then in use, without taking into consideration the charm there has always been in a well toned and well regulated voice.

As language improved and expanded, the noun and the verb, the first elements of language, were found insufficient, with all their declinations and inflections, to convey thought accurately and forcibly. The connecting links, the qualifying terms, the affirmations and negations, with the prefixes and affixes, to increase, change, or qualify the power of the words, were sought for, and obtained; sometimes by a happy hit, which by frequent repetitions in time became usage, and usage law; or by the elaborate reasonings of the scholar upon the doctrines of analogies, or the principles of an easy composition or arrangement of sentences. Sometimes the understanding directed in this work of composition and structure of language, but oftener the ear; and when at times the wise and the learned reasoned and laid down the rule, the great mass of the people changed it for euphony sake, and the learned at length came into the same use; for custom is the despot over language. In the laws of language, as well as in those of national policy, the people, after all, are the revising tribunals; not by their sudden impulses, but by the sober reflection of years; and even their own opinions are revised by their own experience.

The English literature received its share of the acquisitions of learning made by the crusaders; and the language of course was greatly benefitted by the taste which these heroic adventurers awakened and cherished. In these epochs of delicacy and refinement, many of the coarse words were disused, and those better chosen and more appropriate became fashionable. The English language gained much from the days of Chaucer to those of Spencer; and more by the taste of Shakspeare than by any other person.

It is a matter of some singularity that so little of the Saxon language is known by our scholars, when on a strict examination we find that our poets and prose writers have used so many words derived from the Saxon. In Shakspeare, taking out the proper names, eight words out of nine are found to be of Saxon origin, as exemplified by several quotations taken promiscuously from the works of the great dramatist. Milton, tried by the same rule, would give the proportion of six out of seven. Johnson's works, as he coined Latin words and used them freely, about five sixths are Saxon.

In our translation of the Bible, and the writings of Addison and Goldsmith, and other writers of simplicity and purity, the proportion of words of Saxon origin is still greater than in Shakspeare or Milton. Our own declaration of Independence, and many other American productions, are written in the style which contains a great proportion of these words of pure Saxon origin. I will give a few specimens of the use of Saxon words among our best writers; fair samples of their style, and the use of good old English. The Saxon words are in italics.

But no! the freshness of that past shall still
Sacred to memory's holiest musings be;
When through the ideal fields of song at will,
He roved, and gather'd chaplets wild with thee;
When, reckless of the world, alone and free,
Like two proud barks, we kept our careless way,
That sail by moonlight o'er the tranquil sea;
Their white apparel and their streamers gay,
Bright gleaming o'er the main, beneath the ghostly ray.

SANDS.

While thus the shepherds watch'd the host of night,
O'er heaven's blue concave flash'd a sudden light,
The unrolling glory spread its folds divine,
O'er the green hills and vales of Palestine;
And lo! descending angels hovering there,
Stretch'd their loose wings, and in the purple air
Hung o'er the sleepless guardians of the fold:
When that high anthem clear, and strong and bold,
On wavy paths of trembling ether ran:
Glory to God—Benevolence to man—
Peace to the world.———

PIERPONT.

A good man's piety and virtue are not distinct possessions; they are himself, and all the glory which belongs to them belongs to himself. What is religion? not a foreign inhabitant, not something alien to our nature, which comes and takes up its abode in the soul. It is the soul itself, lifting itself up to its maker. What is virtue? It is the soul listening to, and revering and obeying, a law, which belongs to its very essence, the law of duty. We sometimes smile when we hear men decrying human nature, and in the same breathing exalting religion to the skies, as if religion were anything more than human nature, acting in obedience to its chief law.

CHANNING.

There are some poems in the Saxon language which strongly show the rude, bold, and superstitious character of the Saxons before christianity was introduced among them, or had generally spread through the island. The Volupsa, the sybil of the Saxons was called Vola, is a poem given in an English translation by Turner, from whom, with Bede, Ellis, Tooke, and Campbell, I have derived much of my information on this subject of Saxon literature. It is a rhapsody on the creation according to the Saxon notions of it, and the first lessons of wisdom given to man from his maker. The successive generations, with their history, are introduced, but only as a landscape is seen by the transitory flashes of the lightning amid the darkness of the storm. The Welch wrote at the same time with abruptness, and threw the fire and fanaticism of their Druids into the form of some wild and magic strain.

True poetry cannot exist until there is a considerable degree of mental cultivation in the bard who makes it. Men must think and feel, and reason, too, from cause to effect, before any delicacies of poetry can be developed; but the strong ebullitions of genius raving to soar to the regions of light and futurity, are scattered through the early ages of poetry; and time gives these productions, perhaps, an interest beyond their real merits.

The English language is now so enriched from the sources I have mentioned, and other sources more recondite, and also from some more recently made contributions to our stock of words, particularly in terms of banking, trade, and revenue, that it may challenge any other language to show more words of clear and definite significations, than we have legitimatized and secured. The terms of art are every day increasing, as well as those of the sciences, and are constantly added for common use to our vocabulary. These, in general, have been formed by new applications of old words to the subjects, or by new compounds made to convey the idea of the use of the invention.

The English language is full of strength. There are no feeble words in it, such as are often made by an effeminate people; but every part of the fabric is of good old materials or approved new ones. There is no thought, or shade of a thought, that the English language is not capable of conveying to the mind, if used by a judicious, learned, and spirited writer. In the use of language to gain, or to defend a point, much depends upon the skill and judgement of the writer or speaker. The vocabulary of angels would fail to propagate a thought, *that would wake the genius or mend the heart,* in the mouth of dulness or apathy. The soul of the writer or speaker must breathe into his language the breath of life. The earthly particles must be melted, as it were, into the ethereal, to give a composition the spirit of intelligence and genius. The following extracts, the first from Shakspeare, and the other from Milton, show the natural strength of the English language; for without any apparent effort, or artful selection, the words admirably convey the elevated thoughts which the authors had in their minds, and intended to put into an imperishable form.

> " The cloud-capt towers, the gorgeous palaces,
> The solemn temples, the great globe itself;
> Yea, all which it inherit, shall dissolve,
> And, like the baseless fabric of a vision,
> Leave not a wreck behind."———
>
> Tempest, Act iv. Scene 4.

> " For in those days might only shall be admir'd,
> And valour an heroic virtue call'd:
> To overcome in battle, and subdue
> Nations, and bring home spoils with infinite
> Manslaughter, shall be held the highest pitch
> Of human glory, and for glory done
> Of triumph, to be styl'd great conquerors,
> Patrons of mankind, gods, and sons of gods,
> Destroyers rightlier call'd, and plagues of men.
> Thus fame shall be achieved, renown on earth,
> And what most merits fame in silence hid."
>
> Milton, b. xi.

The beauty of the English language is conspicuous in English poetry and prose. It is fortunate for our vernacular, that the language of poetry does not differ, except in a few words, and perhaps in no one, from our prose; for in such a formation of language, all that is gained in the interchange with other nations in prose, is transferred to verse; and all that is created or refined by verse, is given over to prose, after due trial and final judgement of its use or beauty, at the tribunal of public criticism. The following poem is a specimen of that powerful, graceful beauty, which excites admiration for its elegance, and respect for its strength. It seems to come upon us with that calmness and divinity which it describes in the god of wisdom and taste, in his easy victory over the Python. What a beautiful fable this is; it was made to show how easily refinement and wisdom can overcome and destroy that monster of the literary world—a depraved taste.

PRIZE POEM.—THE BELVIDERE APOLLO. (1812.)

> " HEARD ye the arrow hurtle in the sky?
> Heard ye the dragon monster's deathful cry?
> In settled majesty of fierce disdain,
> Proud of his might, yet scornful of the slain,

The heavenly archer stands—no human birth,
No perishable denizen of earth!
Youth blooms immortal in his beardless face,
A god in strength, with more than god-like grace!
All, all divine—no struggling muscle glows,
Through heaving vein no mantling life-blood flows;
But animate with deity alone,
In deathless glory lives the breathing stone.

Bright-kindling with a conqueror's stern delight,
His keen eye tracks the arrow's fateful flight;
Burns his indignant cheek with vengeful fire,
And his lip quivers with insulting ire;
Firm-fix'd his tread, yet light, as when on high
He walks the impalpable and pathless sky;
The rich luxuriance of his hair, confined
In graceful ringlets, wantons on the wind,
That lifts in sport his mantles, drooping fold,
Proud to display that form of faultless mould.

Mighty Ephesian! with an eagle's flight
Thy proud soul mounted through the fields of light,
Viewed the bright conclave of Heaven's blest abode,
And the cold marble leapt to life a God:
Contagious awe through breathless myriads ran,
And nations bowed before the work of man.
For mild he seemed as in Elysian bowers,
Wasting in careless ease the joyous hours;
Haughty, as bards have sung, with princely sway,
Curbing the fierce flame-breathing steeds of day;
Beauteous as vision seen in dreamy sleep
By holy maid on Delphis' haunted steep;
'Mid the dim twilight of the laurel grove,
Too fair to worship, too divine to love.

Yet on that form, in wild delirious trance,
With more than reverence gazed the maid of France;
Day after day the love-sick dreamer stood
With him alone, nor thought it solitude;
To cherish grief, her task, her dearest care,
Her one fond hope—to perish—or despair.
Oft as the shining light her sight beguiled,
Blushing she shrunk, and thought the marble smiled:
Oft, breathless listening, heard, or seemed to hear,
A voice of musick melt upon the ear.
Slowly she wan'd, and cold and senseless grown,
Closed her dim eyes, herself benumbed to stone.
Yet love in death a sickly strength supplied,
Once more she gaz'd, then feebly smiled, and died.

Sweetness in a language is intimately connected with beauty. Beauty may perhaps consist without sweetness; no one of taste would say that the head of Apollo was a sweet one, while all agree that the face of Venus is full of sweetness; yet, if beauty can exist without sweetness, the converse of the proposition would be offensive to taste and truth, to say that sweetness was ever found without beauty. The impression which beauty leaves on the mind, is pleasure and admiration; but when sweetness is superadded, the charm is increased to love and rapture. I have mentioned images that strike the senses to illustrate those which are sentimental. This is the only method by which anything ethereal can be made to affect us forcibly, as we are now constituted. The dirge in Cymbeline is full of sweetness and delicacy.

To fair Fidele's grassy tomb
  Soft maids and village hinds shall bring
Each opening sweet of earliest bloom,
  And rifle all the breathing spring.

No wailing ghost shall dare appear
  To vex with shrieks this quiet grove;
But shepherd lads assemble here,
  And melting virgins own their love.

No wither'd witch shall here be seen;
  No goblins lead their nightly crew;
The female fays shall haunt the green,
  And dress thy grave with pearly dew!

The redbreast oft, at evening hours,
  Shall kindly lend his little aid,
With hoary moss, and gathered flowers,
  To deck the ground where thou art laid.

When howling winds, and beating rain,
  In tempests shake thy sylvan cell;
Or 'midst the chase, on every plain,
  The tender thought on thee shall dwell;

Each lonely scene shall thee restore;
  For thee the tear be duly shed;
Belov'd, till life can charm no more,
  And mourn'd, till Pity's self be dead.

The *wailing ghost*—The *withered witch*—The *howling winds*, which at first thought seem to injure the loveliness of the picture, form a fine contrast to all the tender and affectionate images which are grouped around the grassy death-bed of beauty and innocence.   The effect of this contrast is forcibly seen in the picture of Prospero, with the snow of many winters upon his reverend head, in the majesty of science and wisdom, and paternal affection, contrasted with the manly youth of Ferdinand, and the delicacy and beauty of Miranda; and the finishing of the whole is the ugliness and ferocity of Sycorax, with her fiend-begotten Caliban, " *whose nature nurture would not stick to.*"

The majesty of the English language is conspicuous in the following extract from Akenside :

> "Look then abroad through nature, to the range
> Of planets, suns, and adamantine spheres,
> Wheeling unshaken through the void immense ;
> And speak, O man ! does this capacious scene
> With half that kindling majesty dilate
> Thy strong conception, as when Brutus rose
> Refulgent from the stroke of Cæsar's fate
> Amid the crowd of patriots ; and his arm
> Aloft extending, like eternal Jove
> When guilt brings down the thunder, call'd aloud
> On Tully's name, and shook his crimson steel,
> And bade the father of his country hail !
> For lo ! the tyrant prostrate on the dust,
> And Rome again is free !"

The majesty of the language is conspicuous also in the following extract :

> ————" Different minds
> Incline to different objects : one pursues
> The vast alone, the wonderful, the wild ;
> Another sighs for harmony, and grace,
> And gentlest beauty.   Hence, when lightning fires
> The arch of Heaven, and thunders rock the ground ;
> When furious whirlwinds rend the howling air,
> And ocean, groaning from his lowest bed,
> Heaves his tempestuous billows to the sky ;
> Amid the mighty uproar, while below
> The nations tremble, Shakspeare looks abroad
> From some high clift superiour, and enjoys
> The elemental war."

Our own writers furnish numerous specimens of the various characteristicks of our language.   The chaste, pure, classical language, abounds in Hamilton's prose, and Pierpont's poetry.   For sweetness, we might look into Ames's prose, and Percival's verse.   Robert

Treat Paine would furnish us with many sentences in strong language in both prose and verse. Dr. Dwight's works might also be mentioned as exhibiting a fine selection of words and phrases in communicating his thoughts. In fact, an hundred others among our distinguished writers might be quoted for our purpose, to illustrate the statement that our language is copious, beautiful, sweet, majestick, strong, &c. but we will not at this time make these selections, for my audience will probably call to mind as many instances of all these traits in our writers as I can.

I need not dwell long on the importance of cultivating our mother tongue, nor attempt to prove that it is becoming the triumphant language of mankind, when it is known to all that it is now spoken by fifty millions of enlightened freemen, who keep it purer than that used by any other nation; and that the number now, to whom it is vernacular, is five fold greater than it was fifty years ago. As Empire travels westward with us, or over the immense plains of Asia with the English, this language, whose origin and history, copiousness, strength, beauty, sweetness, and importance, have occupied our past hour, will carry with it the blessings of sound political and civil institutions, the blessings of letters and science, of virtue and religion.

As our knowledge, political, civil, and religious, expands, and our arts and sciences are extended; and the comforts and luxuries of life increase, words of new significations and aptitude are required to correspond with these advancements. A poverty of words is a sure sign of poverty of thought in those who have had advantages to acquire a full supply. Not only the progress of knowledge, but the fashion of society, has its influence over language; and the time has arrived with us, that no word found in the Dictionary of our language, that is used with good taste and judgement, can be considered as too learned for the social circle. It is neither affectation or pedantry to use any proper word in a proper sense. There is too much information diffused through the country, to require that condescension in the learned which strives to be simple and plain in language in order to accommodate their hearers. The vocabulary of the scholar and the publick man, should be opulent and well arranged. There should be no " res angusta domi" for an excuse for himself to the publick, in his possession of the stores of his mother tongue. These are at his command. Every one's warehouse of words should not only be well stocked, but well sorted and arranged. Every synonyme should be classed for a ready selection. Still, however, I would not be understood to commend that fastidiousness that wakes to contentious valour in defence of an accent, or strives to martyrdom for the support of the pronunciation of a doubtful word or syllable. No, it is only that free, generous, tasteful use of language, and common regard to a just pronunciation, which shows at once the affluence of thought, and the extent and polish of education, that I contend for. The conversation of the social circle is now often rich and elegant, and even when it relaxes to trifling and playfulness. Formerly there was a great difference between the written language and that used in common conversation; but these styles are more nearly assimilated, and both have been benefitted by it. Eloquence has ceased to strut in corsets, and to walk only in measured steps, and to speak only in affected cadences. Nature has assumed her sway, and ease and grace prevail. Strong, beautiful, neat, or delicate thoughts, should each have their appropriate dress. The lion's skin to throw loosely over the shoulders, the succinct tunick, the flowing toga, the sweeping robe, and the transparent veil, should all be ready for clothing for the thoughts of the conversationist, the poet, or the orator, as these thoughts arise in their imaginations, and are marshalled forth by their understandings for use and display. Words should be the vassals of the mind, at the call of memory; but at the same time should always, like the slaves of the faithful, be used only in rigid justness or innocent familiarity. Once profaned by an indecent use, their character is degraded for ever. Necessity is the only true mother of invention in words as well as in other things: wit and profligacy often degrade appropriate words by indelicate uses. The languages of polished nations alone are liable to this misuse or profanation. It is in the reckless plenitude of genius that words are violated. A host of instances might be adduced to illustrate my meaning, if it were proper; but this is rather a subject for the eye, or the imagination, than the ear. One or two instances might be named.

The voluptuaries of the Court of Louis 14th, called a pure white wine Virginis Lac; this was going far enough in all conscience; but another of a purple colour they called Lachryma Christi. To compare the ruddy, joyous drops of the wine-cup, to the tears of a suffering Saviour, was reaching the confines of blasphemy.

Every pure and elegant mind ought to rejoice in a freedom from the fetters of bigotry and the prudery of excessive puritanism; but should never relax his vigils over the chastity of his mother tongue. Morals depend more on taste, than philosophy, in her analysis of the human character, is willing to allow; but no one will deny the correctness of the maxim of inspiration, that *"words fitly spoken are like apples of gold in pictures of silver."*

For many centuries, in the early history of letters, much time and labour were spent by the industrious and learned, in making Lexicons, Dictionaries, Vocabularies, and Glossaries, or works on languages, by whatever name the compilers chose to give them. They were of great use to the world in abbreviating the labour of acquiring a knowledge of languages. Perhaps, the first that was put into a good form for the learner, and for the learned, was an Arabick dictionary, made in the ninth century by the scholars of Grand Cairo; a great number of Greek lexicons and glossaries had preceded it. This work, it is said by their historians, was done by order of the Caliph, who was supervisor as well as patron of the work. At the same time, or soon afterwards, an encyclopedia was compiled at the same place, which was unquestionably the first of its kind ever known. Other nations soon followed the example; and the scholar who had pecuniary means might have had the advantages of such a work, but he alone; and it was not until after the art of printing was discovered, about the middle of the fifteenth century, that dictionaries came into common use. From this there was a succession of dictionaries in our vernacular, down to Johnson, who set himself to the task with a gigantick genius and a philosophick mind; well read in all the best works in the English language, with a memory stored with apt examples and felicitous illustrations, and patient of the most tedious details, he wrought day and night, for many years, in the deep mines of etymology; and by analysis and comparison, solved a thousand difficulties that his predecessors were unable to grapple with. He had neither the aid of the learned or the opulent, and when his work was finished, all who would have been pleased with his fame, or benefitted by the emoluments of his pains, had gone to another world. Such are the common results of the exertions of genius and learning.

On this great work all the lexicographers of our vernacular have modelled their labours; and if, at times, they have added or amended, still their ground-work was Johnson. The learned Todd has, with great labour, brought Johnson down to the present day, with many additions and some corrections.

It has fallen to the lot of an American scholar to follow those great men with success. To this mighty task he has devoted the flower of his youth, the prime of his manhood, and the wisdom of the gray head: Webster's dictionary has been the labour of nearly half a century. Like the Arabick dictionary, it might well be called "AN OCEAN OF WORDS," for it contains about seventy thousand. About eight thousand of these, in common use, are derived from the Greek, Latin, and French languages, and about forty thousand from the Saxon and other kindred languages of the North, with the Hebrew, Arabick, Sanscrit, Coptick, &c. of eastern origin. The remainder of the words in his dictionary have been taken from the arts, sciences, and the learned professions, which are, in general, compounds from various languages. Although grown old, and exhausted by long and intense application, by frequent disappointments, by coarse criticisms, petty insults, and heavy expenditures, yet he does not, like his great prototype, dismiss his work *with frigid indifference;* he is not solitary or disconsolate, for he has those about him, and connected with him, who can rejoice in his fame, and share his rewards.

The study of the languages is not, in this country, confined to a few learned men, but is pursued by many of those engaged in professional business. Duponceau and Pickering, have written learnedly on this subject; and many others, who have as yet offered nothing to the public, have with them, in addition to their labours in the common track, made considerable progress in the examination of the languages spoken by the various tribes of North American Indians; and it is now fully believed, that this examination will afford the only clue to their origin, if ever one is found.

The Indians themselves are becoming philologists and grammarians, and exciting the wonder of the world, by the invention of letters. The invention of the Cherokee alphabet, has excited the astonishment of the philosopher in this country and in Europe; but as I have not as yet seen any satisfactory account of the progress and history of this greatest effort of genius of the present day, I will state what I know of it, from the lips of the inventor himself.

In the winter of 1828, a delegation of the Cherokees visited the city of Washington, in order to make a treaty with the United States, and among them was See-quah-yah, the inventor of the Cherokee alphabet. His English name was George Guess; he was a half-blood; but had never, from his own account, spoken a single word of English up to the time of his invention, nor since. Prompted by my own curiosity, and urged by several literary friends, I applied to See-quah-yah, through the medium of two interpreters, one a half-blood, Capt. Rogers, and the other a full-blood chief, whose assumed English name was John Maw, to relate to me, as minutely as possible, the mental operations and all the facts in his discovery. He cheerfully complied with my request, and gave very deliberate and satisfactory answers to every question; and was at the same time careful to know from the interpreters if I distinctly understood his answers. No stoick could have been more grave in his demeanour than was See-quah-yah; he pondered, according to the Indian custom, for a considerable time after each question was put, before he made his reply, and often took a whiff of his calumet, while reflecting on an answer. The details of the examination are too long for the closing paragraph of this lecture; but the substance of it was this: That he, See-quah-yah, was now about sixty-five

years old, but could not precisely say ; that in early life he was gay
and talkative ; and although he never attempted to speak in Council
but once, yet was often, from the strength of his memory, his easy
colloquial powers, and ready command of his vernacular, story-teller
of the convivial party. His reputation for talents of every kind gave
him some distinction when he was quite young, so long ago as St.
Clair's defeat. In this campaign, or some one that soon followed it,
a letter was found on the person of a prisoner, which was wrongly
read by him to the Indians. In some of their deliberations on this
subject, the question arose among them, whether this mysterious
power of *the talking leaf*, was the gift of the Great Spirit to the
white man, or a discovery of the white man himself? Most of his
companions were of the former opinion, while he as strenuously
maintained the latter. This frequently became a subject of contemplation with him afterwards, as well as many other things which
he knew, or had heard, that the white man could do ; but he never
sat down seriously to reflect on the subject, until a swelling on his
knee confined him to his cabin, and which at length made him a
cripple for life, by shortening the diseased leg. Deprived of the excitements of war, and the pleasures of the chase, in the long nights
of his confinement, his mind was again directed to the mystery of
the power of *speaking by letters.* The very name of which, of
course, was not to be found in his language. From the cries of wild
beasts, from the talents of the mocking-bird, from the voices of his
children and his companions, he knew that feelings and passions
were conveyed by different sounds, from one intelligent being to
another. The thought struck him to try to ascertain all the sounds
in the Cherokee language. His own ear was not remarkably discriminating, and he called to his aid the more acute ears of his wife
and children. He found great assistance from them. When he
thought that he had distinguished all the different sounds in their
language, he attempted to use pictorial signs, images of birds and
beasts, to convey these sounds to others, or to mark them in his own
mind. He soon dropped this method, as difficult or impossible, and
tried arbitrary signs, without any regard to appearances, except
such as might assist him in recollecting them, and distinguishing
them from each other. At first, these signs were very numerous ; and
when he got so far as to think his invention was nearly accomplished, he had about two hundred characters in his Alphabet. By the
aid of his daughter, who seemed to enter in the genius of his
labours, he reduced them, at last, to eighty-six, the number he now
uses. He then set to work to make these characters more comely
to the eye, and succeeded. As yet he had not the knowledge of the
pen as an instrument, but made his characters on a piece of bark,

with a knife or nail. At this time he sent to the Indian agent, or some trader in the nation, for paper and pen. His ink was easily made from some of the bark of the forest trees, whose colouring properties he had previously known; and after seeing the construction of the pen, he soon learnt to make one; but at first he made it without a slit; this inconvenience was, however, quickly removed by his sagacity. His next difficulty was to make his invention known to his countrymen; for by this time he had become so abstracted from his tribe and their usual pursuits, that he was viewed with an eye of suspicion. His former companions passed his wigwam without entering it, and mentioned his name as one who was practising improper spells, for notoriety or mischievous purposes; and he seems to think that he should have been hardly dealt with, if his docile and unambitious disposition had not been so generally acknowledged by his tribe. At length he summoned some of the most distinguished of his nation, in order to make his communication to them—and after giving them the best explanation of his discovery that he could, stripping it of all supernatural influence, he proceeded to demonstrate to them, in good earnest, that he had made a discovery. His daughter, who was now his only pupil, was ordered to go out of hearing, while he requested his friends to name a word or sentiment which he put down, and then she was called in and read it to them; then the father retired, and the daughter wrote; the Indians were wonder struck; but not entirely satisfied. See-quah-yah then proposed, that the tribe should select several youths from among their brightest young men, that he might communicate the mystery to them. This was at length agreed to, although there was some lurking suspicion of necromancy in the whole business. John Maw, (his Indian name I have forgotten,) a full-blood, with several others, were selected for this purpose. The tribes watched the youths for several months with anxiety; and when they offered themselves for examination, the feelings of all were wrought up to the highest pitch. The youths were separated from their master, and from each other, and watched with great care. The uninitiated directed what the master and pupil should write to each other, and these tests were varied in such a manner, as not only to destroy their infidelity, but most firmly to fix their faith. The Indians, on this, ordered a great feast, and made See-quah-yah conspicuous at it. How nearly is man alike in every age! Pythagoras did the same on the discovery of an important principle in geometry. See-quah-yah became at once school-master, professor, philosopher, and a chief. His countrymen were proud of his talents, and held him in reverence as one favoured by the Great Spirit. The inventions of early times were shrouded in mystery.

See-quah-yah disdained all quackery. He did not stop here, but carried his discoveries to numbers. He of course knew nothing of the Arabick digits, nor of the power of Roman letters in the science. The Cherokees had mental numerals to one hundred, and had words for all numbers up to that; but they had no signs or characters to assist them in enumerating, adding, subtracting, multiplying, or dividing. He reflected upon this until he had created their element-ary principle in his mind; but he was at first obliged to make words to express his meaning, and then signs to explain it. By this pro-cess he soon had a clear conception of numbers up to a million. His great difficulty was at the threshold, to fix the powers of his signs according to their places. When this was overcome, his next step was in adding up his different numbers in order to put down the fraction of the decimal, and give the whole number to his next place. But when I knew him, he had overcome all these difficulties, and was quite a ready arithmetician in the fundamental rules. This was the result of my interview; and I can safely say, that I have seldom met a man of more shrewdness than See-quah-yah. He adhered to all the customs of his country; and when his asso-ciate chiefs on the mission assumed our costume, he was dressed in all respects like an Indian. See-quah-yah is a man of diversified talents; he passes from metaphysical and philosophical investiga-tion to mechanical occupations, with the greatest ease. The only practical mechanics he was acquainted with, were a few bungling blacksmiths, who could make a rough tomahawk, or tinker the lock of a rifle; yet he became a white and silver smith, without any in-struction, and made spurs and silver spoons with neatness and skill, to the great admiration of people of the Cherokee nation. See-quah-yah has also a great taste for painting. He mixes his colours with skill; taking all the art and science of his tribe upon the subject, he added to it many chemical experiments of his own, and some of them were very successful, and would be worth being known to our painters. For his drawings he had no model but what nature furnished, and he often copied them with astonishing faithfulness. His resemblances of the human form, it is true, are coarse, but often spirited and correct; and he gave action, and some-times grace, to his representations of animals. He had never seen a camel hair pencil, when he made use of the hair of wild animals for his brushes. Some of his productions discover a considerable practical knowledge of perspective; but he could not have formed rules for this. The painters in the early ages were many years coming to a knowledge of this part of their art; and even now they are more successful in the art than perfect in the rules of it. The manners of the American Cadmus are the most easy, and his habits those of the most assiduous scholar, and his disposition is more lively than that of any Indian I ever saw. He understood and felt the advantages the white man had long enjoyed, of having the accumulations of every branch of knowledge, from generation to generation, by means of a written language, while the red man could only commit his thoughts to uncertain tradition. He reasoned correctly, when he urged this to his friends as the cause why the red man had made so few advances in knowledge in comparison with us; and to remedy this was one of his great aims, and one which he has accomplished beyond that of any other man living, or perhaps any other who ever existed in a rude state of nature.

It perhaps may not be known that the government of the United States had a fount of types cast for his alphabet; and that a newspaper, printed partly in the Cherokee language, and partly in the English, has been established at New Echota, and is characterized by decency and good sense; and thus many of the Cherokees are able to read both languages. After putting these remarks to paper, I had the pleasure of seeing the head chief of the Cherokees, who confirmed the statement of See-quah-yah, and added, that he was an Indian of the strictest veracity and sobriety. The western wilderness is not only to blossom like the rose; but there, man has started up, and proved that he has not degenerated since the primitive days of Cecrops, and the romantic ages of wonderful effort and god-like renown.

LECTURE II.

"They say that thou wert lovely from thy birth,
Of glorious parents."——

THE literature of a nation, thoroughly studied, affords the best criterion, by which may be judged the principles and powers of a people, as well as their rank in the scale of civilization: I mean literature in its extended sense. In endeavouring to execute my task, I shall show those men, and something of their works, who have added to the stock of our learning, from time to time; or those who, by their eloquence or industry in teaching, or by the productions of their pens, have left us an account of the deeds of their predecessors or contemporaries. I shall divide our history into

C 2

four periods, of half a century each, for the sake of more easily managing my subject. These periods are, indeed, arbitrary, it may be said, and will not correspond with any remarkable events in politicks or literature. This is very true; but still the division may aid my labours. The skilful painter of a panorama, divides his canvass into portions before he takes up the pencil; but these mechanical arrangements are not seen when the whole surface glows with life and action. A writer may profit by such an example.

All civilized nations have made great exertions, in some period of their history, to discover the origin of their literature, and have rejoiced at every successful effort to trace up and open the fountains, from whence the streams of knowledge have issued to gladden successive generations. With many matters of well authenticated fact, there has been much of fable and conjecture commingled. The farthest East, the birth-place of science and letters, has been overhung with clouds for thirty centuries; and if, for a moment, the eye of genius has sometimes attempted to pierce them, it succeeded for a moment only, and the splendid vision it unfolded was soon covered again with a thicker mantle.

Even Greece, so dear to us by many sweet associations, can boast of but little accuracy in her early history; she has often substituted for truth, the loveliest visions of fancy, and given the history of her earliest worthies, from golden streams of fiction, rather than from a series of facts. The portraits of heroes and demigods, have generally been shown in the twilight of history, and the glories of their acts have been seen in the faint rays of the sun; while men, mere men, have only been exhibited in the fulness of the perfect day. But in every age there has been a disposition to know much of former times; the persons, dress, minds, manners, and modes of thinking, of those of former days, are sought after by us; and no subject delights us more than a history of their intellectual treasures. This remark would have applied with equal effect to our own country, if we had not been under the erroneous impression, that after the most painful search, nothing of value could be found.

In the early ages, the curious examined nature in all her virgin loveliness; and her beautiful forms made indelible impressions upon the minds of those enamoured of her charms. We always love to look back and contemplate things as they were. In the philosophical days of Pericles, the Athenians went back with enthusiasm to the days of Homer; and when the Thebans were in a high state of military discipline, and not so much depended upon individual prowess as in the earlier ages of their warfare, and every event was more a matter of calculation, the great objects of their admiration were placed in a more romantick period. They went back to the

Trojan war; when hand to hand, and foot to foot, the sons of gods contended in mortal strife, and fought and bled for the possession of the daughters of men, as well as their own individual fame, governed by such passions as are found in the breasts of mortal men now-a-days. But if fiction be mingled with history, and it is impossible to make the great men of antiquity appear as they really were, still it is delightful to look back upon ages past, and catch a glimpse of them through the medium of their thoughts and opinions, which do not deceive us, if their history does. This we have a right to do; it is no waste of time, no dereliction of duty, and is not injuring any one, if we do not dwell on them so long as to forget the opinions and the subjects of contemplation of the great men of our own times. A man's business, most assuredly, is with those about him; but it is for the interest of himself, and those around him, to draw knowledge and instruction from those who have gone before him. The industrious husbandman who rises early, may, before he enters his fields to labour in the furrow, or to gather in his harvest, indulge himself for a few moments in turning to the rising sun, and in extending his view over the distant landscape to enjoy the sight of the afar-off mountain, the flowing stream, or the lofty spire; or may, if his taste should so direct him, cast a glance at the solemn mansions of the dead, as the rays of light fall on their crumbling tombs. Such contemplations will not enfeeble his hands, or sicken his heart, or make him go reluctantly to his labours; no, it will teach him what he is, and what he has to do, and the necessity of setting about it, that his task may be finished in season, before *the night cometh in which no man can work.*

The lover of literature, who confines himself to the smallest corner of the vineyard, may, strange as it may seem, refresh himself by viewing the fields where others have toiled through many a weary day. The stores of literature lie before him, and from which he may collect, for use, many lessons of wisdom; for literature, in its proper sense, is the transcript of the head and the heart of man, in the thoughts of the one and the workings of the other, in every age of his existence: all his sufferings, his joys, his hopes, his reasonings, his anticipations, and even his imaginings, belong to the literature of the world; yea, more—the descriptions of his country, of his kindred and friends; of the flowers on which he treads, and of the fountains which flow at his feet, and the dews which fall on his head, and the atmosphere which he breathes, are incorporated in his literature. Thus, thoughts embalmed in words, and principles in thoughts and expressions, make the heir-looms of one generation for another, and to which something is added every day.

It is by literature that we live, as it were, in the ages past as well as in the present. The well educated man brings into the narrow compass of human life the knowledge of many years, and examines in a single day the events of centuries. He travels back to the wisdom of Egypt, and measures the mind and weighs the science of those who erected the pyramids and etched the hieroglyphics upon them. He dwells upon the literature of the Hebrews, and reads in the books they have left an instructive lesson of human powers and of human virtues and frailties; and enjoys the verses of the poets who sang the glories of that God who delivered them from the *yoke of Egypt and the house of bondage;* and where can be found pictures of a brighter colouring, or flowers of a sweeter flavour? In these early writings, all the images at once strike the mind as natural, and all the sentiments flow directly from the heart. Their religion, their morals, their whole history, are directly before us, and are monuments of intellect that rise sublimely in the lapse of centuries, a wonder to man.

The Greeks, too, drawing from the same fountains, have left us a literature which cannot be named without emotions of pleasure. Having a language of their own, their literature was seemingly indigenous, however deeply they might have been indebted to the oriental store-houses that had been long open to them. The growth of Greek literature was like all other improvements, progressive; for more than seven hundred years it was so. The Greeks were a peculiar people; their taste was pure, and their discrimination exquisite; and their understandings were the most acute of any people who have ever lived. Their language proves this; for so well was it formed, that science and art are obliged to resort to it at this present day for terms to convey a proper idea of their inventions and improvements. If we could forget their ambition, their volatility, and frequent acts of injustice, the reader might think that he was coursing over fields of light with beings of a superior creation, while he was making himself acquainted with Greek literature. The Greeks multiplied books to inform the judgment and warm the heart, and which gave immortality to themselves and information to all succeeding generations. They created a code of laws for taste and the imagination. What can exceed their permanent fictions? Their mountains still drop with honey, their springs still flow, and will forever flow, with waters impregnated with inspiration; and their groves are still vocal with song. These creations of literary taste are as imperishable as the mind of man; and Attica may be, as it has been for ages, a den of pirates and a place of skulls—yet no matter, a thousand successive pachas could not pluck from our minds the lovely country which literature created, and has preserved. In this form, and under these fascinating guises, the people of that age found out a method by which they have preserved every shade of thought, and every change of feeling, of which human nature is susceptible. Fiction has given truth some of her ornaments; but they were disposed of so tastefully, that she has been made more beautiful for receiving and wearing them. This is emphatically the triumph of letters; but this triumph was not confined to that region alone; letters assumed their empire not only at Athens, but also at Rome they claimed the wreaths of immortality. The conquests of that mistress of the world have passed away, but her literature never will.

When the Greek was no longer a free man on his own soil, or was an exile in another land, and when the Roman eagles had drooped their wings, literature found her altars among the Arabs; her form in some degree was altered, but her spirit was the same. This people threw all their fierce nature into the pursuits of learning, and surpassed their predecessors not only in works of imagination, but in those connected with the sciences. They spurned the narrow bounds of time and space, and imagined worlds of their own, and peopled them with matchless beings, unshackled by mortal functions, and human laws, and gave them powers and virtues of an angelick nature. But in the midst of these delightful fictions of literature, they forgot not the sciences, but pursued them with a poetick passion. They invented the laws of numbers, and proved the truth of them by the invention itself. They pursued, through the alembick, the visionary doctrines of alchymy to the satisfactory results of chymistry; and, by experiments, brought science from the dreams of avarice to enlighten mankind. That warmth of imagination which saw the times in the stars, found, by the light of the mind which accompanied it, the precise movements of the heavenly bodies; and the delirium of the magician was changed to the devout reverence of the scientifick astronomer. The choicest names in the Arabic language were given to the constellations; and these have been preserved by those who knew but little of their origin. The literature of Spain and Italy was the same in a new form, gaining something at times, but losing much of its ethereal fire in every new transformation. The Gauls and Britains at length came in for their share, and have repaid the world for what they received. The light they borrowed from the East is now reflected back, and the nations of Egypt are learning the arts of war and peace from those they once instructed. It would require volumes to trace the march of science and letters through every age in its progress round this world of ours.

It may seem to some that I am taking a wide range in these remarks, to get at our literature and science; but there is not a page of it, however humble, that is not indebted to every one of these sources for some thought, word, or expression. The literature of the present day is made, in a good degree, out of the ruins of the literature of former ages. There are words in our vernacular from the Arabick, the Hebrew, the Coptick, the Greek, and Latin, and many other languages; our arts, too, claim a lineal kindred, and our numbers are theirs unchanged. And shall we say that our literature is nothing, because we have not in it the production of numerous centuries? Shall we, who have inherited all these spoils of time, continue to avow our poverty, merely because we do not wish to examine our treasures? Or shall we, because others possess more, think and say that we have nothing? No man, when the question is put to him, will acknowledge that he is willing that we should be so supine or neglectful. What then is to be done? Why, there is but one course to take in this business. In the first place, examine thoroughly into what we have had of learning among us; in what shapes it has appeared; of what utility it has been to the country; of what to mankind at large. And how is this to be done? Why, in the way that knowledge has ever been acquired; by painful investigation into the history of our country's mind, and the pursuits of that mind; and this by carefully collecting what fruits of it are left, and by examining its nature and growth. I grant that it is not to be accomplished in a day, or by one man, nor by one course of means. The historian must take his part; the biographer his; the antiquarian his; and the lecturer his part of it also. This latter mode of diffusing instruction is not a novel one. Lectures were given on national literature and on national glory in the walks of the academy, in the groves of Egeira, and at the olympic games. The doctrines of religion have been so promulgated; those of the Old Testament and the New; those also of the koran, and those of every sect in every age of the world. The lecture gives in one respect a better form than history, to the knowledge we may communicate; for the facts of the former may be interspersed with free and particular remarks on men and their deeds, as the lecturer passes on to matters which the historian cannot condescend to, consistent with the dignity of his subject. It is a better mode than that of the sermon, in some respects; because a sermon is properly a discourse made on some particular subject, and, in general, drawn from aphorisms or texts, and should be confined to them. The lecture is a better mode of conveying information than the oration, strictly speaking. The orator cannot, without compromising the dignity of his subject, descend to minute details; he is obliged to glance at these, and throw them aside as understood by his audience, while the lecturer has a right to enter into the most minute details, to reason upon them when he chooses, and to draw inferences from such axioms and principles as may chance to come in his way. The lecturer has a right to the same ornaments as the orator; the same facts as the historian; the same minute relations as the biographer; and the same moral strain as the sermonizer. It is difficult, most certainly, to pass from details to generalizing; from figures of dates to figures of rhetorick, and still seem to preserve unity of design with proper effect; yet it has been done by many, and of course the attempt is not preposterous. In the numerous literary and scientifick institutions in Germany, this mode of diffusing information is in general use, and is considered of high importance in the acquisition of knowledge. The habit is growing up in our seminaries, and will, I have no doubt, come into general use. It is not so much the mass of information that a well digested lecture contains on any subject of literature and science that renders it valuable; the excellency consists, if it have any merit, in directing the mind to such topicks as are worthy of investigation at another time.

The fields of literature have aptly been compared to a garden; we walk through it and partake of its flowers and fruit. Such wanderings are delightful; but how much more information might be obtained in the same time, if the exoticks were designated and separated from the native; if the trivial and classical names of plants were given at the same time; and the merely ornamental distinguished from those which combine both characteristicks. The lectures of Sir Joshua Reynolds are models of this species of composition. But to return to the subject of my own exertions; the literature of our country is incorporated with the character of our ancestors. In our own history, it is true, we cannot go back into regions of fiction, and indulge in the reveries of the imagination; for solemn, well authenticated facts, meet us at every turn, and we must trace them from date to date, and from man to man. Still, the highway is full of subjects of deep interest, and the mind will find food for contemplation at every step.

The spirit of inquiry had been abroad for more than a century previous to the first date in the history of these American colonies. The doctrine of civil and religious liberty had been broached and diffused. The light of science and reason, and the love of letters, were found in the ecclesiastical states; and the sovereign pontiff Leo X. was among the great patrons of improvements, before our ancestors came to these shores. The German monks had commenced the work of reforming the church, with an intelligence and an earnestness that baffled all control. The little republicks of Italy were contending with each other and the world, by exertions in favour of the arts and letters; and the United Provinces of the

Netherlands were teaching the nations of Europe, that commerce
and freedom, and the rights of man, were not the mere offspring of
a heated imagination. Then the doctrines of a representative
government were beginning to be understood and valued; and
amid the storm of contending factions, the principles of civil and
religious liberty were seen to be taking root. England, after struggling with the strength of Spain, was rising in power and influence,
and advancing, even by her acts of persecution, the progress of
liberty. At this moment, the people in England felt more than they
dared to express, and sighed for more than they enjoyed. Some
were ready to emigrate from a love of change and a spirit of enterprise; while others were anxious to find an asylum from religious
persecution.

That the end depends on the beginning—" *Finis origine
pendet*"—is an axiom more applicable, if possible, to nations than
to individuals. This country had an auspicious beginning, when
considered in connexion with its destinies. It has been held as true
to history, that nations have their rise and decline in some regard
to centuries, as the human constitution to shorter periods of time.
History does indeed produce some examples to illustrate this posi-
tion; but their beginnings and their elements were different from
those which are found in our history. Our beginnings were indeed
different from those of other nations in many respects; we did not
pass through the long and painful stages of civilization, from the
dawn of knowledge to the full day of light, but commenced with
the possession of all the knowledge which had been left by departed
nations, or treasured up in later times. Our ancestors came not to
this country as the savage hordes of the north came down upon the
cultivated grounds of Italy; who took possession of the tasteful
villas, the vine-covered hills, the magnificent palaces, and the superb
temples; and subdued by the charms of voluptuousness, and the
sweets of refinement, grew pliant, tasteful, and effeminate, and well
informed; and throwing aside their swords and coats of mail,
seized the pencil, the chisel, and the lute, and made an abode for the
graces in the bosom of the arts.

Our ancestors were not, like some colonists, disgorged from the
mother country to keep the remaining population sound and pure;
they were not a surplus mass thrown off to prevent national apo-
plexy, or political spasms; such a population as sometimes went
from Attica to take possession of the islands in the numerous seas
about them, or to the more distant shores of Africa; nor were they
sent by the parent country to extend her commerce, or to gain a
footing on, or near, the territories of other nations.

They did not come to this country as the Spanish and French

colonists to the "summer isles," allured by the golden dreams of avarice, or by the glowing description of the luxuriance of the soil, abounding in perpetual fruits and flowers; an earthly paradise, teeming with all that could satisfy the appetite or regale the senses; which for centuries have been the abodes of luxury, superstition, profligacy, and crime. No; the sober calculations of forming a thrifty settlement, which would make a good home for themselves and their descendants, operated upon some of the early colonists of this country. A spirit of enterprise natural to enlightened men, induced others to come and see, and in doing this, they became attached and fixed to these shores which their posterity now inhabit. Others had different motives for emigration; a love of freedom in thought and speech. They were fully sensible of their situation. They could not anticipate all the occurrences which might happen in their destinies, but they were determined to commence upon the broad principle, that knowledge and virtue are the pillars of power and security in every national code. They saw physical means about them for an almost interminable increase of population. The sea was on one side, and boundless forests on the other. Navigable rivers were flowing into the oceans. Nothing but a thinly scattered race of rude men stood in their way to the founding of an empire larger than the world had ever seen. Nature seemed to have waited from her birth until this hour for their coming, to give them possession of her bounties. This was the place for contemplation, and a place to originate a new course of thoughts upon political and civil liberty. There were, in these retreats, no shouts of the conqueror, no moans of the conquered; the time resembled the cool of the evening, and the place the abode of innocence, when and where other beings were at rest, and God walked with man in his primeval state. Every thing, in America, was to be begun, and every thing seemed to depend on themselves; with this happy difference, however, between us and those in paradise, for our safety and happiness were to depend upon eating freely of the tree of knowledge, which was forbidden to him who first sprang from the dust of the earth. Here was offered the opportunity to cultivate the mind without the trammels and fetters which embarrass and bind those born in aged and decaying communities. Here, plains, and vales, and hills, offered opportunities for all the experiments of agriculture. No agrarian law was needed to give men an equality; there was one passed already by nature without stint. The sites for cities were unoccupied; and they exercised their judgments upon this subject of a proper place to build them, without statutes or restraints. The political compact was to be formed and altered as the covenanters could agree; for there was no other lawgiver

D

than their own understandings; no *Solons* but their own *wisdom*,
no *Lycurguses* but the severe discussions of their own judgements.
There was no syren to allure them from their duties to the rocks on
which they might split; no soft laps of pleasure on which they
might sleep until their locks of strength were shorn.   There were
no beds of flowers beneath which the serpents flattery and fashion
might glide to wound their naked feet with sharp stings.   Indolence
to them would have been death ; and labour, that supposed curse on
man, was a blessing.   Thus stripped of every shackle, they began
their work of founding an empire.   By the lights emitted from their
minds shall we trace the path they pursued, and the deeds they
performed.   The light of the sun passes away with the going down
of the same; but the accumulated light of successive ages of intellect, like the precious stones which adorn the city of God, chases
away all darkness, and beams in eternal splendour.

But to descend from general remarks to more particular details,
and follow our country through its infancy, youth, and manhood, in
the progress of knowledge and growth of intellect, is more distinctly
the duties we prescribed as a course to pursue.

In 1584, Sir Walter Raleigh visited this continent, and, naturally
of a romantic turn, he gave such favourable accounts of it, as kept
alive the disposition to emigrate; and which were also sufficient to
feed the hopes of speculators, who had turned their attention to
this country.

The first settlement of any importance was not, however, made for
several years after his return.   It took some time for the adventurers
to pluck up at home, and transplant themselves in an almost unknown world.

In 1606 the Virginia settlement began.   It was not at first prosperous, but at length succeeded.   The Dutch soon formed another
settlement on the Hudson river.   The next settlement was made at
Plymouth by the pilgrims, as they were called by the historians of
that day ; and which appropriate name they have ever since retained.
The settlers of Virginia were allured by a love of gold, and the prospect of aggrandizement, to commence their labours.   They had a
leader in Capt. John Smith, more capable of commanding an enterprise, than any person history or fable has ever described.

He was acquainted with man in various countries, and had deeply
read the human heart.   Full of resources, he was capable of keeping
his followers together, when they would have deserted any other
man ; and of supporting them, when under any other leader they
would have starved.   He did not confine his reserches to one small
region, but coursed along the seaboard to a high northern latitude ;
and in the spirit of a great adventurer, drew a chart of his voyage,

and set down most judicious remarks upon all he saw or did. Thus Virginia has the honour of a founder, who was at once a hero, a scholar, a man of science, and a man of the world; and what is more, "*a most right honest man.*"

The old world were soon made acquainted with the new, through the medium of his pen. He published his sixth voyage to Virginia in 1608; the first voyage to New England, with the old and new names, 1614; a relation of his second voyage to New-England, 1615; and a description of the country, in 1617; New-England's trials, in 1620, and the general history of Virginia, New-England, and the Summer Isles. Purchas had previously published Smith's adventures in other parts of the world.

Such a man might be supposed to have given an impulse to an infant settlement, beyond that of common adventurers; but his followers wanted concert and sympathy with each other, and did not profit by his example and advice, as they ought to have done.

The pilgrims were of a different class. They had left England for religious freedom; had sojourned for a time in Holland; and had ventured upon these shores, in an inclement season, buoyed up by the belief, that the God they worshipped would go before them, and help them in the wilderness.

They had quarrelled with the church of England, and abhorred the church of Rome. From the austerity of their lives, and the simplicity of their manners and habits, they had in their own country received the name of Puritans, and had received it as a common appellation. The doctrines they professed, it is not my intention now to discuss, or offer an opinion upon them. No matter who were right or who were wrong; these Puritans had opened a discussion, which ages will not close. A handful of men were landed on the coast of New-England, and as it often happens in human events, their very feebleness became their protection. If their numbers had been considerable, the Indians would have been jealous of them, and associated then, as they did fifty years afterwards, to destroy them. They were at first to the natives rather subjects of curiosity than fear. These emigrants were a reading and a thinking people. They had been bred in the warfare of religious controversy, and each, and all, could give the reasons for the faith within them. They had left numerous connexions in England, who were anxious to hear from them; and religious friends, who were desirous of knowing how they prospered in building up a church.

On the return of every vessel to their native land, men, women, and children, wrote of all they had seen, suffered, or enjoyed, to the most minute circumstance. The extraordinary events of every changing season, (and every event is extraordinary, when men are placed in new and singular situations,) were faithfully recorded by the leaders of this little band, with the minuteness of a missionary journalist, of the character of which they were. Distance of place, and novelty of situation, give importance to trifles in themselves; and all the small things have become great, from the greatness of their results. But from whatever cause it may have happened, the fact is certain, that every thing relating to these early settlers, has come down to us in the most authentic form.

The next settlement, was that of the colony of Massachusetts Bay, in 1630. These people came able handed, with wealth and wise men, whose objects were of this world and the next united. They were men of distinction in their own land; were also learned in all the wisdom of the age, and had well defined plans of religious associations and political institutions. They began their labours at once with courage, and pursued them with success. Here was at once opened the widest field for their exertions. They could here reason upon the divine right of kings without fear of the axe, and speak of the Pope without fear of the faggot. They construed the *Magna Charta* as they pleased, and interpreted the Scriptures as the Spirit gave them light and utterance. These second comers were in full communion, in most things, with the pilgrims; and the course they followed was so nearly alike, that in the further view of our subject, we shall not make any discrimination between them, in a moral point of view; for if these streams were not then united, they ran side by side until their waters commingled and flowed on together.

I have said that they were acquainted with the literature of the age; but the great fountain of their knowledge was the Bible. From this they drew their morals; and where could purer morality be found? From this they supplied their religious creed; and from whence shall revelation come, if not from the sacred word? From this they drew their political creed, that "*those who ruled over men should be just, ruling in the fear of God.*" From the scriptures they drew their knowledge of men; and what history is so full of the workings of the human heart? From this book they derived their knowledge of their vernacular tongue; and I would ask, what book there is to be found of purer English, than the translation of the Bible? I am not contending for the accuracy of every translation; but it will not be denied, when I say, that a very copious vocabulary of good English words may be made from the pages of the common version of the Bible.

Their philosophy of the mind, and their knowledge of the character of the Supreme Being, was also sought for in the hallowed pages of the Bible; precisely where they ought to have been sought for.

It is by example as well as precept that we profit in our lives and conversation, and what book can be found that will furnish us with so many models of meekness, patience, honourable feeling, generosity, and affection, as the sacred volume? It is full of historical detail, of incident, and dramatic effect. There is in it every species of writing from the simplest narrative to the most affecting tragedy. The sweetness of its verse, the loftiness of its poetry, the boldness of its delineations, and, above all, the warmth of its descriptions, and the depth of its inspiration, all conspire to suit, in some part or other, every taste and capacity. The child is delighted with reading the Bible. The young man, yea, all men look into it for lessons of elocution; and the poets dwell upon it for models of composition. Many of our fathers read the scriptures in the original Hebrew; for they were more than any other race of men of this country versed in all the niceties and beauties of that language. It is a primitive tongue, if any one can be called so, and it seems to carry you back to the elements of thinking and speaking. I perhaps dwell on this subject with enthusiastic fondness, but I love to come often and drink of the

"Sweet waters welling from the sacred spring."

The settlers of the province of Massachusetts Bay had as much piety, more learning, and more ambition, than the pilgrims; they began stronger handed, and if with no more fixedness of purpose, certainly, with more clearness of design, than the pilgrims; but no men could have higher claims to moral worth than the first settlers of Plymouth. The leader and first Governor of this bay province, was a lawyer, and a most eloquent and learned man. There was a precision and a legal cast of character in all their proceedings, which show that the framers of their laws were not unacquainted with the technical language of the English statute books, and the courts of justice. Their religious opinions prevented them from being favourites at home; but they were not forced to come abroad. There was as much of adventure as of necessity in their emigration. With their prayers for protection and prosperity were mingled visions of their future glories. They had learned from the sacred volume that means were necessary to produce ends, even when God himself had ordered the thing to be done, and the connection between them could not be seen by the limited understandings of men. The hands of Moses must be raised, that Moab might be smitten, although his hand grasped no sword, and he was afar from the field of battle. They fixed on the means which, in the ordinary

D 2
6

course of providence produced such ends as they prayed for. To watch the humble mansion as it was erected; to listen to all the patriarchal instruction as it flowed at the family altar; to contemplate the rude structure in which public worship was at first performed; to note the infant seminaries of instruction as they arose; to watch the police, apparently as simple as that of the barbarians around them, yet still guarded by every great principle embraced in the charter of British liberties, and the still greater principles of the moral law, founded upon justice, and written on the human heart; to do all this, and more, would be a delightful task; but it is the privilege of but few to indulge minutely in these retrospections, so honourable to our fathers and so useful to us. Our fathers had failings, for they were but men. It will be found, however, that the more they are inspected, and tried, the more conspicuous will be their merits, and the deeper will be the sense of our obligations to them for what they did.

I will endeavour, with as much justice and impartiality as I can, to go up to the springs of our institutions, and trace the sources of our literature and sciences; and will, as fairly as I am able, give the brief history of the merits of the colonies as they arose and flourished; but as I proceed through details of the history of their minds and its productions, I shall ask for the candid remarks of the enlightened and liberal, and I promise to profit by judicious hints and honest criticisms. I am nothing more than one of the pioneers in the great work of redeeming our fame from the foul aspersions of our enemies. I have written for the instruction of the rising, and to awake the recollections of the risen generation. I invoke the scholar and the patriot to aid me in this undertaking, that justice may be done to our common country. The fond hope of sometimes catching the ear of taste, and of eliciting the approving smile of beauty, has often cheered me in my labours, but if the patriotick should not hear my invocations, or taste lend her ear, nor loveliness lavish her smiles, still I can console myself with a consciousness that my admiration of the reputation of our ancestors, and the wish to do some good to my fellow-men, were the strongest motives for my exertions.

LECTURE III.

'So Providence for us, high, infinite,
Makes our necessities its watchful task,
Hearkens to all our prayers,helps all our wants;
And e'en if it denies what seems our right,
Either denies because 'twould have us ask,
Or seems but to deny, or in denying grants."

IN making our researches, for the literature of any particular period, we must necessarily go to the men of that age; for who they were, and what they did, are so intimately connected with what they wrote, that it may be the better course to name some of those, together with their works, who first enlightened the country by their literary and religious labours.

In the little band of pilgrims, there were several men of cultivated minds. The venerable Brewster, who was chosen the ruling elder among them, had been educated in the school of diplomacy; having been secretary to one of the ambassadors of Elizabeth. He was a brave soldier, and well acquainted with the military tacticks of his time. His talents, united to his gravity, age, and sanctity, made him a very proper person for a leader. Carver, the first governor of Plymouth, was also a man of enterprise, intelligence, and great benevolence, and quite a business man; and his letters upon the contract he had made with the Virginia Company, show him to be a well educated one.

Bradford, who was governor after the death of Carver, was a man of sense; was bred a lawyer; was a good scholar, well read in the modern languages, and knew something of the classicks. This gentleman kept a most minute and faithful journal of events; but they were not all published, and most of them have been lost. Some few scraps have been found, which are now in the Massachusetts Historical collection; but Moreton and others had read his manuscripts, and it is probable, we have no small portion of their substance in other works.

Miles Standish, their military captain, was not only a good soldier, but highly respectable in point of acquirements; having been appointed, in difficult times, an agent for the company in England, and sent over as a financier; and it was thought his mission was well executed when he was able to hire money at fifty pounds on the hundred; so low was the credit of the colony. He probably loved to fight better than to pray, exhort, or teach; and of course he was not so much celebrated in the churches, as he might have been, had he been more of a saint and less of a hero; but a braver man never lived, than Miles Standish, nor a more useful one for an infant settlement.

Edward Winslow, another of these hero-pilgrims, was also governor of the colony, and esteemed a fine scholar. He was one of the most active and intelligent of the first emigrants. He journeyed from place to place, visiting the several tribes of Indians, to keep them in peace and quietness, and always managed them with great discretion, being at once fearless of their power, and tender of their feelings. He visited England also, for the good of the colony, and suffered imprisonment for the cause during the arbitrary rule of Laud. His writings were valuable, and are now highly esteemed; for he was one of those few, in that age, who showed a true spirit of philosophy in the midst of religious zeal. Purchas has preserved some of his writings in his collections.

To be assured that this people were well informed, and understood their civil as well as religious rights, we only need look to their contracts, drawn up and signed on board the May-flower, on the 11th of November, 1620. This was the very first instance of power, coming without influence or control from the people themselves; and the style and matter of this *Magna Charta* of American liberties, do honour to the intellects of those who formed it. The whole superstructure they designed and reared, was based on knowledge and virtue, and implied the establishment of schools and a supply of teachers; and of course we find, among their first acts, after the immediate wants of nature were supplied, was the establishment of schools, with penalties for any breach of their ordinances.

The records of this colony, kept during the time they were distinct and separate from the colony of Massachusetts Bay, and which was so for more than seventy years, has been lately copied by the order of the legislature of Massachusetts; and it is found to contain many excellent ordinances, decrees, or laws, well adapted to their character and situation. The thorough-bred politician of the day might smile at the simplicity of some of them; but they were suited to the age and the people for which they were made; and this is the true philosophy of all law making. The histories which we now have of that age and people, are the best authenticated of any histories extant. Morton's memorial, which is often referred to, is an invaluable work. The writer, who was in that colony from early life to the time of his death, was a relation of Governor Bradford. He was also secretary of the colony, which gave him a fine opportunity to know the passing events. The memorial was printed in the life time of the author, in 1669. It went through an ordeal of criticism before it was sent to the press, being inspected by two learned, grave divines, Mr. Higginson of Salem, and Mr. Thatcher of Weymouth; and the work and the author were commended to the faithful. In 1721, it was reprinted and published by Josiah Cotton, register of deeds for the county of Plymouth. The editor, Mr. Cotton, was an antiquarian, and he made an appendix to the work, but did not do so much as he might have done at that day for his author, or for himself. From this edition there have been reprints; one in 1772, at Newport, R. I., and another in 1826, at Plymouth.

This year, 1827, an improved edition of the memorial has issued from the press in Boston, under the sanction of a name now connected with the literature of our country, in its earlier and latter days; as an antiquarian, Judge Davis has but few equals; as a writer of taste and talent, no superiour among the literati of the United States. Besides the *Memorial*, and Winslow's *Good News from New-England*, and others we have mentioned, there is a work called *Mourt's Journal*, whose history seems to have been involved in some mystery; but the fortunate circumstance of finding a complete copy of this work in 1819, has, in a good measure, removed all difficulties about it. To Mr. Duponceau, of Philadelphia, we are indebted for this, as the country is for some of the most learned and satisfactory essays upon its history and literature which have ever been published in it. The name of the journalist was not to be found in the catalogue of the first settlers, but a critical writer in the North American Review, with much plausibility, places him among the "*Merchant adventurers*" of that day, who had been assiduous in obtaining information from the New World. It was a time of great curiosity in Europe respecting this country. The avaricious were still indulging dreams of gold, although there had been so many disappointments; the lovers of religious freedom looked to it as an asylum for the persecuted of all nations; and the political economists were hailing it as the future receptacle of the surplus population of decayed and falling nations. These were favourable auguries, but there were no certainties in the destinies of these adventurers. Numerous tribes of Indians surrounded them, and it was uncertain how much they would be assisted by more distant tribes, in some future day, in case of war; and it was still doubtful what course the nations of Europe might pursue in some remote period towards these settlements, when urged by love of power, or gain, or revenge. The seed sown had indeed come up well, the plants were thriving, but what frosts, or blights, or mildews might come, it was beyond human foresight to divine; but their hopes were in the God of their fathers, and in his promises to those who sought aright and followed his precepts in singleness of heart.

The transition is easy from individuals of the pilgrims to those of the Massachusetts colonists. This colony was contemplated earlier, but not much was done until the summer of 1630, when Governor Winthrop and Deputy-Governor Dudley, Sir Richard Saltonstall, Mr. Johnson, and others, several of them learned divines and eminent physicians, sailed from England in a fleet of twelve ships, containing fifteen hundred souls. Many of these adventurers died, during a long voyage, by the small pox, and other diseases; and there were no ready accommodations for them when they reached these shores, and of course many died soon after their landing. But notwithstanding every discouragement, they instantly set about organizing themselves into churches, and, trusting in heaven, went on as if in the utmost prosperity. Winthrop was truly a great man, and so were many of his coadjutors. Winthrop had been a distinguished lawyer in Groton, in the county of Suffolk, before he came to this country. It was thought a great acquisition to the enterprise when he was induced to join it. He was well acquainted with the great doctrines of civil liberty, which had just begun to be thoroughly examined by the most eminent jurists of Europe. The works of *Grotius* had been dispersed though the civilized world, and the strong minded had profited by them.

Winthrop not only attended to his duty as a chief magistrate, but kept a journal of his proceedings, and the general current of events, from the commencement of his voyage to the time of his death, or nearly to it, embracing the period from 1630 to 1649. A portion of this journal was preserved among his descendants, but not published until 179%; and other parts of it were lost. It had often been alluded to as having been a guide to others; but all hopes of finding it were given up, when, in the spring of 1816, the lost manuscript was discovered in the tower of the old south church, in Boston. It had slept among the rubbish of a church library until this time. The antiquarian considered it a God-send, and the lovers of American literature at large were much delighted at this discovery. Here was something authentick; a history written day by day, as the events transpired, by one who knew the whole matter, and in which he acted no small part: a journal not written to please any set of men, or to assist the designs of a party. This valuable manuscript was put into the hands of James Savage, Esq., a lawyer of distinction at the Suffolk bar, whose taste and talents fitted him for the task of arranging and commenting upon it. The learned notes given to the world by that gentleman, in his edition of this journal, justly entitle him to the thanks and respect of his countrymen. The life of Winthrop was one of great activity, magnanimity, and suffering, and adds another fact to prove that the pioneers in all great enterprises must be actuated by high motives and patriotic feelings; for their enjoyment is scanty, and the sun of glory bursts not from the cloud to cheer their parting souls, but shines only on their mouldering monuments.

Dudley, the deputy governor, was a man well educated, and from his letters, appears to have had a correct view of the undertaking of building up a church in the wilderness, although he did not rank with the very learned men of his time. He had more learning, however, than tolerance. It was not an age of liberal feeling.

Sir Richard Saltonstall did not come out with any pretensions to learning; he was a statesman of no small parts, but from his report, which is to be found in the appendix to Winthrop's journal, Savage's edition, he appears to have been well educated; for it is written in better English, and in a more elegant style, than other specimens of that period; except perhaps some of Winthrop's works.

John Wilson, the pastor of the first church in Boston, was a learned man—spoke Latin with great fluency. He was a firm friend to liberality and science, and was, generally, both the friend of Winthrop and of Cotton; but when called to decide in the antinomian controversy, he joined with Winthrop against his ecclesiastical senior.

John Elliot, generally styled "*the apostle to the Indians,*" deserves to be remembered among the good and learned men of that age. He came to Boston in 1631; and although he intended settling at Boston, chose to live at Roxbury, and was there a great favourite of his congregation throughout his long life. But one opinion has ever been entertained of this great scholar and christian philanthropist. Gifted by nature with quick perceptions, and a strong memory, to which was added the most untiring industry, he became an admirable linguist; and soon made himself master of the Indian language. He preached to the Indians, who readily understood him; and, with immense labour, he succeeded in translating the Bible and several religious tracts into their vernacular tongue. This Indian Bible is now a great curiosity. Probably there is not three men living who can do more than pick out a few words which they can read and understand. Elliot was a man of great simplicity of character; zealous in his profession, and ardent in his desire to convert the Indians; but this was destined to be of more benefit to the whites than to the Indians; for, in the Pequod war, these "*praying Indians,*" as those converted by Mr. Elliot were called, were either neutral or friendly to the whites; and a different feeling towards the colonies would have been dangerous to the new settlement. Elliot was well acquainted with the rights of man, in his civil as well as religious character. He wrote the first political pamphlet which was published in this country, entitled "The Christian Commonwealth." This work is full of free and noble principles; but the magistrates took alarm at it, and the good man had to recant his opinions, or rather apologize for this publication. He lived to the age of eighty-six; to a time when the colonies had grown to a large and flourishing people. The tribe of Indians which he instructed is now nearly extinct. There are not more than a dozen of them left. One of these Naticks was tried, a few years ago, for murdering his grandmother, and then all that were left of the tribe assembled. The Indians are fated to fade away before the progress of civilization: it was so written in the destiny of nations.

Cotton, Haynes, and Hooker, all came to this country in 1633, in the same ship. The former settled in Boston, "and in compliment to him, in the expectation of his coming from Boston, in Lincolnshire, did that ancient town in New-England receive its name." Mr. Cotton was, until the time of his death, the chief of the apostles to the new world. "A mighty fame as a scholar and preacher had preceded him," and this expectation was not tarnished nor diminished by his conduct in the colony. Hooker went with Haynes to Connecticut, after three years residence in Massachusetts, as ministers at Newton. Haynes was one year governor of the colony before he removed. Hooker wrote many sermons which were printed, but his greatest work was on "Church Discipline."

Thomas Parker, another of the New-England fathers, came to the country in 1634, and was for a year an assistant to Mr. Ward of Ipswich, and then removed to Newbury, on a river which now bears his name. James Noyes, his friend, was teacher to the same people; and these learned men did much good in their settlement. Noyes acted in the capacity of a schoolmaster, and did much to enlighten his flock. It is a remarkable fact that, in later times, this spot has been noted for being the birth place of several learned men. Judge Parsons, Professor Pearson, Professor Webber, Professor John Smith, and several others of fame, were natives of Newbury, and born near the old farm of Mr. Parker. While Noyes was training the youthful mind, Parker was deep in the mysteries of the profession, and produced a treatise which was much read by the learned of that day. Mr. Parker was an amiable man, but some of his writings brought him into the field of controversy with President Chauncey. It is not to be presumed that these controversies had really so much bitterness in them as, at this distance of time, we may suppose them to have had. It was the fashion of the day to break a lance with a neighbouring divine merely to try each others' skill and strength, and to acquire a fame for shrewdness and learning. This habit has, in some measure, continued to the present day. It is a bloodless war of words, and the discussion will be read by many who would perhaps read nothing else.

The name of Shephard is intimately connected with the early history of American literature. Thomas, the first in the catalogue, came to Boston and Cambridge, in 1635, as successor to Hooker, who had left this vineyard abounding in labourers, and had set out, through the wilderness, to form a settlement on Connecticut river, at Hartford. Mr. Shephard was an excellent scholar, particularly deep in metaphysicks, and yet he wrote without that obscurity which is often found in the writings of men of that cast of mind. He died in the forty-fourth year of his age, but he lived long enough to publish many works of merit. Several of them were very popular. "*The Morality of the Sabbath,*" "*New-England's Lamentation for Old England's Errours,*" and also, "*An Explanation of the Parable of the Ten Virgins.*" From this latter fountain, the great Doctor Edwards acknowledged that he drew copiously in writing his "*Treatise on the Affections.*" Thomas Shephard's eldest son bore his father's christian name, and was heir to his father's talents and virtues, but he joined the congregation of the dead still younger than his parent. President Oakes delivered an elegant Latin oration upon his death. His days were devoted to literature and religion. There were two other sons of the elder Thomas Shephard, Samuel and Jeremiah. The first of these died at the age of twenty-seven. Mitchell wrote his eulogy. The latter Shephard lived to a good old age. These three sons were educated at Harvard College. Cotton Mather speaks of them with admiration, and says, "that having three such excellent ministers is something better than to have three orators, like the Curii of Rome."

Our ancestors had among them men of all casts of mind, and some who, fearless of the austerity of the times, often indulged in wit and satire. Of this class no one was more distinguished than Nathaniel Ward. He was a lawyer, a divine, and a satirist, who came to this country, and for a while, was settled at Ipswich; was invited to preach the election sermon by the freemen, without consulting the magistrates, and also to draw up a code of laws, which he did. This code consisted of one hundred laws, called "*the body of the liberties.*" Among his satirical works is one called "*The simple Cobbler of Agawam.*" He was a high royalist, and this was in part written to abuse the enemies of Charles I. It had been admired for its causticity, but its coarseness is equal to its pungency.

Peter Bulkeley was a gentleman who came to this country to enjoy the liberty of conscience and the liberty to preach. He was a clergyman in Bedfordshire, and continued his labours there for

E   7

twenty years; but on being silenced for non-conformity, he left England and gathered a church in Concord, within twenty miles of Boston. His fortune was large and his benevolence unbounded. He
was said to have been very learned. He wrote Latin poetry; some
scraps of which Cotton Mather has handed down to us. He also
published a celebrated work on "*the covenant of grace opened.*"
This work went through many editions, and was praised by the great
theologians of that day.

Nathaniel Rogers, minister of Ipswich, was a descendant of John
Rogers, the martyr in Queen Mary's time. He came to this country
in 1636. He was one of the greatest of that distinguished band of
christian emigrants who suffered by the persecutions of Laud. He
is mentioned in high terms by Johnson, Winthrop, and Mather.

Ezekiel Rogers came about the year 1638, and settled in Rowley,
and was held in veneration by the people of Rowley and throughout
the colony. He preached the election sermon in 1643. In this he
advocated the pure democratick doctrine of rotation in office, and
strenuously urged the good people not to choose a governor twice
in succession: but they did not regard his advice. He was a publick
benefactor, giving his library by will to Harvard College, and leaving
considerable property for the support of a clergyman in the town
of Rowley.

Many more of these founders of the republick might be named, if
our time would allow it, who, for liberty of conscience, left ease,
plenty, and friends in their native land, and all the charms of elevated society, and threw themselves upon the wilds of America.
Their hardships can never be fully told. They spent their lives in
subduing nature, and teaching an humble flock; acting as patrons,
pastors, physicians, lawyers, and often as nurses to mind and body. A
lively sense of duty, and a full measure of grace, could alone have
supported them in their labours, while in their hearts they sighed
for the country they had left. Even in their dreams they visited
the shores of England, and could not but acknowledge that *with all
her faults they loved her still.*

One of the most remarkable events in the history of our early
literature was the founding of a college in the Massachusetts colony
at Cambridge, in the year 1636. Scarcely had they cultivated sufficient ground to supply the wants of nature, before they began this
great work of establishing an institution of learning, that theological
learning should not be lost among them for want of education. The
projectors were wise men, and laid a good foundation. They were
unfortunate in their first president, who proved a tyrant; but he was
soon dismissed, and an excellent man, President Dunster, entered
upon the duties of his office. He was a man of learning and great

mildness of character; but, differing with the great proportion of the clergymen of that day on the subject of baptism, he retired from office, about fourteen years after his appointment. Chauncey succeeded Dunster. He had been a minister at Situate in the old colony. Dunster was a fine oriental scholar, particularly well learned in the Hebrew; and he set about revising the psalms which Elliot and his friends had versified from David's. This corrected version of Dunster's passed through many editions, and were used until the version of Tate and Brady, and that of Dr. Watts, more particularly took the place of them. Under the administration of Dunster the college flourished greatly, and acquired such fame in England, that the sons of the puritans were desirous of coming to this country for an education. President Chauncey had been distinguished in England, but falling under the displeasure of archbishop Laud, he came to this country in 1638. This was a judicious appointment; for he stood *primus inter pares*, as a scholar. Besides the dead languages usually acquired, he was acquainted with some of the living oriental languages, which were studied in England in his time by many of the great lights of their universities. He was president for seventeen years, and the college prospered under his care. He had six sons, all of whom graduated at Cambridge, and were eminent in their day as divines and scholars. Dr. Hoar succeeded President Chauncey. He was a learned man, of amiable manners, who had moved in polished society; but he had not enough of the sternness of the pedagogue to succeed in the government of youths, and he was obliged to leave his office in a rebellion of the students. This was too great a shock for his delicate nerves, and he sunk under this affliction in the same year of his resignation, at the age of forty-five. Many learned men want the spirit of discipline to govern boys; and, in fact, every instructor has found this the most difficult part of his duty. He was the first president who was graduated at Harvard college.

President Oaks, who succeeded Hoar, was also one of the sons of Harvard. The office of president he held, and still continued pastor of the church at Cambridge. His official life was short, for he died in 1681. Dr. Rogers was his successor: but he died also within a year after his installation.

Increase Mather was now appointed President, and although tainted with the bigotry of the age, for he had entered deeply into the delusions of the belief of witchcraft, yet he was a very excellent president: fond of encouraging the emulous youths under his care.

Thus, this college, for the first half century of the existence of the colony, had flourished beyond a parallel in the annals of letters; had been blessed with the munificence of the wealthy and the good, in

New-England; had secured friends and patrons in the mother country; had supplied the churches with learned divines to fill the places created by the increase of population and those made vacant by the death of the fathers of the American church; and others of various pursuits were found among the Alumni of Harvard. Every man in the province considered this institution as a monument he had assisted to rear, and it became incorporated with every branch of church and state. The temporalities were remembered in the testaments of the wealthy, and the righteous were unceasing in their prayers that, from this fountain, might flow streams refreshing to the body politic, and such as would gladden the city of our God. The government of the commonwealth have, from the beginning, made, from time to time, liberal grants for its support, and have constantly extended its protecting hand in every hour of its existence.

Mathematical science flourished in the colony of Massachusetts at a very early period. John Sherman, who came to this country in 1634, and was for a short time assistant to the Rev. Mr. Phillips, at Watertown, was eminently learned in the science of numbers. He left Watertown, and sojourned for several years in Connecticut, and there preached occasionally, but generally was employed in public life; but after the death of Mr. Phillips, he was invited to return to Watertown, to his old parish; and he accepted the invitation, and took upon himself the duties of a clergyman once more; but his active mind could not be confined to his parochial duties, for he wished to do good in every way he could. On being appointed fellow of Harvard college, he delivered lectures on scientifick, moral, and religious subjects, which were attended by the students of the university, and others. These were the first lectures delivered on such subjects in this country. During this time, he published an almanack, interspersed with religious remarks, which was a work of much talent. If Cotton Mather may be taken as authority, he was profoundly skilled in mathematics, and its kindred branches of knowledge, natural philosophy and astronomy. His style of writing had nothing of mathematical dryness in it, but was lofty, flowing, and eloquent. (Mr. Sherman was blessed with a numerous family, having twenty-six children, and some of his descendants are among the first people in New-England; a greater number from the female branches than from the male.)

Of the progress of the literature of the ancient dominion, during the first half century, after it was so far settled as to form a regular government, which was in 1620, I am not able to give much account; not that I have not been sedulous in my inquiries, and constant in my researches for this purpose; but, as they were all churchmen in Virginia at this period, and did not enter into the polemicks of the day, and no extraordinary man was driven by persecution to her shores, it is but fair to suppose that they thought it wiser to enjoy the hour, than to trouble themselves to record the occurrences of their lives for posterity. They could not have been destitute of classical men, when, in 1641, there were about forty clergymen in Virginia extremely well paid for their services. The salary of a clergyman was then ten thousand pounds of tobacco a year; forty shillings being a fee for a funeral service, and twenty for a marriage one. Among these divines, as well as among the magistrates, there must have been some men of high attainments. There was no tolerably accurate history of Virginia until Beverley's, which was published in England in 1665. He was a man of intelligence, and seems to have written merely to correct the error, which was prevalent in England, on the subject of Virginia history.

Maryland was settled not far from the time of the planting of the colony of Massachusetts Bay. For this enterprise the world are indebted to the first and second Lords Baltimore. The adventurers were catholicks, and are said to have been of high respectability. They were as talented as any of the early colonists, and reserved to this day extensive lands for the purposes of education. But there are but few traces of their advancement in the cultivation of letters, for the first half century of their existence. Yet to this state, as well as to Virginia, many of the royalists fled during the time of Cromwell's commonwealth; and surely, many of these must have been fine scholars; but how they employed their time, during that period, they have left us nothing but conjecture, as far as I can discover.

New-York, being all the time, from its settlement to 1664, in the hands of the Dutch, we can say nothing of its literature; but there is no reason to suppose that it was not very considerable. If the country does not owe much to the Dutch, in the way of its literary establishments, it certainly has cause to respect them for an industrious progeny, always a blessing to any country. It is stated by Lamberchtsen, a late historian of New-Netherlands, that this colony was partly settled by the Waldenses of Piedmont, subjects of the duke of Savoy, who fled from the persecutions of their sovereign; and Milton, and other writers, speak of them as among the most virtuous and intelligent of mankind. Lamberchtsen's work has been made known to us, for it was locked up in a language unknown to most scholars, by one of the first writers among us, whose taste and researches have done honour to his country, G. Verplank, of the city of New-York; and to whom others, as well as myself, stand deeply indebted for much instruction, and many a fine model of composition. He has burnished up the bullion of his ancestors with admirable skill, and stamped it with inscriptions of classical taste.

E 2

Connecticut was an emanation from the colony of Massachusetts, and, like the former, was commenced by enlightened men. Winthrop, the son of the governor of Massachusetts, an accomplished scholar, came out from England with an agency of the Lords Say and Brook, in 1635, and was chosen governor of Hartford colony. Hopkins, Haynes, Wyllys, Thomas, Wells, and Webster, were governors after him. The colony of New-Haven was begun in 1637, and was governed by Seton, Newman, and Leet, until the union between the two colonies. Winthrop was the most scientific man of his time among the colonists. He was intimate with Boyle and Wilkins, and assisted in founding the " *Royal Society of London.*" Douglass, who praises no one heartily, and abuses as many as he can, says, " Winthrop, who died in Boston, March 26, 1649, was much given to experimental philosophy and medicine." Several of his receipts are still used by that family in charity to the poor. Some of his pieces are to be found amongst the first philosophical transactions of the London Royal Society. In fact, one of the volumes of the transactions of that society was dedicated to him. He was the principal correspondent of this society in the West, and they had chosen the first men in every country for this office.

Leet was a lawyer, and a man of talents and firmness. He, long after his acting as deputy to Winthrop, protected Whally and Goffe, the regicides, and behaved with high honour, and great kindness and firmness, in this critical time. Hooker we have previously mentioned. Eaton was a liberal man, and gave largely for the support of education. Five hundred pounds of his estate went, by a decree of chancery, to Harvard college; and twice that sum was given for the support of schools in New-Haven, Hartford, and Hadley. These early settlements paid the same attention to education that was bestowed upon this important subject in Massachusetts, and, with them, it has been equally successful. They began wisely, and have proceeded judiciously: but, as during the half century we are now treating, they had neither university nor press, still they were imbibing the elements of that knowledge, and cherishing those principles, which, in the next half century, were to develope themselves so beautifully.

New-Hampshire can hardly be considered, for the first half century, as separate from the colony of Massachusetts, in a political point of view, being then virtually under the government of the former. The settlers were the same sort of men; and, in proportion to their means, they pursued the same course in religion and letters. In a few towns near Portsmouth, churches were gathered and instruction commenced; and, by the second half century, York, Wells, and other places, were in a hopeful forwardness, and were able to sustain their part in the labours and trials of extending the blessings of civilization and knowledge.

Rhode Island was first settled by Roger Williams, a native of Wales. He came to this country in 1631, and was engaged in the ministry in Salem, in Massachusetts. Some difficulties arising respecting his doctrines, he went to Plymouth colony, and from thence returned to Salem; but he became so bold in preaching his tenets, both religious and political, that they could not endure to hear them. He came out fully, and said that the charter of Massachusetts was good for nothing, as the soil and sovereignty was not purchased of the natives. These were unpalatable doctrines in that day. He would not desist for the threats of enemies nor the entreaty of friends; and the magistrates passed sentence of banishment on him, and he was exiled from the godly; and, after many tribulations, he settled in Providence, a name he gave the place of his rest, in gratitude to a kind providence that had directed him to so goodly an heritage. He began by a noble act, which contained at once the spirit of a true religion, and the dictates of a sound philosophy. He began by tolerating all religious creeds. Toleration was then considered a plant of a strange growth, that had sprung up in errour, and would soon die in shame. The zealous dreaded it, as a poisonous weed that would blight all the sweet-scented flowers in the garden of God; one that would change the balmy breath of religion to moral pestilence and death. How often have good men been mistaken. This spirit of toleration is the bond of harmony, and the protection of all religion. The liberty this great founder of a state gave to others he took for himself; for he changed his own sentiments of baptism, and thought that man must wait for the ordinance until it was intimated to him from heaven. From religion, he bent his mind to the politics of his settlement; and went, in 1643, and afterwards, to England as agent for his colony, and, on his return, was made president of it. He was as magnanimous as he was tolerant; for living in the neighbourhood of several formidable tribes of Indians, he could at any time have stirred them up to avenge himself for his banishment; but, so far from taking this course, he kept them in peace with the Plymouth and Massachusetts Bay colonies; but, what is more particularly to our purpose, Roger Williams wrote a key to the Indian language, which is a very learned, well written book, and gives the present generation a better knowledge of the advancement of the savages in their moral and social, as well as political and warlike relations, than any other book of that age. He attacked, as a controversial writer on religious subjects, Mr. Cotton, Endicot, George Fox, and others, with great power and sagacity. He tolerated all, but followed none. His own opinions were, perhaps, never very fully settled in his own mind, and this he did not conceal from others. His whole soul seemed constantly struggling with a spirit beyond the feelings and the knowledge of the age in which he lived. The eccentricities of the intelligent are often nothing more than the agitation of the mind, pregnant with new principles and inventions, to which accident may give birth.

During the first fifty years of the existence of our settlements, the useful arts as well as letters flourished among them to a very considerable extent. The private dwelling houses were made more comfortable; prosperous villages grew up; a thrifty commerce, commencing in the fisheries, was established; merchant vessels and ships for defence were built; (three, before 1645, of 300 tons;) several public edifices were erected; and school-houses convenient for the great work of publick instruction were built in various parts of the country. Much of this prosperity, with the blessing of God, was undoubtedly the effect of the mental energies and moral character of the men who conceived and achieved the enterprise of establishing an asylum in this newly discovered world.

But it ought not to be forgotten that the character of the women of that age, had much to do with the success of the undertaking. At the time of the first emigration to this country, the females of England were well educated, and had a higher rank in the scale of mind, than at any previous age in British history. This had been effected, in no small degree, by the long and prosperous reign of Queen Elizabeth, and her high reputation for talents and learning. Fashion has often the same control over the mind, as over the dress and equipage of a people. It was fashionable during the reign of this extraordinary queen, to think women as capable of reasoning upon public affairs as men. Our mothers brought something of this spirit with them. They knew from history, how much their sex had done in the advancement of civilization and christianity; and here was the finest field to prove that they still had the power and inclination. Naturally generous and enthusiastick, women have in every age been attached to the hero and the saint; and have followed the former to the battle-field, to bind up his wounds, and to sing his praises after victory; and the latter to the cross and the tomb. The wives of the pilgrims who landed at Plymouth discovered more than Spartan fortitude in braving dangers and in supporting calamities. They were well educated women.

Among those who came after the pilgrims to settle the province of Massachusetts Bay, were several women of high rank and superior refinement; Lady Arabella Johnson, daughter of the Earl of Lincoln, and the wives of the gentlemen who formed the board of magistrates, were high bred dames; as well as the wives of the .

clergy, and many of the wives of their associates. Some of their chirography has reached us. It resembles the easy, flowing, fashionable hand of the present day, while the writing of the men of that day, is difficult to be read. We have all seen the needle-work of that age in embroidered armorials, and genealogical trees; and these ancient records bear ample testimony to the industry, talent and skill of the fair who wrought them. They shared the hardship of the times. Many a lovely daughter, in that day, who had been brought up in affluence, and with tenderness, on her marriage, moved from her home and parents, to some new settlement where her bridal serenade was the howlings of the beasts of prey, as they nightly roamed the desert.

If our mothers had a share, and a great share they had, in the trials of those days, why should they not be remembered in the history of this new-born empire? I contend, and who will deny it, that it required more courage and fortitude to stay on the skirts of the forest, unprotected by moat, ditch, or stockade, in the half built cabin, with decrepitude and infancy, listening to every step, anxious for the coming in of those who had gone forth in search of the foe, than it did to fight the foe when he was met. This was more than Spartan fortitude; for the enemy seldom saw the dwelling where the heroick mother of Sparta waited to hear the fate of her husband or children; but ours were in constant danger of an attack from the savages.

Such were our progenitors: such the race who came to a wilderness, and broke it into fertility and made it a garden. Men who, living, exercised the rights of freemen, and who died with the spirit of the brave, in the hopes of the just: and if no monument mark the sacred ground in which their ashes repose, yet, their labours, their struggles, and their virtues, are matters of distinct history. The monuments they left behind, are more durable than brass, and will retain their polish longer than marble. They consist in the institutions they founded and cherished, in their day and generation, and bequeathed as a rich legacy to their posterity. There is not a principle of religion, of liberty, or law, among us, at this day, whose germ cannot be traced to them. The foundation stones of our schools of learning, of our halls of justice, and of the temples of our God, were laid by them in every hallowed right of consecration. This goodly heritage, has been cherished and defended in good faith, and has come down, extending wider and growing more valuable with every passing day: and when distant ages to us shall come blessed with wealth, with dominion, and power, and shall be covered with new intellectual glory, surrounded by arts yet unknown, and sciences yet untaught, these early fathers of the land

8

shall receive an increased measure of fame. Then may it be said,
of this generation, that they were daughters worthy of their mothers,
and sons who did not disgrace their fathers; a people who had
transmitted unimpaired the blessings they had received.

LECTURE IV.

Antiquities, or remnants of history, are tanquam tabula naufragii, when industrious persons, by an exact and scrupulous diligence and observation, out
of monuments, names, words, proverbs, traditions, private records, and evidences, fragments of stories, passages of books that concern not story, and the
like, do save and recover somewhat from the deluge of time.

Verulam.

In this second half century, from the settlement of the country,
flourished the Mathers. The father, Increase Mather, has been
already mentioned as president of Harvard College; but, in a literary view, the father and son may be said to have been contemporaries. They died about the same time, within five years of each
other, the elder 85, the younger 65. They were the most voluminous writers of the age in which they lived, and have never been
exceeded by many in the variety of their subjects, nor in the amount
of their matter. The concerns of religion and literature, the duties
of political and domestick life, the subjects of the passing day, and
the most abstruse questions of science, all fell within their grasp,
and were honoured with their attention. It is no wonder, then, that
the estimates of their merits were various; some influenced by one
motive and some by another. They felt every thing, and received
every measure of attention, from adoration to hatred, from individuals of the same community, at the same time. But after all, it is
not so very difficult to form a just estimate of them at this day, although it must be confessed, that some, who agree in other things,
disagree in regard to the merits of the Mathers. They were more
exclusively our own scholars, than most of those we have mentioned; both were born on the soil, and were educated at the same
university. The father was born at Dorchester, 1639, and the son
in Boston, in 1663. Their minds were in a great degree alike; but
the father had seen more of the world than the son, having been

several times in England, and mixed much in society, from the very nature of his profession and offices; and certainly had a better taste, either natural or cultivated. Both were indefatigable students, and were devoted to the same pursuits in letters and religion. The father wrote more than an hundred works, which issued from the press in this country or in England; nothing escaped them, from *cometographia* to *witchcraft;* from wizards to angels. They *shot off an arrow at profane dancing*, and threw off a pamphlet *in favour of innoculation for the small-pox*. The father had a rich imagination, great stores of learning, with great industry and aptitude for study; which often arises from equanimity of temper, which he had in a greater degree than his son; and he possessed, what indeed is a great acquirement, a happy facility of moulding the minds of his pupils to virtue, and at the same time of stimulating their appetites for knowledge. He was happy in his own exertions; happy in his own success; and still happier in a long life, to mature his plans, and to give efficiency to his efforts. This was not all; he was thrice blessed in his son Cotton, who arose from the swaddling clothes of the cradle a prodigy. In his father's mind, the Arabian tale of the birth of Solomon was no longer a fable, of whom it was said, that the first word he spoke, was the awful name of the *Most High*, and the first sentence he uttered, was a confession of faith. Cotton Mather, when an infant, checked the wandering and reproved the vicious; and received the blessing of the seer and sage, at every corner and in every temple. At fifteen years of age, he had finished his collegiate course, and was before the world as a scholar. His piety was superiour to his talents and learning; for he read fifteen chapters a day in the bible, and reading, with him, was nearly committing to memory; and multiplied his fastings and vigils, with the zeal and perseverance of an hermit, who is destined to grace the calendar of saints. He coursed over the whole circle of sciences with great speed, and formed systems of his own, which, probably, he thought at the time would endure with sun and moon, and be as necessary to mankind as seed time and harvest. He became a colleague with his father in the ministry, and they lived and laboured, each in the sunshine of the other. He preached sermons, of great length, every Sunday, and spent several afternoons in the week in visiting his parishoners, for the purpose of devising something for their mental, temporal, and spiritual comfort. He wrote treatises with almost incredible celerity, and scattered them profusely, in the hope of doing good. One of his biographers says, that the number of his works was three hundred and eighty-three. It were vain to attempt to characterize all of them by any general class. The subjects, as well as the execution, were of different character. Franklin ascribes to one of Mather's essays, *all his usefulness in life*. This alone, one would think, were praise enough for one man; but, in addition to this, many have added, if possible, higher praise; namely, that the preacher, by his writings, had led them into the way of life everlasting. If any thing could exceed his industry, it was his wish to be useful; and, if any thing could be imagined to transcend that desire, it was his credulity. His mind was rich and fruitful, well cultivated, but without regularity or order. He mistook method, or arrangement and order, in the distribution of his time, for method and order in the classification of his thoughts. This mistake is not an uncommon one. His intellectual store-house was full to overflowing; but nothing there was threshed, winnowed, binned, or labelled. Whenever he attempted to spread before the public his own thoughts, there came rushing to his memory ten thousand thoughts of other men; probably not so good as his own, but which, from the pride of learning, must be used. These thoughts often dazzled his own vision, and obscured or misled his understanding. Thus the children of his own brain were bedizzened with the flaming colours of all costumes, and were half-smothered in the tatters of outlandish wardrobes. His logick was often overlaid by illustration, and the force of his eloquence lost by vanity, quaintness, and punning. Acquainted with the pure fountains of classical literature, and often refreshed with copious draughts from them, he feared his piety might be questioned by having this generally known; and therefore he drew his quotations, and, in fact, formed his taste, from the literature of scholastick divinity; forgetting, that some waters may be fit to bathe in, which might be deleterious to drink. Credulity, which is often the concomitant of quick genius, and which is, generally, in itself harmless, was to him a sore evil, and left a stain on his escutcheon, which will go down to posterity with his name forever. When he was in the plenitude of his influence, in church and state, the delusion of witchcraft was at its height. He had the keeping of the conscience of the new governor, Sir William Phipps, who was an uneducated man, and never rose, though a man of strong mind naturally, above the errours of vulgar life. With the ignorant, he believed in demonology, and his confessor established his belief; "*for who should know all about these things better than Doctor Mather.*" This was the natural course of the governor's reflections. The statesman and divine acted in concert, and the country was ransacked for instances, to show the great power of the devil; and all these instances Mather *noted and conned by heart*. The victims died with imprecations upon their heads. The sober and thinking part of the community reasoned on the subject, and sifted the arguments and statements of the clergyman and the judges, and, at length, common sense prevailed, and the actors in the tragedy were driven from the scene with scorn and detestation. The delusion passed off, but the stigma never will; no man has ever visited the tomb of the Mathers, without thinking of these things, and, perhaps, thousands who have visited it, knew nothing else of them than the part they took in this sad affair. But why Mather, Phipps, and the New-England judges here, should be more condemned, than the judges in old England, who, not far from the same time, both before and after, condemned unhappy creatures for the same crime, in the same way, is not easily explained. The part Cotton Mather took in this persecution has had a great influence on the minds of succeeding generations; even in their estimate of his literary and religious reputation. All men can judge of a deficiency of common sense, while few are capable of appreciating the depths of learning.

That the riper years of Cotton Mather should not have fulfilled the promise of his earlier, is not wonderful, when we reflect, that from his leaving college he had no rival; for, like the Turk, *he could bear no brother near the throne.* For a mighty mind to be able to produce its best efforts, it must come in collision with those of full growth and maturity; and gain the mastery by mental struggles, with others of similar character. But, so situated was Cotton Mather, that, although others could, and did often mortify him by neglect, yet he was still acknowledged by the people to be first and foremost in every thing wonderful in science, or rare in letters. Calef chastised him with much severity, in an admirable piece of argument and satire, and fearlessly held him up to the world as bigoted and vain. A few joined with Calef, but the great mass of the good people found ready excuses for the great divine. In a few years after his death, and even in his life time, the sour, caustick, unprincipled, but talented Douglass, sneered at his learning and laughed at his vanity. The dull and vapid Oldmixon thought he could mend his works; and, in his own collections, has attempted to remodel Mather, in style and manner; and in attempting to remove his excrescences, such as *quaint sayings,* and *inapt quotations,* and *useless pun,* he left him a sinewless and marrowless skeleton of deformity. In modern times, Cotton Mather has been treated by some with severity, and by others with more justice, and, perhaps, by some, with a measure of kindness. Honest Elliot speaks fully of his faults, but is not unmindful of his virtues and his acquirements. With faithful and intelligent Allen, there was no disposition to exaggerate his faults; and it will not be said, that he was unmindful of his merits. The learned Savage, passes him without much respect, for honesty as a literary man, or for his value as a historian. In the hands of the late editor of Morton's Memorial, he fares better than

F

he has before, for a long time. His estimate of this singular writer
is candid, and, in our judgement, more accurate than many others.
His virtues and his failings sleep together, and we would not have
any of his errours or bad taste propagated at the present day ; and
we believe there is no great danger of it, for his faults are not fashionable with us. To imitate his very errors, would be very difficult,
and would require more learning than men commonly have; for
those faults cost much labour and great memory. It is the fashion
to neglect such writers as Mather; the dress is antiquated, but we
hope never to be entirely debarred, by the tyranny of fashion, from
once in a while looking over Bunyan, and keeping company, for an
hour or so, with Christian and his wife, in their homely progress on
the way to heaven; nor be obliged to throw away the quaint emblems of the pious Quarles, or any of his thoughtful brethren,
because they may seem, to some, uncouth in their guise.

At the commencement of the second half century, from the first
settlement of Massachusetts Bay, Penn began his colony, and laid
out his city of Philadelphia, which grew more rapidly than any
previous settlement on the continent. The founder was a rare man ;
possessing talents, virtue, fortitude, perseverance, caution, benevolence, and toleration, with great political sagacity. He made a treaty
with the natives, founded upon reciprocal advantages, which was
faithfully kept for seventy years. He was a lawgiver, who built all
his maxims on the principles of justice and a knowledge of human
nature. His aim was for the best interests of man, as a reasonable
being. He had suffered, and knew how to forgive. He had been
persecuted, and had seen that persecution begot opposition, and
opposition, strifes and bloodshed. He saw that knowledge and virtue were the pillars on which every political fabrick must be built, to
endure any length of time. With broad and just views, this great
lawgiver began his commonwealth; and its rapid growth justified
his claim to superiour sagacity and wisdom. In the course of fifty
years, Philadelphia took the start of older settlements; and has
never, in the slightest degree, lost her high claims to distinction.
In 1749, Douglass says, that Philadelphia had two thousand and
seventy dwelling houses, and eleven places of publick worship; and
that some deserving gentlemen had established " a laudable academy
in Philadelphia, with a publick spirited design of encouraging literature; that is, political and natural knowledge;" and mentions,
also, that it was in a flourishing condition. This is the seminary,
which was commenced by Franklin and his associates in 1742; extended in 1749; and in 1753 was established as a college, and put
under the charge of Rev. Dr. William Smith, who had a great reputation for polite literature; and, at the same time, the Rev. Francis

Allison was called in, as vice provost, and his labours contributed much to the prospects of the institution, and the general diffusion of literature in Pennsylvania and the neighbouring states. The city of Philadelphia has been more rapid, and, at the same time, more solid, in its growth, than any other in the annals of modern times. At the period when the first temple of learning was erected in the Athens of America, the ivy had mantled the age-stricken edifices of Cambridge.

While Harvard College was continuing to flourish, under the fostering care of all classes in society; Connecticut, having increased in population, sufficiently to begin to think of no longer being indebted to her neighbours for seminaries of learning, commenced a collegiate institution in 1701. The first charter was a narrow one. It confined the trustees to the holding of lands, not exceeding five hundred pounds in value. One hundred pounds currency was granted, yearly, to support the seminary, and Saybrook was resolved upon, as the proper place to begin the undertaking. Mr. Pierson, minister of Killingworth, was made rector. The assembling of students, generally, was at his house, while some remained under tutors at Saybrook. This division, at the threshold, was inauspicious, but, after several serious disasters, the trustees fixed on New-Haven, for its location; and in September, 1717, the first commencement was held there; but it did not receive its name until September 12, 1718, when a splendid commencement was got up for the occasion of giving it a name, and spreading its fame through the state. As at the establishment of Harvard College, requisitions were made, not only upon the government of the state, but on the friends of learning in England and in America. Elihu Yale, Esq., an East India merchant, bestowed stocks and books, to a considerable amount, and gave something of importance, by will; but this bequest was, in some way, frustrated. Distinguished individuals in Connecticut gave freely, as did many others in Massachusetts and Rhode Island. Dummer, of the former province, and Brenton, of the latter, gave liberally in money and books. The patrons of the college abroad, were Sir Richard Blackmore, Sir Richard Steel, Drs. Bennett, Calamy, Woodman, Halley, Bentley, Kennett, Edwards, and Mr. Henery, and Mr. Whiston. Mr. Cutler was the second rector, but soon resigned on becoming an episcopalian. In 1723, the charter was enlarged. In 1725, Elisha Williams was chosen rector. In 1732, the general assembly of Connecticut granted the college fifteen hundred acres of land. They intended to follow in the precise steps of Harvard, in the great work of education; for it was expressly "ordered, at the first founding of the college, that when no special provision was made by the trustees, the laws of Harvard college, in the province of Massachusetts Bay, should be the rule."

In 1728, the Rev. Dr. George Berkley, dean of Derry, afterwards bishop of Cloyne, fired by the most enthusiastic visions of the coming glories of the new world, left England for these western shores, with a charter for a college, to be established either at Bermuda, or on the American continent. He soon saw that Bermuda would not answer his purpose, and came to Rhode Island, and there purchased a fine country seat, where he might reside, while he could take a view of the country at large. Liberal funds had been granted to the bishop and his associates for the noble undertaking, (it is said, to the amount of ninety thousand pounds sterling,) and which had been paid into the treasury. While the benevolent dean was casting about him, for the best place to fix himself and build his college, the British minister seized all the funds, for a marriage portion for the princess royal, and at one dash of his pen, destroyed the whole plan. The dean, finding all his hopes at an end, in 1732 made a deed of gift of his farm in Rhode Island, to the trustees of Yale College; and directed that the income from it, should be appropriated to the support of three scholarships, to be bestowed upon the best classical scholars, in each year. This gift is called the *Dean's Bounty*, and has had a fine effect on the students of that college, by exciting a spirit of emulation among them. In 1740, Thomas Clapp succeeded Elisha Williams, who had resigned. In 1744, the charter was again enlarged, and the rector, by this charter, was in future to be called president; and the president and trustees of Yale, has been the style of the corporation, ever since. The reputation of the bishop of Cloyne, has been a subject of panegyric, ever since his friend Pope ascribed,

"To Berkley every virtue under heaven;"

and his name is commemorated at Yale, by the poets and orators of every passing year. Thus was the second literary institution of our country established by the exertions of the learned and the wise; and has ever been a national blessing. Bishop Berkley was a scholar and a poet. A quotation, of a single line, from a short poem of his, is often made by the friends of this country:

"Westward the course of empire takes its way."

As the little poem is extremely scarce, having seldom been published in this country, I have transcribed the whole of it from the "Anniversary discourse, delivered before the New-York Historical Society," by one of the most distinguished scholars of our country,

Gulian C. Verplank, Esq., now member of congress from the city of New-York. This single discourse is a mine of information to the lovers of American literature; and to this work I am much indebted for many valuable facts.

> The muse, disgusted at an age and clime
> Barren of every glorious theme,
> In distant lands now waits a better time,
> Producing subjects worthy fame.

> In happy climes, where from the genial sun,
> And virgin earth, such scenes ensue,
> The force of art by nature seems outdone,
> And fancied beauties, by the true.

> In happy climes, the seat of innocence,
> Where nature guides, and virtue rules;
> Where men shall not impose, for truth and sense,
> The pedantry of courts and schools.

> There, shall be sung another golden age,
> The rise of empires and of arts;
> The good and great, inspiring epick rage;
> The wisest heads and noblest hearts.

> Not such as Europe breeds, in her decay
> Such as she bred, when fresh and young;
> When heavenly flame did animate her clay,
> By future poets shall be sung.

> Westward the course of empire takes its way;
> The four first acts already past,
> A fifth shall close the drama with the day;
> Time's noblest offspring is the last.

While this institution was rising up by the zeal of the benevolent and the good; Connecticut was blessed by the government of Gurdon Saltonstall, as chief magistrate. He was a grandson of Sir Richard Saltonstall, one of the first settlers of Massachusetts Bay. The governor had been a preacher, but his fame for wisdom, in matters of civil and political life, was so extraordinary, that he was taken, as it were, by force, and made chief magistrate; and his case is an exception from the general charge of volatility in the people: for he was chosen from 1707 to 1724, without any diminution of publick respect, or without a rival. He was indeed a rare man; with a noble and commanding person—a generous and sympathizing heart, a fascinating eloquence, with profound erudition and courteous manners; he was irresistible among the people, and first also in the synod, the council-chamber, and the judgement-hall. His wife was equally renowned, and lived longer to do good. She was a patroness of Yale and Harvard Colleges, to several churches, and other institutions of piety and learning. The house of Madam Saltonstall was resorted to by the intelligent and the good, as the abode of a prophetess, or a mother in Israel. It was a high honour to be accounted one of her friends; for her discernment was such, that the hypocrite in religion, or the pretender in knowledge, was soon discovered and discarded.

In every age of darkness and superstition, we find some minds superiour to prejudice, and which fearlessly rise above the mists around them. Such an one was Robert Calef, a merchant of Boston, who was in business at the time of the delusion of witchcraft. He saw how the people were misled, by some of the higher classes in society. The governor, Sir William Phipps, was the most zealous prosecutor, aided and directed by his father confessor, Cotton Mather, and assisted by most of the commission, who tried those unfortunate persons, who suffered for this supposed crime. Calef wrote many private letters, and published some communications in a pamphlet form; but as the printers were alarmed at publishing frequently, he was induced to issue a volume on the subject. He opposed reason and common sense, to fanaticism and overstrained constructions of scripture; and had many readers and more converts, than at that time dared avow their sentiments. The attack upon the Mathers, was considered by the parishioners of these influential divines, as the most imprudent and wicked of all slanders; and they published a defence of their pastor, and treated Calef as a vile free-thinker. The Rev. Increase Mather, President of Harvard College, to show the students in what horrour such a man as Calef should be held, had some of Calef's works burnt in the college yard; as impious and infidel productions were by the common hangman in England. But after all, common sense prevailed, and in fact, was never entirely lost sight of in the community; for in looking over the records of the trials for witchcraft in 1692, I find that the court found it difficult to bring the jury to convict the persons charged; and that one foreman of the jury was dismissed by the court, for refusing to find a verdict on "the spectral evidence," as he could not justify it to his own understanding, nor find it sanctioned by any fact or rule in the scriptures. Calef lived to see his views of this delusion become the general opinion, and that of most of the commission; for they were tried by judges, under a special commission, as is generally the case in England, when state policy requires such a course should be pursued. Calef died in Portsmouth, New-Hampshire, to which place he had removed to spend his old age with some of his children, loved and respected by all liberal minded men.

Among the most accomplished scholars and writers of the age, in which he lived, was William Burnet; who was for some time governor of New-York and New-Jersey. His first speech to the legislature, after he came to that government, was celebrated for its ease, dignity, and elegance, and has seldom been equalled in this species of composition, now so common throughout the land. On the accession of George 2d, he was removed from his government to that of Massachusetts. In this office he had some difficulties; but with him, as a politician, we have nothing to do at this time, but only as a scholar. His eloquence was of the first order; his manners were most polished, which gave a grace to his great learning. He had laid the foundation of his knowledge, under the care of his father, a learned prelate, and of Sir Isaac Newton. In such a school, he was taught to think for himself, and he improved upon his lessons. Governor Burnet wrote several works of celebrity, one of which is, "an essay on the scripture prophecies." His taste, and talents, had a very salutary effect upon the literature of his day. He every where ridiculed the quaint style of the ecclesiastical writers of his time; and the Mathers were the persons, generally, against whose writings his polished shafts were levelled. He outlived Cotton Mather about a year and a half.

Contemporary with Burnet, was Jeremy Dummer, who was an honour to the literature of our country. While he was in college, the President, Dr. Increase Mather declared him "by far the best scholar that had ever been there;" which his succeeding reputation evinced to be a just encomium. From Harvard, he went to study theology at Leyden; but, although he was considered as great in this science, he preferred politics and jurisprudence to the creeds of Calvin, or the annotations of Whitsius, the professor of theology at Leyden. As agent for the province of Massachusetts Bay, his services were greater than his rewards; for while he was writing most ably *in defence of the charter*, he was dismissed from his office; not for any alleged misconduct, or neglect of his duties; but he had been employed by Bolingbroke, and that was sufficient to destroy his popularity in Massachusetts. He had the misfortune, which is indeed a great one, to be in advance of the knowledge of the times. In the ages of rusticity and ignorance, the elegance of Chesterfield would have passed for egregious foppery, and the science of Sir Humphrey Davy for necromancy. Jeremy Dummer was a great friend to learning in this country, and was a very considerable patron to Yale College.

Lt. Governor Dummer, who was in office under Burnet, and was for a while, *locum tenens* of the chief magistracy, after the death of the governor, as he was before his arrival, was a man of considerable acquirements, and a very good officer. A friend to learning and piety, he gave a considerable sum to build the first house of publick worship in Hollis-street, in Boston; and also, a noble farm in New-bury, in the county of Essex, to establish an academy in that town; at which seminary, some of the first scholars of the present age received the rudiments of their education; and it is now, notwithstanding the larger seminaries which have grown up in New-England, in very good credit. The building in which the school is kept, is on the farm which supports the instructors; and is shaded by the trees, which more than a century ago, the munificent benefactor of learning planted with his own hand.

The charter of William and Mary, 1692, although opposed by many of the first settlers, was undoubtedly advantageous in many respects. The union of the old colony with that of Massachusetts Bay, was one of the beneficial results. A more parliamentary shape was given to legislative proceedings; and a more distinct line was drawn between legislative, judicial, and executive proceedings. The patriarchal form, which is admissible in a small and infant community, is not sufficiently powerful or regular when that community has considerably increased. As Cotton Mather would have said in such a case, the commands of Jacob were not sufficient to restrain the ungoverned passions of his sons, Simeon and Levi, when his family had became large, and the Patriarch had grown old. The profession of the law, had been confined to a few, and those few were restrained by the rules and regulations of the magistrates; but when this charter went into operation, the courts assumed a more legal character. It was under this charter, that the witches were tried; but it should be remembered, at the same time, that this delusion was arrested in its course, by the happy thought, of bringing actions of defamation against those who made the foul and false aspersions upon their neighbours; charging them with being united to the devil, and working deeds of darkness. In all the trials for the crime of witchcraft, there is no mention made of counsel to the prisoners, or of their having counsel to advise or argue for them.

Soon after this charter went into operation, a luminary arose in the law, whose fame will be as enduring with us as the names of Lyttleton, Coke, or Mansfield. John Read was graduated at Harvard College in 1697, and prepared himself for the pulpit, and did actually preach for some time; but indulging himself in a little wit and satire in his discourse, he was suspected of liberal, tolerant feelings in his creed, and that would not do. From the pulpit, he went to the bar, and here he effected a complete revolution, or rather began a new era, in the history of American law. The long deed, conveying real estate, which then covered a sheet of parchment, he reduced to its present simple and intelligible form ; and the ease and convenience of it was so apparent, that it was soon adopted. Read was often in the legislature from Boston, and for several years in the council. In either place, his opinions were law, for he was as fearless as intellectual ; and spoke as he thought, in great honesty of soul. He lived to a good old age, and died about twelve years before the late venerable John Adams came to the bar, who informed me, that he never saw Read ; but that his seniors, Gridley, Kent, Putnam, Pynchon, and others, had treasured many anecdotes of his wit, and many axioms of his law. Shirley, who was himself a lawyer, thought him the greatest lawyer that ever lived, and consulted him as an oracle. After his appearance on the stage, the profession of the law shared the publick honours with the clergy ; and by degrees, the spirit of the times gently crowded the clergy out of civil appointments ; and brought in those better acquainted with the practical things of life, and the ordinary business of men. New-York, had not an opportunity to advance, in this half century, as the other colonies. After the final settlement, by which the colony was ceded to the English, the people were frequently annoyed by bad governors ; this continued for several years after the commencement of the 18th century. Lord Cornbury greatly retarded the prospects of New-York, by his ignorance, avarice, and faithlessness to his duties ; but the statute book of the state, and the history of the quarrel with Burnet on his chancery decisions, prove that there were some good lawyers among them ; and probably, much other learning. The clergymen of the Dutch Reformed Church were, in general, well educated men ; but preaching in their own language, their usefulness was in a great measure lost to the people from New-England, who flocked in as emigrants to share so goodly a heritage.

During the second half century, the literature of South Carolina began to be respectable. The professional men, before this time, had been educated in Europe ; and now found the want of a library, to keep pace, in some measure, with the improvements of the European continent. In the year 1700, a provincial library was established in Charleston, by the liberality of the lords proprietors and of the Rev. Thomas Bray. This introduced a love for reading, and made an impression upon the minds and tastes of that people, which has never been lost. In 1712, a free school was established, which was an extensive grammar-school, and where a good foundation for classical education was laid. Several private academies were set up, within a few years. England and the eastern colonies supplied them with teachers, for many years. A printer settled at Charleston, between the years 1720 and 1730. The first newspaper was printed there in 1730. The professions were, at that time, filled with men of learning, many of them from Europe. Mark Catesby, an English naturalist, came to South Carolina in 1722, and resided four years in the colony ; and was assiduous in promoting the knowledge of botany and zoology. He had lived in Virginia seven years previously, engaged in the same pursuit; Sir Hans Sloan was his patron. James Blair began to lay the foundation of William and Mary College in 1691 ; but he was many years in getting it under way, for he did not take upon himself the duties of president, until 1729, and then continued them until 1742. This good man laboured hard in his duties, but many of the youth of Virginia still went to England for an education. Dr. Blair was an able man. He published a work, the year he died, in London, in four volumes octavo, " Our Saviour's divine sermon on the mount explained, and the practice of it recommended." It was, in that day, esteemed a work of great merit.

As we have taken a survey of our forefathers from their first landing on these shores, particularly as men of letters and science, and have given sketches of their characters as individuals, and have made some general remarks on the communities as they grew up, it will not be going out of the path I have prescribed to myself in the lectures, to take a summary view of them at the close of the first century of their existence. I have mentioned the little poem of the good Bishop of Cloyne, which at the period it was published was considered only a compliment from a pure and highly intellectual ecclesiastick, to a race of people he was fond of praising—it is now thought to have been prophetick—particularly the closing canto :

> " Westward the star of empire takes its way;
>   The four first acts already past,
> The fifth shall close the drama with the day—
>   Time's noblest offspring is his last."

But it was only the sagacity of a great man, reasoning from cause to effect ; and we will, for a moment, see how far he was justified in making these predictions, as a sagacious observer of human nature, deeply read in the history of man.

The century from the settlement of the northern province closed, exhibiting a people extended along the sea coast, for more than a thousand miles, of more or less maturity, some being of a more recent date, and others a few years older than those of Massachusetts. Although not precisely alike in their manners and customs, yet these provincials were so nearly alike as to be embraced under general remarks, applicable to the most advanced portions of the country. They were, at this period, comparatively at ease, for the dread of extermination from the aborigines had entirely passed away. They had fought the savages, and had driven them back to remote forests and distant hunting grounds; and though often vexed and distressed by the hostile incursions of the Indians, still they had no fears of being destroyed by them. The Indians had, in the infancy of the colonies, come down upon them in their full strength and best possible concert, and were then beaten and broken, and if not destroyed, were so far dispirited and enfeebled, that nothing like regular warfare was afterwards carried on against the most populous parts of the country. The people, it is true, were often distressed at the complaints of the frontier settler, and were frequently called out to avenge his wrongs, which was generally done in such a manner as to keep the tribe of Indians who perpetrated them quiet for some time. The growth of this country was indeed marked by wonders to the people themselves; for the most sanguine of the emigrants did not contemplate so rapid a progress in their growth and strength. They had, in this century, not only fought the Indians for self-preservation, but after little more than fifty years of their existence, assisted the mother country in an attempt to wrest Canada from the hands of the French, which fortunately did not succeed; for an intermixture of the French and English at that time would, in all probability, have had no good effect on the nationality of the provincials; but as it was, the primitive character of the people had not essentially changed from that of their fathers, when the century closed. They had wisely adopted new rules and regulations in the administration of justice, and greatly expanded their views, and thoroughly changed their opinions on many subjects, but still the same spirit remained, and the same hardihood of character was apparent. They had, before this time, separated church from state, and had found many blessings flowing from this division. Men of distinction grew up in both departments of these intellectual and moral pursuits, who laboured hard for the general good, and have left their deeds on record.

They had also established courts under their various charters, and civil justice took a new form. The primitive courts, though believed by the people themselves, when first instituted, to be the best method of getting at justice that could then be devised, had, long before the close of the century, become rather offensive to the good sense of the people at large. They found that there was something very arbitrary in *discretion*, that which the magistrates possessed of defining the crime and of fixing the punishment at the same time; and often making that criminal, which had never been considered a crime, misdemeanour, or offence, in any written code of laws that had ever been given to the world. It is amusing to look back to their records now, when the judges and those they condemned have gone to a perfect tribunal, and to mark the course of proceedings in those early days, when the magistracy, on the suspicion of an offence against what they thought the decorum of society, would often decree a more severe punishment than against a crime of a felonious nature. The people were too shrewd to be so governed forever; and they found the courts of law, established upon proper principles, with judges sworn to administer justice according to fixed and settled laws, either the wisdom of many years experience, or the written law of the statute book, were far better than the arbitrary opinions and decisions of those esteemed even as wise and good, who had no barrier against caprice, and who were imperfect, because they were men.

At this period, the day of delusion had passed away, and the mists of superstition were fast dispersing before the rays of reason and the reign of common sense. This very delusion, however, was made a mean, under Providence, of hastening on the age of philosophical inquiry into the nature of man, and of the permissions of Deity in his government of the world. The blood of the victims of delusion, though they were few in number, was not without its use. It did not cry from the ground for vengeance, for it was shed by infatuated honesty; but ages of eloquence and reasoning could not have done so much for the advancement of rational thinking as the sacrifice of these few lives did. There was an image of error left in the minds of the community which was held up against misguided zeal, and a too ready desire to punish offences, which has had a most salutary effect ever since. The shades of immolated innocence haunted the severe in disposition, who are always inclined to superstition, and restrained them from attempting to influence publick feeling, which they had a secret wish, no doubt, at all times to do. The momentary folly of the few was the permanent security of the whole.

At this period, publick schools had been long in operation in New-England, and the rich were made to educate the poor, not only in the common elements of learning, but in the higher walks of literature, when they aspired to it. The colleges that had been established were fountains of useful knowledge, whose streams were flowing in all directions. The young men educated in these colleges were, most of them, engaged, for several years after they had graduated, in the useful employment of teaching school in those places required by law to maintain a grammar school, and almost every town was sufficiently large to require one. Among other duties, the clergy, too, assisted in preparing youths for college. The influence of their labours had entered into every thing temporal, as well as spiritual; and being now confined, by the separation of the government of the church from that of the state, to their own distinct duties, they had much more leisure to attend to improving their own minds, and those of their parishioners, than ever; and to them, present generations are indebted for no inconsiderable portion of the literature of that day. By this time, the law had become a distinct profession, and several luminaries had arisen, who had changed the modes of transacting the business of the courts, and driven the race of pettifoggers, which generally abound in a new country, (and did in this to a considerable extent,) at the first establishment of courts, into disgrace and neglect. Learned physicians had grown up, who were not only devoted to the healing art, but were making researches in the phenomena of nature, with great assiduity and success.

The press was well supported by the people, and held as one of the great safeguards of the rights and interests of freemen. The literati were fond of seeing themselves in print, and pamphlets and tracts issued, to gratify the curiosity and taste of the people. At this period, newspapers had been established, and were most valuable vehicles of information. They were, in general, edited with no ordinary share of talent, and some of the first men in the country were engaged directly or indirectly in their support. Political rights were freely discussed in them, and their influence was felt in the most remote settlement of the country. Not only the proceedings of the British Parliament were communicated to the public through their columns, with the news of the day; but they were made serviceable in giving the people a knowledge and taste for the current English literature. Long extracts from authors of standard value were weekly diffused by these papers. England was, during this century, prolific in men of genius, and the great doctrines of civil liberty were taught in their writings, which in this country had a free circulation, if not in their own. Texts are often graced, and sometimes amended, by their commentaries; it was so in this country, in regard to every work on British liberty; for here it was read without prejudice, and scanned without fear. The mind of man was awake to its true interests, in a country where there was neither hierarchy, nor aristocracy, nor furious democracy, to disturb the smooth and equal current of thinking and acting. They had often quarrelled with governors, and complained of royal neglect,

G
10

and sometimes were gravely debating upon heresies and schisms; but these things were not more than sufficient to give force and activity to their intellectual powers, and had no withering effect. The people, although prudent and saving, were not goaded by avarice, or sunk in voluptuousness, or dissipated by trifling amusements; and these political and religious excitements were necessary to give proper tone to the mind.

Commerce had, during this century, extended its humanizing influence among the people, and trade was now doing what war previously had done—making them acquainted with each other's wants and capacities. Their commercial enterprise, considering their means, was astonishing.*

Their fisheries and lumber trade, with their ship building, produced them a very considerable surplus over their importations from the mother country and the West India islands. They had found that the bosom of the earth was rich in iron ore, the true gold of a primitive people; and they at this early period had established foundries, or bloomeries, as the works for manufacturing iron were then called, which were in a prosperous condition for many years afterwards. The clothing of the great mass of the people was from their own flax and wool, wrought at their own firesides; and if it did not allow them to dress sumptuously, it made comfortable articles of wearing apparel. The forests were then abundant, and their dwellings were warm and convenient. The purest of streams watered their grounds, and their orchards produced in abundance, so that there was but little use of ardent spirits.

Their military system was simple, yet perfect; every man was enrolled who could carry a musket, and all were accustomed to the use of it. They obeyed the calls of their country with alacrity, and fought as long as their services were necessary: braver troops never stood on the battle field; they were valiant without ferocity, and endured the hardships of war without the hopes of plunder. Military glory was with them a principle, not a passion. Military knowledge was with them a habit, not a profession. The plough, the axe, the saw, and the hammer, were the tools of their handy-craft—necessary implements of their daily avocation; and the musket, and the sword, only implements of defence; and they were expert in all. They asked no wreath for their victories, they obtained no heraldric honours for their numerous instances of valour; a consciousness of having discharged their duties as citizen soldiers, was all their reward. At the time we are now describing, they exhibited in their character all that is now embraced in the hopes and desires of na-

* See Appendix, note A.

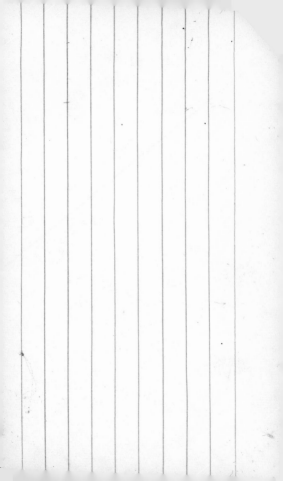

tions, for liberty, for moral dignity, and for the rights of man. They were sons of trial, of perseverance, and enterprise, who had turned their afflictions and their exertions to advantage ; and made not only their enjoyments and privileges, but even their misfortunes, a truly valuable lesson for themselves and for their posterity.

LECTURE V.

——— See their sons
Before the bulwark of their dear rights drawn,
Proud in their simple dignity, as runs
The courser to the fair stream—on their thrones
They sat, all kings, all people—they were free,
For they were strong and temperate, and in tones
Deep and canorous, nature's melody,
They sung in one full voice the hymn of liberty.
PERCIVAL.

FROM the beginning of the second century, reckoning from the commencement of the settlement of the province of Massachusetts Bay, there could not have been more than half a million of inhabitants in the colonies.   Douglass, as late as 1749, calculates that there were three hundred and fifty-four thousand souls in New-England; and it must be recollected, that it was the policy of the country to magnify these numbers, to appear as formidable as possible to the French in Canada, and their allies the Indians.   This is very evident when Douglass says there were ninety thousand fighting men in New-England at the time.   This was too erroneous to deceive for a moment.   The growth of all the colonies had been much retarded by sickness and wars.   Nearly one half the pilgrims died the first three months after their landing.   A wasting sickness came among the settlers of the province of Massachusetts Bay.   Virginia had her share of sickness and the disasters of war.   In 1622, three hundred and forty-seven of the Virginia colonists were massacred by the Indians in one day, and a famine and pestilence ensued.   The other colonies were sickly : in fact, all new settlements are so ; numerous causes conspire to make them unhealthy.   The population of the colonies was very much overrated at the commencement of the revolutionary war.   Burke and Chatham state the population to have been three millions; but Franklin, who had better means of judging, puts the population at two; and this was too high for the free white population.   The expeditions to take Canada, and the Indian wars, had proved fatal to the young men engaged in defending their country.   They were just about settling in life: but after all, this may not have been so great an evil as it was then thought to have been. If the Indians had not been constantly harrassing the settlers on the frontiers, the people would have settled extensively in this new country, and the advantage of schools, churches, and the good habits of a dense population, would have been lost.   Their march of improvement was slow, but the elements of their growth were pure; and if they gained slowly, they held their gains securely.   The early settlers, who thought this a place of sojourning, not a home, were dead.   A race had come up who knew no other country, except in sympathy with the feelings of their fathers, and who were content with their birth place.   They had been, as they conceived, neglected and ill-treated in every change of affairs in the mother country. They had suffered from the bigotry and tyranny of the house of Stuart, and had been almost forgotten during the continuance of the Commonwealth.   The colonies had, among themselves, no common bond of union, nor concert in action.   Virginia had harboured the royalists in the days of Cromwell, and New-England the regicides at the restoration of royalty.   At the restoration, Charles II. was too much engaged in his pleasures to look after these colonies, from whence he did not expect to receive any money to support his love of indulgence.   When the Stuarts were driven from the throne, the house of Orange was too busy in continental wars to think any more of us than as growing auxiliaries in future contests with France.   When the house of Brunswick came to the throne, the policy of fighting France in this country was still pursued, and in fact become necessary; for France had a stupendous line of fortifications from Cape Breton to the Mississippi.   These must be conquered at all hazards, and at any expense.   The colonies were loyal from principle and from habit; but their hearts were not so warm for their mother country as they once had been.   The seeds of the revolution were scattered about the land at every act of unkindness or hardship they had felt from England.   Some of her patriots and philosophers had taken a deep interest in the growth of the western world; and unquestionably looked forward when injured virtue would find here a safe retreat.   Berkley, Milton, Sidney, and Hollis, saw sufficient promise in the New World to induce them to believe that we should soon become an important people.

With a little bickering about some disputed points, the colonies went on as usual in the course of knowledge and civilization.   If

they were sometimes a little turbulent, no fears of permanent difficulties were entertained by the British nation. The nation at large
knew but little about us; and in truth they have always been found
dull of comprehension in relation to this country. They knew
nothing of the "fine spirits touch'd to fine issues" who had grown
up here. They did not believe that a handful of people who had
been romantick and silly enough to leave the delights of polished society, could have been the progenitors of such a race of men as then
lived in this country. They could not believe that we had enlarged
the great lessons of freedom, and at the same time had practised on
them.

Among those to whom the country is much indebted for an attempt at diffusing knowledge, was Thomas Prince, the chronologist.
He was graduated at Harvard College, in 1707. He studied divinity,
and in 1709 commenced his travels in Europe, and did not return
until 1717. His manners were formed in the best society, and his
information was of the most extensive range. He was said to be
the most learned man of his time, excepting Dr. Cotton Mather; and
even Mather's eulogists would acknowledge that Prince had more
common sense than their Magnus Apollo, and had in all respects a
better balanced mind. The writings of Prince are numerous and
valuable. He published an account of the first appearance of the
Aurora borealis; a great many sermons, obituary notices, and works
on occasional subjects; but his great work is what he called a Chronological History of New-England. He began at the creation of
the world, and he made a work of immense research and learning,
but it is to be regretted that he did not bring it down to a later period.
This would probably have been effected if he had not felt mortified
that his great labours were not more highly appreciated at the time.
The present age, however, has honoured Prince with a new edition
of the "chronological history;" and the work is examined with great
interest. His was a common fate then. The popular productions
have gone down to oblivion, or many of them, while this work is
considered among the most valuable of the kind. This chronology
was commenced early in life, and finished late. The whole of it
was not published until 1736.

Those distinguished in political and civil life had hitherto been
found among those learned in all the wisdom of the schools; but at
the commencement of this half century, a youth appeared in the
common walks of life, who had never visited the academick shades,
nor gone up to the fountains of learning, who was destined to produce almost a new era of thinking and reasoning in the moral world.
This man was Benjamin Franklin. He was born in Boston, in 1706,
and began his publick course when quite a boy. Being connected

G 2

with a newspaper, he tried his juvenile hand at commentaries and criticisms on the current topics of the day, and soon found that this great world was not so wisely governed as it was thought to be. At midnight he wrote papers and threw the manuscript into his brother's office, who often published them, supposing them to have come from very high authority. Flattered by his success, he determined to become a mender and director of the great world himself; and his destiny was in accordance with his determination. In looking about him, he found that he had touched the hallowed vessels of the Lord with too bold a hand, and that *the thrift* he bent his mind to, would not so readily be found in New-England as elsewhere, after this offence. He wandered to Pennsylvania, and from thence found his way to England, and back to Philadelphia. In that city he matured his plans, and lived to see them all successful. Shrewd, cautious, enterprising, and watchful of the signs of the times, with a business talent, and great industry, he had the advantage of most men. Educated as he was, he could readily associate with all classes of society, and understood them all perfectly. He knew the wants, wishes, habits, and powers of every grade of life, from the labourer in the log cabin, anxious to secure "the sustaining crust of bread" for his helpless children, to the splendid wretchedness of the palaces of princes, and to the thorny pillow of the ambitious statesman. He conversed upon all the affairs of life in a more practical manner than Socrates ever did with the Athenians; and at the same time he carried on his plans for his country with the ability of Pericles, and without one particle of that ancient statesman's profusion. The gods permitted him to serve the public for a very long life. He sometimes wrote for the humblest capacities, as in Poor Richard's Sayings, and at other times, taught the philosophers of Europe to bring the fire from the heavens and confine it in harmless jars of glass. He examined minds as one would take a survey of a field, and could at once tell what was the natural soil, and what had been the culture of it. It could not be said of him, that he was a great man in a small village, for he belonged to his country, and acted for mankind. He was an economist in all things; he would use the lightning's flash he had stolen from the heavens to assist him in picking up a pin in the street; not from avarice, although he knew the worth of property, but to set an example to others. He not only wished, like the good king of France, that every one might have a fowl in his pot for dinner, but Franklin added to the same hearty wish, the means of procuring it in an honest way.

Among the self-taught men of that age was David Mason, a follower of Franklin, and perhaps his pupil. It is certain they held a correspondence upon the subject of electricity; he was the first who erected lightning rods in New-England, and also the first who delivered lectures on natural philosophy as connected with electricity. His experiments excited the wonder of some of the good people of Massachusetts, and they required the opinion of a number of the clergy upon the morality and propriety of attending his lectures, intimating something more than a suspicion that such things must have been performed by the "*black art.*" The clergy, as they have generally been, were on the side of science; and the lectures went on unmolested, but with some suspicions still lingering among the ignorant. In the war of 1755, Mason was an officer in the corps of engineers, and was distinguished for bravery and science. When the American revolution opened, he was foremost among the patriots; and his knowledge of practical gunnery, and of fortification, was of incalculable service to the army. Chemistry then was but little known in this country, but he was acquainted with the science as then understood in Europe; and was called upon by the makers of gun powder and cannon to assist them in the art. He was field-officer, teacher of tacticks, and superintendant of arsenals during the whole war; such a man as Colonel Mason was wanted every where. The character of this distinguished officer should find a place in his country's list of heroes; it is only as a man of intellect and science we name him.

Amidst the attentions of our people to all theological speculations, the exact sciences were not neglected. They had received a great deal of attention ever since the first settlement of the country. Sherman, we have already mentioned, was followed by Danforth, who was also distinguished in this branch of science : in 1644, he published an almanack, and a calculation of the orbits of comets. He has been distinguished as one of the most sentimental preachers of his time, and his eloquence was of the first order. He died in 1674, at the age of forty-eight. Who filled up the space as an almanack maker from his time to that of Daniel Travis, I have not as yet discovered. The earliest number of the series of almanacks I have yet seen of Travis' is one of 1721, which I have now in my possession; and on comparing it with the almanacks of 1827, I have no hesitation in saying that it is no ways inferiour to the latter.

In 1731, Nathaniel Ames, who then styled himself " Student in Physic and Astronomy," published an almanack, which was continued until his death, in 1765. It was a most useful book, filled with all the necessary astronomical calculations for the year, and with patriotic remarks and moral reflections. In one of his numbers, I think that of 1745, he indulges in a prophecy of the future glories of his country. Nothing can exceed the accuracy of his calculations in the records of human anticipation. Perhaps he had shown among the common people a little quackery in displaying his knowledge, but this was harmless, for the most enlightened of his friends esteemed him as a sagacious and valuable man; and one who was consulted in domestick and political arrangements, by all around him. After the speech of Lord Chatham on the repeal of the Stamp Act, Ames got up a subscription to erect him a statue. It exhibited the gratitude of the good yeomanry of Dedham to the eloquent premier, but did not show any great advancement in the art of sculpture. Nathaniel Ames was the father of Fisher Ames, whose name and writings we shall have occasion to mention in another lecture.

Almanacks were more connected with literature, and particularly with history, in that day, than at the present time; for it was the general practice of learned men to keep an almanack in which to record all the passing events on blank leaves, or in marginal notes. I have one of these in my possession which belonged to Samuel Sewall, chief-justice of Massachusetts, in 1718, filled from the beginning to the end with notes upon current affairs, domestick, publick, or national, both in English and Latin. This same chief justice Sewall was himself a writer of distinction at that time, and had before, in 1690, published "answers to inquiries respecting America;" a work of great merit for its accuracy in its details. No man could think of leaving the world at that period, without leaving something on some subject, in divinity, which was in after ages to be the basis of his fame; but which, most probably, these after ages will not give themselves much trouble about. Judge Sewall, a learned and great man in his profession, wrote "proposal touching the accomplishment of prophecies;" "Phœnomina quædam Apocalyptica, or a description of the new heavens and new earth."

While mathematicks and theology were in a prosperous state, history was not neglected. William Douglass, M. D., a physician in Boston, was one of the number who were publishing accounts of this country. He was noticed for the freedom of his thoughts and remarks. Every one acknowledged that he was learned; but his sarcasms made him many enemies. He was indefatigable in collecting materials for a history of the colonies; and he published what he called "a summary," or an historical account of the British settlements in 1749 and 1753. Honest Elliot says, that Douglass wrote in a slovenly style; but he had caught something of the prejudice which tradition had brought down to his own time. Douglass had, it is seen by his writings, no great regard for the strict doctrines of the Mathers, or perhaps for any religious principles taught at that time. The weight of private character in one's own neighbourhood enters very fully into his public fame, and it is impossible to separate them entirely even at a distance; but as nearly a century has elapsed since these impressions were made upon the minds of the good people of Boston, it may be proper now for us to give them up, and look at his productions alone. His learning was not confined to one branch of information. He was a botanist, more learned than his predecessors, and advocated the doctrine, at that early period, on which Darwin founded, half a century afterwards, his splendid poem, "The Loves of the Plants." Douglass turned his attention to statisticks, and political economy, before the latter science had received a name; and this information is scattered through his historical works; but it did not suit the taste of the times as well as wonderful events and miraculous providences. He was the decided enemy of Cotton Mather, and they were at daggers-drawn while Mather was living, and Douglass did not spare the fame of his enemy when he was dead.

The natural history of New-England, and her botanical treasures, had attracted the attention of Paul Dudley, F. R. S., chief justice of Massachusetts, who wrote some papers upon these subjects, which were published in the philosophical transactions of the Royal Society, London, 1720 and 1721, which are of a high order of writing, and show great observation and acuteness. Douglass pursued his inquiries perhaps farther than his neighbour Dudley, the subject being more intimately connected with his professional pursuits. The historians of this country have been more indebted to Douglass than they have been willing to allow. The most enlightened physicians acknowledge that he wrote upon professional subjects with great talent and information. Among his papers on medical subjects is a dissertation on the "Cynanche Maligna," which prevailed in Boston in the year 1736; and in that and subsequent years swept off a great many of the children, and some full grown persons. Mathematicians, too, consider Douglass as in the front rank of their host; and as proofs of the correctness of these opinions they refer to the almanack he published in 1733-4, styled the "Mercurius Novanglicanus, by William Nadir, S. X. Q." This work, besides all the astronomical calculations common in such a publication, contains a catalogue of historical events in chronological order, which has saved his successors, in writing history, a great many laborious hours. It is unsafe to trust to the opinions which Douglass gave of his contemporaries, for he was often goaded to bitter resentments against those who attempted to diminish his influence and tarnish his fame for want of conformity to the creeds of the day. His writings do not directly show either infidelity or absolute laxity of morals, both of which he was charged with; and, if tradition may be relied on, with justice. In matters of a general nature, or of a professional cast, where his enmities did not enter, he is the best authority of the times in which he wrote, notwithstanding all the

11

imputations which have been cast on his fame. I have been more particular in this notice of Douglass, because he has been so often plundered and so long neglected; leaving the great Author of his being to judge of his morals and religion.

One branch of metaphysicks, that which treats of superiour beings, and of the abstract nature and the attributes of God, had long been a study with the divines of every denomination in this country; but that part of the science which analyzes the human mind, and treats of its capacities, affections, passions, and reasoning powers, had not been studied in this, nor in any other country, until the great metaphysician, John Locke, arose in England, who brought the energies of the most comprehensive power to bear upon the philosophy of the mind; and gave new views to the enlightened upon this subject. Some of the distinguished men in America, delighted with this study, so congenial to their habits of investigation of spiritual essences, pursued the path of Locke with great ability and success. Among these was Jonathan Edwards, who was a native of Connecticut, and was born about the year 1702, and was graduated at Yale College, 1720. He was for some time settled in Northampton, in Massachusetts, afterwards at Stockbridge, in the same commonwealth; and from this latter place was removed to Princeton, New-Jersey, as president of that college, to succeed President Burr; but President Edwards did not live long to serve his fellow men in that conspicuous situation. The great work of President Edwards is entitled "The Freedom of the Will." This raised his reputation to an equality with the first metaphysicians of his age in this country and in Europe. This work was for many years read as a classick in metaphysicks in several of our colleges. The style in many parts of this work is obscure and involved; and it is thought, by some teachers, too abstruse for young men in that science; and in fact it is now almost entirely superseded by Stewart, Locke, Reed, Brown, and others. It requires the grasp of a vigorous and mature mind to master such a work as Edwards on the Will, without previous training in the more simple elements of the science. The freedom of the will is a subject of inquiry which commenced with the first man, and will end only with the last; and will never be thoroughly explained by any one; but most certainly it is no common mind that can produce any thing worthy of notice on such a mysterious subject.

President Edwards wrote other treatises; one on "the history of redemption;" "a defence of the doctrine of original sin;" and also "a treatise on the affections," a work much read by all classes of christians of the present day; and another upon the "nature of virtue;" in the whole, eight volumes. When Edwards wrote, it was thought that abstruse subjects were not susceptible of embellishment; but Stewart has convinced the world that there is no subject so knotty and knarled which the skill of a master cannot adorn and polish with the charms of imagination.—Poetry is now the handmaid of philosophy.

President Edwards had a son, Jonathan Edwards, D. D., who was president of Schenectady College, and distinguished himself as a writer upon metaphysicks. He wrote an answer to Dr. Chauncey's work, "Salvation for all men," and likewise to Dr. Samuel West's essays upon liberty and necessity, and many think he was superior to his father; certainly, his writings are more lucid than his father's; but few men ever equalled the author of the Freedom of the Will in strength and depth.

Since the invention of printing, the world has been flooded with scholastick and controversial divinity; which has been read for a while, and then dropped into oblivion, without the regrets of any one. Then some new subject, in the same field, would be started and pursued with great animation, for a while, and then take the fate of the preceding one. We may talk, with a smile, of the dulness of the " convent's shade," and ridicule tomes written upon monosyllables. It is easy to condemn, with a word, what we have not seen, and do not understand; but no one, well acquainted with the works of these laborious metaphysicians, and wranglers upon every thing of matter and mind, will hesitate, notwithstanding all their quaintness, far-fetched illustrations, and singular inductions, to ascribe to them the merit of laying the foundations of modern knowledge. There is now to be found, in their moth-eaten pages, wit, satire, argument, and, sometimes, taste, sentiment, and even elegance, with worlds of learning. There are other considerations, which should make this class of men dear to us, for, in all their religious discussions, some glorious scintillations of thought, upon civil and political rights, were struck out, and were caught by, and illumed other minds, engaged in other pursuits.

About the year 1763, a question respecting the introduction of episcopal bishops in the American colonies, was agitated in this country, which brought out some of the first literary characters then in it. The publications on this controversy were much read at the time, and infused into the people a love of attending to every thing relating to their rights in religious and political matters. The Rev. East Apthorp, rector of the episcopal church in Cambridge, near Boston, was the champion for the introduction of the bishops; he was seconded in this, by several able and conscientious men; Dr. Samuel Seabury, afterwards the first bishop of Connecticut; Dr. Samuel Johnson, and others, gentlemen known for their learning and piety. The opposition to this doctrine consisted of the most powerful array of talents which ever appeared on any question, in this country, except that of independence. Dr. Chauncey, of Boston, a great scholar and divine, was among this number; he was then in the full maturity of his faculties; he wrote with erudition, firmness, and decision; and all were delighted with his display of learning and patriotism. He was then nearly sixty years of age. Dr. Jonathan Mayhew, of Boston, engaged in this controversy. He was the ablest metaphysical gladiator of the age in which he lived. He was then in the prime of manhood, possessing a fearlessness, and a hardihood of character, which nothing but death could subdue; rich in the learning of his day, and ready, at any moment, to take his part in any thing which would benefit his country. He saw the Apocalypse of liberty, and felt its inspiration. The signs of the times were full of moment and importance. He was in communion with the bold spirits on the other side of the water, Lardner, Benson, Hollis, Kippis, and others. In the pride of his strength, he came down upon ecclesiastical corruptions, and the tyranny of religious establishments: with the zeal of a reformer, he tore the tiara and broke the crosier for interfering with civil matters. His temper was warm, and, like other reformers, he often went farther than he intended, but no one could charge him with the slightest degree of hypocrisy. He dared to think for himself, and openly to avow his thoughts on every subject relating to religion or civil policy. He discovered no regard for the divine rights of kings; and in a sermon preached on the 31st day of January, the anniversary of the death of Charles I., he spake more freely than any one had ventured to speak before, upon the character of the monarch who had been styled the royal martyr. There seemed not the slightest disposition in his mind to canonize him. Mayhew died at the age of forty-six, with a nervous fever, brought on by intense application to his studies and parochial duties. His heart was a noble and fearless one, as ever palpitated in the bosom of man, and his grave was wet by the tears of patriots. Religious freedom is connected with civil in this and other countries, and at all times. In the memoirs of Thomas Hollis, there is a fine miniature likeness of Dr. Mayhew, with a short notice of him as a christian and patriot; and in the library of Harvard university, a portrait from the pencil of Smibert. Dr. Mayhew published voluminously upon controversial divinity; and his works are very considerably read by the scholars of our time, who are desirous of estimating the talents of those who are gone, and to whom we are indebted for the light they left us. After all, the fears these good men entertained of English bishops were probably imaginary; what harm have the catholick bishops done since ?

In this third half century, there were several colleges founded in this country. The first of these was Nassau Hall, or the college of New-Jersey. This institution was founded in 1746, at Elizabethtown; from this place it was removed to Newark, in 1747, and in 1757 to Princeton, where it now is. It was then under the superintendance of Aaron Burr, who was a graduate of Yale College, in the class of 1735. To have found such a man was a most auspicious beginning, for he was learned, and indefatigable in his duties, and fulfilled them from inclination as well as from principle. Such a man does much by example, as well as by precept, to make his pupils scholars and christians. He was considered as an eloquent man, and, it is said, that many of the preachers who came from that college, kept his manner alive for a series of years after the good man's death. President Burr was succeeded by his father-in-law, Jonathan Edwards, of whom we have spoken in this lecture, and under his care the college continued to flourish, and sent forth well-informed young men for church and state.

Columbia College, in the city of New-York, was founded in 1754, and was then called King's College. The change of name was made at the revolution. This institution was founded by several pious, learned, and enterprising gentlemen at New-York, consisting of Lieut. Governor De Lancy, Dr. Barclay, Drs. Johnson, of Connecticut, and Chandler, of New-Jersey, Joseph Murray, the attorney general of the province, and most of the literati of the state, who lent a helping hand to the good work. It requires a great deal of nursing to build up an institution of learning. Dr. Samuel Johnson, renowned at that time and since in the republick of letters, was the first president, and under his care the college grew into repute, and has since that period had the honour of producing some of our first-rate statesmen and orators, and men of letters. Dr. Johnson was an author, and wrote a treatise upon logick, and one upon ethicks, which were issued from the press of Dr. Franklin, then residing at Philadelphia, 1752. Dr. Johnson afterwards published a Hebrew grammar, which was in use in some of the colleges until it was superseded by the Hebrew grammar of the learned Dr. John Smith, professor of the languages at Dartmouth College.

In 1764, a college was founded in Rhode-Island ; the Rev. James Manning, of New-Jersey, had the honour of being the prime mover in this enterprise, and was elected the first president of this college. Samuel Elam, Esq., was one of its principal benefactors in its infancy, but the college now bears the name of its present patron,

H

Nicholas Brown, Esq., of Providence. It is at this moment under happy auspices.

Dartmouth college was incorporated in 1762. It is situated in the town of Hanover, in the state of New-Hampshire. This college was founded by Dr. Eleazer Wheelock, a man of great benevolence and learning. A school had been established at Stockbridge, in Massachusetts, by the Rev. John Sergeant, about the year 1743. This seminary was commenced for the benefit of the Stockbridge tribe of Indians; but he had hardly begun this pious labour, when he was removed from it by death. Dr. Wheelock attempted to revive this school, and, for this purpose, solicited donations in Europe and America. He opened it at Lebanon, and called it Moore's academy. Before this time, Dr. Wheelock had contemplated founding a college somewhere on Connecticut river, and the Earl of Dartmouth had promised his assistance to the undertaking. Hanover was fixed upon as the most suitable place for its site. Moore's school was removed there also, but was not connected with the college. Besides the Earl of Dartmouth, there were several other benefactors, King George III., the Countess of Huntingdon, and others of eminence, in England; and John Adams, Dr. Franklin, John Phillips, and Samuel Phillips, with others, of this country, lent a helping hand to the establishment of this seminary. Dr. Wheelock was going on prosperously, when the revolutionary war broke out. The students necessarily became soldiers, and the building a garrison. The scholars read the classicks with arms in their hands, and, to use an expression of the second president, "MARS was made the protector of MERCURY." After the war was over, this institution flourished, and has sent forth her proportion of eminent men, in every age of her struggles, of which she has had her share. Out of her history has grown one of the most important decisions, in fixing the stability of property and the rights of charters, that is to be found on the records of our federal judiciary.

It is greatly to the honour of our country, that, on every occasion that has required talents of any sort, she has readily produced them, whether the subject presented was literary, scientific, or political. We have already spoken of our mathematicians, and of their labours in various ways; but in no instance was their merits more conspicuous, or their knowledge so thoroughly tested, as when the planet Venus made a transit over the disk of the sun in 1761. Great preparations were made in England and France, as well as in this country, to seek the best places on the globe for observations at the time. In this country, some of our first minds were deeply engaged in making the most minute and accurate notices of this event. Ewing, Rittenhouse, Smith, Williamson, West, and Winthrop, and many others, published accounts of this phenomenon; and the philosophers of Europe have acknowledged, that those of America were the most accurate of all that were published. These men were not mere mathematicians, but were also distinguished for their knowledge of letters. The Rev. John Ewing, D. D., a native of Maryland, born in 1732, and graduated at New-York College, in 1755. He was settled as a minister in Philadelphia, and was chosen provost of the university of Pennsylvania in 1777, and lived to a good old age. John Blair Linn, D. D., his colleague, wrote the obituary of his venerable friend in a style of surpassing elegance. Of Rittenhouse, it is difficult to speak without seeming exaggeration. He was a self-taught man; born in Pennsylvania in 1752, he was a mathematician from his cradle. He perfected himself in the art of clock-making by his own ingenuity. Newton's principia was mastered by him without any assistance. From that he went to *fluxions*, and, for awhile, thought himself the original inventor. It is true, he was in a good degree a genuine inventor, but not an original one. It is often the fate of uneducated geniuses, to spend much time on subjects, the discovery of which was unknown to them, but with which former ages have been familiar. He invented an orrery, as he called his planetarium, which far exceeded, in accuracy and extent, all that had been known before. After his publication of his observations on the transit of Venus, he became extensively known in Europe as well as in this country, and loaded with academic honours—L. L. D., F. R. S., &c., were added to his name. He was president of the philosophical society of Philadelphia. Dr. Rush wrote his obituary notice, and others strove to make his fame bear some proportion to his merit. Barlow, in his Vision of Columbus, speaks of him among the great men that the hero saw in "coming time," who were to bless their country by the power of their understanding.

> "Thus heard the hero—while his roving view
> Traced other crowds that liberal arts pursue;
> When thus the Seraph—Lo, a favourite band,
> The torch of science flaming in their hand!
> Through nature's range their ardent soul inspire,
> Or wake to life the canvass and the lyre.
> Fixt in sublimest thought, behold them rise,
> Superiour worlds unfolding to their eyes;
> Heav'n, in their view, unveils the eternal plan,
> And gives new guidance to the paths of man.
>
> See the sage Rittenhouse, with ardent eye,
> Lift the long tube and pierce the starry sky;

Clear in his view the circling systems roll,
And broader splendours gild the central pole.
He marks what laws the eccentrick wanderers bind,
Copies creation in his forming mind,
And bids, beneath his hand, in semblance rise,
With mimick orbs, the labours of the skies;
There wondering crowds with raptured eye behold
The spangled heavens their mystick maze unfold;
While each glad sage his splendid hall shall grace,
With all the spheres that cleave the ethereal space."

Benjamin West, another eminent mathematician, was also a self-taught philosopher. He was for sometime a professor of mathematicks and natural philosophy in Providence college, and very much distinguished in his branches. Pike, the author of the Arithmetick, which most of us have dozed, plodded, or fretted over, informed me, that West was one of the most extraordinary men in the science of numbers he had ever met with. This talent for mathematical inquiries is almost as common in our country as the inventive capacity. There is scarcely a village which does not contain *some gifted man in that way.* I have known a malt-seller, and a school master in an obscure country town, teaching at six dollars per month, who were among the best instructors in mathematicks that I ever knew: and at the present time the island of Nantucket is distinguished for mathematicks. The Folgers have, for more than a century through successive generations, watched the phenomena of the heavens, and given the result of their observations to the publick.

Professor Winthrop, of Harvard College, probably made the highest exertions to notice the transit of Venus, of any American. In 1761, he sailed to St. Johns, in Newfoundland, for that purpose, and on the sixth day of June of that year, had a fine clear morning to make his observations. Winthrop was an accomplished scholar, in most branches of learning, and wrote Latin with great facility and in great purity. He published treatises on comets, earthquakes, &c. was deeply read in divinity, and was a very pious man. He said of revelation, perhaps, what no mathematician ever said before —"the light thrown upon the doctrine of a future state, (meaning by revelation,) amounts with me to demonstration." It has been too often supposed that philosophy and deep research were inimical to religion; but this has seldom been the case, certainly not in our country; for the wise and the learned, have seen and felt the necessity of a future state, to satisfy their longings after that knowledge which they believed existed, and yet was unfathomable by the intellect of man, in his present state of existence. The weak followers of some human creed, have too often taken a denial of its truth and efficacy, for a disbelief in the great doctrines of revelation. The higher the views, the more penetrating the ken; and the greater the ability to examine, the more forcibly does man feel his nature, and the more ardent are his aspirations that it may be purified and elevated.

LECTURE VI.

God gave to man power to feel, to think, to will, and to act; and made him responsible for this prerogative; whoever, then, has the gift of tongues, let him use it; whoever holds the pen of a ready writer, let him dip it in the ink-horn; or whoever has a sword, let him gird it on, for the crisis demands our highest efforts, both physical and mental. The soul has its nerves as well as the body, and both must be put in tono for service.

Old Sermon.

THE next epoch, that called forth the talents of our countrymen, was the attempt of the British ministry to tax the colonies without their consent. Not content with the monopoly of the trade of the colonies, they wished to draw a revenue from them, by imposing taxes in the form of duties on certain articles of common consumption. This was at first resisted by petitions, remonstrances, and arguments from every portion of the country. They did not regard as a grevious matter the duties imposed: it was the declaration which accompanied this taxation which was so offensive, of their right to tax the colonies, at all times, and in all cases whatsoever. The manner of enforcing these acts of Parliament was equally offensive. The custom-houses, which had been regulated with the usual lenity of collecting all colonial duties, were instructed to use all sorts of severity to bring the people at once to their allegiance and obedience. Informers and spies were scattered through the country, and behaved with all the insolence of petty tyrants; still their fears of the resentments of a people, never known for timidity, induced them to wish to have the appearance of acting legally, if unkindly. To do this, they applied to the courts for *writs of assistance.* The courts hesitated: this process had never been known before in the colonies. The writ was considered in the nature of a star-chamber proceeding, and against the great principles of *Magna*

H 2   12

Charta. The custom-house petitioners obtained a rule on those interested to show cause why the petition should not be granted. Gridley was attorney-general, and of course, was bound by the duties of his office, to appear for the officers of his Majesty's customs. Otis was employed on the side of the merchants. This was in 1761. The cause of the petitioners was ably argued by Gridley: he brought all his learning into the cause, which was considerable, and the whole weight of his character, which was greater with the court. Otis made a most eloquent and learned answer, the fame of which is not lost by the lapse of years. The court were in doubt, and took time for advisement; and the subject has never been settled to this day, in that or in any other court. This was the speech which John Adams has told us, " *breathed into the nation the breath of life.*" I am not engaging in a political discussion at this time, but this statement is made to show the causes of the development of talent in this country. Immediately after this, the papers waxed warm upon this subject, and others connected with it, and the press teemed with pamphlets, which discovered no small degree of political information. Otis was not content with employing his eloquence alone, but he took up his pen also in defence of our rights; and if his pen was not equal to his tongue, it was sufficiently pointed and powerful to arouse his countrymen, and to excite the vengeance of those he called her oppressors. Otis affixed his name boldly to whatever he wrote; before this time, most political writings had come to the world anonymously. Others followed the example which Otis had set them, and wrote over their own names, when it was thought they could do more good by this course, than by taking an assumed name. He was not only a patriot, but, what is more to my immediate purpose, he was a splendid scholar, and wrote several elementary works, and works of taste. His talents, his misfortunes, his death, are so familiar to us all, that I will not stop to recount them.

Samuel Adams was the contemporary of Otis, born only three years before him, but formed altogether on a different model. The energy of Adams was equal to that of Otis, but it was united to sanctity, as Otis's was to passion. Adams gained by a sage demeanour, while Otis lost by openness of manner and freedom of remark. They were both patriots, and brave to martyrdom; but while Otis rushed upon his enemies in a whirlwind, trusting to his powers and to his impetuosity for success, Adams approached with caution, and struck with guarded certainty.

Thomas Hutchinson, a native of the town of Boston, was at this period a secret opposer of these patriots; with declarations of love for his native country, he was holding a correspondence with the ministry, and encouraging them to persevere in their strong measures. He had been an idol of the people, and they were unwilling to give him up at once. Feeling himself well fixed in the confidence of men in power, he threw off the mask, and boldly met his accusers. He was a man of learning and abilities, and possessed a very great aptitude for all kinds of public business, and was industrious in all its details. The history of the country was familiar to him, for he had made it a particular study, and was for many years employing his leisure hours in writing the history of the province of Massachusetts Bay. The storm burst upon his head when he was Lieutenant Governor, and his house was demolished by the infuriated populace : but he was not easily daunted. The ministry came to his support, and raised him to the office of chief magistrate. His correspondence with the government in England, which the patriots considered as full of treachery to the colonies, was, by some adroitness or accident, obtained, and it was impossible for any one to withstand the effect. The populace, the legislature, the statesmen, old and young, brought their indignation to bear upon him, and he left our shores for England, where his services were forgotten ; and neglect and a broken heart awaited him. He was unquestionably the most efficient man the royal cause could boast of in this country, at that period. For his history, we are much indebted to him. This will live, when his political course will only be remembered as a common occurrence.

The late President Adams was another of the distinguished writers, in the days preceding the revolution. He was ardent in the cause of liberty, but he never " run with bare-headed debasement the scrub race of popularity." He was of counsel for Preston and his men, in 1770, and, regardless of popular clamour, discharged his duty with ability and firmness. He was consistent, unwavering, and determined from the first, and employed his pen in defence of the colonies from his earliest manhood. He was engaged in controversy with those who took the side of the crown, until a few months previous to the battle of Lexington. He wrote over the signature "NOVANGLUS," in answer to one who had taken the signature "MASSACHUTENSIS," and whom he supposed to be Jonathan Sewall, then attorney-general, but it has lately been stated, on the authority of Sampson Salter Blowers, chief justice of the supreme court of Halifax, who, with Mr. Adams, was at that time a member of the Suffolk bar, that " *massachutensis*" was written by Mr. Leonard, a younger member of that bar than either Adams or Sewall, and afterwards a judge in one of the English West India islands. These were able papers on the great questions then before the people, full of striking thoughts and plain and direct arguments: we speak thus freely of both of these writers; they managed their causes well. Mr. Adams was, at all times, a bold straight-forward writer, and sometimes was quite prophetick in his conjectures.

Among the writers of that day, no man was more conspicuous than Doctor Samuel Cooper. He was a most acceptable preacher and a fine scholar; probably more refined in his style than most other writers in our country; but he did not confine himself to religious subjects alone. He saw that encroachments on civil liberty would reach, in no distant day, the liberty of conscience, and hierarchies would grow up when the elective franchise had become a nullity. His polished style had reached Paris, and his fame as a fine writer was among the first circles of taste and fashion. He was a friend to learning, and was a member of the corporation of Harvard College; but he did not content himself, on the score of duty, with college halls or religious temples, but threw out the strong emotions of his clear mind into the political excitements of the day. He wrote frequently in the publick journals, particularly in the Boston Gazette, on all the current topicks of the day. These pieces of composition were remarkable for perspicuity and elegance; and the good people were looking out as each paper came from the press, for something from his pen, as a charm and a guide. He wrote a pamphlet called "*the Crisis*," which contained a great share of neat and forcible argument, but is not equal to many of his other compositions. All his works have a political bearing, or, at least, a great portion of them. The most popular works of Doctor Cooper, were the following discourses: on the Artillery election, 1751; and in 1753, an address for encouraging industry; this contained the true principles of political economy; that is, for the rich to study to find work for the poor as a preventive of further distress; and many others, upon occasional subjects, were printed by his friends, as he delivered them before the several societies which called his talents to their aid. A sermon on the reduction of Quebec, was a very popular discourse in this country and in England; and one on the commencement of the new constitution of Massachusetts, October 25th, 1780, was thought, by statesmen, to be a very correct exposition of the great doctrines of a free government. This political discourse was translated into the French and German languages, and perhaps many others. It was no less admired for its bold and generous principles, than for its polished style and elegant composition. It was sent through Europe, as at once a specimen of the mode of thinking and writing in the American states. One of his great maxims was, that knowledge and virtue are the pillars of a free government; and these were only to be had and supported by institutions of learning and religion: he was therefore foremost in raising and in supporting seminaries of letters, arts, and sciences in the country ; and the American Academy of Arts and Sciences was honoured by his being elected the first president of that body. The political influence of such a man is noiseless, but effective. The truths he teaches steal into the minds of the reading part of the community, and are transmitted with theirs to less enlightened minds, and so on, as far as any think or reason at all upon such matters. The letters, the reasoning, the current of feeling in his extensive circle, for several years after Dr. Cooper wrote, bore marks of his works having been text-books and standards all around him.

Among the distinguished political writers of that day, as well as a great Fanuiel Hall orator, was Josiah Quincy. He had graduated in 1763, with a splendid reputation for his early years. A reputation, at his period of life, is so full of promise, that in many cases it falls short of the ardent hopes of friends, and often disappoints the calculations of the community ; but it was not so with Mr. Quincy; his fame increased until his death, in 1775. At the bar he was conspicuous, yielding to none in fluency and energy ; his voice and person were much in his favour, and his fearless course of independence, with or against the current of popular feeling, gave him the confidence of all sides. Never was there a more ardent or inflexible whig than Mr. Quincy. He was not content with raising his voice in the primary assemblies of the people, but took up his pen to assist them in giving their complaints to the world. *The Boston Port-bill*, an act of parliament to punish the people of Boston for destroying the tea, and other acts of a rebellious nature, as they were considered by the British ministry, made its appearance in 1774, in this country, and the port of Boston was shut up in obedience to it. This was a violent measure, and raised a clamour through the country. Mr. Quincy seized the opportunity, and wrote a review of this measure, entitled, " Thoughts on the Boston Port-bill, &c. addressed to the freeholders and yeomanry of Massachusetts." This was well written for the times ; a tame discussion would not have met the exigencies of that day. He closes the notice with these bold remarks, evidently emanating from a mind made up to meet the coming crisis, however bloody or lasting. " America has her Bruti and Cassii, her Hambdens and Sidneys, patriots and heroes, who will form a band of brothers ; men who will have memories and feelings, courage that shall inflame their ardent bosoms, till their hands cleave to their swords, and their swords to their enemies hearts."

The publick had so long been in training for the evil times which came upon them, that every one was thoroughly prepared for all the difficulties which he had to encounter. From 1761 to 1775, knowledge was disseminated, feelings were communicated, and mutual pledges, in the best of all forms, that of general sympathy and similarity of opinions, were given.   There were no discordant notes in the concert; all were in tune to any master hand that struck the chords.

The massacre, as the death of those who fell on the 5th of March, 1770, by the firing on the inhabitants of Boston, by a platoon of Captain Preston's company, has ever been called, was made an admirable cause to rouse the people to arms, or rather to prepare them to resist further aggressions.   It is a law of nature, that the blood of unarmed citizens *should cry from the ground* for vengeance.   It is a voice that ages cannot stifle.   The patriot leaders, at that time, restrained the sudden vengeance of the people, but still kept alive the feelings of a just resentment, with great address. On the 5th of March, 1771, a number of the citizens of Boston assembled to mourn the fate of those who had fallen the preceding year.   It was then thought by some, that an oration should be delivered on the occasion, and James Lovell, A. M., a much respected grammar schoolmaster, renowned for his learning and eloquence, a very decided whig, was selected for the task; and, on the 9th of April, 1771, the next month, he was ready, and delivered his oration on the *massacre.*   This address was a serious political dissertation upon the rights, duties, and feelings of the American people.

The next year, on the 5th of March, 1772, Dr. Joseph Warren was selected as the orator.   He explained, in his oration, the nature of the social compact, spoke of the struggles Britain herself had made for liberty, and of the excellence of the British constitution, of which he considered that of Massachusetts, and, in fact, that of all the colonies, a copy.   He proceeded to try the acts of Britain by her own constitution, and found them wanting in justice and law.   The ruinous consequences of standing armies were dwelt upon with great severity and openness.   The tragedy of that fatal night was depicted in glowing colours, and managed with a master's skill.   The appeal to his countrymen, in this address, was received as a hallowed burst of feeling from a patriot's heart, which reached every pulse in the hearts of his hearers.

In 1773, Dr. Benjamin Church, a physician in Boston, a gentleman distinguished for his learning, talents, and, at that time, for patriotism, was selected as orator for the anniversary of the 5th of March.   His oration was written in a fine style, and was a good commentary upon the great doctrines of liberty.   In this production, Junius is quoted as an authority, for the first time I ever remember to have seen his name in a solemn address.   Church was a poet, and closes his oration, after a pathetic burst of eloquence upon the " foul deed" of a standing army, done in a time of peace, upon a defenceless populace, in the following lines, which were undoubtedly his own:

> "Thou who yon bloody walk shalt traverse, there
> Where troops of *Britain's* king on Britain's sons
> Discharg'd the leaden vengeance : pass not on
> Ere thou hast blest their memory, and paid
> Those hallowed tears which soothe the virtuous dead:
> O *stranger!* stay thee, and the scene around
> Contemplate well; and if, perchance, thy home
> Salute thee with a father's honour'd name,
> Go call thy sons—instruct them what a debt
> They owe their ancestors, and make them swear
> To pay it, by transmitting down entire
> Those sacred rights, to which themselves were born."

In 1774, John Hancock was appointed orator for the 5th of March. This oration has been much read and admired ; it was impassioned in the parts relating to the events of that particular day ; but less florid and swelling than some others on the occasion.

In 1775, Joseph Warren was, for the second time, the orator. He wrote with the fire of genius and the boldness of a hero. The papers had teemed with writings which were easily traced by his enemies to him, for they contained a spirit which could not be mistaken. This last oration was the knell of his own obsequies, for in a few months he was slain in supporting the doctrines he, on this 5th of March, promulgated to his countrymen. The martyr's blood sealed the patriot's sincerity ; and the soil that drank the stream of life, grows holier with every passing age. There was something in this second appointment, that deserves commemoration. It was at his own solicitation that he was appointed to this duty a second time. The fact is illustrative of his character. Some British officers of the army, then in Boston, had publickly declared, that it should be at the price of the life of any man to speak of the event of the 5th of March, 1770, on that anniversary. Warren's soul took fire at such a threat, so openly made, and he wished for the honour of braving it. This was readily granted, for, at such a time, a man would probably find but few rivals. Many, who would spurn the thought of personal fear, might be apprehensive that they would be so far disconcerted as to forget their discourse. It is easier to fight bravely, than to think clearly and correctly in danger. Passion sometimes nerves the arm to fight, but disturbs the regular current of thought. The day came, and the weather was remarkably fine. The old south meeting-house was crowded at an early hour. The British officers occupied the aisles, the flight of steps to the pulpit, and several of them were within it. It was not precisely known, whether this was accident or design. The orator, with the assistance of his friends, made his entrance at the pulpit window by a ladder. The officers, seeing his coolness and intrepidity, made way for him to advance and address the audience. An awful stillness preceded his exordium. Each man felt the palpitations of his own heart, and saw the pale, but determined, face of his neighbour. The speaker began his oration in a firm tone of voice, and proceeded with great energy and pathos. Warren and his friends were prepared to chastise contumely, prevent disgrace, and avenge an attempt at assassination. The scene was sublime; a patriot, in whom the flush of youth, and the grace and dignity of manhood were combined, stood armed in the sanctuary of God, to animate and encourage the sons of liberty, and to hurl defiance at their oppressors. The orator commenced with the early history of the country, described the tenure by which we held our liberties and property; the affection we had constantly shown the parent country, and boldly told them how, and by whom, these blessings of life had been violated. There was, in this appeal to Britain, in this description of suffering, agony, and horror, a calm and high-souled defiance, which must have chilled the blood of every sensible foe. Such another hour has seldom happened in the history of man, and is not surpassed in the records of nations. The thunders of Demosthenes rolled at a distance from Philip and his host, and Tully poured the fiercest torrent of his invective, when Cataline was at a distance, and his dagger no longer to be feared; but Warren's speech was made to proud oppressors, resting on their arms, whose errand it was to overawe, and whose business it was to fight.

If the deed of Brutus deserved to be commemorated by history, poetry, painting, and sculpture, should not this instance of patriotism and bravery be held in lasting remembrance? If he "that struck the foremost man of all this world," was hailed as the first of freemen, what honours are not due to him, who, undismayed, bearded the British lion, to show the world what his countrymen dared to do in the cause of liberty? If the statue of Brutus was placed amongst those of the gods, who were the preservers of Roman freedom, should not that of Warren fill a lofty niche in the temple reared to perpetuate the remembrance of our birth as a nation?

In 1776, the anniversary of the massacre was kept at Watertown, Boston being then in the almost exclusive possession of the British. The Rev. Peter Thatcher was the orator. The same subject naturally led to the consideration and discussion of the same general principles. The times and the events of the day, provided the orator with some additional topicks, and he happily introduced the fate of Warren and Montgomery, whose premature deaths were mourned by all classes of people in the country, as those who were near and dear to liberty and to them. The people of Boston kept up the practice of noticing this anniversary until the close of the war, and then it was discontinued, and the celebration of the fourth of July succeeded. In 1778, Benjamin Hitchborn, Esq. was orator, and Jonathan Loring Austin, William Tudor, Esq., Jonathan Mason, Jun., Thomas Dawes, Jun., George Richards Minot, and Dr. Thomas Welsh, were called to address the public on this occasion, in succession. All these productions breathed the same spirit, and made the same pledges to the world to support them; and they spoke the language of the great mass of the people. I have mentioned these orations particularly, as showing the subjects of a nation's thoughts, and the literary form in which they were spoken.

In other colonies, at the same time, the same spirit was awake, and information was diffused in every form by which intelligence is communicated. In 1764, John Dickinson, a member of the assembly of Pennsylvania, made an impression upon the publick as a patriot of distinguished talents. In November of 1767, he began to publish his letters against the acts of the British parliament, laying duties on paper, glass, and other necessaries of life. They were written in a bold and dauntless spirit. He was no leveller, but a loyal subject, who considered it his right to discuss these great matters at all times. These letters were at that time read by all classes in the community, and were quoted as being the true sentiments of the great mass of the thinking people in America. He was a member of congress in 1774, and was the author of that petition of congress to the king, which breathes so loyal and yet so firm a spirit, and which extorted praise from the lips of our enemies, and warm congratulations from our friends. When the proposition was before congress for the declaration of our independence, Dickinson was opposed to it, and made a long and powerful speech against it, as a premature measure, inasmuch as we were not prepared for it; and that the hope of reconciliation was not extinct. His argument was a manly one, and did not impair his reputation any farther than this, that his constituents were not of the same opinion, and did not re-elect him until they were satisfied that he would act generally with those who advocated the declaration of independence. When Mr. Dickinson was fully convinced, that a large majority of the people were willing to risk all on the question of independence, he came into it cordially. He was president of Pennsylvania from November, 1783, to 1785. He afterwards removed from Pennsylvania to Delaware, his native state, and was sent from there

I   13

to congress under the old confederation. He was a republican, firmly attached to his country, and laboured heartily for her welfare. He was powerful in argument, bland in manners, rich in learning, and happy in his taste as a writer on almost every passing matter, as well as of a more profound nature. His works have been published, in two volumes, and should be more often referred to than they are by the present generation. He was equally a favourite with his native and with his adopted state. Even in the violence of party, his sincerity was never questioned.

Daniel Galloway, Esq. was a native of the same state, and was also a member of congress from Pennsylvania in 1776, and was opposed altogether to the declaration of independence. He was a writer of respectable talents, and, after fully ascertaining what the people, and their representatives in congress, intended, he differed with them entirely, and wrote on the British side of the question, and, after a while, left Philadelphia to join our enemies. At that time, it must have been very unpopular to have said a word on the side of our opposers; and Mr. Galloway must have been a man of high moral integrity to have got off with so little abuse as he received. But his fate was an unfortunate one, for he left us from principle, but was treated with great rudeness and severity by the ministry of England.

Another writer on the other side of the question, who claims our attention and gratitude, was William Henry Drayton, of South Carolina. He exerted his literary acquirements and talents in the cause of his country. In 1774, he was the author of a pamphlet addressed to the American Congress, signed "A Freeman." In 1776, in his judicial capacity, he made a charge to a grand jury, which contained a full and fair view of the situation of our country at that time, and the duties devolving on every citizen who laid any claims to love of country. The whole of this charge has been preserved by Dr. Ramsay in his historical works. This able and valuable statesman and patriot died while attending his duties as a member of congress, in Philadelphia, in 1779, at the early age of thirty-seven. He was truly a great man, and his death was deeply deplored in every part of the country.

New-York and New-Jersey were happy in having a share in the fame of William Livingston, governor of the latter state, but a native of the former, and a writer and politician of distinction before he took up his residence in New-Jersey. Livingston was an elegant scholar, and wrote with great pungency and effect in those times, in which every form of argument was required to rouse the spirit of the people, to discharge their awful responsibilities. The effect of his exertions were seen in the good conduct of the Jersey militia, in the most perilous moments of the revolutionary war, when their territory was overrun by the enemy, and despondency was extending her paralyzing influences over the whole country, from Georgia to Maine.

Maryland produced, among her numerous patriots and writers, one who was very celebrated at the time, in Daniel Dulany, Esq., a writer on political subjects; and he has had the credit of having done much good. He was a lawyer of Annapolis, and distinguished at the Maryland bar.

Virginia had her share of writers previous to the revolution, although she did not for some time feel much of the arbitrary power of Great Britain. Thomas Jefferson, when quite a young man, wrote upon the great questions then agitated, but his whole history is so well known that it would be useless to restate it. Richard Bland, Arthur Lee, and Robert Carter Nicholas, were also known as writers on the popular side of the question in Virginia. Bland was a distinguished member of the house of burgesses, in 1776, and at that time published an inquiry into the rights of the British colonies in America, in answer to a pamphlet published in London in the preceding year, entitled "regulations lately made concerning the colonies, and the taxes imposed on them considered." Arthur Lee wrote, in 1769, "the monitor's letters," which were extensively read, not only in Virginia, but in other parts of the country. There were others of note and worth who wielded their pens in the great cause of American freedom, whom we have not had time to mention, particularly many of the clergymen, who were then in active life, such as Witherspoon, Webster, and a host of good patriots, who mingled their ardent wishes for their country with their morning and evening prayers to heaven for salvation. While the statesman called upon his countrymen from the halls of legislation, to come forward and act valiantly, the zealous clergyman entered the citizen's dwelling, preached a homily on the duties of a patriot before the fire-side and at the family altar, and roused father and son to gird on their swords and march for the defence of their country; and not unfrequently, when his flock were ready for the field, joined them himself with the *sword of Gideon and the Lord*, to encourage their hearts and strengthen their hands.

During all these preparations for the coming conflict, the subject of education was more attended to than ever it had been. In addition to the common course of instruction, the Oriental languages, which are now opening their inexhaustible treasures of learning to the world, were assiduously cultivated. After the resignation of Morris, as Hebrew instucter in Harvard University, a professorship of Oriental Literature was established by the munificence of Thomas

Hancock, uncle to John Hancock, the patriot, and Stephen Sewall, was selected for the Oriental chair. He was indeed well qualified for the office, being probably the best linguist of his age. He was bred a mechanick, a house-joiner, until he was one and twenty years of age, and was distinguished for his skill in his trade. He had been fond of books, and had made many curious philological researches that attracted the attention of a learned divine in his vicinity, who gave him every aid in his power. The pupil made the most rapid advances in the languages, and studied them so deeply and carefully, that he became unquestionably the first critick of his time in this country. He wrote Greek odes, which were noticed in England. He went perhaps as learnedly into the philosophical constitution of that beautiful language as Porson and Parr have since done. He pursued his philological studies farther, and made himself master of the Syriack, Arabick, Chaldee, Samaritan, Ethiopick, Persiack, and Coptick. He left some accurate notes on all these languages in his lectures, and made many remarks on them in a correspondence held with the learned Orientalists in Europe, which received from these professors the highest commendations. He made a lexicon of some of these languages, and translated a part of Young's Night Thoughts into Latin hexameter. It was in no small degree owing to this fine classical scholar that Hebrew retained its rank among the languages, when the spirit of modern philosophy strove to banish it from the dignity of those languages worthy the attention of a learned man. The day of proscription has passed ; the inquiring mind has found some of the richest gems of thought, some of the loveliest flowers of poetry, and many touches of a profound philosophy, in the immense fields of eastern literature, through which the scholars of the present day are travelling with inexpressible pleasure.

For many years previous to the revolution, the science of government and the rights of man were subjects of discussion at Harvard University, in every form of their literary exercises, from dialogues to orations, not only on quarter-days and commencements, but at all other times. The students examined all the principles of political and civil liberty of the ancient republicks, and were well read in the English constitution, and also in that of the United Provinces of the Netherlands; and the forms of liberty in the Italian cities, such as had boasted of their freedom in modern days, were commented upon with the spirit of reformers ; the right to resist oppression was often taken as a theme for declamation, and the loudest applause was bestowed on the boldest of the advocates for the doctrine. I name not this fact as wishing to consider them as models for the student at the present day : the present times demand other directions of the human mind, but simply to show how intimately our literature and national existence have been connected.

It was a mutual and most felicitous thought, to call the learned men of all times and nations a Republick of Letters; for with them, in every age, have been found the true doctrines of political liberty and the seeds of civil institutions. The learned, as a body, have favoured freedom of opinion, and the sacred rights of man, even in the courts of tyrants, and in the faces of their creatures. The learned priests of Egypt wrested from their kings rights for themselves, and protection for the people. In the walks of the academy and the halls of science, the mind threw off its shackles; and in the contemplation of the laws of nature, and of the moral world, and in the pursuit of science and the arts, it lost its reverence for hereditary claims to eminence, and looked directly with a philosophical eye to the fitness of things, thoughtless of arbitrary distinctions among men. In a community where the operations of the mind may be watched in its advancements in knowledge, those cast by nature in a superiour mould will attract the attention and receive that homage which in some form or other genius will for ever secure. The institutions of learning in our country had, it is true, some of the forms and shows of the relicks of aristocracy, in the arrangements of their catalogues, or some trifling ceremonies; but there never existed purer fountains of political justice, and true equality, than were to be found in them. The right once established to judge of religious doctrines, of reasoning upon human, angelick, and divine natures, embraces in it the right of judging upon the political, civil, and moral conduct of men, in, or out of power. The student, surrounded by the lights of mind which had illumined the world in every age, and holding, every day, converse, through their works, with the mighty dead, felt no great respect or reverence for empty-headed vanity, or ignorant pride, however bloated by consequence, or elated by the possession of power; for he knew that, at best, for him who possessed it, power could not be permanent, or with us hereditary; he therefore saw, as he looked forward into his country's history, one generation of little oppressors pass off after another, as insects of a day, or creatures of a moment. If all the scholar felt could not have been fully communicated to his fellow actors as he entered into life, yet sufficient of his spirit might have been diffused to have given a similarity to the feelings and reasonings of others, and to have prepared the community to reason and think for themselves on all subjects involving their rights and privileges. Every educated man who had left these walks of learning, became a Hierophant of liberty among the people, and taught them, at once, the means and the blessings of freedom. The love of freedom with them was no phosphorick light

I 2

or flickering blaze from putrescent masses, or occasional ignition, but a steady flame, which burnt like the sacred fire on the altars of Greece, in the temple of liberty, or that holier flame of the lamp of God in the house of the Lord, which burnt day and night to keep the hallowed fane from darkness and pollution. The liberty they asked was only British liberty, such as the people of England enjoyed, and still enjoy: that they should be taxed by their own representatives, and by none others.

LECTURE VII.

———

" The true patriot is found in all classes of men ; his name is sacred, his deeds are glorious ; he is not seduced by honours or rewards ; he is above all bribes ; he is destitute of all selfishness ; he is ready to pour out his blood as water for his country's good ; he labours for great ends by honest means ; he fears luxury as a national evil ; he dreads parsimony as a national curse ; he thinks no man lives for himself alone ; he subdues his pride, and humbles his sense of importance, by thinking how short is human life ; he represses his vanity by knowing how many are his superiours ; he feels rightly ; thinks correctly ; judges candidly ; acts wisely ; hopes humbly ; and dies in the full assurance of immortality—favoured by men, or if not that, beloved by God."

The Patriot's Manual.

DURING the long agony of our revolutionary conflict, our small seminaries of learning were generally closed, and the course of instruction in colleges and high schools was interrupted ; yet the minds of the people were never more active. Every publick square and every private dwelling, were places of discussion, and of inquiry into the general principles of liberty of thinking, and acting. The fervour of passion had passed away ; and that cool determination succeeded, which denotes a firmness of purpose, and which is not to be shaken, and that high resolve which nothing can break down. The publick documents of that day, fully show this calm and quiet temper, for in them there is nothing spiteful, irritable, or feverish. A careless observer might think that the hearts of the people were not in this cause, all things were conducted with such serenity. It is a fact worthy of notice, that on the 17th of June, 1775, the provincial congress of Massachusetts was in session at Watertown, not more than six miles, if so much, from Charlestown heights; yet their records show that they were busy throughout that eventful day, in their deliberations. Notwithstanding the incessant roar of musketry and cannon, and the awful conflagration of Charlestown, the dwellings of their friends and neighbours, yet not a man left his seat; and the journal of their proceedings on that day is very full, and marked with precision and fine chirography. Not the slightest allusion is to be found on these records, to the alarm of the neighbourhood, or the possibility of defeat in the contest. It was not until three days after the fight, that even the probability of the death of their President, General Warren, was suggested, and that only on a motion to proceed to the choice of another, to fill his place. These conscript fathers would not give the people any intimation that they would shrink from personal danger, while in the discharge of their duties as statesmen. Their first account of this event is prepared with great deliberation; not a word of boasting is contained in it, nor is there even a just account of American bravery to be found in it. In fact, they were not apprised of the honour of that fight, at that time. The language of the continental congress also, at that time, is full of the same modesty, which the enemy took for timidity and fear. The addresses which came from this body were not tinctured with the slightest boasting, even when arguing with friends or foes. They made no flattering appeal to the people they wished to arouse to action, and prepare for disasters and blood-shed, in every form of attack, from their enemies.

The petitions and addresses to the king of Great Britain were modest, patient, and manly; those to the people of England, affectionate and full of sorrow, that such times should have come, and such evils, as they suffered, should exist. The declaration of independence, in which, it might be supposed, was concentrated all their wrongs and sufferings, is still expressed in the calm language of enduring philosophy and patriotism, without one particle of rage or vengeance, but still strong, clear, bold, and impressive.

The pamphlets and letters of that period are, with a few exceptions, models of plain unsophisticated reasoning, and addressed to the understandings of the people, rather than to their passions. Nothing of the tumid, vapouring, trash of the electioneering style of later days was known to those who brought on our independence, at the price of blood and treasure, which price was not fixed to any limits, nor bounded by any measure. The addresses of the governors, presidents, and commanders-in-chief of the militia of the several states, partook of the same spirit; and as strange as it may seem, a better day of taste in literary composition had never been known amongst us, than that when the danger was the greatest, and the minds of men might be thought to be the most perturbed.

The authors of that day, not only availed themselves of the productions of the philosophers and sages of antiquity, whose works abound in all the doctrines of liberty, expressed in every beauty of language and charm of literature, but also of those pithy writers of a later date, that political circumstances had brought out, in Italy, France, and England; but particularly those of the United Netherlands; these last were of great service, their history resembling our own more distinctly than that of any other nation. Their articles of confederation were, confessedly, the basis of ours, at the commencement of the revolution.

Charleston, in South Carolina, has the honour of making the first celebration of the 4th of July. This was in 1778, two years only after the declaration of independence. On that day, Doctor Ramsay, since so well known to every child in the United States, as a politician and historian, appeared as the orator. Whoever will turn over the pages of that excellent address, will rejoice to find how fairly and faithfully the blessings of independence are enumerated in it; not in the swollen language of vanity, striving for importance, but in the strong, bold, flowing periods, of one who had reasoned and felt upon all the great matters he was discussing. In all probability, this custom has been kept alive there ever since; if not exactly annually, yet with sufficient regularity to answer the purpose of a proper political stimulant. In 1785, on the 4th of July, Doctor Josiah B. Ladd, a gentleman of high standing in the literary world, was solicited in that city, to make an address before the executive authority of South Carolina. This tasteful effort has been preserved for our instruction and guide.

In every stage of the contest, the literary men of our country did every thing in their power, to raise the flame of patriotism in the breasts of their countrymen. The aphorisms of the poets and sages of all times and countries were brought forth to enlighten and animate our people; and the striking instances of patriotism in history were made also to bear upon every crisis in our political affairs, with great judgement. An instance of this I will give you. On the 5th of July, the fourth having been Sunday, in the year 1779, Judge Breckenridge, of Philadelphia, delivered an " EULOGIUM ON THE BRAVE MEN WHO HAD FALLEN IN THE CONTEST WITH GREAT BRITAIN." It was a happy thought; the subject was natural and classical, and was treated with great taste and effect. There was a law of the Athenians, that after a battle in which her brave men had fallen, an orator should be elected by the court of Areopagus, to pronounce an eulogy on the deceased before the citizens of the Republic. In the 87th Olympiad, 431 years before the christian era, Pericles was appointed by the court to pronounce an eulogium upon those citizen-soldiers who fell in the first Peloponnesian war. The oration of this eminent scholar and statesman has been preserved in the pages of Thucydides, and is one of the noblest specimens of eloquence which has come down to us from antiquity. He began with commending to the notice of his audience their ancestors—the Athenians of other times; their valour, their love of liberty, their attention to arts and arms, were touched with the skill of a master hand. The charms of civil society, of refined manners, and of the sweets of intellectual superiority, were admirably portrayed. The privileges of the people of Greece, above all other men, were not forgotten, nor the value of existence kept out of view; but at the same time, the honour of dying in the field of glory was fully set forth. The duty of the publick to the offspring of those who were slain fighting the battles of the country, was distinctly stated, and the ordinance on that subject recited; "*that those children made fatherless by such a cause, should be educated at the public expense.*"

The American orator had a still more noble theme. The Athenians had engaged in this war, not from necessity, but from pride and a love of military glory. They might have avoided it, and yet have retained their splendour and liberties, and all those charms which the orator dwelt upon, as sweetening life. The mighty Athenian said, that one of the great motives which influenced the brave citizens, and led them to rush on death, was *revenge, revenge.* The citizen-soldiers of our republic had nothing of *revenge* in their dispositions, which brought them to the ensanguined field, and laid them low in the dust. To use the American orator's words, "it was the pure love of *virtue* and *freedom,* burning bright within their minds, that alone could engage them to embark in an undertaking of so bold and perilous a nature. They were not soldiers by profession; they were men in the easy walks of life, mechanicks of the city, merchants of the counting-house, youths engaged in literary studies, and husbandmen, peaceful cultivators of the soil, happy in the sociability and conversation of the town, the simplicity of the country village, or the philosophick ease of academick leisure, and the sweets of social life; they wished not a change of these scenes of pleasure for the dangers and calamities of war."

The American orator is more impassioned than his great prototype of Athens; his language glows with more warmth; there was less ambition in his strain of eloquence, and more of humanity than the orator of Athens allowed in his philosophy. Both orators called up the fathers and the sons of those who fell, to comfort them by

14

different forms of reasoning. The American orator had the advantage in the closing part of his oration, for the Athenian, in a few cold and ungallant sentences addressed to the widows, advised them " *to keep as much out of publick view, and as far from publick remark, as possible.*" The American mothers and widows required no such advice. In the time of Pericles, the christian religion which gives to women all their true influence, was unknown. Our orator took leave of the mighty dead, with the heart of a patriot, and with the views of a prophet. " Who in after times (says he) shall speak of those who have risen to renown ? I will charge it to the golden-winged and silver-tongued bards : that they recollect and set in order every circumstance, the causes of the war, early and just exertions, the toils, hazardous achievements, noble resolutions, unshaken perseverance, unabated ardour, hopes in the worst of times, triumphs of victory, humanity to an enemy ; all these will I charge it, that they recollect and set in order, and give them bright and unsullied to the coming ages. The bards I know will hear me ; and you, my gallant countrymen, shall go down to posterity with exceeding honour. Your fame shall ascend on the stream of time ; it shall play with the breezes of the morning. Men at rest in the cool age of life, from the fury of a thousand wars, finished by their fathers, shall observe the spreading ensign. They shall hail it, as it waves with variegated glories, and feeling all the warm rapture of the heart, shall give their plaudits from the shores."

The Athenians did redeem their pledge ; the orphans were educated at the publick expense ; but where are the children of those who fell in our revolutionary war ? We leave those to answer who can, satisfactorily to themselves.

The literature of the revolution is scattered throughout the history of all the transactions of that eventful period ; but in no instance does it shine more conspicuously than in the productions of Washington ; he was not a scholar by education or profession ; his information was miscellaneous, and by no means extensive, when his early publick services began. He knew something of history and mathematicks, and something of the military tacticks of the day. He, from his youth, saw things, at all times, through a clear medium, and expressed his thoughts with clearness, force, and honesty. His history of his journey to the Ohio, undertaken by the order of Dinwiddie, proves that his judgment was the master trait of his mind. The object of his mission is not a moment forgotten ; he looked with a single eye to that object, and he never, for a moment, turned himself, to think of his dangers or his sufferings. At every step such a mind improves. His first address to his army in July, 1775, is full of excellent military rules, but is wanting in that felicitous elegance which he afterwards acquired. He never suffered a sentiment to come from his pen negligently written; all was worked into ease and dignity. No commander that ever lived had so much need of this talent. Others have had to issue orders and to give an account of proceedings; Washington had not only to do these, but other things besides. He had, at times, to perform every duty incident to war, and more, from a pioneer to a field marshal; and from a sutler to a chancellor of the exchequer, at least with his pen; not only this, he had to use every argument to collect troops, and to keep them together, even for the shortest time; apathy was to be aroused; vaulting ambition to be struck down; individual bickerings to be silenced; sectional irritations to be soothed; the quarrelsome and high mettled to be controlled, that the service should not suffer; the faint and despairing to be encouraged; the living to be supported, and heaven, sometimes, only knew how; and the dead were to be duly honoured, according to military usages, when the army had hardly powder enough to fire a volley at the enemy. In all this, the address of Washington was conspicuous, but the productions of his pen were more so. He wrote to all, he reasoned with all, and he conquered all. Congress was not at all times in a proper temper to render him the most efficient aid; he was obliged to come upon them in all forms of entreaty; alarming them, at times, by his intimations of leaving the army, using every suggestion which could reach their pride, their patriotism, their honour, courage, or any other faculty, property, or sympathy, about them. There is not a form of reasoning that he was not obliged to assume; still, every form was pure English, good common sense, in his mother tongue. Cesar wrote his commentaries in the camp, and they are a fine model of chaste and elegant writing; but it must be remembered, that Cesar was a high bred Roman scholar. He was as proud of his eloquence and fine writing, as he was of his fame as a great leader of armies. Wolfe made his addresses and wrote his despatches in the toils and distresses incident to a camp; but these productions are but few, compared with those of Washington. Burgoyne's letters, written in the field, are said to surpass those written in the closet; Nelson's account of the battle of the Nile is sublime; and Buonaparte's address to his soldiers under the pyramids, is full of epick grandeur. But these are momentary bursts of chivalrous feelings; while Washington's addresses, despatches, and letters, to every one, in every part of the country, was a continued exertion of reason, to save his country. When the memory of individual exertion shall be lost, and history shall only speak, in general terms, of the revolutionary conflict, these letters and addresses of Washington will preserve the particular scenes of that day, and bring them at once to the understanding of men. In looking carefully over his productions already published, I cannot find in them one word that is not pure, legitimate English; good Saxon English, through which runs the best currents of true liberty in thinking and acting of any language that can be found, at any time or place.

The close of the war of independence, when the people fondly thought that they were about to be rewarded for all their sacrifices, was the most painful period of our history. At that time, from 1783 to 1789, almost every one found his affairs in a deranged state. The state debts which had been made in hopes of prosperous times, then operated severely on all classes in the community. To pay their debts with promptness was impossible, and every relief-act only made the matter worse. It was then that the people found that the great work of independence, as contemplated at the beginning of the conflict, was only half done; a form of government was to be fixed upon to give energy to national power, and success to individual and national enterprise. This portentous crisis formed another epoch for the display of the literary and political attainments of the active and patriotick minds in our country. New men appeared on the important discussion of the adoption of the federal constitution in the several state conventions; and it was found that the quantity of talent and information in the country had greatly increased during the war; and that its standard quality was equally good and precious as that which had been assayed at the commencement of the difficulties. A thousand intellectual lamps were lighted up along our shores, to show the people in what darkness they were groping, and to what a precipice they were hastening. A baleful meteor now and then led the people for a moment astray, but at length the right path was found, and the nation commenced its march onward to prosperity and honour.

Perhaps it were well to pause a moment and name a few of those who displayed their literature and eloquence at this important period. They left unexplored no portion of history. They passed by no lesson of experience; all were faithfully examined and thoroughly sifted, and the people had the benefits of the results. That nation cannot be long in danger that can, on any great event, command her physical and mental powers for her safety and guide.

It was felt by all thinking men, in every part of the country, that the old confederation was no longer a sufficient bond of union. The great pressure of common danger, which had kept all secure, had in a great measure ceased, and the people were hurrying fast on to anarchy, for want of a government that could enforce its requisitions.

From these conventions much of the nature of our people, their habits of thinking, and reasoning, and feeling, may be gathered. In looking over the debates in the several conventions in the different states, we find a great deal of talent displayed, from New-Hampshire to Georgia; and we may also see that the education of each state had been nearly on the same model; for in reading the speeches of all, a foreigner would at once pronounce that the orators were trained in the same school. The style of eloquence may vary a little, but the language used in the debates is all in the good old English books. They had the same jealousies, the same hopes and fears, and the same determinations. These jealousies had taken rank hold of common minds in every portion of the country; but it is not too much to say, that those in favour of adopting the constitution were generally of the higher classes of intellect, and those who had most at stake, although it must be conceded that there were many exceptions to this remark. The speakers in favour of adopting the constitution far outnumbered those opposed to it, in proportion to the majority obtained for the final vote.

In the convention of Massachusetts, there were, out of three hundred and fifty-five members, sixty-seven speakers, and not more than eight or ten ventured to oppose the constitution in debate; and yet there were, after every exertion, but a majority of nineteen in favour of the adoption of it. In the convention of New-York, which consisted of about sixty members, there was only a majority of two in favour of the adoption; and among the thirteen speakers there were only two or three in the negative. The talents were certainly on the side of the adoption; the impressions of the people were at first decidedly against it, from the fear that they were giving up too much of their hard earned liberty, and not from any wish to live in a state of anarchy. A bookseller of the city of Washington has, with a very enterprising spirit, commenced the publication of the debates in the several conventions; and has issued one volume, containing those in the conventions of Massachusetts and New-York. This is a laudable enterprise, and we wish him the success which he deserves. It must, however, be taken into consideration, that forty years have elapsed since these debates were reported; and at that time the art of reporting speeches was but little known; and it cannot be supposed that in cases where the speakers did not assist the reporters, that we have any thing more than the skeletons of the speeches delivered. The convention of Massachusetts were together from the 9th of January, 1788, to February 7th, twenty-nine days, at which time there were nearly two hundred speeches made; and among the orators some of the first men New-England ever produced. Parsons, Ames, Cabot, Gore, King, Dana, Jarvis, Strong, Brooks, Dawes, and others, who exhausted every subject they dis-

K

cussed. The whole of these speeches is comprised in one hundred and fifty octavo pages; and from a comparison of their different styles of speaking on other subjects, I find that the reporter's, not the speaker's style, is to be seen; still, however, much credit is due to him for getting these debates up so well as he did at that time. The New-York orators were fortunate, for they undertook to assist the reporter, and of course posterity will have a fair view of their arguments. It must be granted that the New-York convention was a highly intellectual body.

Virginia, always true to her native talents, had an experienced reporter in the convention to take down the debates; and fortunately for us, he extended them to three volumes, amounting to six hundred and twelve closely printed pages; and although that body was in session but twenty-six days, and only thirteen or fourteen members attempted to speak, yet we have more matter from these speeches than from the Massachusetts and New-York reports together. Those in the Virginia convention, in favour of adopting the proposed constitution, who distinguished themselves by their speeches, were Messrs. Nicholas, Randolph, Madison, Pendleton, Marshall, and Tyler. Those opposed to its adoption, were Patrick Henry, Mason, Munroe, Grayson, and Dawson. Mr. Madison took a very active part, and spoke more than any other member in the convention; although all those mentioned were deeply engaged. It will not be denied, at this day, that throughout the thirteen United States, in these debates on establishing a form of government, a majority of the talents was on the side of the constitution; yet there were able men opposed to it. When the main question was taken, the plurality in Virginia was only ten—eighty-nine voting in the affirmative, and seventy-nine in the negative. The question was ably argued on both sides, and the objections very honestly given. Patrick Henry, and those who acted with him, were fearful of the loss of state influence. They were alarmed at the expression " we, the people." They saw in this phrase a consolidation of interests which was not consistent with state pride; while, in many states, the people were afraid that individual rights would be lost. These different jealousies were shown at every movement of the states; but at last were happily overcome by the perseverance of the friends of the constitution. A victory was obtained more difficult to achieve than any; yea, than all those of arms which had been gained in the revolutionary struggle. These jealousies were natural, but the conquest over them was glorious.

I should proceed to give the best information I have upon the conventions of the other states, if the publick were not soon to be in possession of all that remains of their history from the press of

Mr. J. Elliott, of Washington, whose labours and research in this undertaking deserve the patronage of the publick.

It is to be regretted, that so many of the speeches of the members of the different conventions, are irrecoverably lost for the want of a proper reporter at the time, and from inattention since. It is a mortifying truth that more of our history, or more of the minute facts of which our history has been composed, have been preserved by other nations than by ourselves. The nations of Europe considered our case a new one in the annals of the world; and some of their curious speculators on the progress of events, took infinite pains to procure all the information to be had in respect to us and our proceedings. The Italian historian, Botta, not only procured all the information he could, but set down and wrote the history of our revolution with great fairness, and with tolerable accuracy. Professor Ebeling, of Germany, had the intention, it is said, of writing out our whole history, and collected a great mass of materials for that purpose. The history he did not write; but we have, through the medium of an individual, the benefit of his collections; they having been purchased and brought to this country.

There is one work which deserves our notice, and which ought to be republished, as there are but few copies of it in this country. "The Remembrancer, or an Impartial Repository of Publick Events." This work was begun by J. Almon, and published in monthly numbers, in London. It extends over the whole time of the revolution, from 1775 to 1783, and amounts to fourteen volumes, as collected and bound. The work was friendly to the cause of America, and was supported by the friends of this country at that time, and is remarkable for its candour, truth, and fidelity. One already possessed of the general outlines of the great contest between the colonies and the mother country, will find in this work more valuable documents, of a particular and circumstantial nature, to aid him in getting a minute history of his country at that period, than he can in any other work extant. Every one who has read history with attention, and with a desire to gain knowledge, will frequently find that there are a thousand little chinks left by the general writer that he could wish to see filled up; but knows not where to seek for the facts he is anxious to find. As to the history of our revolution, these volumes will greatly assist him. It has been a fruitful source for the historians themselves. The Remembrancer is something like Niles' Register, and is now what that will be to the future historians of our country. We are deeply indebted to the friends of our cause, at that period, in every part of the world, for their helping hand and good wishes; without which we might have fainted in reaching the goal and obtaining the prize; gratitude should remember what benevolence has forgotten.

After these great exertions for the adoption of the federal constitution had been made in the state conventions, and indeed while they were making, and the question was under discussion, a great deal was written by men of enlightened minds, and given to the public, to clear up the difficulties which had been suggested by those opposed to the form of government provided for in the constitution. Mr. Jay, Mr. Madison, and Mr. Hamilton, brought all the powers of their mighty minds, to satisfy the people that they were doing wisely to support the constitution, not only in convention, but by a series of letters in the publick prints. These periodicals, now acknowledged as their productions, unite the soundest maxims of good government, with the clearest and best illustrations of the best forms in which it could appear. These productions may be said to have fixed the publick mind. The relations and bearings of the provisions of the constitution, were so distinctly pointed out in them, that all could understand; and such was the correctness and beauty of the style of these numbers, that by them the taste of the country was refined, as well as the views of the citizens enlarged, and their understandings enlightened. I shall not stop, at this moment, to point out the part each one took in this great labour; but simply make this passing remark, that the *Federalist* stands foremost among American literary productions, whether we consider the subject, the matter, or style of the work, or its usefulness in explaining the views of those learned statesmen who achieved the second part of our independence. The effect of this work was such, that in a few years after it gained general circulation, there was scarcely a man to be found who questioned the propriety of the adoption of the constitution.

The valour which fought out the battles of the revolutionary war, and finally drove the enemy from our shore, and the wisdom which suggested our excellent form of government, and the address and perseverance which led to its adoption, were more than equalled by the wisdom and prudence with which the machinery was set in motion. The first congress, under the constitution, was composed of great men; most of them had been reared in the school of experience, and had been employed previously in considering that instrument; in order to assist in forwarding its adoption, they came to their congressional duties with a spirit of forbearance, ready to sacrifice all local prejudices on the altar of their country's good. What the knowledge and experience of one did not reach, the ingenuity of the other suggested, and all went on harmoniously and successfully. There was a delicacy shown to each other in that body, generally speaking, which has never been felt or exhibited since; and perhaps it has never since been so necessary as at that time. The eyes of the community were turned towards congress as towards the trying of an experiment, of which there were nearly as many fears as hopes. To use a phrase from the laws of the solar system, its polarity was inclined towards democracy, as being more congenial to the feelings of the people, and more consistent with the elements of our society, than a stronger government would have been. The people reasoned from expanded views of human nature, and a thorough acquaintance with history. They saw that despotick power destroys the oak of liberty, by cutting up root and branch, and by striking the soil on which it grows with dead sterility; while anarchy, if it comes at all, comes in a whirlwind with an hundred hands, and scatters the leaves and breaks the branches; but the root is not always left sapless; and the acorn, trodden under foot, may burst its germ and spring into life, and flourish in a new generation. Violent political discussions often pass away, and leave the lessons of experience to be felt and regarded; but nations rarely recover from the paralysis of despotism. Our ancestors saw the mother country, even in all the disasters and horrors of civil wars, advance in power and influence, while Spain, in the quiet of arbitrary power, was fast sinking into a secondary importance. In England the most useful institutions, and many of her learned men, grew up immediately after a civil war, or in it; while with all the influx of gold from the new world, learning and the arts declined at the same time, in the calm of Spanish despotism.

The literature of nations may be seen, in some measure, in the style in which their laws are written, and by their state papers. We judge of the state of the Romans by the style of the Justinian code, as well as by the poets of the Augustan age. In fact, the style of the laws is a better proof of the general advancement of knowledge, than that of the works of a few poets. The laws reflect the general intelligence, while poetry is perhaps only the reflected imagery of a few individual minds. The laws of the United States show a great extent of knowledge in the civil and commercial relations of society and nations. No country ever produced so many laws in so short a period of time. These laws and regulations are, in general, clear and explicit; sometimes they are marked with the peculiar phraseology of a particular state, as borrowed from the statute book of that state; but this is not perceptible to any one but those deeply read in these state laws. Every day's business is giving a more entire national stamp to the statute book of the United States; and the numerous and lucid decisions of the supreme court have produced uniform constructions in the laws which were in some degree differently construed in different sections of this extended country at the commencement of our national career.

The style of our state papers has been of a high order, in point of clearness and correctness, the great requisites in communications of a publick nature. The first secretaries were men of industry and learning, and they spared no pains to leave on record proofs of their abilities as makers of precedents. A responsible situation, indeed; several of these men were prime scholars, and felt that they were making models for future ages. It is a subject of congratulation to us, that so many patient, industrious, and learned men were, at that period, found for the discharge of such important duties. The anxiety of the first president to have every thing well matured, and clearly expressed, was favourable for the commencement of such an order of things. The duties of high political offices are always laborious and painful; but when there were but few or no landmarks to guide them, it must have been difficult indeed to have steered so correctly.

Much debating talent had been shown in congress in every stage of organizing and making these laws, the passage of which circumstances imperiously demanded; but there was no particular display of eloquence from any side of the house, until the British treaty called it forth; and perhaps, at no time since, have higher powers been developed in our national assembly, than on that subject. The champions, for and against, came forward and fought valiantly. It was a new question; and there might have been some honest differences; but it was debated upon party grounds, and so decided. Who were right or who were wrong it matters not, as it regards these lectures; it is mentioned as an era in our eloquence, so memorable, that American talent, in speaking, is never mentioned without some allusion to the debate on Jay's treaty.

Literature and science are near in their relationship, and seldom known to be far separated. Literature has generally received more attention in the early ages of nations than science. The sweet influences of Orion and Pleiades had been sung for ages in poetry, before science had marked their courses or weighed them in her balance; and science, after all the discoveries she has made, has adopted the terms used by taste and imagination, long before these discoveries were thought of. Every profession, to be respectable, must unite both in some degree. Without both, they are only trades, possessing neither dignity, nor refinement, nor interest. Bacon was the first among the lawyers who brought taste into the science of the profession. For this, he was derided by Coke as unsound and fanciful. Bacon could do nothing without leaving the impressions of mind, taste, and elegant novelty upon it. He laid hold of all the fabulous history of gods and demigods, and heroes, and laid bare its hidden meaning, and, by his explanations, gave utility, point, and beauty, to that which before seemed useless, dull, and extravagant. It is the pride of the present day, that his fame has been defended, and his honesty proved, by one of our own countrymen, after it had been surrounded by falsehood and prejudice, for more than a century and a half. A writer of the first talents, in the North American Review, a few years since, had the honour of showing the world, that Bacon deserved the epithets *brightest, wisest of mankind*; but that "*meanest*" was added at first by *wickedness*, and perpetuated by one who cared but little whether the epithet was just or unjust, if he could make the libel "*paint a moral, or adorn a tale.*" Bacon treated the law as a science capable of employing the graces of literature. After a considerable interval, Blackstone wrote his commentaries, which proved that the fundamental principles of law might be conveyed, even in a choice and clear style, without any quaintness, abruptness, or tedious repetition; and, like other subjects of less gravity, Lord Mansfield delivered his opinions in the best phraseology the English language would permit of in argument or illustration. The lawyers of our own country were men of learning before the revolution, but the manner of arguing at the bar, to the court or jury, was not remarkable for refinement or delicacy. Coarse attacks and sharp retorts were common between members of the bar; and the court either maintained a hard-featured silence, or broke in upon their sparrings with surly dignity. That gentlemanly courtesy, which reigns from one part of our country to another, among judges and advocates, was, for many years, unknown, or thought improper for a tribunal of justice. Not only the arguments of counsel, but the opinions of the bench, are now given with some regard to literary taste; and one not acquainted with law terms, may read the reports without being offended with a parade of technical terms or involved sentences. This branch of science is rapidly increasing; already we have more than three hundred volumes of American reports in law and equity; and, as the present generation of lawyers must go through such a mass of American law decisions, it is fortunate that some regard has been paid to the style in which these cases are made up. Some of these opinions might be selected, which have the freshness and spirit of animated truth conveyed in exquisite taste. Facts are not the less forcible, because they are happily arranged, nor reasonings less convincing, because they are well expressed. The professional men are trying to diffuse as much intelligence and taste in the community as possible, in order that a day of purer literature should succeed. Much has been done, and much more has been planned to be effected hereafter; the

numerous agents are busy, and in concert and harmony, in the
great work of spreading the sciences and literature throughout the
land.

The literature of theology in this country suffered, as well as the
literature and science of other professions, during the revolution.
The pulpit rang with patriotism and politicks, and harangues upon
the good and sound christian duty of fighting for freedom; all very
excellent lessons for the times, and which certainly had their uses.
After the warning appeals to the brave defenders of the country, it
was dull to go back to detailing the enormities of papal power, or
speaking of the *great beast of seven heads and ten horns;* therefore his holiness was left quite alone, except now and then in some
good man's form of prayer, from which the epithets of abhorrence
for Babylon never had been expunged. Dissertations on Antino-
mians, Pelagians, and all the host of sectarians, had begun to grow
stale, and the doctrines of eternal decrees and predestination were
not so attractive to the new generations as they had been to their
fathers. From all appearances, the timid began to fear that the pulpit had lost its legitimate, primitive influences. Under this impression, many were turned from the study of this profession, who
were intended for it by their parents, and engaged in medicine or
law. At this weak moment, if the defenders of the faith will allow
that there ever were such moments, infidelity reared its monstrous head, and stalked through our part of christendom with gigantick strides; but, as it has often happened, that which threatened
destruction to the altar and the priest, was the cause of giving new and
lasting honour to both. Infidelity had for years been disseminated by
the philosophers into inquisitive minds, but had never come upon
us in the form of popular eloquence, and had not reached common
minds engaged in ordinary pursuits, until about the time of the
French revolution; it now came under the potential form of superiour wisdom, free from the thraldom of error. It dealt out a
strong denial of the great truths of the gospel, and made impu-
dence, with now and then a flash of witty scurrility, pass for common sense and true reasoning upon the revelations of God to man,
through nature and her laws, and by the inspirations of holy writ.
At first, great shipwreck was made of the faith of thousands; the
weak were bewildered, and the unlearned entangled. The truly
pious still believed that the church was built upon a rock, and that
the gates of hell should not, finally, prevail against it, yet they were
discouraged at the progress of infidelity, and were cut to the heart
at hearing the authenticity of the scriptures doubted, and the ministers of our holy religion ridiculed in every possible form of con-
tempt; called by opprobrious epithets; charged with ignorance and

hypocrisy; and their downfall prophesied with confidence and joy. For a while there was some confusion in the church, but the purest men soon roused themselves from idleness, or rather from idle disputes about trifles, or non-essentials, and many of them plunged into the depths of learning, to answer the falsehoods and sneers of the scoffers, who laid pretensions to having penetrated into the recesses of oriental literature, and having detected the errours of christianity. The contest was animated, and the ministers of light struggled hard with the ministers of darkness. Great minds entered the contest, and, after a while, the dreams of Condorcet and the scurrilities of Paine, were swept away together, and infidelity was first scouted by learning, piety, and taste, and, at length, proscribed by the irresistible power of fashion. The works of Watson and Tytler, and, towards the close of the struggle, of many others, were found, not only in the hands of the polemick, or in the library of the speculative, but on the toilets of the fair, with the last work of the imagination from Southey or Campbell; for the ecclesiastical writers had added to the science of theology the most sublime of all contemplations, the charms of literature and taste. The reading and thinking part of the community were delighted to witness the commencement of a new era in the rhetorick, eloquence, and logick of the pulpit; useless divisions and subdivisions, and their scholastick divinity, with loose and spongy declamation, gave place to fair, inductions, correct illustrations, and philanthropick views. The ways of God to man were satisfactorily justified to the understandings of the mighty in intellect, and to the humble and lowly seekers of the truth. Religion wore the smile of innocence and the robe of purity, as she was destined to do from the beginning. The charms of a delicate and finished literature now came from the pulpit, and the temple of God became, as it ought ever to be, a place of instruction for the mind and for the affections, as well as for learning the great doctrines of salvation.

LECTURE VIII.

"The poet grieves to find his page grow scant,
And he must stint the praise of those he loves;
Nor number half that cluster round his pen."

AMONG the literati of our country, in the different ages of her growth, may be numbered many eminent physicians, who were not only useful in their profession, but distinguished for a spirit of inquiry and a knowledge of letters. At the first settlement of the provinces, the clergy were the physicians, and often the surgeons of the community. They practised, in general, without fees, from a religious belief that they ought not to receive any compensation for their services, as what they could do for the body was intimately connected with the cure of souls. This union of the professions had long been in use in Europe. The confessors of the convents and monasteries had made, in many orders, the healing art a part of their vows; and after the suppression of the religious houses in England, by Henry VIII., the clergy still continued the art among the people; and, after the reformation was entirely effected, kept up the custom without any dread from the bulls against the practice of dissection.

The first settlers of Plymouth and Massachusetts Bay, as well as those of Jamestown, had physicians and surgeons with them. Gager, an eminent surgeon, came to Charleston in 1630, but soon fell a victim to what has since been called the spotted fever. He practised physick as well as surgery. Firmin, a physician and surgeon, in 1639, was settled at Ipswich, but left the profession for that of divinity, which was the safest road to distinction in those days.

The skill of the early physicians was speedily put to the test, for, besides the fevers incident to the hard living of new settlers, the small-pox and yellow fever were soon brought among them from the West-Indies; and, after several years, the "cynanche maligna" baffled all their skill for a time. The measles, often an obstinate disease, was constantly among the new settlements. The yellow fever, which we now trust has left for ever most of our cities, prevailed, in its most malignant form, in Charleston, South Carolina, in 1699, 1703, 1732, 1739, 1740, 1745, 1748; and Dr. Harris says it was there in 1761 and 1764. This fever prevailed in Philadelphia in 1741, 1747, 1762, and 1793; in New-York in 1792, 1798, and several times since. Hutchenson says, that, as early as 1693, it was prevalent in Boston. It came from the West-Indies in the fleet of Sir Francis Wheeler, which was sent from that station to join the New-England forces, destined against Quebeck. This fleet lost 1300 sailors out of 2100, and 1800 soldiers out of 2400. Previous to this period, a disease swept through the country in 1647; its precise character has never been known; the Indians fell victims to it, as well as the European colonists; and in 1655 it was nearly as extensive and fatal. The small-pox was a great scourge; it prevailed in Boston in 1689, 1702, 1721, 1730, 1752, 1764, 1776, and in 1792; and the probability is, that it was as frequent in other cities. We state these facts, to show that there were constantly subjects for the inquiries of the medical mind; and as early as 1647, Thomas Thatcher, of Weymouth, in Massachusetts, turned his attention to the subjects of diseases, and wrote a treatise on the small-pox and measles, called "a brief guide in the small-pox and measles." He was a great man, learned as a mathematician, and a practical mechanick, whose inventive genius was equal to his scientifick acquirements. He was also a profound oriental scholar, and had explored all the wisdom of the East in the healing art. This treatise of Thatcher's was probably the first book written in this country, upon any of the diseases incident to it. This eminent physician, scholar, and divine, died at the age of fifty-eight; a greater man than whom, this country has not since produced. At this time, some of the physicians educated abroad, attracted by the novelty of a new country, or dissatisfied with the old world, came among our ancestors to diffuse their information, and to find new sources of knowledge. Robert Child, educated at the university of Padua, came to Massachusetts as early as 1646. The name of this physician was connected with an attempt made to diffuse a spirit of religious toleration, which received the censures of the magistrates, but which may form his eulogium now, however severe they were thought to be at that time. The next physician and surgeon of note in our annals, is Gershom Bulkley, of Connecticut, son of the learned Mr. Bulkley, of Concord, in Massachusetts. He was a clergyman; in Philip's war of 1676, was appointed surgeon to the Connecticut troops, and such was the confidence of the legislature in his abilities, that he was made, by their order, one of the council of war.

The next publication from a professor of medicine, that I can find, but probably my researches may not have been so thorough on this subject as on some other subjects, was one of Dr. Douglass' on the small-pox, whose character I have sketched in a former lecture. He was opposed to inoculation, and ridiculed Boyleston, who was there in 1721, introducing the practice of it. This provoked Boyleston to a defence. Cotton Mather had his share in the dispute; he was in favour of the practice. At this time, Nathaniel Williams, a clergyman, a schoolmaster, successor to old master Cheever, and a distinguished physician also, being a good-natured man, wrote a humourous dialogue upon this dispute, entitled "Mundungus, Sawney, Academicus, a debate;" these names glanced at the different characters who had been distinguished in the dispute; and it is said to contain the arguments on both sides of the question, as far as facts had then developed principles. The old physicians spoke of this work with great respect. Williams was a man of such benevolence and sincerity, that in that day of gratuitous epithets, he was called "the beloved physician." The next work was a treatise on pharmacy, by Thomas Harwood, a good medical writer of some eminence. This work was published in 1732. In 1740, Dr. Thomas Cadwallader published an essay on the "Iliack Passion," which gave him great celebrity in this country and in England. In 1745, he published some medical papers in the "Royal Transactions, London." This was the mode pursued by eminent physicians in this country; for the fact of appearing in such a publication, was sufficient to ensure the attention of the publick, or that part of it one would wish to attract. Dr. Cadwallader was one of the first professors in the medical art, who, in this country, taught his pupils from hospital practice; being one of the visiting physicians in the Philadelphia hospital, which was founded in 1752.

Previously, the subject of plants had attracted the attention of men fond of pursuing nature in "the herb and flower." Mark Catesby had the honour of being among the first engaged in this pursuit in this country. He was sagacious and indefatigable, but his works are far inferior to Clayton's Flora Virginiana. The history of the labours of this great botanical work is very singular. The art of printing and engraving in this country, would not admit of printing a flora here; he therefore sent his production to Leyden, to professor Gronovius, who published it in several editions; the first of them in 1739, the second in 1743, the third in 1762. Clayton began this work in 1705, when the forests were extensive, and when the lily of the valley and the mountain daisy breathed their fragrance on the same gale. Dudley and Douglass, whom we have named before, were at the same time engaged in the same pursuit. Clayton's descriptions of the plants he collected are remarkable for neatness and accuracy, and often beautiful and elegant. It is a fact worthy of notice, that some of the finest descriptions to be found any where, are in the works of naturalists and botanists. Some descriptions of plants by Linnæus, Darwin, and their fellow-labourers in the garden of nature, are models of beauty; and what can surpass in splendour Buffon's description of the horse, the peacock, and the eagle?

Every part of our country puts in just claims for distinction in the medical profession; Doctor William Ball, of South Carolina, who was a graduate of Harvard college, defended a medical thesis, with ability, at Leyden, in 1734. He was for many years eminent in his native state. Doctors Thomas Bond, and Middleton, made the first publick dissection, in 1750. This was done by leave of a court of law. Josiah Bartlett, of Exeter, New-Hampshire, wrote on the "cynanche maligna," which had been prevalent in New-England; and John Jones wrote at the commencement of the revolutionary war, a treatise "on wounds and fractures," for the use of the army. I have collected these facts, with many others that I shall not trouble you with, respecting the medical faculty, simply to show that this profession has had its share in the literature of our country. Within the half century, it is well known that in Europe and this country, they have raised the standard of the profession, by banishing, as far as possible, all empyricism from their borders. This is a profession in which ignorance has heretofore so often hid herself, and gulled the world by pretensions, that the satirists have in every age, poured out upon it their surcharged vials of wrath; but the historian now sharpens his pen to write their praise. Hippocrates describes a quack, as a being "no laws could reach, and no ignominy disgrace." The medical profession has often wisely resorted to letters for immortality. It is not the cure, but the record of it only, that we can see. To prove the altitude of the medical character in our country, we need only look to the earliest medical school in America. When, in 1768, a medical college was established at Philadelphia, what a cluster of distinguished men were collected to give it popularity. Shippen, Cadwallader, and a host of others, were ready and active ministers of science to diffuse its advantages. "A good physician" (says the scriptures) is from the Lord; and to continue the oriental phraseology—a Hospital well regulated, and bountifully endowed to heal the maladies of the mind and body, may be said to be *a perpetual lamp of life in the temple of nature;* and those whose duty it is to watch, should never slumber or sleep on their posts.

At the time of the revolution, there were a goodly number of active men in the profession of medicine, who took a part in the conflict. Warren, Church, Bull, Finch, and others, had taken the place of Perkins, Cutter, Clarke, and others, in Massachusetts; and in other States, there were also many of the physicians who were an effective and active class of men. They had defects, no doubt, in their education, for they had many difficulties to contend with, but none that could not be overcome. Many of them had distinguished

16

themselves by their writings in favour of civil liberty, and it was
necessary for them to push forward and take an active part. Some
of them entered the army professionally, and others gave up the
lancet for the sword. Among the officers of the army of the revolution, whose profession had been that of physick, were, Warren,
Mercer, St. Clair, Gadsden, Cobb, Brooks, Bricket; and who were
braver than they? In political life, the profession has been conspicuous; before the adoption of the federal constitution, the profession
could number some of the first men in Congress from their body.
And since the constitution has been in operation, there have been also
many of distinction in publick life. As orators, there has been no
small share of eloquence among them. This has been proved in
the halls of legislation often, but more often, and more happily, in
the lecture room; there the subjects are neither artificial nor con-
ventional, but natural, and nature makes her votaries eloquent.

As poets as well as warriors, the medical faculty has been distinguished. We have, in our account of American poets, mentioned
Hopkins, Church, Warren, Ladd, Bryant, Shaw, Boyd, Percival, and
other bards, who, while they plucked the misletoe as Druids, ana-
lysed, as chemists and philosophers, the nut gall of the same oak on
which the parasite had grown. It is impossible to mention all in a
short course of lectures; but I cannot pass over some names
without paying a tribute to their virtues, if it be only in a hasty breath.
In every great enterprise, more depends upon the character of the
few who zealously engage in it, than upon the many, who may take
cursory and imperfect views of it, and with only faint motives for
its prosperity. It was fortunate, that such a man as Rush should
have been found at the close of the revolution, to assist in building
up an American school of medicine. He was fitted for the task.
His temperament was ardent, and his feelings enthusiastick; he
had the rare faculty of communicating this enthusiasm to others;
and his pupils pursued their inquiries with an impetus, derived from
him, which carried them rapidly and pleasantly through the laby-
rinths of science. His eloquence, his arguments, and his love of
labour, did much to break the spell which hung over the profession,
"*that no man could be qualified for a professor, in any of the
branches of medicine, who had not been in a foreign school.*" He
taught that nature was the same in every country, and that when
she was properly interrogated, her responses would be the same at
all times.

The medical school at New-York has had a share of the intelligence of the country in every stage of its growth; James, Middleton, and others, distinguished in their day, have been succeeded by
men of science and letters.

The medical school of Harvard University, was in contemplation for many years, and liberal donations had been made for the purpose of its establishment, but the situation of the country forbade its commencement until 1782. Doctor John Warren, brother of General Warren who fell at Bunkerhill, ardent in his patriotism as any man that ever lived, who entered the army as a common soldier after the death of his brother, probably from the strong excitement at this event, and continued in it as a surgeon for several years, was at the head of this school. He had at this time left the army and settled in Boston, in his profession, among his brother's friends, and had before 1782 delivered a course of lectures on anatomy. The students of Harvard University had an opportunity of attending them. When the school was opened at Cambridge within the college walls, Warren was put at the head of the newly established institution, and Doctors Dexter and Waterhouse were also appointed professors. Doctor Warren was well qualified for this important situation; he had genius, patience, industry, and eloquence, and all were required for the commencement of such a school. He secured the understanding of his hearers, while he charmed their imaginations, and without a struggle he led them through the course of his lectures with pleasure, admiration, and profit. The army had been a good school for him, for there he had witnessed the diseases of camps and the wounds of battles, and no lesson was lost on such a mind. He, like Rush, had the faculty of inspiring his pupils with love, confidence, and admiration, and, at the same time, with an ardent passion to excel in their profession. The influence of his example was more powerful than his precepts, in teaching the many axioms he wished to inculcate. Independent of his professional fame, he has left some excellent specimens of his taste and talents as a classical writer. He has left a son who is among the first of his profession, and who does great credit to the advantages which his father gave him, and who, by his attention to the progress of knowledge, has quartered new honours on his arms as a professional man.

The medical school of Dartmouth College was the fourth institution of the kind which was founded in this country. In 1798, Dr. Nathan Smith was appointed sole professor, and for many years lectured on all the usual branches of medicine taught in a course of medical instruction. This was indeed a Herculean task, but he met it manfully, passing from one subject to another with astonishing ease. His labours were often embarrassed by the cavils of the suspicious and envious; but he marched on, in the dignity of conscious genius, and conquered a prejudice at every step. He, too, had a spice of that enthusiasm which distinguished his great predecessors and coadjutors in the task of building up the schools of medicine.

He, too, had eloquence to assist him in making his way against a thousand evils. He passed from the grave to the pleasant with such readiness, that the delicate shades of the transitions were not always noticed; but when the history of our great men is written out, the enterprise, genius, perseverance, and success of Dr. Nathan Smith, will be remembered by every lover of science.

It will not be necessary to speak of others, or to follow up the progress of the healing art to the present day, as this has been done with great ability by several distinguished medical gentlemen; my only object in these details being to show the course of intelligence in this country, in this department of knowledge, as well as in other branches which are more directly in our path, in the pursuit of whatever can give us pleasure, intelligence, or profit.

One other memorable name I must here mention: the patriarch of the physicians of the present age, Dr. Holyoke, has just gone down to the tomb, having numbered among men more than an hundred years. He lived in an eventful period, for during his time, the various branches of his profession had advanced more than for twenty preceding centuries; and yet, it may be said, that he not only knew what had previously been taught, but had kept up with the progress of knowledge to the last year of his life. I first knew him when he was near eighty, healthy and intellectual, and anxious to be possessed of all that was going on in the literary and scientifick world, as well as of all matters in his own profession. He acquired information with great ease; for besides a natural quickness of perception, he had a thorough early education; for being the son of a literary man, he was made a scholar from the cradle; was graduated from college early in life, and commenced his professional career while in his minority. He made it, for many years, a practice to read some portion of the classicks daily; but his mind was rather mathematical, inquisitive, and philosophical, than creative or tasteful; not that he was deficient in imagination or taste, but these properties of the mind were not his distinguishing characteristicks.

His moral and social habits were commendable and attractive; for a pure philanthropy was seen running through the whole course of his conduct. His disposition was bland and fraternal; and like most true philosophers, he loved to find himself surrounded by young, vigorous, fruitful minds; and in the early times, when custom had established an awful distance between master and pupil, he drew his so near him by the cords of affection, that he had no difficulty in ascertaining the number of their talents, and the weight of their arguments. He was singular, perhaps, in making Euclid a part of their professional studies; but he examined them as often in this work as in Hippocrates; and it was a maxim with him, which he constantly gave to his pupils, *never lose sight of ancient philosophy in modern improvements;* yet he rejoiced in all the lights that were bursting in upon the profession of medicine and surgery; and he was not far behind the reformers themselves, in adopting whatever was found salutary by a well tried practice; and he was an admirable judge of what was good, for he brought an honest and serene mind to bear upon every subject of discussion. He was not satisfied with brilliant theories unassisted by well tested facts, properly authenticated by careful and intelligent men, competent in every respect to decide a case upon professional and philosophical principles.

He never sought honours or distinctions, and never meddled with politicks any farther than to show his patriotism, and his willingness to trust his fortune and freedom with others of his choice. A deep sense of duty sometimes brought him out; for there were some situations he could not refuse—such as that of president of the American Academy; and also that of president of the Massachusetts Medical Society, when it was first organized; but the greatest portion of his time was devoted to his professional duties. His publications were not numerous, but were of a very high character for a careful arrangement of facts, and a pure induction of principles.

Such a protracted life as Dr. Holyoke's—a union of a sound mind with a healthy body, is seldom enjoyed by man in the present age. Indeed, it has rarely happened that any seer, or sage, at any period of time, since the days of the primitive patriarchs, has been permitted to look on, or mingle in the affairs of men, active and strong, for more than thirty years beyond the threescore and ten—that boundary in the revised code of nature. It is pleasant, however, now and then, to contemplate the course of such a favoured being;—a philosopher, philanthropist, and christian, who had reasoned so much, and felt and acted so long; one whose disciples of every age, from decrepitude to youth, were around him; from those who had thrown the lancet and the bolus aside, to young aspirants for Esculapian honours, in whose trembling hands these emblems of art and science were yet unused. To exhibit such a character fully is difficult, if not impossible; there seems to be nothing in the common pathway of our experience for illustration; nothing to liken him to; we turn necessarily to the muses for aid, and adopting the language of the Persian poet, say, that such a man resembles *the god of day lingering long in the western skies to catch the incense and to receive the homage of the flowers as they gratefully turn to him in his decline; flowers which his warmer rays had awakened to life and beauty;* or to soar to higher similitudes in the regions of inspiration and prophesy, a hale, virtuous, intellectual man of an hundred years old, communing with heaven and dispensing wisdom on earth,

L 2

who seems to have the power and favour of the GOD OF ISRAEL vouchsafed to him, to stay the course of time, and to say, "*Sun, stand thou still upon Gibeon; and thou, moon, in the valley of Ajalon*," *until reason, religion, and philosophy, have avenged themselves on their enemies.*

In quitting this class of intelligent men, we pass to that of our historians, particularly those who have written since the revolution, as we have mentioned those who wrote before that time; like all others, this class has various claims to distinction; most of them have shown some industry in collecting materials, and some few of them talents for arranging them, and giving them in a proper dress to the publick. We will take them as they come to our recollection, without regard to the order of the time in which they were written.

Belknap's history of New-Hampshire, is a well written work; the author was a good scholar, a man of great honesty and generous feelings; as well educated for an historian as any one who has ever undertaken the task in this country. His materials were scanty, and scattered over a thinly settled territory; one half of what was to be said was in tradition, and the other on scanty records; but the narrations were honest and the records true; and by the help of a thorough knowledge of the people, and an intimate acquaintance with contemporaneous records, he was enabled to get at the truth, and nearly the whole truth; but although his history is of a high order, we think that his biographical works are better than his history or his sermons, which have been for many years highly valued. Those who knew this amiable and accomplished writer, will hardly hear a criticism upon his works; for the sweetness of his disposition, and the blandishments of his manners, went much farther in the estimation of his character than the elegance of his pen.

The history of Maine, by Sullivan, is the ground work for a future history of that growing state. Sullivan was a man of genius and research; but was too much employed as a politician and a lawyer, to devote much time to literary labours; but if he did not find time to give a finishing touch to his history of that province, the publick are much indebted for that which he did write.

The history of Massachusetts has been more fully written than that of any other province. It was the theatre of important events, and the nursery of many other settlements in New-England, and in the latter period of more distant places. After the historians we have already mentioned, come Hubbard's History, Church's Indian Wars, and historical sketches of a smaller kind. There are many well written historical works of particular periods, such as Minott's, Bradford's, and others. Morse and Parish have written a school book history of New-England, and Hannah Adams has published a very neat and accurate compendium of New-England history. When the historian shall appear to write a full account of us, there will be found many excellent materials in the collections of the Massachusetts historical society. It is a subject of congratulation, that other states are following the example of Massachusetts, and rescuing from oblivion valuable facts for the future historians of our country. Our activity cannot be too great, for every hour as it passes shrouds some circumstance in obscurity, and the grave-digger, time, is always busy in burying the deeds as well as the generations of man.

The history of Vermont has been written by Professor Williams, and no one will say that he has not made the most of the scanty materials he had for his work. When he wrote, the state was in its infancy. It would be well now to continue this history; for the rapid growth of that portion of our country, in population, wealth, and intelligence, has made its history a subject of interest and inquiry.

The history of Rhode Island has not yet been fully written. The great father of toleration in this country, Roger Williams, made that state, as is well known, an asylum for those disturbed by the narrow views and bigoted feelings of other states. This great philanthropist, R. Williams, wrote a valuable treatise upon the language, manners, and customs of the Indians in his vicinity, which, after having been locked up for ages in some library in England, has at length reached us as a matter of information and curiosity. The Rev. Mr. Callender published a curious sermon, which, when enlarged, made a very excellent historical sketch of Rhode Island, for the time. And the Hon. Mr. Hunter, in a fourth of July oration, favoured the publick with some vivid sketches of their revolutionary history; but it remains for his pen, or that of some other intelligent Rhode Islander, to write out her history.

The history of Connecticut has been written with talents and taste, and perhaps as minutely as was required at the time when Trumbull published his work. The old libraries of the ancient families of that state must certainly contain matter for a most circumstantial and minute history of it. The first settlers were of a literary class. They left Massachusetts to take up their residence on the Connecticut and the Thames; and carried their axes on their shoulders, and their ink-horns in their pockets; and sat down to write a full journal of their travels through the wilderness, to satisfy the anxious friends they left at Massachusetts Bay, before they had finished the log-hut to shelter them from the wind and rain.

Of the history of New-York it may be said, that the historian did as much towards making a good history as could be expected from any one, at the time in which he wrote; when he had but few aids from extensive collections of books. The Dutch history of the colony, if he ever saw it, was probably a sealed book to him, from an ignorance of the language in which it was written. M'Cullock has written one lately.

The history of New-Jersey is not sufficiently full or particular to satisfy the age;—nor can that of Maryland as yet lay greater claims to distinction. These states have many who can supply all deficiencies if they will look about.

The history of Virginia has been written at different periods, by several hands; Smith's, Stith's, and Beverley's, we have already noticed. Burk and Geradin have continued the subject, and in fact, have gone over most, or all, of the same ground with their predecessors. Mr. Jefferson's Notes on Virginia, which are partly statistical, as well as historical, are highly valuable to those who wish to be acquainted with that state. Chief Justice Marshall, in his life of Washington, has done great justice to the history of Virginia. It has been said of Cæsar, *that his biography was the history of Rome while Cæsar lived;* but in the case of Washington, the biographer found it necessary for his subject to write nearly the whole history of his country; this is a great work; it has nothing in it of the splendour of Robertson, the grandiloquence of Gibbon, or the sweetness of Goldsmith; but it is a monument of stability—a pyramid of granite, of majestick dimensions, that will stand in the waste of time on the frontiers of our history; but ages may pass away before the merits of this great mental labour will be justly appreciated.

The history of South Carolina is from the pen of Dr. Ramsay. The bare mention of this fact is sufficient assurance of its excellence. Dr. Ramsay possessed, in an eminent degree, the qualifications of an historian; learning, memory, research, readiness, a love of labour, with an easy, elegant style of composition, and a mind naturally active and free from prejudices. The history of the American war from his hand is, in all things considered, the best for general use extant. He lived in the time in which he wrote; "all of which he saw, and a part of which he was," may be said of him, in connexion with the events of that period. He had means which other historians did not enjoy, an intimate acquaintance with the principal actors in the scenes he describes. After he had written his history, the manuscript was read to those capable of judging of its correctness; and of course, any errours of time or circumstance were detected and corrected. This historian did not stop at the revolutionary war, but gave his country an account of her history from the earliest settlements; and then a succinct universal history, most happily condensed. Of late years, Prentis, Hale, and others, have written succinct histories of the United States, which are of a respectable character. That from the pen of Mr. Hale received a premium from some historical society, for its superiority over others as adapted to youths.

The productions of our theologians, perhaps, have not been so numerous as in former times; but those sermons and polemick discussions which we have had of late, are marked with high characteristicks of mind and taste. Emmons, Dwight, Freeman, Buckminster, Griffin, and many others, evince deep erudition and evangelical piety; and the controversial writings of Channing, Stewart, and others, who have lately been engaged in the unitarian and trinitarian controversy, have discovered that biblical literature is a favourite study among the clergy of the present day, and that they have pushed their examinations into other times, and made themselves masters of ancient lore. If some are grieved, all are instructed, and a free inquiry cannot in the end be useless. Irreverential inquisitiveness is a species of profanity, but a holy wrestling with God to obtain the dispositions of his nature, and the determinations of his will, is the amount of what is called the study of theology, which is at once the prerogative and the duty of intellectual beings. We have now in this country more than seven thousand teachers of divinity, who form the upper class of instructors in this community. If these are enlightened as they should be, we cannot perish for lack of vision.

In the biographical department of literature, we have had several writers of talents, who have as patiently as possible, when we consider the scanty remuneration they generally receive, collected facts for the purpose of illustrating the lives of some of our distinguished men: Belknap, Elliott, Allen, Hardie, and several others, have published their collections, much to the advantage of the community. Belknap was a smooth Addisonian writer of great sincerity and faithfulness, without a single particle of bitterness in his nature. He wrote his faithful chronicles with an admiration of the great discoverers and settlers of this country; but he had no motive to make them other than they were. These lives are not so much known and read as they would have been, if they had come from some ordinary novelist, and had been portraits of fictitious personages.

Elliott was a great antiquarian, and a very honest man; he had treasured up a great many facts, and knew all the traditions of his country; but he knew but little of book-making, and, in truth, paid but little attention to the style of his sketches. Dr. Elliott was esteemed, among his literary friends, as a most admirable antiquarian

17

and a fair-minded critick; and his volume of biography, although carelessly written, and more carelessly printed, will do honour to his memory, and will be in the hands of all who wish to know any thing of the character of the early worthies of New-England. Allen was educated in modern times, and had a more extensive acquaintance with facts than most biographers. He was patient of labour, and collected his facts, and wrote his commentaries upon events, and sketched his traits of character, while a librarian of Cambridge university, with the best library on American history and American biography in the world, at his full command. It is said, that the publick are soon to be favoured with a new edition of this work; we hope they will not be disappointed. His whole life has been devoted to literary pursuits or to literary duties, and there are but few more capable of doing justice to the mighty dead of our country than President Allen, of Maine.

One of the most valuable among American books is Holmes's Annals. In its first editions it was a very correct chronicle of successive events, but the last edition is enriched by biographical notices and pertinent remarks, and is not only history in itself, but a manual for future historians. Dr. Holmes is a profound antiquarian and a sound scholar, and is happy in living to find his labours duly appreciated.

The nine volumes of the lives of the signers of the declaration of independence, contain no small share of fine writing. These productions are from different hands and of unequal excellence. It is well to have an opportunity of seeing these worthies at one view, and to be able, as it were, to enter the venerable group; but as the writers were necessarily confined to one signal period of time, that certainly a very eventful one, the information conveyed by the perusal of the whole is not, of course, so great nor so diversified as it would have been had the writers been engaged in the biography of the great men of our country who had lived in different epochs of our history.

We have some exquisite morsels of single biographical sketches; Kirkland's Life of Ames is a miniature of admirable workmanship. The shades are so disposed of as to give relief to the prominent features; the true evidence of a master's work. Thatcher's memoir of Buckminster is of the same class, and, perhaps, superior in finish if not in conception; and Greenwood's obituary notice of Thatcher has something of a kindred spirit in it.

Several writers have given the publick the life of Washington, and some of them are felicitous compositions. Dr. Bancroft's, of Worcester, in Massachusetts, is one of those which will be read with interest in future days, as it is now. The Doctor has published a volume of sermons of much merit. The work is remarkable for liberality of sentiment, purity of style, and for strong direct reasoning on difficult matters of belief. There is something refreshing in his candid, bold, and pleasant manner of treating his subject, and you are satisfied with the writer, even when you refuse to become a convert to his argument. Whatever comes from the pen of this venerable philanthropist and christian, is finely marked with delicate and discriminating touches.

It is difficult to speak, at the present time, of Mr. Adams' Lectures on Rhetorick. As an orator and statesmen, his fame is in every court. For more than forty years he has been known to the republick of letters as a splendid scholar. With his political life we have nothing to do here; but we venture to predict, that, when these lectures are read hereafter, free from those prejudices or partialities which are almost necessarily incorporated with our opinions of the works of living politicians, that they will add to the honour of American literature; and, if not considered as faultless in style, will be ranked among the most vigorous efforts of American genius and learning.

Pitkin's political and civil history of the United States is a valuable work. The writer has laboured more to show causes and to develope principles, than to round periods and polish metaphors. He came to his work with much knowledge of our history, and a sound discriminating judgement. The practical politician should be thoroughly master of the contents of these volumes. There is a deplorable ignorance of constitutional history among us. It should not be so. We have had frequent occasions, in the course of these lectures, to speak of medical works, and of the medical mind in our country, with great respect. They deserve it. The journals of that profession, though more directly belonging to scientifick and professional knowledge than to general literature, are of a high literary grade. The writers in these periodicals have certainly acquired the art or mystery, for it partakes of both, of preserving uninteresting, and even revolting facts, if seen too nakedly, in the beauties of language and the charms of style. They have perfumed and cleansed the lazar-house; ornamented the cinerary urn, and so tastefully sculptured the sarcophagi, that one of delicate nerves may walk among the ravings of disease and the victims of death, and reason upon the phenomena without disgust or terrour. Of this character is the work of Dr. Beck, of Albany, on *Medical Jurisprudence.* It was the first work on that subject that issued from the American press. The order pursued is natural, the style is easy, and the facts appear to have been cautiously examined, and the inferences from them fairly drawn; and the illustrations are generally happy.

This work should be found in every lawyer's library. There has been many a victim,.innocent of crime, sacrificed to an ignorance of the science of medical jurisprudence. Their blood must rest somewhere.

The life of Fulton, by Colden, is much esteemed, and comes timely to ward off many criticisms upon the course Fulton had pursued.

Judge Johnson's life of Green, is a work of research and extent; but it has not suited all tastes. Perhaps too much was expected from the circumstance of official elevation.

Brown's life of Dr. Linn, is superiour to most writings of the kind. Brown excelled in drawing characters, and his subject was full of romantic beauty. The melancholy of the mind and imagination of both Brown and Linn is slightly incorporated in the colouring of the picture. The light falls upon it as passing through the painted glass of a gothick window into the chancel of a monastery, throwing a religious solemnity over the group of the painting, and the artist, and all the scene around them.

DUNLAP'S LIFE OF BROWN, is a very fair and honest narrative of the events in the life of the American novelist and sentimental writer; who laboured, and suffered, and died, without receiving from his countrymen the rewards he deserved. Dunlap is a man of genius as a painter, as well as a writer, and second to but few in either profession.

We claim Washington Irving as one of our literati; and are proud to rank him among the first of our authors. He began his literary career here, and for many years was a contributor to our best periodical journals. He left this country with a high reputation as a man of taste and talents, and with the affection and respect of the first circles among us; but in Europe he has more widely extended his fame, by his sketch book, and other works. His tales abound in deep interest, his plots are finely conceived, and his descriptions felicitous. His delineations of character are just and striking; and every article from his pen has some fine touches of the pathetick; in this he is singularly successful. His language is choice, good, pure old English; and his style is polished with the most exquisite care. He was not, however, satisfied by resting his fame on these works, but looked around him for some unoccupied portion of history on which to seize for a lasting work; but at length most wisely took an old subject, but one which will never be exhausted—the life and adventures of Christopher Columbus. This subject contained incidents already related, sufficient in his hands for the purposes of making a most entertaining and instructive work; and these were at his command without going out of his library for them; but he was not content to rely on any garnishments of this subject for reputation, but added the results of long and assiduous research to new philosophical views, and more minute incidents. Fired with his theme, he sought the fountains for information, and drew his knowledge from them, all pure and fresh for his uses. The national archives of Spain, so long shut up from the world, were opened to him; and the family papers of Columbus, that had been preserved with great care, were now thoroughly examined. His success has fully justified his devotion to the cause. This was precisely such a subject as should have engaged the attention of such a mind. Poetry and fiction had nothing more splendid to offer, nor history to hold up, for the contemplation of man, than the life of Columbus; there was enough of vicissitude, of glory, of heart-ache, of degradation, of apotheosis, to have suited an epick bard, or an oriental enthusiast. Had the great discoverer been "wrapt into future times," as poets have imagined him to have been, one of the most delightful visions he could have had, would have been a sight of his own great historian. Not a misery of his existence could now be spared by his biographer, for they were all wanted to finish so noble a character. Who is there now so dull as would wish to find that all the troubles of Columbus were fictitious; and that, full-fed with wealth, and overloaded with honours, he had sunk to "*the vulgar level of the great;*" and had passed the last of his days in the stately magnificence of a Spanish grandee? Not one; his chains, his dungeon, his death, his obscure grave, are all sacred appendages to his fame; nor were his honours and his virtues to shine in that age of superstition and ignorance; three centuries, in the course of time, were required to bring forth a historian for him; for it was a decree of fate, that the events of the life of the discoverer of the new world, should be fully written by one who should arise in it.

Dr. Thatcher, author of a medical work, and a military journal of considerable celebrity, has published "The Biography of American Physicians:"—the preface, containing a succinct history of the medical profession, is learned and interesting; and the lives are written with great fairness, with fraternal feeling, and discover touches of discrimination and literary taste; and from the sources from whence the Doctor derived his information, and the pains he has taken to compose and correct whatever he had gathered, there can be no doubt of its being the most authentick of all our works on American biography. The Doctor did not begin this work until well advanced in years; and of course had a very extensive acquaintance with distinguished men in his profession. The work is a valuable addition to our stock of biography.

Several instructive works, in the form of letters, have appeared

M

among us from time to time; one from the pen of **Mr. J. Q. A**dams when abroad, to his son in this country, which is full of parental tenderness and valuable instructions and advice; it ought to be read by all young men.

Nathaniel H. Carter, who is distinguished among our scholars for delicacy, taste, and learning, has favoured the publick with two volumes of letters, written while on his travels through Europe, full of brilliant observations, classical allusions, and neat, graphick descriptions. Few volumes have given so much pleasure and instruction as these productions. They have a sweet and gentle spirit running throughout their contents, which, if it adds nothing to the author's fame at the present moment, will preserve them for future use, and make them more precious to the reader, when the writer, with his contemporaries, has passed away. Such works are pleasant to read at home, and useful as guides abroad.

The life of Doctor Dwight, prefixed to his sermons, supposed to be from the pen of his brother, Theodore Dwight, is full of incident, and well written. Dwight was an excellent subject, and his biographer was equal to his undertaking. It is more difficult to detail what may happen in the life of a literary man, than in that of a politician, who is in some measure identified with every passing event. The history of thought, and of such publications as a literary man may make from time to time; or the occurrences of a school, or a church, or a college, all of which are important to the individual, and of deep interest to the community in their social and literary relations, are not easily traced, nor the bearing of any one circumstance distinctly seen; yet, as a whole, they often make up an important life—as in the case of the distinguished individual we have mentioned.

Within a few years past, the literati of the United States, following up the English, have issued periodicals of great taste and beauty of execution, under the name of *Souvenirs, Tokens, Forget Me Nots, Talismans, &c.*; which have called forth much of the youthful and vigorous literature of our country; and if they cannot be put exactly in competition with some of those of the same class on the other side of the water, still they approximate so closely, that in a few years they may be equal in every respect. It is delightful to look over these fashionable publications, and find so much fine writing in them. A gem of prose is followed by a floweret of poesy, in which sweet descriptions and chaste fancies, give evidence of the improving state of taste among our scholars. Nor is the honour conferred on our writers alone; the artists of our country deservedly share in it. These objects of luxury have not, like many others, any improper effect upon the publick mind. The appetite for knowledge may become dainty by a perpetual feast of good things, but there is no danger of destroying the digestive faculty by pure food, properly served up. The magazines assume a tasteful appearance, and the careful printer makes a careful writer.

In one species of literature we surpass all other countries, that is, in our newspapers; we have more of them, most certainly, than any other country in the world. The increase has no parallel. The first paper printed in the United States was called the Boston Newsletter; this appeared on the 24th of April, 1704, at Boston, in Massachusetts, by B. Green. The second was commenced in 1720, at the same place, and called the Boston Gazette, by Samuel Kneeland. In 1721, the New-England Courant was set up by James Franklin, an elder brother of the philosopher. In this printing-office the Doctor began his apprenticeship at an early age. In the course of seven or eight years several other papers were printed in that town. The Greens had supported a press at Cambridge, near the college, from the earliest settlement of the country. Elliott's Indian Bible was published there in little more than six months after it was begun.

The first newspaper printed in Philadelphia, was commenced December 22d, 1719. The first printed in New-York, is dated October 16th, 1725. The first was under the direction of Andrew Bradford; and the second was edited and published by William Bradford. They were relations, and served their apprenticeship in the same office. The Philadelphia paper was called "The American Weekly Mercury," and that of New-York, "The New-York Gazette." The Rhode Island Gazette was set up by James Franklin, in October, 1732. The first in Connecticut, by James Parker, in 1755. The first in New-Hampshire, by Daniel Fowle, in 1756. It is somewhat surprising that a paper should not have before this time been established at Portsmouth, the principal town in the province; as it was a favourite harbour for the British naval commanders, and a place of fashion and intelligence. And their governor, at that time, was a splendid officer. In the time of the Boston massacre, March 5th, 1770, the statement of facts were to be sent to all the papers in the American provinces under Great Britain; which were calculated to be about five or six and twenty. In eighteen years after the peace of 1783, there were about one hundred and eighty. Since that period, a period of twenty-six years, they have increased to seven hundred at least; more than one hundred of them have been established within sixteen months past.

The circulation of these vehicles of information are truly astonishing. More than fifty millions a year are constantly issued in this country; the cost of which cannot be less than two millions of dollars annually to the people. In moments of party strife, these sources of information, it must be confessed, are often tinged with party rancour, and in some instances polluted by slander and falsehood; but in general they diffuse information of all sorts to the community, and make up a considerable share in that general knowledge which our busy people possess, after having obtained the general elements in the common schools of the country.

Until lately, periodical journals were not so successful as newspapers among the good people of this country. The first published in the provinces, was in the year 1741, by Benjamin Franklin, then of Philadelphia, just ten years after Edward Cave, of London, commenced the *Gentleman's Magazine.* The English publication has continued until this time; but the American was soon discontinued. Franklin knew that such a work was wanted in the country, and he thought that he would try it, at that early date; but it was in advance of the age.

After the peace of 1783, there were several magazines started in different sections of the country, in New-York, Boston, and Philadelphia, and flourished for some time with considerable success. Some of them are read with great pleasure at the present day. Matthew Carey, and his associates, published the Museum, a repository of literature, which flourished until the whole amounted to several large volumes. This was commenced in 1787, and contained the productions of Trumbull, Humphrey, and Dr. Ladd, with many other solutions of prose and verse. This work did not expire for want of patronage, but ceased because the publishers found better business. New-York and Boston have supported a review in some shape or other ever since 1790. There were many well written pieces in these works; but the business of reviewing had not then assumed its shape, and form, and power, which it has since. The writers touched with a faltering hand upon the errours of others; but their general course was to pass in silence those they did not like in sentiment or manner. A bolder hand was soon tried, and the publick supported freedom and vivacity in discussing the merits of authors; but this privilege has, since that period, often degenerated into dogmatism and censoriousness.

About the year 1801, the Port Folio was commenced by Joseph Dennie, in the city of Philadelphia. He had been known as the editor of a piquant and tasteful paper in the interiour of New-England, on the banks of the Connecticut river. He was then in a circle of wits, who threw their productions on the winds with careless profusion. Royal Tyler, long known as the Bonnel Thornton of America, who wrote that which the muses sometimes inspired in the shades of the evening, and blushed to acknowledge at the light of the morning sun, was one of the number. Dennie was free, easy, and readily excited to a stretch of thought, and latitude of expression, pardonable only, if ever, at the "*noctes cœnæque Deum;*" but his feelings were naturally pure and sincere; and if, for a moment, his mind, like the cloth made of the asbestos, received a stain by contiguity with impurity, the blaze of his genius, like the operation of fire upon the imperishable texture of the web, burnt it all pure again at its first kindling up. If Dennie had not that intellectual vigour which crushes to obtain an essence, or dissolves to develope a principle; he had judgement and taste to arrange a sentence and to polish a period. His imagination was rich and excursive; it knew no thraldom, and spurned at all narrow bounds. He had that which the country wanted more than any thing else, *a refined taste.* The Port Folio was then in full circulation; and this, more than any other work in the country, had an influence on the style of writing in our seminaries of learning. The young aspirants for fame saw how much the writings of Dennie were read, and they imitated him in their productions. This was fortunate. It is better for youths to emulate the flexible motions of the dancing master, to give grace and ease to their movements, than to practise the measured steps and stately demeanour of the knight in armour, before they have bone and muscle for the fight. Modern education, it may be said, has found a happy mean, or rather, has taught us how to unite both. Dennie did not live many years to continue his work. Since that period the Port Folio has fallen into other hands; and although it has frequently exhibited talent, yet it has lost its relative standing in the republick of letters. In 1802, the Anthology was established at Boston. It had a very considerable character from its commencement. It was often interesting, and sometimes learned; at times it assumed a consequential air and manner; but it cannot be said that it had as much weight as a leading journal ought to have had in the country at that time. It took another shape, and a milder character, in the North American Review, and has since been a well conducted journal; many times rivaling the first works of European fame; and if an imitation, in some degree, of the Edinburgh, it has no servility of thought or tone. The Edinburgh was the first of this class of works which are now so popular; and without which the literary world would be at a loss to fix on a course of reading to keep up with the literature of the day. The Edinburgh Review began its course as Hercules did his labours, not exactly when he was most wanted, but when his prowess could be most distinctly seen, and noted. The Edinburgh Reviewers course every field of literature, ancient or modern, often-times merely to show their speed and bottom. They come upon the literati as their conquerors and protec-

M 2   18

tors; and if they deny the divine right of kings in political governments, they assume the office of perpetual dictators in the community of letters.   When they commenced their labours, the literary
world was indeed overrun with monsters; and they laid aside the
sword and the spear, and pursued their prey with club and blun-
derbuss, from jungle to crag, regardless of trespassing on rice-
ground or cane-patch; but it must be acknowledged that they did
more good than mischief in their sport.   The Quarterly followed
with as much ferocity, but not with more power, and our country
became the object of their direst vengeance.   They saw us rising
rapidly in the scale of nations, and thought it wise, prudent, and,
probably, fair in politicks, to check our growth.   They had no control over the progress of population, none over the increase of
wealth, which was greater than they could imagine, or understand.
Nothing was left but to attack our institutions, or *manners* and
habits ; and this was done with rancour and profligacy, and without
regard to truth.   They seized upon worthless tales of travellers,
who wrote solely for the purpose of furnishing food for the cormo-
rant appetites of these haters of America; the writers knowing that
by such means they would be favourably noticed by the Reviewers,
and of course their trash would find a ready market.   Part of the
people of England were with them from ancient prejudices, a part
opposed to them from information and principle; but a still greater
part were ignorant of the true state of facts.   This evil was only for
a season; and instead of disgracing our country, as the Reviewers
intended, they raised up a host of able vindicators of American mind
and literature, which they little expected.   Dwight, sensitive upon
this subject, came out in our defence with spirit and effect.   And
Walsh, a name identified with our literature, appealed to the common sense of the nations who knew us, and manfully repelled the
coarse and wicked assaults which had been made upon us.   Others,
too, were engaged to repel these vile slanders.   Much was felt, much
was said and written upon the subject at home, and a reaction took
place abroad; and in no place was this reaction greater than in England.   Our novels, which had not gone farther than a second edition
here, *there* passed through several editions with great eclat.   Brown,
whose grave could hardly be traced by us, was there ranked among
the finest writers of fiction that any age or nation had produced.   There
are still a few traces of this malignity left, as may be seen in the miserable libel of De Roos, and a slight disposition to keep it alive, as
seen in the patronage given him by the British admiralty; but no
matter for that, this prejudice is, we pronounce, nearly over and
gone.   The literature of our country is increasing with a most astonishing rapidity; and knowledge is pouring upon us in its lesser

and greater streams from all parts of the land; besides weekly and monthly magazines, which are profusely scattered throughout all our territories, we have several journals in medicine and law; and six established quarterly reviews, extensively read, and well supported. The editors of these quarterly works are pursuing a wise course, in repelling the attacks which have been made upon our literature, rather by exhibiting fine specimens of thought and taste in composition, than by retort and vituperation.

LECTURE IX.

'Tis not the chime and flow of words, that move
In measured file, and metrical array;
'Tis not the union of returning sounds,
Nor all the pleasing artifice of rhyme,
And quantity, and accent, that can give
This all-pervading spirit to the ear,
Or blend it with the movings of the soul;
'Tis a mysterious feeling, which combines
Man with the world around him in a chain
Woven of flowers, and dipped in sweetness, till
He taste the high communion of his thoughts,
With all existences, in earth and heaven,
That meet him in the charm of grace and power.

PERCIVAL.

In order to have a fair view of American poetry, we must go up to the springs from whence it flowed. Poetry is natural to man. It is a sympathy of the human mind with the invisible world, in which the spirit is active in expanding, exalting, and reforming the realities it witnesses to something which belongs to upper natures, or divine essences. Most things around the primitive poet were above his comprehension, for he had but little philosophy to assist him in analyzing appearances, and he therefore mingled the known with the doubtful, and the real with the imaginary. He was a poet of sensibility long before he had learnt to express any of his emotions, or combinations in language. When he had proceeded so far as to give his thoughts utterance in words, he selected the best and most favourable he could find as a medium of his thoughts, and probably for ages his words rather designated than expressed his feelings and conceptions. As he grew more and more intelligent, he became dissatisfied with his first expressions, and sought new ones more comprehensive and more pleasing to his ear; and verbal beauties became as necessary to please himself and his hearers as impassioned conceptions; and measure, cadence, and tone, were studied. The passions taught him their languages; joy had his sprightly note, and sorrow her melancholy one; pity, as she melted the mind, softened her words; and rage and revenge were regardless of the harshness of theirs. Even in early days the consonancy of words was sought, and rhyme was added to the other properties of verse; but not much used until after the christian era, though, probably, more than is generally believed. Every nation has found the advantages of poetry. It enlarged the compass of language; it selected words of greater beauty and energy than were in common use; it was the medium of heroick sentiments and devotional feelings; it multiplied appropriate phrases, and melodious sentences; and was constantly improving the language with synonymes, new combinations, and niceties of expression. It would be a delightful task to trace the progress of the mind, through the history of poetry, from the earliest times to the classical ages, and from them down to this of philosophy and criticism; but this would lead us into a wide field, too wide for our present purposes; I shall, therefore, only give a brief account of English poetry, to show its rise and progress, in order to have a fuller view of our own. Poetry generally exhibits the best state of the language of the day in which it was written. One set of poets pass off after another, and the succeeding generation is indebted to the preceding for much of the excellence it possesses, as the fine and rich mould of the earth is formed from the successive productions of a prior age. By examining the works of English poets, we can trace, very satisfactorily, the several stages of our vernacular tongue. It is agreed, on all hands, that the English language had its origin in the first century after the Norman conquest, in 1066. In the reign of William, and his immediate successors, the poetry of the country, which was nothing more than ballads, was in Norman. The Saxon legends were preserved in Norman rhyme; but the Anglo-Saxon mind was superiour in strength and invention to that of the conquerors, and the English vernacular grew up with a few Norman features; but in body and spirit it was Saxon. This fact is proved by the earliest English poets. Layamon wrote somewhere between 1135 and 1180. He was the author of the work called "Arthur's Account of his Dream." After the time of Layamon, there is a poem consisting of a dialogue between an owl and a nightingale, disputing for superiority; this, more distinctly than the works of Layamon, makes the change which had taken place in the tongue of the Britons. From 1300, English poetry, and of course the whole language, took a definite, positive existence.

At this period, Robert de Brunne, or Robert Mannyng, wrote a metrical chronicle of England, taking his facts from several old historians. This same writer composed tales in verse; these have not been printed until lately; but copies of his manuscripts have been preserved. The antiquarians say that the English language was copious then, and give as a specimen his tale of the " Lady, a Lord's Wyfe." This work may be read with tolerable ease by any English scholar. He deals largely in satire, but is at times full of tenderness, and is not a little romantick.

In the twelfth, thirteenth, and fourteenth centuries, the English romances constituted the reading of the age. The heroes of King Arthur and Charlemagne, Richard Cœur de Lion, Amadis de Gaul, and others, had their day, and passed away; but they were great in their time—quite equal to the Waverly novels of the present day; and, like the latter at present, were read by clergy and laity, the fair and the wise. It was the fashion to read them; and fashion is irresistible. Romance and poetry are kindred spirits, and are generally found together. In that age, the old ballads were renovated, and were in the mouths of every one who had any pretensions to taste. These writers aimed at the beau ideal in their compositions, and that was suited to the taste of the times. The habit of reading these fictions and ballads entered into college-halls by grave permission from the guardians of literature and religion.

Chaucer, who is called the father of English poetry, who died in 1400, was preceded by John Gower, who was celebrated before Chaucer was known; he out lived Chaucer, however, and died old and blind, but not poor. He wrote a poem in English, called "Confessio Amantis." It contains thirty-five thousand lines; it was composed at the request of King Richard II. He had more knowledge of ethicks than of poetry; and is named by Chaucer, in these words: "O! Moral Gower!" He united the moral philosopher with the minstrel; and he may now be called the Cowper of his age. He enlarged and disciplined the intellectual taste of his countrymen. Gower was the first poet that wrote in the English language, who gave his lovers a good share of learning, as an indispensable requisite for success in winning the affections of the fair, to whom they were devoted. Would that it had been more often imitated. On the tales of Gower, Byron and Scott have founded their Laras, Corsairs, Brides of Abydos, and Marmions. Who ever was, or who ever can be, entirely original?

Chaucer was a politician as well as a poet, and was sent an ambassador to the Doge of Genoa, about 1370. He was for many years a favourite of his king, Edward III.—but by some accident, lost his good will, and suffered imprisonment; but was restored to favour on the accession of Henry. He wrote Troilus and Creseide, and the Canterbury tales.

The next English poet, was *John the Chaplain.* He translated Boetius, and his language is remarkably good English; much less obsolete at this day than Chaucer's. He lived in the reign of Henry IV.

The next poet, contemporary with *John the Chaplain,* was Thomas Occleve. He considered Chaucer as his father in poetry; and was a scholar worthy his master; he added many beauties of language to English poetry. He wrote for Henry IV. and his gallant son, Henry V., who employed Occleve as a clerk in the office of the privy seal. He had the grant of an annuity, but it was badly paid, for Hal had robbed the exchequer for his wars. He wrote a poem on government, for Henry V., which is said to contain many fine sentiments and correct principles.

Lydgate, a Benedictine monk, was another of the poets of the days of these Henries. He wrote the "Storie of Thebes," and "Siege of Troy." He is the first English poet who complains of the criticks, a common grief since his time. He says that Chaucer did not care for them; so much the better for him, and, perhaps, for us; for he might not have published so many of his works, if he had been as sensitive as Lydgate. About this time, there were several very clever poets in Scotland; Dunbar, and others; but we are now looking only for those familiar to our ancestors.

A spirit of criticism is a strong symptom of an age of intellectual advancement and literary taste. The publick grew fastidious in proportion to the frequency of their mental banquets. The brightest parts of the most successful writer make the world less tolerant of his defects.

From Lydgate to Spenser, there were several poets of considerable celebrity in those times, but not much known to us. Spenser was born in 1553, and died in 1599. He was nine years seinor to Marlowe, and eleven to Shakspeare. Marlowe was the most popular dramatick writer of his age. His plays caught the popular gale before Shakspeare's were known. He was learned, and understood the laws of rhythm, and of course his measure is smooth and finished. He brought more care and beauty into blank verse, than any of his predecessors. He was killed, at the age of thirty-one, in a brawl. He was a free thinker, and his death was held by the pious of that age, as a judgement for his want of principle; and for many years his works were neglected; indeed, it could hardly have been otherwise, if there had been no blot on his fame, as Shakspeare was so near him.

When our ancestors came to this country, Shakspeare had been known to a few only in the circles of court fashion, and those who frequented the theatre; but the religious part of the community, who abhorred plays, and every thing connected with the drama, knew but little of this great poet at that time. There were not many of Shakspeare's plays then in print. An entire edition of them was not published until the year 1623, seven years after the death of the author; and, after this time, it was many years before his works were much read. During the puritanical times of the Commonwealth, the great dramatist was almost lost sight of; and, as strange as it may seem to us of the present day, there were only four editions of his works printed in all the seventeenth century.

I believe that there is hardly a quotation to be found from Shakspeare in any American author, until after the commencement of the eighteenth century. Beaumont, and Fletcher, and Ben Jonson, were less known, at that time, than some itinerant ballad-singers. The prose writings of Milton, from his political character, were more extensively circulated in his life time. These, after a while, were neglected, and his poetry made its way slowly in the literary world. At first it attracted no crowd of imitators, and made no visible change in the poetical rules of the age. Milton stood alone and aloof above his time, the bard of immortal subjects; and, as far as there is perpetuity in language, of immortal fame.

Dryden flourished at the time of the restoration, and was the harbinger of the Augustan age which followed; when Swift, Addison, Pope, Arbuthnot, and others of distinction in the walks of literature, shone upon the world. This was truly an age of poetry; for many then, who are scarcely known at this day, wrote good verses. Fenton and Broome assisted in the translation of the Illiad, and their labours are not much inferiour to Pope's share of it; and yet they held quite a secondary rank in the galaxy of genius which graced that period.

Pope was first known this side of the Atlantick in April, 1717, as appears by a poetical epistle addressed to the author of *Windsor Forest*, from Watertown, in the province of Massachusetts Bay. The other works of Pope soon followed, and were much admired in this country. Most of his productions had passed through numerous editions before the death of the poet, which was in 1744.

Sir Richard Blackmoore, who was a physician to William and Mary, and a poet of more loyalty than genius, wrote before Pope; and was, from his stately hexameter, and general strain of piety, much admired in this country. He is often quoted by Cotton Mather and others, with great respect and fondness. But of all the poets at the commencement of the eighteenth century, no one was more read in this country than Dr. Watts. His fame for piety was co-extensive with christendom, among the protestants. His poetry was found in the hands of all classes in this country. His lyricks were well spoken of by the learned, and all joined in thinking his psalms and hymns far superiour to the works of all his predecessors, in the same line. The American booksellers reprinted his works as they appeared, for they were sure of a rapid sale of them.

The works of Young were read with avidity on their first appearance, particularly his *Night Thoughts.* Addison was not so generally read, but he had many admirers. It is amusing for us, at this day, to look over the early newspapers in our country, and find criticisms and quotations exciting the people to read these works of rare excellence. Franklin formed his style on Addison, as far as he could, being of a very different cast of mind. The youthful American anticipated the advice of the great English critick, and literally *read the works of Addison day and night*, to assist him in forming a style. The intensity with which some of those works were read by the people of only a common school education, is almost beyond the belief of those unacquainted with the fact. Many of the aged people we have seen, could repeat whole books of Milton and of Young; and the works of Watts were in the mouth of every man, woman, and child; and, at the time when his psalms and hymns came into general use in the churches, there were but few who required a book to join the choir in their devotions.

The history of American poetry is more curious than is generally believed. Many writers have declared that we had no poetry until after the commencement of the last century. The people of a prior age, however, did not think themselves destitute of poetical talent. It has been said that the austerity of the manners of the puritans was not congenial to the muse; that when they dethroned the pope, and broke down the altars, and destroyed the groves of papal worship, they waged war also with the lovely creations of the classical ages. The theory has some plausibility in it at first sight, but it is not true to any great extent; although the first exhibitions of our own poetry were religious and scriptural, and mostly made on mournful occasions; yet the muses were often invoked, and inspiration looked for from the *Nine* by our puritan fathers; and, most certainly, Milton had none of these scruples of availing himself of the works of heathen authors, for he has plundered every heaven and earth, and mid-way territory, of Pagan creation, to adorn his own wonderful and lovely universe. Good poetry, like other possessions of knowledge, more often belongs to the age in which it was written than to the genius of the individual poet. There are a great number of young ladies in the United States, who can write better poetry now, than the most distinguished poet among us could half a century ago.

I propose to offer you some specimens of poetry written in this country, at different periods of our history, that you may compare them with each other, and judge for yourselves of their merits; interspersing a few remarks of my own upon the writers and their productions.

Our first quotation shall be from the muse of John Smith, who was the Æneas of the new world. One would think, from the character of the man, that his poetry would be of the first order. He was fitted by nature and education for a poet; generous, noble, and full of genius, he saw every thing in a chivalrous light; not the flitting, irregular, meteorick light of a perturbed mind, which is so often found to mistake the agitations of feebleness for the workings of the divinity within; but one which saw things in the blaze of intellectual day. He had been a philosopher, a hero, and a lover in every clime; and a favourite of the fair in every path of the sun. The veiled beauties of Asia, whose hearts melt with romantick tenderness within the harem walls—the refined and accomplished women of his own country, and the simple, honest, and noble daughters of the forest, were enamoured with the blaze of his fame, and charmed with the martial elegance of his person. His whole life was an epick. From his work, we have culled a few scraps of his poetry. He probably wrote much which has not reached us.

Smith, speaking of his journeying around the country—or rather giving an account of it, says,

> " Thus have I walked a wayless way, with uncouth pace,
> Which no Christian man did ever trace;
> But yet I know this not affects the minde
> Which cares doth heare; as that which eyes doe finde.

Mentioning the superstition of the Indians, and their temples and tombs, and of their offerings to their god Okee, for fear of him, he gives his readers a couplet:

> "Thus, Feare was the first their gods begot:
> Till fear began, their gods were not."

And, speaking of their devotions, "which the priests begin, while the rest follow him; sometimes he maketh invocations, with broken sentences, by starts and strange passions, and, at every pause, gives a short groane,"

N   19

" Thus seeke they in deepe foolishnesse,
To climbe the height of happinesse."

And further,

'Though god begetting fear,
Man's blinded mind did raise
A hell-god to the ghosts :
A heaven-god to the hoasts,
Yea, God unto the seas ;
Feare did create all these."

Again; speaking of the mischiefs which sprung from ignorance,
and the exertion of good men to counteract the influence of fanaticism and wickedness, he says,

" Good men did ne'er their countries ruine bring
But when evill men shall injuries beginne,
Not caring to corrupt and violate
The judgements'-seat for their own lucre's sake ;
Then looke that country cannot long have peace,
Though for the present it have rest and ease."

In describing the scene in which Pocahontas saved his life, the
emperour, thinking he could do all work, kept him to make hatchets
and bells, the former for the father's, and the latter for the daughter's use ; and the captain, assuming as lively a countenance as possible, gives us the following poetical version of his situation :

"They say he bore a pleasant shew,
But sure his heart was sad
For who can pleasant be, and rest,
That lives in feare and dread :
And having life suspected, doth
It still suspected lead."

Touching, sarcastically, upon Master Wingfield and Captaine
Archer, who had been too fond of titles and places, and were now
sent home with Captaine Newport, he offers his readers the following verses :

"Oh cursed gold, these hunger-starved movers,
To what misfortunes lead'st thou all these lovers ;
For all the China wealth, nor Indies' can
Suffice the minde of an av'ritious man."

On Captain Martin, who wished to load his ship with something resembling gold dust contrary to Smith's opinion, he writes,

> "But, the God of heaven, he eas'ly can
> Immortalize a mortall man
> With glory and with fame.
> The same God even as eas'ly may
> Afflict a mortall man, I say,
> With sorrow and with shame."

In speaking of the factions in the colonies, the historian bursts out in a fine thought, such as might have furnished a subject for a long poem.

> "Till treachery, and faction, and avarice be gone,
> Till envy, and ambition, and backbiting be none,
> Till perjury, and idlenesse, and injury be out,
> And, truly, till that villany, the work of all that rout ;
> Unlesse those vices banished be, whatever forts you have,
> A hundred walls together put will not have power to save."

The bards who wrote congratulatory epistles, after the custom of the day, were numerous. Their lines are preserved in Smith's work, and, by tacking them to his name, it is now known that such men as R. Brathwait, Anthony Fereby, Ed. Jordan, Richard James, M. Hawkins, Richard Meade, Ed. Ingham, and a host of others, ever existed or tuned a stave; and yet they probably were very considerable men in their time, for we observe the name of old Purchas, the historian, among them, whose congratulatory ode is the most stiff, awkward, and wretched piece of affectation, ever written in any age, or by any hand. Some of the others have a few scintillations of genius about them, but this has none.

In " Mortion's New-England Memorial" of the pilgrim fathers, published in the first half century of their history, may be found several acrosticks and elegies of that early period. The following lines on Mr. Thos. Hooker, pastor of the church at Hartford, (Conn.) were probably written by John Cotton, the first minister of Boston, one of the most distinguished men of the Massachusetts Colony.

> "To see three things was holy *Austin's* wish,
> *Rome* in her *Flower*, *Christ Jesus* in the *Flesh*,
> And *Paul* in *Pulpit ;* lately, men might see,
> Two first and more in *Hooker's* ministry.
>
> *Zion*, in *Beauty*, is a fairer sight,
> Than *Rome* in *Flower*, with all her glory dight,

Yet *Zion's* Beauty did most clearly shine
In *Hooker's* Rule and Doctrine; both divine.

Christ i' the *Spirit's* more than *Christ* in *Flesh*,
Our *souls* to quicken, and our *states* to bless !
Yet *Christ* in *spirit*, broke forth mightily,
In faithful *Hooker's* searching ministry.

Paul, in the *pulpit, Hooker* could not reach;
Yet did he Christ in spirit, so lively preach,
That living hearers thought he did inherit
A double portion of *Paul's* lively spirit.

Prudent in rule, in argument quick,
Fervent in prayer, in preaching powerful;
That well did learned *Ames* record bear,
The like to him he never wont to hear.

'Twas of *Geneva's* worthies said, with wonder,
(Those worthies three) *Farell* was wont to thunder;
Viret, like rain, on tender grass to shower;
But *Calvin*, lively oracles to pour.

All these in *Hooker's* spirit did remain,
A son of thunder, and a shower of rain;'
A pourer forth of lively oracles,
In saving souls, the sum of *miracles*.

Now blessed *Hooker*, thou'rt set on high,
Above the thankless world, and cloudy sky;
Do thou of all thy labour, reap the crown,
Whilst we, here, reap the seed which thou hast sown!"

The following is an extract from the pen of Peter Bulkeley, of Concord, whose reputation as a latin poet and scholar, we have mentioned in another lecture.

"A lamentation for the death of that precious and worthy minister of Jesus Christ, Mr. John Hooker, Anno Domini, 1647."

"Come sighs, come sorrows, let's lament this rod,
Which hath bereaved us of this man of God;
A man of God, which came from God to men,
And now from them, is gone to God agen.
Bid joy depart: bid merriment begone;
Bid friends stand by; sit mournful and alone.
But oh! what sorrow can be to suffice,
Though heaven and earth were filled with our cries.

*   *   *   *   *   *   *   *   *

Let Hartford sigh, and say, 'I've lost a treasure;'
Let all New-England mourn at God's displeasure,
In taking from us one more gracious
Than is the gold of Ophir precious.
Sweet was the savour which his grace did give,
It seasoned all the place where he did live.
His name did, as an ointment, give it's smell,
And all bare witness that it savoured well."

* * * * * *

In a few years after writing the elegy of his friend, Hooker, Mr.
Cotton died in Boston;

"Poets themselves must fall like those they sung;
"Deaf the praised ear, and mute the tuneful tongue;"

and was mourned and praised in a funeral elegy, by his friend, John
Norton, from which we make an extract:

"And after *Winthrop's, Hooker's, Sheppard's hearse,*
Doth *Cotton's* death call for a mourning verse!
Thy will be done! yet, Lord, who deal'st thus,
Make this great death expedient for us.
Luther pulled down the *pope, Calvin,* the *prelate* slew;
Of *Calvin's lapse,* chief *cures* to *Cotton* due.
Cotton, whose learning, temper, godliness,
The *German Phœnix,* lively did express.
Melancthon's all—may *Luther's* word but pass
Melancthon's all in our great *Cotton* was;
Than him in flesh, scarce dwelt a better one,
So great's our loss, when such a spirit's gone.
Whilst he was here, life was more life to me;
Now he is not, death hence, less death shall be.
That comets great men's death do oft forego,
This present comet doth too sadly shew;
This prophet dead, yet must in's doctrine speak,
This comet saith, else must New-England break.
Whate'er it be, may heaven avert it far,
That meteors should succeed our greatest star.
In Boston's orb, Winthrop and Cotton were;
These lights extinct, dark is our hemisphere.
In Boston, once, how much shined of our glory,
We now lament, *posterity will story.*
Let *Boston* live, who had and saw their worth,
And did them honour, both in life and death.
To him New-England trust in this distress,
Who will not leave his exiles comfortless.

N 2

The following lines were written upon the same occasion, by **B. WOODBRIDGE.**

*   *   *   *   *   *   *   *   *   *   *

> A living, breathing bible; tables, where
> Both covenants at large, engraven were.
> Gospel and law in 's heart had each its *column*,
> His head, an *index* to the sacred *volumn*.
> His very name a *title-page ;* and next,
> His life, a *commentary* on the *text*.
> O, what a monument of glorious *work*,
> When, in a *new edition*, he comes forth,
> Without *errata*, may we think he'll be,
> In *leaves* and *covers* of eternitie !
> A man of might, at heavenly eloquence
> To fix the ear, and charm the conscience ;
> As if *Apollos* were revived in him,
> Or he had learned of a *Seraphim ;*
> Spake many tongues in one : one voice and sense
> Wrought joy and sorrow, fear and confidence.

*   *   *   *   *   *   *   *   *   *   *

> A star, that in our Eastern England rose,
> Thence hurried by the blast of stupid foes,
> Whose foggy darkness and benumbed senses
> Brooked not his dazzling influences.
> Thus did he move on earth, from east to west ;
> Here he went down, and up to heaven for rest.
> Nor from himself, whilst living, doth he vary,
> His death hath made him an *ubiquitary*.
> Where is his sepulchre, is hard to tell,
> Who in a thousand sepulchres doth dwell,
> (Their hearts, I mean, whom he hath left behind)
> In them his sacred relick's now enshrined.

Governor Bradford, of the old colony, was another of the primitive poets. His muse was rather timid ; for it does not appear that he published many of his productions in rhyme ; but he certainly left some of them to his posterity. They were narrative and descriptive. Some portions of his poetic pains had a most singular fate. The manuscript was carried to Boston by some of his descendants, and there it remained for more than a century ; but, when the British forces left Boston, they took it to Halifax ; and, some years since, an American gentleman found a portion of his " Account of New England in verse," in the shop of a pastry cook ; no uncommon highway to oblivion. The relict contained three or four hundred lines, and is well worth preserving, which has been done by the Massachusetts Historical Society, in their valuable collections. I shall introduce his lamentation on the avarice of traders getting the better of their patriotism and prudence. It has much of good sense about it, if not of harmonious verse.

* * * * * *

"But a most desperate mischief here is grown,
And a great shame it is it should be known;
But why should I conceal so foul a thing
That quickly may our hurt and ruin bring!
For base covetousness hath got such a sway,
As our own safety we ourselves betray;
For these fierce natives, they are now so fill'd
With guns and muskets, and in them so skill'd,
As that they may keep the English well in awe,
And when they please, give to them the law;
And of powder and shot they have such store,
As sometimes they refuse e'en to buy more;
Flints, screw-plates, and moulds for all sorts of shot
They have, and skill to use them they have got;
And mend and new stock their pieces they can
As well in most things as an Englishman.

"Thus, like madmen, we have put them in a way,
With our own weapons, us to kill and slay;
That gain hereof to make they know so well,
The fowl to kill and us the feathers sell,
For us to seek for deer, it doth not boot,
Since now, with guns, themselves at them can shoot.
The garbage of which we no use did make,
They have been glad to gather up and take;
But now they can themselves fully supply,
And the English of them are glad to buy.
And yet, if that was all, it might be borne,
Though hereby the English make themselves a scorn."

It has lately been discovered that Roger Williams, the first settler of Providence, was a poet, and a very good one too. There are some fine specimens of his poetical powers in his treatise upon the Indian language. It has more directness and ease, without the quaintness, which was common to the times.

Thomas Wilde and John Elliott, the first ministers of Roxbury, were considered as among the great poets of their time. They, with Mather, made a version of the psalms. The work was wretched enough; but Wilde sometimes wrote with some spirit, and even taste, for that period. Some of his lines on Danforth are quite tolerable, and Cotton Mather has quoted them in his account of Samuel Danforth, who was a scholar, and second fellow of Harvard College. A few of them are given from the Magnalia.

> "Mighty in scripture, searching out the sense,
> All the hard things of it, unfolding thence;
> He lived each truth; his faith, love, tenderness,
> None can to th' life, as did his life express:
> Our minds with gospel his rich lecture fed;
> Luke and his life, at once are finished:
> Our NEW BUILT CHURCH now suffers too by this,
> Larger its windows, but its lights are less."

The apostle to the Indians, the colleague of Wilde, had a most unconquerable propensity to deal in verse. The burying grounds, in Roxbury, bear testimony to this. He furnished epitaphs for all his dear departed friends. One of his biographers thinks it is best to let his poetry moulder and sink into the ground with the stones on which it was engraven. He is fearful, if his epitaphs were discovered, their uncouth verses might excite a little merriment in the present generation; and, using Cotton Mather's expression, "lest the children might play with the beards of their fathers," *which old Mather seems to think a grievous thing.* It would have grieved him, indeed, could he have foreseen that the beard of reverend age would not only be *played with,* but often plucked and scattered to the winds; not, indeed, *irreverently,* but in the search of truth;— Mather's opinions on witchcraft, for instance. Elliott is not the only instance of a great man making a ludicrous, if not a silly, poet; but, if not the only, he is certainly the most conspicuous example. He was deeply imbued with every beautiful sentiment in the classicks. The romantick tales of suffering love, and unyielding fortitude, and deathless friendship, were familiar to him; not only these, but he had read, in the original, the loves of David and Jonathan, and the sweet psalmist's lamentations over the bodies of Saul and his son; surpassing, when rightly understood, all other elegies. He had heard the lamentations of the Indian father, who had received his warrior-son a corse from the battle-field; had listened to the murmurings and bursts of grief which filled the wigwam through the long watches of the night; and had, by his eloquence and his prayers, soothed the convulsions of nature, and given repose to the parental heart. Yet, with every poetick image in his mind, the moment he attempted to put a thought into verse, every particle of inspiration vanished. I leave to philosophy to analyze such a mind, and to give a reason why an attempt at measure should stupify such an intellect, and why such a passion should be for ever operating on such a mind.

Michael Wigglesworth, who was graduated in 1651, and whose name I have mentioned in another lecture, was a poet of great renown in his day. He published a work, "The Day of Doom, or a Poetical Description of the Great and Last Judgement." This had reached the fourth edition in 1701; and, of course, could not have been, as it has sometimes been asserted, an imitation of Young's "Last Day," which was written several years afterwards. The poet of the old world had read the work of the new, as every thing published in this country soon found its way home.

About the commencement of the eighteenth century, Thomas Makin was known as a poet. He had been a teacher of the first school established in Pennsylvania, and wrote a Latin poem in very good taste. It was a descriptive, sylvan, and statistical account of the settlement of Pennsylvania; which was translated by Proud, the first regular historian of that state, and inserted, together with the translation, in his work. In 1717, Francis Knapp, who was educated at Oxford, wrote, from Watertown, a poetical address, congratulating Pope on the publication of his Windsor Forest. This epistle was written in the best style of poetry which had then appeared in this country; but this rather shows the general progress of poetry in England than in this country, for he had settled here only a few years before. In that day the writing of verses in Latin and English formed a part of the academical exercises in the English universities. They had not then come so fully into the erroneous doctrine that a taste for poetry was rather natural than acquired, as their successors have affected to believe. The united efforts of nature and education are required to reach distinction as an orator or a poet. It is education as well as nature which makes the Indian orator. The most distinguished aboriginal orator I ever heard, an Osage, once told me, that he had spent more than half of his life, (he was then, he said, fifty years of age,) in communing with the great Spirit, in contemplating his works, and in listening to the speech of the old and the wise, to make himself an orator. What is this but education?

Among the most extraordinary productions of the early part of the last century, are those of Roger Wolcott, of Connecticut. He published a volume of poems in 1725, when he was forty-six years of age, one or more of them being of considerable length. Mr. Bulkley, of Colchester, wrote a preface for the poem. Bulkley was a poet himself, as was also the Reverend Timothy Edwards, to whom it was dedicated by a poetical address. The writer of a preface, and the person to whom a volume was dedicated, were considered as sponsors for the moral tendency, at least, of the production; and as these friends of the author were distinguished scholars in their day and generation, their opinions were, of course, decisive of the merits of the work at the time. Wolcott was a self-taught man. He raised himself from the humblest walks of life, without a single day's instruction in any school, and became an orator, a poet, a commissary-general in the expedition to Canada, in 1740; a major-general, in 1745, at Louisburg; and a chief-justice, and chief-magistrate of his native state. This did not satisfy him. He must be an author also; not only an author, but a poet's wreath was wanting to fill up the measure of his desire for glory. The following is his dedicatory address to Edwards, which shows that he could praise as well as command and fight, and had no ordinary appetency for poetick fame.

To the Reverend Mr. Timothy Edwards.

Sir,

At sight of this, you scarcely will excuse
My broken numbers should affront your muse,
Whose single elegance outdoes the Nine,
And all their off'rings at Apollo's shrine.

But, sir, they come not to AFFRONT, but stand
Trembling before your awful seat to hear
From you their sentence that's definitive,
Whether they shall be killed, or saved alive.

Yet, where you censure, sir, don't make the verse
You pinned to Glover's venerable hearse,
The standard for their trial; nor enact
You never will acquit what's less exact.

Sir, that will never do; rules so severe
Would ever leave Apollo's altars bare,
His priests no service: all must starve together,
And fair Parnassus' verdant tops must wither.

Sure that was not the purpose or design
Of the fair sisters when they did combine
Themselves in your assistance; no, their mind
In that great work, was otherwise designed.

They, having often to their trouble seen
Many bold poets launch on Hippocrene,
Men that might a handsome voyage made,
Had they but kept them to the coasting trade;

But ranging far upon those swelling seas,
Came home with broken lines and voyages;
Grieved at their losses and miscarriages,
A council met at Hippocrenides;

They vote a remedy; which to effect,
That their Herculean pillar to erect,
And, to advise adventurers once for all,
Wrote *ne plus ultra* on its pedestal.

Since which, there's none that dare presume to go
Beyond that wonder then set up by you;
No, nor attain it in their navigation :—
That sacred work is not for IMITATION !

Conscious of this, you see my muse ne'er soars
To *Hibla's top*, nor the *Aonian shores;*
Nor doth pretend to raptures that might suit
Pindarus' muse or great *Apollo's lute.*

Then weigh them candidly, and if that you
Shall once pronounce a longer life their due;
And, for their patron, will yourself engage,
They may, perhaps, adventure on the stage:
But if deny'd, they, blushing, back retire
To burn themselves on their own funeral pyre.

Windsor, Jan. 4, 1722-3.   R. W.

There are to be found at the present day, many of the old narrative pieces, written something after the manner of the old English Ballad; and are considered as veritable scraps of history. It was then a fundamental law of the muse, which she has not always regarded, in every age of her communications, to tell nothing but the truth. The Indian wars, began, in good earnest, in 1635, and continued, with only a few intervals, until 1763; during which time, there were many "bloody massacres" of our people by the foe, sometimes by the Indians alone, but oftener by the Indians and French together. These fights were full of savage vengeance, and what was thought to be retaliatory justice. Instances of great courage and suffering often occurred, and afforded many excellent opportunities for those disposed to exercise their poetical talents. In fact, these instances imposed upon them the necessity of trying their hands at narration and elegy. There have been a thousand descriptions of single combats which have delighted the reading world in every age; but few have ever attempted to awaken the sympathies of mankind by poetical descriptions of such awful exterminations of the human race, as those of Austerlitz, Jena, Wagram, or Waterloo. Hector and Achilles, Æneas and Turnus, Smith and his Turks, Boon and his Indians; combats in which every movement may be seen at once; these are such as are attractive to all minds. We can sympathize and take a part in such actions; but not so in those tremendous instances of the carnage of the human race. These individual cases could easily be brought to bear on families and villages, for there was hardly a family that had not been called to mourn the loss of some one of its members; and there were but few villages on the frontiers that had escaped savage vengeance, during the long period of these bloody conflicts. All these events were then commemorated by some village poet, set to some mournful measure, and were so preserved, perhaps for many years, before they got into print, if they ever did. Some of these doleful ditties were, at length, seized upon by the ballad-mongers, and exhibited at their windows, in sheets, with two columns, and were called "A Pair of Verses." These sheets were often adorned with coffins and cross-bones, and sometimes, by way of high attraction, were surmounted with the "effigies of salvages," who were exhibited

> " Like fierce barbarians, grinning o'er their prey,"

or, with bended bow, or glittering tomahawk, ready to destroy decrepitude and infancy, when their sturdy opposers had bit the dust. They figured, at these shops, with *Chevy Chase*, *Handsome Harry*, *Captain Kidd*, and others of the same class.

Among the most respectable of these productions, is one which has come down to us, certainly to me, anonymously; an account of Captain Lovewell's fight at Pigwacket, on the 8th of May, 1724. This battle excited a great deal of sympathy at the time, and the event has been oftener commemorated than others, from the fact that every minute circumstance of the battle has been more faithfully described than other occurrences in the Indian wars. Symmes, a learned divine, of Bradford, which was on the highway taken by the relict of Lovewell's men, as they journeyed homeward, collected from them the history of the fight, as he entertained them at his hospitable mansion, and gave it in a spirited sermon to his parishioners from the pulpit, which was afterwards published with notes. Penhallow, of Portsmouth, who was then writing a history of Indian Wars, took the narrative from some one of the survivors, and his statement varies but little from the others; but, if all these had been lost, the ballad I have selected would have given to the present generation a very correct idea of the fight. At that time, there were other circumstances, also, which gave this battle much celebrity. The character of the men who figured in it was one.

Lovewell himself was a man of note. The very act of venturing, with only a handful of men, so far in the wilderness, was considered heroick; and such was the state of feeling, that nothing could be considered as presumptuous at that time. All his men were of the most virtuous and religious class of society, and were well connected. Many of them were heads of families, whose loss was severely felt in that thinly settled population. Among the number who fell, was Mr. Jonathan Frye, a student in divinity, who was Lovewell's chaplain, and who had joined this little band, from some affair of the heart. He made himself conspicuous in the fight, and, as described, acted with reckless valour, which is often found to belong to such a state of mind. The fair one to whom he was thought by his friends to be imprudently attached, was not content with the praise others were ready to bestow upon the lost object of her affections; and although only fourteen years of age, struck her harp, in mournful lays, upon her Philander's fate, and produced an elegy which has survived to this day, being lately found in an ancient manuscript of a gentleman of the native place of the lovers, and lately transmitted to me. If it does not burn with a Sapphic blaze, it gives more of the light of history than all the odes of the Lesbian dame on her lost Phaon. Miss Susannah Rogers calls on the muse to assist her in describing the youthful warrior, who afar off was resting without his shroud on the field of glory. She says, that his person was comely, his age just twenty-one, his genius of the highest excellence, and that he was the only son of his parents, beloved by all who knew him. His valour, his piety, his prayers amidst the fight, his wounds all bleeding, pass in review before her streaming eyes, and she sees the "howling wilderness" where he fell. She notes the fortitude and resignation with which he died, or rather his exhibition of it, when they left him to die, for he was not dead, when his companions were under the necessity of leaving him to perish. The parental grief is not forgotten, and her own loss is touched upon, with truth and delicacy. Thus every age furnishes matter for grief and subjects for the poet of a melancholy cast. I will give you the whole of the balled on the fight, for it is a fair specimen of that style of writing; but the elegy of the bereaved fair, is too long for my purpose.

Of worthy Captain Lovewell, I purpose now to sing,
How valiantly he served his country and his king;
He and his valiant soldiers did range the woods full wide,
And hardships they endured to quell the Indian's pride.

O

'Twas nigh unto Pigwacket, on the eighth day of May,
They spied a rebel Indian, soon after break of day;
He on a bank was walking, upon a neck of land,
Which leads into a pond, as we're made to understand.

Our men resolved to have him, and travelled two miles round,
Until they met the Indian, who boldly stood his ground;
Then spoke up Captain Lovewell, "Take you good heed," says he,
"This rogue is to decoy us, I very plainly see.

"The Indians lie in ambush, in some place nigh at hand,
In order to surround us, upon this neck of land;
Therefore we'll march in order, and each man leave his pack,
That we may briskly fight them, when they make their attack."

They came unto the Indian, who did them thus defy,
As soon as they came nigh him, two guns he did let fly,
Which wounded Captain Lovewell, and likewise one man more,
But when this rogue was running, they laid him in his gore.

When they had scalped the Indian, they went back to the spot
Where they had laid their packs down, but there they found them not;
For the Indians having spy'd them, when they them down did lay,
Did seize them for their plunder, and carry them away.

These rebels lay in ambush, this very place hard by,
So that an English soldier did one of them espy,
And cried out, "here's an Indian," with that they started out,
As fiercely as old lions, and hideously did shout.

With that our valiant English, all gave a loud huzza,
To shew the rebel Indians they feared them not a straw;
So now the fight began, and as fiercely as could be,
The Indians ran up to them, but soon were forced to flee.

Then spoke up Captain Lovewell, when first the fight began,
"Fight on, my valiant heroes! you see they fall like rain."
For as we are informed, the Indians were so thick,
A man could scarcely fire a gun and not some of them hit.

Then did the rebels try their best, our soldiers to surround,
But they could not accomplish it, because there was a pond
To which our men retreated, and covered all the rear,
The rogues were forced to flee them, although they skulked for fear.

Two logs there were behind them, that close together lay,
Without being discovered, they could not get away;

Therefore our valiant English, they travell'd in a row,
And at a handsome distance, as they were wont to go.

'Twas ten o'clock in the morning, when first the fight began,
And fiercely did continue until the setting sun ;
Excepting that the Indians, some hours before 'twas night,
Drew off into the bushes, and ceased awhile to fight.

But soon again returned, in fierce and furious mood,
Shouting as in the morning, but yet not half so loud ;
For as we are informed, so thick and fast they fell,
Scarce twenty of their number at night could get home well.

And our valiant English, till midnight there did stay,
To see whether the rebels would have another fray ;
But they no more returning, they made off towards their home,
And brought away their wounded, as far as they could come.

Mather Byles was born in Boston in 1706. He was settled as a clergyman in the south end of his native town, was distinguished for his wit and talents, and was a poet of no ordinary character. He wrote with taste, but did not write much. He was one of the correspondents of Dr. Watts; and also one of the first in America, to induce his parishioners to introduce the Psalms and Hymns of that pious divine and respectable poet, who laboured in almost every branch of literature, for every age, from lisping infancy to full grown philosophers. Contemporary with Byles, was Joseph Green, born in the same year, and graduated in 1726. He was a wit, a classical scholar, and a poet. He was also an intelligent merchant, of great integrity, and soon became a man of fortune. He annoyed the politicians of the time with satire. He put Belcher's speeches into rhyme, and Shirley did not escape his lash. Among his poetical pieces, was an "Elegy on Mr. Old Tenor," and a satire upon a procession of freemasons, which were much admired at the time, from the happy delineations they contained. But masonry in that quarter has changed its character since that time. Green cared nothing for immortality as a wit or poet. To enjoy the hour of recreation was the extent of his wishes ; and, stranger still, though often solicited to take offices of political honour, he laughed at them also. He was appointed a Counsellor by *mandamus*, and so soon as he received the summons, sent his resignation to Gov. Gage. And, before he filed his summons in mercantile exactness, as it was his habit to do with every communication he received, he wrote, as a gentleman well acquainted with him informed me, a short ode on the back of the document, that was an elegant satire upon the times, and which, like a two-edged sword, cut both ways. He belonged to a club of wits, who satirized every one they chose to make amusement of; and, frequently, threw a squib at each other. Some of Green's companions made this epitaph on him.

> " Siste, viator ; here lies one,
> Whose life was whim, whose soul was pun ;
> And, if you go too near his hearse,
> He'll joke you, both in prose and verse."
> 1743.

John Osborn was born in the year 1713, and was graduated in 1735. He studied divinity, but it was supposed he found himself not sufficiently orthodox to be popular in Massachussetts, at that time. He read medicine, was of a sickly constitution, and died at about forty years of age. He was a poet of considerable talent. He wrote, about the time he left college, a beautiful elegy on the death of a young sister. It is tender and philosophical. He wrote also a whaling song, which has been sung a thousand times in the North and South Pacific, and in the Norwegian Seas. It is a good description of the manly sport of hunting the monarch of the mighty deep.

Thomas Godfrey, who died about the year 1761, was the son of Thomas Godfrey, the mathematician, mentioned by Franklin as the inventor of the Quadrant now so much in use, called Hadley's Quadrant ; Hadley having had the honour of giving a name to the instrument which he stole from Godfrey, and, for a while, the credit of the invention also. The elder Godfrey belonged to a society in Philadelphia, with Dr. Franklin and other men of inquiring minds ; the son was for a time an apprentice to a watchmaker, but preferring letters to the mechanick arts, he left the business of a watchmaker, and obtained a subaltern's commission in the Pennsylvania forces raised in 1758 to take Fort Duquesne, three years after Braddock's defeat. He continued in the army until the troops were disbanded, and then he commenced business as a Commission Merchant in North Carolina, where he died, by over exertion in the extremely hot weather of that climate. He was highly esteemed, and his premature death, at the age of twenty-seven, was deeply lamented. He had devoted much of his time to the muses, and had, from time to time, thrown off many fugitive pieces, which were gathered up by his friend Mr. Evans, and published in the year 1763, under the title of juvenile poems, with a dramatick work, called, " The Prince of Parthia, a Tragedy." This is, probably, the first tragedy ever written in this country. Many a bloody one had, however, been enacted from 1755 to 1761, as well as before that time, from Fort Duquesne to the plains of Abraham. The following extract from an ode of his, on friendship, is smooth, easy verse, and is not wanting in spirit. If the writer of such lines had lived, and continued his devotion to the muses, in the maturity of his judgement, we should have had something of note to show from his pen. What he has left is sufficient to give him a rank among the poets of that day. In his pieces, there is abundant evidence that he was acquainted with Dryden and Pope, and, probably, with other writers of the Augustan age of Queen Anne. All his lines are pure in their morality, and delicate in their sentiment; and this is no small matter in a poet; for, in that age, after the writings of Swift were diffused, we had not a few poets, of whom it might be said that "the muses were fond to inspire, but ashamed to avow."

A PINDARICK ODE ON FRIENDSHIP.

By *Thomas Godfrey.*

FRIENDSHIP! all hail! thou dearest tie
We mortals here below can claim,
To blend our else unhappy lives with joy;
 My breast inspire,
 With thy true genuine fire,
 While to thy sacred name,
 I strike the golden lyre.
Clothed in pure empyrean light,
For vulgar eyes thou shin'st too bright:
 For while they gaze,
 Thy dazzling rays
Dim their too feeble light.
But souls uncloyed with sensual toys,
Souls who seek true mental joys,
May, phœnix-like, sublimely soar,
May all thy heavenly charms explore,
And wanton in the glorious blaze.

O, G***! if now no charming maid
Waits thy pencil's powerful aid,
That when her charms shall fade away,
And her pleasing form decay—
That when her eyes no more shall roll,
Or heaving sighs betray her soul—
 Still by thy art,
 The stubborn heart
To melt, and into love betray—

O 2   21

Attend! I sing that power divine,
Whose heavenly influence sways such souls as thine;
Souls by virtue made the same,
Friendship's powerful ties may claim;
And happy they,
Without allay,
Blest in the generous flame.

Dr. Franklin, whose literary and scientifick character we have mentioned elsewhere, would have no small claim to the reputation of a poet, had not his fame as a philosopher, politician, and prose writer, thrown, as it were, into the shade, his occasional offering to the muses. If there is no rhapsody in his inspirations, there is a sweet and beautiful flow of good sense and delicacy of feeling. His love of Addison is discovered in his poetry as well as in his prose. The deep solemnity of Addison was not in the nature and disposition of Franklin; nor had the latter a tithe of the classical information of the former; but a deeper knowledge of human nature, and of the business of life, certainly belonged to Franklin. In the maze of skepticism, Franklin lost, or never cherished, that solemn cast of thought which one so truly pious as Addison always has, and constantly infuses into all he says or writes.

Benjamin Pratt was a scholar who was never fostered into notice, or fed by the flattery of the popular voice. He made his way by energy of mind and firmness of purpose. He was graduated at Harvard, in 1737. He was a first rate lawyer, and most admirable logician. His poetry, written while he was engaged in full practice, shows that he had a fine taste for this elegant accomplishment; for in his compositions are united depth of reasoning, force of illustration, and command of language, with rich imaginings. He died Chief Justice of New York, much admired for the powers of his understanding, and the extent of his information. His communion with the muses was by stealth; another proof of the sacrifice even a great man is under the necessity of making to public sentiment. The poetry on which his fame, as a writer of verse, is built, was found among his papers after his death, and few ever knew that he made these private devotions to the art. His poems on several subjects, are full of point and elegance, and have received the commendations of several judicious cricks.

LECTURE X.

And none are more exquisitely awake
To nature's loveliness, than those who feel
The inspiration of the muse—who take
From her the glowing thoughts, that, as they steal
Around the soul entranced, a goddess make
Of nature, to whose shrine of beauty kneel,
The fond enthusiast, adoring all
Within her, we may dread, or lovely call.

                                                    NACH.

THE events preceding and during the revolution, called out all the poetical talent of our country. I mean those talents which consist in catching at circumstances as they arise, and turning them to advantage. Songs, epitaphs by anticipation, and satire in every form, came flying all abroad, to cut up the tory, and warm up the patriot. Every nation, civilized or barbarous, has used song as an instrument of exciting a love of country, and urging the most popular motives for repelling a foe, and securing that fame which belongs to the brave. Many of these minor American poets have been swept into obscurity by time; and it is, perhaps, too late to rescue their names from oblivion; but there are others of a higher order, whose names will be preserved by the historian of our literature, as having filled their space in the revolution. Among others, Francis Hopkinson, who was born in 1738, was in the full maturity of his intellectual powers when the revolution began, and he brought all of them in aid of the great cause. He was a member of congress from New-Jersey in 1776, and signed that memorable instrument, the Declaration of Independence. He was, afterwards, a judge of admiralty in Pennsylvania. Hopkinson was born for a satirist, and nature had left the most unequivocal marks of her intention in his physiognomy. The quick, twinkling eye, the small animated features, the thin lips and sharp nose, answered the rules of Lavater, for one "*who sees quickly, and combines rapidly, and in such a manner as to produce novel and pleasing effects.*" His "Battle of the Kegs" was much admired for its wit; and even Sir William Howe, who was ridiculed in it, was said to have laughed heartily when it was read to him. Long after the revolutionary conflict was over, he brought his talent to bear occasionally upon the absurdities which are, and always will be, found in every society. Sometimes he turned it upon the follies of a city corporation, and sometimes upon the press itself; and so just, so keen, so powerful, was his satire upon the press, which was then indulging in extreme licentiousness, that, it is said, there was not for months after the publication of some of his satires, a scandalous article to be found in the columns of the newspapers of the day. Juvenal and Pope could not boast of having produced such an effect, with all their fame. It is much easier to "*whip a rascal naked round the world,*" than to awe the conductors of the press, to keep within the pale of decorum, at any time. Hopkinson's poetical effusions were, after his death, collected and published, in three volumes, 8vo. in 1792.

Lemuel Hopkins, a Connecticut poet, whose name and writings, from the similarity of name, are often confused with those of Francis Hopkinson, was several years junior to his brother poet of Pennsylvania. He was a physician, and commenced the practice of his profession in 1776. He was distinguished in his profession, and equally so for his dress and manners. He wrote several occasional pieces, which were much admired, and projected the Anarchiad, a work which was probably the joint production of some of the best poets of the day. The Anarchiad exhibits a thorough knowledge of events, a deep insight into the moving principles of the policy of the statesmen of that period, and an intimate acquaintance with the powers, caprices, and dispositions of the leaders in every party feud. In reading this work, at the present day, we admire the genius of the writers, although many of the points are lost, from our having suffered the minute history of the times when it was written, to escape from our memories, if they were ever treasured there.

At the same time, when the afore-mentioned poets, Hopkinson and Hopkins, were throwing their shafts from vigorous bows, and annoying their enemies—(perhaps, earlier than either,) Trumbull appeared—himself a host in this warfare. His M'Fingal, although modelled on Hudibras, is, in many things, superiour to it. The Tories were not to be met by argument; for they had many arguments drawn from their fears of the success of the American arms, which could not be readily answered; for no one could precisely foretell the issue of the conflict. They were to be conquered by ridicule; no other power could reach them. Wit alone drove them from the field; and the Tories felt a greater hatred to the poet who had made them ridiculous, than to the soldier who destroyed their ranks by hundreds. This poem was decried in England, for many years, but at last acknowledged to belong to the first order of satirical poems. The foreign foe did not claim all the poet's attention; for he spared some of his leisure hours to attack a domestick foe—one much to be dreaded in every age—ignorance. " *The Progress of Dulness*," did much to prevent the multiplication of those characters, sometimes found at the present day, in whose composition dulness is shielded by gravity of face, and ignorance covered by the affectation of piety. The author of M'Fingal is still living, and could now, perhaps, tell us what share the different authors took in the Anarchiad. It is to be hoped that he will do it. Such an intimation would gratify the curious, and injure no one. His co-adjutors in this work are gone, and the parties lashed have passed away; no harm could, therefore, come from such a disclosure.

Humphreys, although he wrote less than many others, has no small claims to the character of a poet. His were mostly hasty pieces written in the hurry of a camp; but constantly abound in energy and patriotism, and must have warmed the soldiers' heart at the time. Some lines are truly poetick, and will hold a permanent place in the poetry of our country. It has certainly been asserted, and never denied, that he was one of the writers of the Anarchiad, and this is enough to give him a rank among " *the tuneful brotherhood*." In the latter part of his life, his muse, accustomed to camps, closed her wings and turned shepherdess: but on an oaten reed she could not play; the trumpet was her instrument. He was, at all times, an enthusiast in the glory and fame of his country, and poured out his prophesies profusely; and of him it must be said too, that he laboured to fulfil them.

Alongside of Trumbull, Humphreys, and Barlow, walked one of a graver mien. His poetry was altogether devoted to learning and piety; and every song, hymn, or occasional verse, is full of pathos and religious dignity. The epick on which he rested his fame was not his happiest effort. He was constituted for epick grandeur, but his piety led him to seize a difficult subject for the trial of his skill. There was no novelty in the vengeance of heaven pouring its chastisements upon a wicked nation. Who can stand before Omnipotence! Who can question the doings of Israel's God! Of course there was no display of machinery; nothing which shows the master-hand of the poet in the invention of his fable; for here was no fable. We must see the mortal in every great work, to be struck with admiration. The lofty dome of St. Peters, the work of man, fills the mind of the beholder with more wonder, than the contemplation of this self-poised earth, wheeling its course, in the "void immense." The works of man are questioned, examined, and criticised, and often remodelled in the mind of the examiner; and his admiration settles at last on the great skill of the builder of an epick, or a temple. But neither philosophy nor religion thinks to set bounds to the power of God, or feels more wonder at one exercise of it than at another.

Dwight's " Conquest of Canaan," notwithstanding the faults inherent in the subject, has not yet had justice done to it ; and one reason for this delay was the superiority of his eloquence to his poetry. No ear will hear *that* again. Mute is the once tuneful tongue; but his verse will be more read than it has been, and the more it is read, the higher will be his fame as a poet. Although his creed was tinged with the severe philosophy of the great Reformer, yet such was the glowing benevolence of his own heart, that none of it was seen in his intercourse with men. He was happy in the affections of the wise, and the good, in the rising as well as in the risen generation, and happier still in the affections of his family. His poetry and his eloquence were pure streams of heart and mind, refreshing to all they reached, both young and old. One of the sweetest morsels of Dwight's poetry was written while he kept an academy for young ladies, to be sung at an examination, previous to a spring vacation of his seminary. His poem, " Greenfield Hill," is much more often read and quoted than the " Conquest of Canaan," and, by many, thought to be a superiour composition.

The following is the hymn to which we referred.

Hail! child of light! returning spring,
Fair image, foretaste sweet of Heaven,
In thee our hearts thy Maker sing,
By whose blest bounty thou wast given.

From thee, the wintry glooms retire,
The skies their purest beams display ;
And winds, and showers, and suns conspire
To clothe the world with life and May.

Hail! knowledge, hail,—the moral Spring
That wakes the verdure of the mind ;
To man thy ways indulgent bring
And fragrant flowers and fruits refined.

Thy progress with the morn began,
Before thee every region smiled;
The savage brightened into man,
And gardens blossomed in the wild.

All hail! fair Virtue! noblest good ;
The bliss and beauty of the skies,

By whom to yonder blest abode
The humble and the faithful rise.

While here, fair Learning's smiles begin,
And Spring leads on the genial year;
From realms of life and peace divine,
Descend; and bloom and flourish here.

And O, thou fount of good supreme,
The Sun that lights eternal spring,
At once of knowledge source and theme;
Thee, first and last, our voices sing!

Virtue, in every charm arrayed,
For this dark world thy sufferings won;
Those charms thy matchless life displayed,
When here, the incarnate splendour shone.

As dews refresh, as suns revive,
When clear and cloudless shines the day,
Command our rising race to live,
And win them from the world away.

Joel Barlow was early distinguished for talents and acquirements of the highest order. He entered the American army as a chaplain, to assist, by every means in his power, the great cause of his country. A chaplain was a very considerable personage in the army at that time, and did much to animate his fellow-citizens to persevere in the struggle. Many of the soldiers of the American army, in that time, were men of capacity and virtue, worthy to command men in any good cause, and, therefore, could more justly appreciate the merits of such men as Barlow. On leaving the army, he became a scholar by profession; and is, perhaps, the only man in the history of our country, who ever brought his learning to a good political market. Poets have been made ambassadors, and peers, and secretaries, in other countries; but few indeed of our country have found emolument or office by their reputation for learning. It will not always be so. It has been said by Barlow's reviewers, that his style lost something of its purity by his enthusiastick attachment to the literature of France, in the boisterous times of her revolution; when phrenzy made havock of taste as well as of aristocracy. If this charge was, in some degree, correct, and perhaps it cannot be fully denied, it did not reach any considerable extent. A few words or phrases may, unquestionably, be found, which smack of that period, but not many. His lines are, in general, vigorous, yet smooth, and full of dignity and moral grandeur. His prose writing had fewer faults of style than his poetry. There is great neatness in some articles from his pen. The preface to the Columbiad is an admirably condensed, historical account of Columbus and his discoveries. Its perspicuity and beauty of language make it a model for succinct narratives of the kind. The Columbiad is, at present, the first American poem extant. There may be defects of style and versification in it; and some of the complaints made by the Abbe Gregoire may be true, "that Barlow was bigoted against superstition." The work was first published at the close of the American war, and was then called *The Vision of Columbus.* It was dedicated to Louis XVI., with some fine remarks upon that monarch's virtues. The Vision was, after the death of Louis, expanded, and called the Columbiad. It would have been quite as well for Barlow's fame, if this had never been done. The Columbiad is, indeed, a great poem; but it does not contain the whole light of Barlow's mind, which was too strongly tinctured with politicks to be kept constantly within the strict laws of measure, or on the classical top of Pindus; for he would be a truant, now and then, from the *sacred groves,* to sacrifice to the goddess of liberty, whether she appeared as a celestial visitant on his own shores, or as a Parisian Elegante, flaunting in meretricious robes. At such a time, Apollo and the nine would call after him in vain; and their promise to bless his offering with a double portion of inspiration were equally disregarded. He was above envy. Mark how sweetly he praises his rivals:

> " To equal fame ascends thy tuneful throng,
> The boast of genius, and the pride of song;
> Warm'd with the scenes that grace their various clime,
> Their lays shall triumph o'er the lapse of time.
> With keen-eyed glance, thro' nature's walks to pierce,
> With all the powers and every charm of verse,
> Each science opening in his ample mind,
> His fancy glowing and his taste refined,
> See Trumbull lead the train. His skilful hand
> Hurls the keen darts of satire thro' the land.
> Pride, knavery, dulness, feel his mortal stings,
> And listening virtue triumphs while he sings.
> Proud Albion's sons, victorious now no more,
> In guilt retiring from the wasted shore,
> Strive their curst cruelties to hide in vain;
> The world shall learn them from his deathless strain."

> " On glory's wing to raise the ravish'd soul,
> Beyond the bounds of earth's benighted pole,

For daring *Dwight* the epick muse sublime
Hails her new empire in the western clime.
Fired by the themes by seers seraphick sung,
Heaven in his eye, and rapture on his tongue,
His voice divine revives the promised land,
The heaven-taught leader, and the chosen band.
In Hanniel's fate proud faction finds her doom;
Ai's midnight flames light nations to their tomb;
In visions bright, supernal joys are given;
And all the dread futurities of Heaven."

Another of that class of poets whose works were of great utility in the revolution, was William Livingston, LL. D., governor of New-Jersey. He held that office after Governor Franklin was deposed and sent off for adhering to the royal cause. Livingston was a scholar and a wit. He was of the Addisonian school in style, but evinced in his writing a thorough acquaintance with all the first authors of his day. He was a satirist of the keenest lash, and quickest hand, and never spared the enemies of his country. His prose writings were numerous and valuable; but it is only as a poet we are now considering his claims to distinction. He published a poem called "Philosophical Solitude;" which, although reposing in some few large libraries unknown to most persons, is full of thought and point, and not destitute of elegance. This work is destined to resuscitation; and when the long neglected works of our country shall take their proper places, the productions of Livingston will be found of no ordinary grade.

Philip Freneau, of Pennsylvania, and some time of New-Jersey, was a poet of the revolution. A great number of his productions evince taste and talent, and were well adapted to the times. Every *old continental* had some of his verses at his tongue's end; and often animated himself and his companions over his bowl, when he had the good fortune to find one that was flowing. Freneau was not confined altogether to poetry of this character. He wrote some fine patriotick pieces of considerable extent, and others of a miscellaneous nature. Soon after the war, he published a volume of his poems on coarse paper and with bad type. Since that time, a handsome and enlarged edition has been given to the publick. Freneau's pieces are very unequal. Some of them were probably thrown off in haste, and others polished with care. The "Address of Columbus to Ferdinand," is a very happy effort, and his Indian death-song has been much admired. The latter effort we will give entire.

"The sun sets in night; and the stars shun the day;
But glory remains, when their lights fade away.

P   22

Begin, ye tormentors; your threats are in vain :
For the son of Alknomock can never complain.

Remember the woods, where in ambush he lay,
And the scalps which he bore from your nation away.
Why do ye delay?...... 'till I shrink from my pain?
Know, the son of Alknomock can never complain.

Remember the arrows he shot from his bow :
Remember your chiefs by his hatchet laid low.
The flame rises high—You exult in my pain :
But the son of Alknomock will never complain.

I go to the land, where my father is gone
His ghost shall exult in the fame of his son.
Death comes like a friend—He relieves me from pain :
And thy son, O Alknomock, has scorned to complain."

Mrs. Warren is well known to the present generation by her
history of the American Revolution ; but perhaps it is not so well
known that she was distinguished for her poetical talents. She
was of patriot blood, and an inflexible republican. If her fame
required heraldrick honours, and connexion with genius, it would
be sufficient to say that she, was sister to James Otis, the great
patriot of the revolution. This lady not only wrote many things
in prose and verse for the encouragement of the work of opposition to arbitrary measures, but she found leisure to write two tragedies in five acts each, and of considerable length. The first was
"The Sack of Rome," and the other, "The Ladies of Castile."
These were written during the war, and published before the close of
it, as early as 1778. These productions abound in heroick sentiments,
and the verse, in many instances, is smooth and strong, without those
extravagant things which injure many of the modern tragedies ;
for instance, Bertram and Cain ; nor is it pretended that they have
as many lofty conceptions and felicitous sentiments as the modern
productions ; but they are very clever, all things considered, and
ought, and will be preserved, in the annals of our poetry. These,
with other poems, were collected in the life time of Mrs. Warren,
and published in a volume, at Boston. This lady also wrote political speeches for some of the members of the Convention, called
for adopting the Federal Constitution, in 1788; and the speaker was
detected in his borrowed plumage by the elegance of the style of
his oration, and from his ignorance of some of her classical allusions. She was well acquainted with all the great men of her
time, and corresponded with many of the most intelligent of them.

She lived to see the country prosperous and happy; and died, in a good old age, surrounded by several generations of her descendants. If not a poetical, certainly an enviable exit.

Thomas Dawes, jr. was a native of Boston, and was graduated at Harvard College in 1777, soon after the revolutionary conflict began. While in college, he devoted some of his leisure hours to poetry, for which he had a strong propensity, but which he then felt he must restrain, if not sacrifice, to the profession for which he was intended; not that he thought a refined taste inimical to the study of the law, or that a man could not make a good special pleader, if he now and then culled a flower from Parnassus; but the world was then in a hurry of industry, and thought that he could not be a business-man, who stopped to polish a period or make a couplet. He was in full practice when quite young, and had powerful patronage. Early in life he was made a Judge of the Supreme Judicial Court, and having resigned this office, he was appointed Judge of Probate; to the duty of which office that of Judge of the Municipal Court was, after a while, added. Once in a while, through life, he stole an hour or two from business or sleep to make an occasional ode or hymn; and when the good people of Boston were attempting to commemorate some fact in the history of the war, on their monuments on Beacon hill, or at the stump of the old tree of Liberty, he was regularly called upon to aid the work by his poetical and classical taste; and those fine inscriptions, which were often read and admired, were from his pen. This medal-style of writing, requires taste, judgement, and imagination; for it must unite in the shortest possible compass, point, fact, dignity and ease. These monuments are razed to the ground: they fell before the spirit of enterprise and speculation; but the inscriptions are preserved as felicitous touches of the patriotism and taste of that period.

The singular and sudden death of that great patriot, James Otis, who had lived, for years, "a mighty mind o'erthrown," called for the poetick talents of Judge Dawes: and he commemorated the virtues and mental energies of the deceased in an ode, worthy of the subject and of the writer. A few lines of it we shall extract, for the purpose of showing the author's tact and discrimination.

> "Blest with a native strength and fire of thought,
> With Greek and Roman learning, richly fraught,
> Up to the fountain head he pushed his view,
> And from first principles his maxims drew.
> 'Spite of the times, this truth he blazed abroad,
> The people's safety is the law of God."

The last effort of his muse, was a hymn to be sung at the dedication of a church in Baltimore. It certainly ranks high in this order of compositions.

Dr. Josiah Brown Ladd, of Charleston, South Carolina, who died on the second of November, 1786, in the thirty-second year of his age, was a poet of the first class in our country. He was born at Little Campton, in Rhode Island. He delivered an oration on the fourth of July, 1785, which is, in part, preserved by Niles, in his " Principles and acts of the Revolution." It is a work of taste and imagination, full of pathos and instruction. In the American Museum, published in Philadelphia, in 1787, there are to be found several specimens of his poetry, which are truly excellent. His " Address to the Sun," a " Runick Ode," as he calls it, is full of genius and skill. He had command of all the laws of rhythm, and sported with his muse in every measure of verse. He passes from grave to gay, with great facility ; from the pun, the jest, or the conundrum, to the solemn appeal of Almasi, the wife of Almaz Ali Cawn, to Warren Hastings, governor general of India ; in which appeal, rage, narrative, vengeance, and power, reign in turns, with intellectual light and vigour. As some persons may not have paid particular attention to Dr. Ladd's poetry, I will give them his " Ode to the Sun," not as his best production, but as one which shows how much he had, not only of the inspiration of the poet, but also of the knowledge and practice of the art of poetry.

A RUNICK ODE,

By Dr. Ladd.

RADIANT orb, revolving round,
Where, O whither art thou bound ?
Thou, that like some shining shield,
Blazing o'er the bloody field,
Dost on high majestick move,
Pouring sunshine all above.

Where, O whither art thou bound,
Rolling now in glory round ?
Red and fiery round thy brow,
Lo ! the western waters glow ;
And behind, across the vales,
Ev'ry length'ning shadow trails.

Where, O whither art thou bound,
Deep in distant surges drowned ?

Evening marches, wrapt in clouds,
And each prospect gaily shrouds;
While on yonder sea-beat shores,
Blacker night in silence pours.

Hark! hear the rushing blast,
What shrieks it mutters round!
It bellows o'er the dreary waste,
And death is in the sound.

See, see what horrid forms,
Like thin gray mists, appear;
They ride at midnight on the storms,
With horrour in the rear.

Hark! hear the feeble shriek,
How shrill the echoes rise!
Ye grim-gray spirits speak, O, speak—
Why—why those dying cries?

What—do you vanish so?
Are ye already gone?
Where, grim-gray shadows, do ye go,
To pour the plaintive moan?

Hushed are the winds—in their dark silent house
The stormy breezes sleep:—save one soft gale
That whistles through the grass, and seems to say,
Hence, bard of sorrow—plaintive poet, hence!

I go, sweet gale—on yon lone echoing shores,
Where, 'midst the foam, sharp-pointed rocks emerge,
To hear the stormy cataract that roars,
Tremendous! answered by the bellowing surge.

And while around the foamy billow's sweep,
The briny wave sheds momentary gleams,
By which the spirits of the awful deep,
Shall court my vision with horrifick screams.

Stay, bard! a moment stay;
For see, the morning ray
Breaks from the eastern sky.
Thus, wand'ring long unseen,
In dim obscurity!

Where, O whither did'st thou stray,
Radiant orb, that giv'st the day.

P 2

Long did we thy absence mourn;
Long we've waited thy return;
Say, refulgent planet, say,
Where, O whither did'st thou stray?

Jonathan Mitchell Sewell, a poet of considerable note, was a lawyer, at the Rockingham Bar, in the state of New-Hampshire.   He
was a man of genius; eloquent and rich in the charms of varied
and happy conversational powers.   He seldom exercised his mind
on any subject, until some strong inducement was offered him;
and those of fame were more powerful with him than those of
money.   He spent more of his strength upon whims and vagaries,
to test his powers, than became a wise man, conscious that *life is
short and science long*.   But his heart was right, when his arguments were extravagant; and the wildest of his eccentricities had
the stamp of genius about them.   His songs are full of the true
spirit of poetry, and were generally produced on the spur of the
occasion.   He was delighted with Ossian, and paraphrased him in
fine, flowing verse.   His version was written before Linn's, and is
more extensive, and, on the whole, better than that of the distinguished poet of Pennsylvania, of whom we shall soon have occasion to say something.   In the latter part of his life, he was often a
prey to gloomy feelings; and his sufferings did not, like Saul's, find
an anodyne in the muse of another, and seldom a transitory gleam
of comfort from his own.   By seasons of melancholy, the mental
fibre may become more attenuated and delicate; but generally
loses in strength more than it gains in sensibility.   The heart must
be pierced by the arrows of affliction, to enable it to pour out the
sweetest strains of sympathy, but it must not be wounded too severely; its pulses must beat regularly in its greatest fulness, to
give to thought its length, and breadth, and depth, and to fancy her
extended wing and purest fire.   It is not philosophically true, beyond a certain extent, that, in the agonies of the heart, *"he best
can paint them who can feel them most."*   They may be felt too
much for the sufferer, however poetical he may be, to describe
them minutely and accurately.

John Blair Linn was born in Pennsylvania, in 1777, but most of
his early life was passed in New York, until he became a preacher
of the gospel.   He possessed the true elements of a poet—strong
affections, quick perceptions, expanded views, with an unquenchable love of distinction.   He felt the full inspiration of genius, but at
the same time acknowledged that, without industry, it was as
useless as the scattered leaves of the Sybil.   He opened upon the
world, after he left college, as a student at law, a poet, a stage

critick, and a dramatick writer. The great dramatick writers were to him, as they are, and have been, to many men of high and cultivated minds, the master spirits of the literary world. To be enrolled among them was then his ambition. There were, at that time, some admirable actors in the United States.

Hodgkinson and his company were then in the height of their fame. Linn was enamoured with the fascinations of the stage, and presented them with a play called Bourville Castle, which was brought out in New-York with considerable success. But, in the midst of his popularity, he changed his views of the moral dignity of the course he was pursuing, and determined on divinity as a profession; and, at once retiring from the gay and fashionable world, and the pleasures of the conversation of the poets and wits with whom he had associated, he began his new pursuits with the warmest visions of future usefulness. Divinity is a noble profession for a man of genius, and of hallowed feelings. He is found at once in the company of saints and martyrs. The visions of glory they saw, he sees also. He converses with the dead, the resurrection, and the life to come; and is, as it were, admitted, by the sanctity of his character, to a familiarity with his God. When in the pulpit, Linn's lips were touch'd with a coal of fire from the altar of the most High. When he dwelt on the loveliness of christianity, and the hopes of those who die in the Lord, age bent with reverence at the truths which came sweetened by his eloquence, and beauty breathed new aspirations for immortality at his pictures of the happiness of the *just made perfect*. In the height of his fame, and in the midst of his usefulness, he forgot not the muse who was so fond of inspiring the moments of his childhood. He wrote a poem on the Death of Washington, and another on the Powers of Genius, which he had commenced some time before. The latter had a high reputation in England, and a splendid edition of it was published in London. The criticks spoke of it in a very favourable manner ; but while the whinings of every baby poet of England have gone through a dozen editions in this country, "The Powers of Genius" has been on the shelf these twenty years. That is not, however, its final destiny. It will find its place soon, and rank high in the annals of American poetry, when that poetry assumes the character which it has a legitimate right to take. John Blair Linn died in the twenty-eighth year of his age, a Doctor of Divinity, beloved by the friends of learning and piety, and honoured by the tears of genius. His fame is preserved for that period when we shall take an interest in our own talent, by the pen of Charles Brockden Brown, "which adorned every thing it touched." The following extract is from the " Powers of Genius;" but the work must be read as a whole for one to form

a correct opinion of its merits as a composition.   In this extract is
a happy offering of one genius to another.

> "While nature howls, and mirth's gay whispers die,
>   Her eye on fire—her soul in ecstacy !
> See bolder Radcliffe take her boundless flight !
> Clothed in the robes of terror and of night !
> O'er wilds, o'er mountains, her high course extends,
> Thro' darkened woods, and thro' banditti's dens.
> At length she lights within some ruined tower,
> While from the turret tolls the midnight hour.
> A thousand phantoms follow at her call,
> And groans ascend along the mouldering wall.
> Dim shadows flutter o'er the sleepy vale ;
> And ghostly musick comes upon the gale !
> A light appears ! some hollow voice is near ;
> Chill terror starts, and every pulse is fear !"

Like other poets of his time, Linn was delighted with Ossian.
This work was one of those which catch the fancy of the day, and
then pass away.   It was a tissue of silver on a cloth of a dark
ground, beautiful and dazzling, but which loses its lustre by too
much exposure, and is tarnished by the very breath of its admirers.
The sound and wholesome taste which had been formed by the
poets of America, by an intimate acquaintance with the best English
writers, from Shakspeare down to Johnson, Cowper, Haley, Beattie,
and others, who grew up after the age of Pope, Arbuthnot, and
Young, was considerably shaken and vitiated by the sudden influence of the Della Cruscan school.   These honied rhymes, without
energy or point, came upon us like a deluge.   They were so easily imitated, and any imitation was so near the original in point of genius,
that a spawn of these namby-pamby verses came from the poets'
corner of every newspaper, in such profusion, that one of taste might
suppose that " *Bedlam or Parnassus was let out.*"   The French
revolution had deranged all the maxims of criticism and morals as
well as of politicks, and jingle and nonsense flowing in mellifluous
currents often passed for true inspiration.   Surrounded and influenced, more or less, by this bad taste, our poets grew up from 1792
to 1800.   In looking at their works, at this moment, the circumstances of the case should be taken into consideration.   Every poet
or orator, in every age, is influenced in his taste by the opinions
then prevalent.   He may in some degree be affected even when he
struggles to oppose it.   Paine, Prentiss, and Lathrop, set their faces
against every thing that was not justified by the canons of Pope ;
but, at the same time, caught something of the rhapsodies of the day.
Robert Treat Paine was, for ten or fifteen years, considered the

first poet of the United States, although he wrote nothing of any considerable length. His most happy effort, the song of "*Adams and Liberty*," gave its author (a copy-right being secured by the friendly and provident printer) more than ten dollars a line; a rare instance of remuneration for literary labours in this country. His "Invention of Letters," was a poem of some length, and was much admired for its reach of thought, boldness of imagery, and smoothness of versification. It has lost cast, however, among the productions of that period, but is still admired by many, and pronounced as holding a very high rank at the present time. The drama called forth his talents, and the ode he wrote for the opening of the Boston theatre, after it was burnt and rebuilt in 1796, ranks with Johnson's at the opening of the Drury Lane theatre. The criticks have pretended that Johnson was not a poet; but whenever the finest geniuses of this country or England have ventured to take the same path in literature, the giant track of the great moralist has never been effaced by a more Herculean foot.

Prentiss (we talk of those poets near our own time with more familiarity, their history being known to all) was a wit who wrote with great ease and neatness. He was without bustle, splendour, pomp, pride, or circumstance, in his literary labours. He manufactured occasional odes, songs, and satires, as the business of the day, and never thought of them again for profit or fame. He was not so capable of lofty flights as Paine, but he was more accurate in his figures, and more easy in his versification. With proper inducements, he was capable of more continued efforts, and more regular and certain results. His knowledge was more extensive and classical than Paine's; but he could not make such an array of it as his rival could, when excited by the corruscations of other minds. Paine, in a flood of mental light, when song and wit went round, was the object of attraction, however numerous were those who contended for victory.

John Lathrop was contemporary with Paine and Prentiss in college; and like them, he studied law, became a writer in the publick, and, then, an editor of a newspaper. He was a man of considerable talent and taste, and a pure, sensible writer, in prose and verse. His poetry was not so lofty as Paine's, nor so witty as Prentiss'; but was more regular, equal, and classical than either. He was a more regular scholar, better acquainted with rules than his rivals; and, probably, most of his productions are destined to more enduring praise than theirs. His life was an eventful one. Ten years, or more, of it were spent in the East Indies, where he experienced much, and learned nothing but how to advise others. He often complained rather of himself than of his acquaintances. Tossed from law to a clerkship; from that to literary fagging; from that to instructing of youths, and from this employment to a clerkship again, and from that to his grave; he knew no rest, from the commencement to the close of his career. He was first known as a writer when the publick taste was vitiated; and bombast and inflation passed for energy and genius. But he stemmed the current manfully, and was not, like many others, carried down by it. His early and his latter pieces have a freedom from singularity and affectation, which show the clearness of his conceptions and the delicacy of his feelings and taste. Among the best of his productions, is the "Vision of Canonicus," the sachem of the Narraganset Indians. This is the first production of that school of poetry, which has since been so prolifick in lovers of the Aboriginals. The Indians of our country, up to his time, had not met with much sympathy, or had many songs of praise or justice lavished on them. If they were mentioned by the poets of "olden time," it was,

"Heard ye yon arrow hurtle through the air?

"Or saw ye the tomahawk or scalping knife, ready to destroy old age and infancy? Or does not the war-cry stiffen your soul with horror?" These were the usual introductions of works on the Indians. The few good things honest Roger Williams, or Elliot, their apostle, had ventured to whisper in their praise, had been forgotten in the succeeding ages of blood and massacre. The day of retribution has, however, come; and some of our poets are making these sons of the forest the heroes of epics and the knights of song. It is no small praise to be called the pioneer in this course of magnanimity and justice.

Soon after the time of Prentiss, Paine, and Lathrop, William Boyd, who died very young, was coming forward with great promise, as a poet. Several of his productions, as an under graduate, have been published, and have been thought by good judges, to be very clever. His poem on woman has many beauties in it; and, considering his youth, at the time he wrote, may be placed high on the list of the works which have given celebrity to some of his compeers. The subject is treated by him with considerable novelty, and without one particle of improper freedom; for he wrote at a time when every one was not so cautious. Boyd was a man of genius, delicate and refined in his feelings, and suffered from having more taste than was then marketable, and more sensibility than could be understood by the common members of society. The most delicate and susceptible are the most readily misunderstood. Their effusions are poured out on all around them, and are too often chilled by the atmosphere they meet. They admire and love by too strong impulses, and act too often without regard to consequences, or never think of contingencies. They are formed to be delighted, and, perhaps, enamoured with the gay, the sentimental and intelligent, who lavish on them their smiles; and these susceptible beings are ready to defend those they love at every risk. They think, at least, that they have made as strong an impression on others, as others have on them; and calculate what others would do for them, by feeling what they would do for others. In addition to this, such a mind is anxious every hour for fear he may offend some of his friends, and spends many a sleepless night in dwelling upon some look of his friend, not so kind as he could expect or wish, and runs his imagination into all possible causes for his supposed alteration, when none exists, nor even a thought of change has entered the mind of him, so strangely altered in the view of the sentimentalist. At one hour the mind of so delicate a man is tortured by thinking that he has done something to diminish his reputation for genius; at another, that his friend may be surfeited, and that were worse than death. This lady did not look so kindly as she was wont to do, and he had lost ground in her good graces, or some such matter. So the too sensitive man is tossed from one wretchedness to another, until he sinks into misery or misanthropy—and falls, perhaps, into a decline, that ends his days and evils together. Many have fallen victims to such a morbid state; and have not had a mourner for their death, nor hardly a follower to the grave, from out of the very circle for which it may be said that they died. Could the victim of sensibility live over the shock of his early heartaches, and look deeply into the world, he would find no excuse for wasting his sympathies on those who had them; for, on a reverse of fortune, he would discover that he had made a false estimate, in many instances, of those with whom he had been associated. Vanity sometimes comes in as an antidote, to assist the sufferer, but pride is a much better support. Boyd had more genius than he had credit for; more sensibility than pride; and felt more of the agonies of love than of the cordials of admiration; and his delicate constitution sunk under them in early life.

Another of these early victims to the consumption, from whom much was expected by the literary part of the community, was William Clifton. He was well known in Philadelphia, in which city he was born, in 1772, and where he died, in 1799, in the twenty-seventh year of his age. His parents were of the society of Friends, but it was never known that he was, after he arrived to manhood, particularly partial to the tenets of the sect. In some things he must have differed widely from them, as he was an advocate for war, or at least a war spirit is strongly breathed in some of his occasional odes and songs of patriotick cast. His father was a man of fortune, and as his constitution was delicate, he never entered much into the details of business, nor had occasion for the emoluments of it. Clifton was just coming to manhood when the French revolution burst out. He was distinctly on the side of legitimacy, and suffered his feelings to get deeply engaged in the affairs of the world at that time. Every thing that had the hoar of antiquity upon it, was likely to be swept away without distinction; not only titles, but habits, laws, and manners were changed. The methods of thinking and writing suffered the greatest changes; and he saw, like Fisher Ames, and other amiable men, nothing but darkness and evil. At this time Gifford's BAVIAD AND MÆVIAD came from the press, and made a great impression upon the literary world. It was a good piece of satire, of old fashioned stuff, of the school of Pope. It was reprinted in this country, and Clifton wrote a poetical epistle to the author, after the practice of former days, which was prefixed to it. This work gave Clifton a high stand among our poets, and the praise bestowed on Gifford was so unequivocal, that the crusty translator of Juvenal was thought to have viewed the epistle of his young admirer with some complacency. The address deplored the situation of letters in our own country, in terms sufficiently distinct and unpretending to suit even Gifford, who could hear of nothing but what was within the sound of Bow bells.

> "———— beneath our shifting skies
> Where fancy sickens, and where genius dies;
> Where few and feeble are the muse's strains,
> And no fine fancy riots in the veins;
> There still are found a FEW to whom belong
> The fire of virtue and the *soul of song*."

It was not to be wondered at, that our poets should have decried our taste for poetry or the fine arts; for all was then bustle and politicks, or calculations and commerce; all the ambitious were striving to be statesmen; and no other path to fame was open. The learned professions had not then taken the stand they now have; they were in the second and third classes in society. The merchant and statesman were very far before them; and literary men by profession were unknown to us. From every line of Clifton it is easily seen, that he was sensitive on this as on other subjects; and as he was above any apprehension for a support, he lashed about him in the most fearless manner. That he had genius, no one who has

read his works will deny.   His poetry was formed in the school of
Dryden and Pope, and long study in the mastery of language, and
in maturing his thoughts, would, if his life had been spared, unquestionably have made him a poet worthy of being ranked with them;
if not on an equality, (for this is to be obtained by a few only,) he
certainly would have been a distinguished follower of these great
English bards.   In patriotick songs, in which most poets have failed,
there being but few good compositions in national songs to be found
in any language, he had considerable tact, as the following will
prove :

> "Soul of Columbia, quenchless spirit come !
> Unroll thy standard to the sullen sky :
> Bind on thy war-robes, beat the furious drum ;
> Rouse, rouse thy lion heart, and fire thy eagle eye !
> Dost thou not hear the hum of gath'ring war ;
> > Dost thou not know
> > The insidious foe
> Yokes her gaunt wolves, and mounts her midnight car !
>
> Dost thou not hear thy tortur'd seamen's cries ?
> Poor hapless souls in dreary dungeons laid ;
> Towards thee they turn their dim imploring eyes ;
> Alas ! they sink—and no kind hand to aid.
>
> > Thou dost, and every son of thine
> > Shall rest in guilty peace no more,
> > With noble rage, they pant to join
> > The conflict's heat, the battle roar.
> Loose to the tempest let thy banner fly,
> Rouse, rouse thy lion heart, and fire thy eagle eye !"

If this is not the best of poetry, it is high spirited sentiment for a
quaker. He saw, at that time, what he considered a crouching
tameness in the people of the United States, to the mighty and ter-
rifick power of France; but he mistook party hesitation for national
imbecility, and seemed to forget that three thousand miles of water
rolled between us and the legions of the Republick, who, in frenzy,
were sweeping along through Germany, and covering the valleys
and hills of Italy.   There were men, and intelligent and amiable
men too, whose dreams were nightly disturbed by images of French
armies ravaging our country, and immolating every opposer, from
infancy to old age.   It was literally the reign of terror among many
of our reflecting part of the community.   In such a state of things
the arts were forgotten, and poetry could only breathe imprecations.

Q   27

Contemporary with Paine, Lathrop, and Prentiss, were several writers of poetry of considerable note, and in the estimation of some persons, if they were not so much known, were fully equal to those who occupied the front rank in publick estimation. Joseph Allen of Worcester, was a class-mate with Paine, and delivered a poem at the Commencement in which he was graduated, that was highly spoken of.

Isaac Story was about the age of Allen. He wrote a considerable number of occasional poems, under the signature of Peter Quince, which were well received. They were written in imitation of Peter Pindar; but Story had more delicacy, if not so much wit, as his original. These pieces were collected into a volume, and have sufficient merit to place him among our poets of this age. He died young, and at a moment when he was fast rising into fame. His death was deeply lamented by the publick; and with the literati and professional men of the day, he was a great favourite.

Paul Allen, lately deceased, devoted most of his days to literary pursuits, and has in his course been a great contributor to the stock of American literature, and a refiner of our taste in good writing. For more than twenty years, he has been pouring out prose and verse for the benefit of the publick in great honesty, purity, and good taste. Many of our periodicals have been enriched with articles from his pen. Several of these journals he established, or was editor of, for sometime. He wrote boldly, but naturally, and did much by example and precept towards breaking down that sesquipedalian style that had become so prevalent in this country, by attempts to imitate Johnson's Rambler, and other works from his pen. Such men as Paul Allen deserve a memoir of no inconsiderable length, written by some friend of taste and talents. The changes in our literary taste and habits, during the time he was engaged as an author, would make a subject of deep interest, accompanied by the incidents in the life of an amiable man and an elegant writer.

Seleck Osborn is a name known to all our readers of poetry; it was found for many years going the rounds in the poets' corner of every newspaper, from one end of the country to the other, and was not unfrequently attached to morsels of exquisite taste. He was naturally an amiable man, but his temper became a little soured by political contests; a political arena is a miserable place for a man of delicate or refined feelings;—he grows acrimonious upon repeated irritations; and all this injures the temper of his muse. The muse can follow, and has been found inspiring, the half-starved wretch in his garret; yea, has accompanied him to a dungeon and softened the weight of his chains. She has gone with the hero to the battle-field, and led side by side with honour and glory, has waded with him through scenes of blood and death, and inspired the song of victory. She has even sometimes looked in a court of justice, and, without being chilled to death among judges and lawyers;—but never could she abide politicks, in the nature of party feuds. In patriotick songs she has often had a magical influence, but her magick is all lost the moment she mingles in party strife. Osborn discovered this, and in the selections he made from his works for a volume, which he printed a few years since, he left out all those poems that had the slightest party bearing in them. This volume was printed at Boston, and contained some very fine poetry; but there never was a poet, who did not suffer by having his fugitive productions brought together in a volume. They wafted more reputation as they flew, than they will praise when caught up and bound together. It is not the fault of the poet; it is in the minds of men; who would not rather sit down, and read Sir Richard Blackmore's Creation, through and through, than to be confined to an equal number of pages in a Hymn Book, in which there is generally some good poetry, and much devotion. This volume of Osborn's, is among the best of our collections of this kind, and is printed in such a form as to ensure its preservation in our libraries.

Captain Spence, a gentleman whose manners, acquirements, and disposition, made him the charm of every circle, was a poet of a fine natural taste. While a midshipman and a junior lieutenant in the navy, he amused himself in writing poetry of a sentimental cast, which bore marks of a powerful intellect. The sea has not been, as one might suppose it would be, a very fine scene to inspire the votaries of song. Even Falconer wrote the Shipwreck, not on shipboard, but from recollections of the dangers of the sea, while he was safe on land. Captain Spense indulged himself but little in the latter part of his life in writing verses, but he was well read in English poetry, which makes up no small part of all that is valuable in our language. The prose productions of the age of Elizabeth, are scarcely ever read, while Kit Marlowe, Ben Jonson, and Shakspeare, are in the mouths of every one. The work, said to be from the pen of Mr. Spence, and I believe it was never denied by him, was called Edwin the Wanderer.

John G. C. Brainard, who has lately deceased, was a poet of superiour talents. The publick thought well of him, but did not know him sufficiently to give him full credit for the high powers of his understanding or the virtues of his heart. He was a native of Connecticut, was graduated at Yale College in the class of 1815; read law, and in regular time opened his office; but felt too strongly the workings of his genius to attend to clients if they called, and too proud to seek them, if they did not; and, as is often the case with such gifted men, hurried himself into an editorship. The Connecticut Mirror, for several years bore marks of his genius and varied learning. His temperament was poetical, restless, and inclined to melancholy; but he so often disguised this, by occasional exuberance of spirits, so common to minds "attuned to strange fancies," that it was not generally known that he ever indulged in gloomy thoughts. In his hours of attick flow, he was a most excellent companion, both entertaining and instructive, but even in these hours of freedom and pleasure, he never offended decency or morals, but poured out his soul in a stream of pure feeling and delicacy. In a youthful mind struggling with difficulties, there is often found confusion, skepticism, and every tumult and doubt respecting this and another world;—at one moment he sees a fiend on the blast, with a vial of wrath, ready to pour it out on every mortal head, particularly his own; at another moment, the clouds burst away, and the joyous rays of hope come on the sunbeams to illumine and beautify every thing; again the evil spirits and the good spirits commingle, and his bosom is torn with conflicting emotions. Such are the wayward feelings of youthful genius. Time, severe occupation, philosophy with her deep streams of wisdom, and religion with her holy influences, are all necessary to calm, to direct, and to keep him in the way of usefulness and honour. He did not live long enough to erect such a reputation as he had talents for. His poetry seemed to breathe a presentiment that this world was not to be his, for any considerable length of time; nor was it. He died on the 20th of September, 1828, in the thirty-third year of his age. His effusions were printed in a volume before his death, and it is left for us to conjecture what he might have done had he lived, from what he had accomplished before his death; and who is prepared to say that this would not have been much?

There is one little anonymous fragment of American poetry extant, which I will ask permission to insert for its truth and loveliness. It is a proposed addition to that exquisite Elegy in a Country Churchyard, by Gray. The author thought that Gray had not given the subjects of his muse enough of a religious character to make the charm complete, and offered the following amendment, although any amendment may be inadmissible, yet what was offered should be preserved. The author suggested, that it should follow the stanza beginning,

" Far from the maddening crowd's ignoble strife."

Would it mar the beauty of the ode if it were added? You must judge.

No airy dreams their simple fancies fired,
No thirst for wealth, nor panting after fame;
But truth divine, sublimer hopes inspired,
And urged them onward to a nobler aim.

From every cottage, with the day arose
The hallowed voice of spirit-breathing prayer;
And artless anthems, at the peaceful close,
Like holy incense, charmed the evening air.

Though they, each tome of human lore unknown,
The brilliant path of science never trod,
The sacred volume claimed their hearts alone,
Which taught the way to glory and to God.

Here they from Truth's eternal fountain drew
The pure and gladdening waters day by day;
Learnt, since our days are evil, fleet, and few,
To walk in wisdom's bright and peaceful way.

In yon lone pile, o'er which hath sternly pass'd
The heavy hand of all-destroying Time,
Through whose low mouldering aisles now sighs the blast,
And round whose altars grass and ivy climb;

They gladly thronged their grateful hymns to raise,
Oft as the calm and holy sabbath shone;
The mingled tribute of their prayers and praise,
In sweet communion rose before the throne.

Here, from those honoured lips, which sacred fire
From heaven's high chancery hath touched, they hear
Truths which their zeal inflame, their hopes inspire,
Give wings to faith, and check affliction's tear!

When life flowed by, and like an angel, Death
Came to release them to the world on high,
Praise trembled still on each expiring breath,
And holy triumph beamed from every eye.

Then gentle hands their "dust to dust" consign;
With quiet tears, the simple rites are said;
And here they sleep, till at the trump divine,
The earth and ocean render up their dead.

Q 2   23

It was fashionable in the latter days of Darwin, and in the early days of Southey, to speak lightly of the productions of Pope. The criticks found that he had sometimes indulged his resentments in the Dunciad, and doomed several characters to infamy who deserved a better fate. The small fry of authors who wished to hide their feebleness in the extravagancies of sentiment then becoming popular by the influence of the French Revolution, and the influx of German literature, which had not been well examined, nor the chaff separated from the wheat, supported by a few men of genius, who had taken up some erroneous impressions on the canons of poetry, did, for a while, obscure the fame of Pope; and it seemed, for a season, that he would at length be found in his own Dunciad. They attacked him as a writer wanting in variety and genius, and boldly called his morals in question. The clouds which obscured his brightness did not last long, but were soon dispersed, and his genius beamed in its ancient majesty. Byron would yield to no one in his reverence of Pope: and almost all the present poets of England, who are the arbiters of taste, have come into the opinion that Pope was a genius and a poet, such as it is seldom the good fortune of nations to produce.

This may be said to be an age of poetry. There are many living writers whose works have secured them wealth and fame, while they were able to enjoy it. Southey's muse has brought forth epicks as common songs; and Scott, before he commenced the Waverly novels, produced Marmion, the Lay of the Last Minstrel, Rokeby, the Lady of the Lake, and the Vision of Don Roderick, with other pieces, in quick succession. Byron from his boyhood never laid aside his pen until the wrongs of Greece seized his heart. Childe Harold, the Corsair, the Gaiour, the Bride of Abydos, Cain, and Don Juan, followed each other as rapidly as the French legions which crossed the Alps with Napoleon. Montgomery, Coleridge, Crabbe, and Moore, have been busy. The polished Campbell, and the Shakspearian Baillie, have not been idle.

The poets of our own country have had these fine models before them; and they have shown the world that they have profited by being in such a school. There is at present much talent, ambition, and information among our poets, and they are getting rid of the ridiculous impressions which have long been prevalent, that genius is every thing, and information nothing, in making a poet. The prophets of old had to build the altar, and lay on it the wood, before they called the fire from heaven to kindle the flame and burn the offering.

My intention, at first, was to have mentioned many of our living poets; two only have I named, Freneau and Trumbull, and these patriotick bards are so near, in the course of nature, to the confines of a better world, that I felt no reluctance to speak of them; but on mature reflection, I gave up the thought of bringing forward any more, fearing that it would be premature to discuss their merits in a work like this, as a fair criticism on these would be in a measure making comparisons between them. I have no hesitation in saying, that we abound in good poets, whose writings will remain to make up the literature of a future age; nor would I yield my admiration for their productions to others who are prodigal of praise whenever their works appear; but at this time I am not prepared to say whether Pierpont or Bryant be the greater poet, or whether Percival has higher claims to immortality than his brethren of the *"enchanted grounds and holy dreams;"* nor whether she of *"the banks of the Connecticut,"* whose strains of poetick thought are as pure and lovely as the adjacent wave touched by the sanctity of a Sabbath's morn, be equal to her tuneful sisters, Hemans and Landor, on the other side of the water, or superiour to her more sprightly rivals on this.

When all classes were busy in building up our national and state governments, the fine arts were neglected; and a few only knew how necessary the cultivation of them was to refine and polish a nation. Even in England, until within half a century, any devotion to them was considered inconsistent with weighty duties. Windham, Talbot, Murray, and Pulteney, "every muse gave o'er," before they entered the temple of justice, and assumed the causes of their clients; and Blackstone dropt a tear at parting with his muse at the vestibule of Westminster Hall. Parsons, of our own country, as great a name as either, who thought that he was made more decidedly for a poet than for any other calling, confined himself to writing a few occasional pieces, generally on some merry-making occurrence, not venturing to trust himself further; while he read with avidity every line that was published on this, or the other side of the Atlantick, in English, French, Italian, or Latin. It is not so now; it is thought quite possible to devote a few hours of relaxation from severe studies to the fine arts, without any fear of being seduced from graver duties. Opinions and taste are changed in many other respects. The good household dames of other days would have turned shuddering from the sight of Cupids, and Venuses, and Graces, which the maiden of the present day, pure as the stainless snow, will sit before whole hours, engaged in her innocent drawing lessons. The mind, properly disciplined, is capable of sustaining much; as the body in full health can support heat and cold. There are no sickly images while there is a sane mind in a sane body. Numerous instances of the facility of passing from severe labour to sportiveness, are now at hand.   Sir Walter Scott wrote all his poetry, and many of his novels, in hours of relaxation from the dull details of a clerkship in a court of justice.   Sir William Jones left Hafiz, and all the enchantments of Arabian poetry, to throw new light upon the black letter of the law, and to give a reason for a principle in Coke upon Littleton, when the two great luminaries of the science had only stated a decision.   Some of the great dignitaries of the church have awakened their zeal by invoking the muse; and the great statesman of England, who has lately become a tenant of the tomb, found his poetry as effective as his eloquence in scattering and subduing his opposers, and in building up his systems, and supporting his policy.   The poetry of the Anti-Jacobin did more than a thousand homilies to defend the cause of old fashioned honesty; and "the Loves of the Triangles," checked the false politicks and the bad taste of the Darwinian school.   Like the eagle, Canning passed from watching the fish-hawks along the coast, to soaring and poising sublimely in the heavens, and to gazing with undazzled eye upon the sun.

We have, by the mistake or modesty of our own writers, been ranked among those nations which have lately become literary.   But avoiding all further deception on that head, it is to be hoped that we have now arrived at that point in our literary history, when it is proper for us to assume some share of independence. Not only our mother country is pouring in her literature by the *bale* upon us, as usual, but other countries are also doing the same. The whole European continent is open to our researches, and yields her literary and scientifick treasures to our enterprise; and our missionaries, in conjunction with those of other countries, are throwing open the door to the immense storehouses of oriental learning, where the treasures of unnumbered ages have been lodged.   Even a key to the mysteries of Egyptian wisdom has been found, and the veil of Isis is about to be removed.   At the same time, all things have become well settled upon true principles among us, and the agitation and bustle of their establishment having passed away, some of the first minds will gratify their ambition by literary distinction; and claim their country's gratitude, by refining our taste, and raising our standard of literary eminence.

Here nature presents her beauties in as delicate forms, and her wonders in as bold relief, as she has in the birth place of the muses. She has laid the foundation of her mountains as broad, and raised their tops as high as in the old world.   What are the Tibers and Scamanders, measured by the Missouri and the Amazon?   Or what the loveliness of Illyssus or Avon, by the Connecticut or the Potomack?   The waters of these American rivers are as pure and sweet, and their names would be as poetical, were they as familiar to us in song, as the others, which have been immortalized for ages. Whenever a nation wills it, prodigies are born. Admiration and patronage create myriads who struggle for the mastery, and for the olympick crown. Encourage the game, and the victors will come. In the smiles of publick favour, poets will arise, yea, have already arisen, whose rays of mental fire will burn out the foul stain upon our reputation, given at first by irritated and neglected genius, and continued by envy and malice—that this is the land

"Where fancy sickens, and where genius dies."

LECTURE XI.

"The sciences which do honour to the human mind—the arts which embellish human life, and transmit illustrious actions to posterity—should be peculiarly respected in all free governments. All men of genius, all who have obtained a distinguished rank in the republick of letters, wherever they were born, are of my country.

"I invite the learned to assemble, and to propose to me their views, their names, or the assistance they may want, to give new life and existence to the sciences and fine arts. My people set a greater value on the acquisition of a learned mathematician, a painter of reputation, or any distinguished man, whatever may be his profession, than in the possession of the richest and most abundant city."—*Buonaparte's letter to the astronomer Oriani.*

THE fine arts can only flourish in the bosom of refinement. They are the latest offsprings of the muse. Poetry is her first born, and painting and statuary the youngest of her children; and there has generally been a long interval between the births of the sisters. Poetry may live in sylvan scenes, and with a primitive people; but the arts must be cherished by wealth and taste, and grow in the sunshine of patronage. A poet may chant his verses for his own pleasure, in his own circle; but the painter and sculptor must be stimulated by the gaze and admiration of intelligence and fashion. Poets may make the solitudes vocal with inspired numbers, to charm some woodland nymph; but no one ever patiently laid his colours on the canvass, or spent long painful years in chiselling the marble, without looking forward to the hour when his labours would be rewarded by a wreath of fame, or a shower of gold.

From the nature of the moral and physical growth of this country, it could not be expected that we should be distinguished in the fine arts, particularly in the early ages of our history; not that our fathers were wanting in taste for the fine arts, but that their situation forbade them from indulging a thought for any thing beyond what was absolutely necessary for a comfortable existence. They brought some pictures with them, but in general, they were nothing more than armorial bearings and family portraits; and, in truth, at that period, in England there was not much attention paid to painting, statuary, architecture, or music. Wren had not then arisen, nor had there been a splendid edifice erected since the gothick ages had passed away; ages in which the solemn piles of religious enthusiasm arose, and with them the massy walls of the feudal castle. The religion of England was changed; the mode of warfare was changed; the monastery was not occupied, and the moat, the drawbridge, and portecullis, were no longer useful for defence; and the Grecian orders, in which reside ease, repose, grace, and beauty, had not then found their way to England; it could not, therefore, be expected that the fine arts, in any of their best forms, could easily have found their way to America, when they were not, at that time, cherished in the mother country. Now and then an Italian painter, or one of the Flemish school, would stray across the Atlantick, and leave some traces of his art here, which have afterwards excited our curiosity, to know from whose hand they came.

The first artist of distinction I can find any record of among us, was Smybert, a painter who came out to this country with Dean Berkley, in 1728. He was at first attached to the family of the good man, and there is now a painting in Yale College, from his pencil. It is a picture of the Dean's family. Smybert was a man of genius, whose talents had attracted the attention of this generous ecclesiastick, and he wished to serve him after he had discovered his merits. Smybert was almost a self-taught artist, having commenced in life as an ornamental chair, clock, or house painter, one grade only above the mechanical part of painting; but feeling the inspiration of a higher ambition, and a capacity for better things, he visited Italy, and returned with much of that knowledge which genius catches by being in the atmosphere of taste and enthusiasm for the arts. On the Dean's leaving this country, Smybert settled in Boston, and commenced in his profession with what was then thought a good patronage, and took quite a respectable rank in society as a citizen. Many of his portraits are in being now, and some of them are very good likenesses, and quite respectable paintings. The poet Green, who, from his taste, talents, wealth, and wit, stood among the first in the society of Boston, at that time, speaks of Smybert with affection and respect, as a citizen and artist. Smybert's head of the Cardinal Bentivolio, and of Dr. Mayhew, are among the first of fine portraits.

Copley followed Smybert in Boston, and must have been distinguished about the time Smybert died. From the best information I can procure, Copley was his pupil for several years. He painted many portraits in this country; probably more than any man except Gilbert Stuart. Full lengths were then the fashion; and many of them, from Copley's pencil, are now to be found in Massachusetts. His likenesses were faithful; but it was in his colouring and drapery that he excelled any other man of modern times. Copley was highly respected for his gentlemanly manners, as well as for his professional eminence; and during the first years of that agitation which preceded the revolutionary conflict, was often instrumental in allaying political excitements, which procured from his neighbours the appellation of peace maker; but the times soon grew too boisterous for an artist, and he departed for England some years before the battle of Lexington. In England he had opportunities of displaying his powers as an historical painter. The number of his pictures is considerable. We will mention a few of his most celebrated works; but we do not profess to be sufficiently acquainted with them, to venture any criticisms. It would not, however, be too much to say, that they were universally admired by those who have had the pleasure of examining them.

1. The Tribute Money.—"Render unto Cæsar the things that are Cæsar's, &c."

2. Samuel and Eli.—"The Lord called unto Samuel."

3. Charles demanding of Parliament the Surrender of the Members.

4. The Nativity of our Saviour.

5. Surrender of Admiral De Winter to Lord Duncan.

6. Sortie from Gibraltar.

7. Death of Chatham.

8. A Youth rescued from a Shark.

9. Death of Major Pierson.

10. Abraham offering up Isaac.

11. Hagar and Ishmael.

He was prosperous in his day and generation; his son, Lord Lyndhurst, is now High Chancellor of England, and his other children eligibly situated in life. He had the good fortune to be as acceptable to the people of England, as he had been in his native country

Haley, in his poetical epistles on the painters, after naming West and his works as he should be named, pays this fine and highly deserved compliment on Copley :

> " With kindred power, a rival hand succeeds,
> For whose just fame, expiring Chatham pleads;
> Like Chatham's language, luminous and bold,
> Thy colours, Copley, the dread scene unfold,
> When that prime spirit, by whose guidance hurl'd,
> Britain's avenging thunder aw'd the world ;
> In patriot cares, employ'd his parting breath,
> Struck in his field of civic fame by death;
> And freedom, happy in the tribute paid
> By art and genius to so dear a shade,
> Shall own, the measure of this praise to fill,
> The awful subject equalled by thy skill."

It is difficult to speak of our countryman, Sir Benjamin West, for his talents were only discovered in this country, but cherished in England. There, for more than half a century, he was a favourite of the British nation, and was patronized by its king. He was admired for the amenity of his manners and the purity of his life, as well as for his excellence in his profession. He was true to his patrons, but he never forgot his country, and was the instructer, friend, and father of the young Americans who flocked to see him, and get advice and direction from him. Perhaps we take too much credit for West as our countryman; for, most certainly, the country that adopts, supports, and honours a man, has a better claim to him than that which gave him birth, and but little more. He was equally the favourite of kings and poets, and both bound his brow with their appropriate wreaths. Like Michael Angelo, he lived long to be the friend and patron of the enterprising young artists of his own and other countries, and he was affectionate and brotherly to the very last hours of his life. The tribute paid him in the " Epistle on the Painters," is not only correct, but in good taste.

> "Supremely skill'd the varied group to place,
> And range the crowded scene with every grace;
> To finish parts, yet not impair the whole,
> But on the impassion'd action fix the soul;
> Through wondering throngs the patriot chief to guide,
> The shame of Carthage, as of Rome the pride;
> Or while the bleeding victor yields his breath,
> Gives the bright lesson of heroick death.
> Such are thy merits, West, by virtue's hand,
> Built on the human heart, thy praise shall stand,

While dear to glory in her guardian fane,
The names of Regulus and Wolfe remain."

The patriarch painter descended full of honours to the grave, leaving a reputation of which both the country of his birth and of his adoption were proud. His biography has been written with taste and interest by Galt, and sketches of him are numerous.

During the revolutionary war, the fine arts in this country were merged in arms, and nothing was thought of, but matters of sustenance and defence. The few who had come to a resolution to devote themselves to the fine arts, and make them a profession, had escaped from the scenes of blood and strife, and were seeking repose and instruction in other countries.

Soon after the peace of 1783, Johnson, who had been a brave officer of our army, took up the pencil as a profession, and made his head quarters at Boston. Johnson was a man of a powerful mind, and had a correct eye and a steady hand, but was, from the nature of his education deficient in drawing, the great defect of self-taught artists. The science of drawing was more rare with our artists formerly, than the faculty of colouring well; Johnson has, however, left many portraits which are strong likenesses, and are more valuable to the present generation than fine paintings would be, if they were but indifferent likenesses of our fathers.

Hancock, a miniature painter, was contemporary with Johnson, and took some fine miniatures of the people of that age. Had his colours been less evanescent, his fame would have been more diffused and permanent. He was at times very happy in catching a good resemblance in the size of half an inch in diameter; some of these, set in finger rings, have been preserved, and give him a claim to be remembered among the artists of his day.

Among the most distinguished of American painters was Gilbert Stuart, who has lately deceased. He was a native of Rhode Island, and, after leaving college, made up his mind to follow painting as a profession, and not being able to find a proper master in this country, Copley being then gone to England, he embarked for that country, in 1775, and put himself under the instruction of Mr. West, who was then in the zenith of his fame. Stuart soon became a favourite pupil of his master, and graduated from his school with a high reputation as a portrait painter; he ranked second to no one, in London, but Sir Joshua Reynolds. While in the metropolis, he had the good fortune to become acquainted with Burke, Fox, Sheridan, and with many of their associates. These men were not only patrons of the arts, but the friends of artists. He painted several of them in a fine style, which spread his fame far and wide. From

25

London he went to Ireland, and spent several years in Dublin. In this city he was without a rival, and had as much business as he could attend to. In the polished society of that hospitable and tasteful place he was a great favourite ; and he relished the wit and gaiety of the Irish beyond measure. Painters seldom feel contented to remain many years in one place. They are anxious to catch the admiration of many cities and different classes of society, to see new faces, and to study expression in every variety. At this time, Washington was, as his name ever will be, the idol of every lover of liberty, and the world were anxious to have a correct likeness of him. The Whigs of England were desirous that Stuart should come to the United States for this purpose. They had seen what were called likenesses of this great man, from painters, engravers, and sculptors, but still were not satisfied ; nothing, as yet, had been produced that reached their idea of him. When Stuart arrived at the city of Washington, the great man had retired from all office, and was in private life at Mount Vernon. He had been so often annoyed by every fledgling artist, that he came to the determination to sit no more for any one ; but Stuart's fame, and Mrs. Washington's solicitations, overruled his resolution, and the hero and statesman was again seated for his picture. In the chair for the painter, Washington was apt to fall into a train of thought, and become abstracted from the things around him, and of course most of the likenesses of him, show more of gravity of muscle, than of the divinity of intelligence. When he sat to Stuart, as the latter has often stated, an apathy seemed to seize him, and a vacuity spread over his countenance, most appalling to the painter. The best portrait painter of the age, was now to take the likeness of the greatest man of all ages ; and the artists and the patriots of all countries were interested in it. To have failed in getting a good likeness would have been death to the artist's fame, and a perpetual source of mortification to the people of the country. Stuart was, like Washington, not easily overcome ; he made several fruitless attempts to awaken the heroick spirit in him, by talking of battles, but in vain ; he next tried to warm up the patriot and sage, by turning the conversation to the republican ages of antiquity ; this was equally unsuccessful. At length the painter struck on the masterkey, and opened a way to his mind which he has so happily transferred to the canvass with the features of his face. In the whole of this picture, in every limb, as well as feature, the martial air of the warrior chief, is admirably mingled with the dignity and majesty of the statesman and sage. It was a proper period in the life of Washington for a good picture. The bloom and beauty of youth have no majesty or greatness in them on the canvass ; maturity and gravity are necessary to give a picture a proper effect; the lines of thought must be in the face; the marks of dangers braved, and duties done, must be there also.   Nor should the painter wait until decrepitude and the dullness of age approaches. There is a period in the life of man, when Nature seems to stop, having matured her work, to contemplate it herself, before she suffers Time to begin his ravages.   This was that moment.   The picture, like the original, was peerless.   The artist himself copied it several times with great success.   It has been copied a thousand times by others, and every copy contains something of the first likeness—no small proof of its excellence and truth.

Stuart tarried a year or two in the city of Washington, and during the time, painted John Adams, Thomas Jefferson, Mr. Madison, and many other distinguished men of our country.   He removed from Washington to Philadelphia, which was then greatly in advance of the other cities and great towns in the United States, in every branch of the fine firts.   Here, too, he was a favourite in society as well as in his profession.   He often spoke of his residence in Philadelphia with great pleasure, and frequently began some of his anecdotes with—"When I resided in the Athens of America."   His next remove was to Boston, where he resided during the remainder of his life.   At first he did not, perhaps, think of making this city a permanent residence; but there have never been many, who were comfortably situated in society there, who ever wished to change it for any other place in this country.   For several years after his coming to Boston, he was overwhelmed with business; many had to wait months for an opportunity of sitting to him; and even in his latter years he frequently had more calls than he could answer, notwithstanding a number of painters, quite eminent in their profession, had collected in Boston, and were active and attentive in their professional pursuits.   All, in his line, looked up to him as their head, and felt no jealousy of him, for his pre-eminence was generally acknowledged.   Most of the opulent families of Boston have pictures from his pencil; a house is hardly considered as properly furnished, or certainly not complete in its ornaments, without some head by Stuart.   Although he often expressed a strong desire to do something in the historical way to leave behind him, yet he never found time for the purpose.   In some of the back grounds of his portraits, he has sketched some emblematick outlines with admirable effect.   These sketches go far to show what he might have done in the historical line, if he had pursued it.

The number of his portraits is wonderful, and are, in general, fine likenesses; some few are failures; but "*Homer sometimes nods.*" He had the power of giving the best expression of a face. The mind and character of the original seems to breathe from his canvass; and if there be a fault in his best pictures, it is, that he sometimes, in the plentitude of his power in the art, threw a ray of his own genius into a countenance in which nature had given no indication that she had stolen the fire from heaven to light it up. For forty years, or more, he stood at the head of his profession as a painter of *the human face divine.*

In his person, Stuart was rather large, and his movements, in the latter part of his life, were slow and heavy, but not ungraceful. His manners had something of the formality of the old school; but it was evident, at the first blush, that he had been conversant with good society. He loved to display his powers as a conversationist, and to come in friendly collision with intelligence and wit, in order to sparkle and shine. He was sometimes a little fastidious and eccentrick: but he never lost the manners of a gentleman on any occasion. His literary acquirements were of a high order, for a professional man, constantly employed; but his early education was good, and the foundations of a classical education were well laid. His penetration was acute; for he saw at a glance the qualities of the mind of the person who came only to have an image of his person struck out. He had often accurately weighed the intellect of his sitting subject before he had finished the mechanical operation of measuring the size of his head. He reasoned upon the principles of his profession with a depth of philosophy worthy of a master ; and he always contended that a regard should be had to the moral as well as physical, in making a just portrait of a man. The capacities of his art were all known to him, and he ridiculed the numerous futile attempts to go beyond them.

The lives and works of the great artists of all ages were familiar to him as his pallet. He discoursed upon their excellences, defects, and peculiarities, as one who had read and examined them all most thoroughly. His eloquence was peculiar and attractive ; his voice was strong and deep; his enunciation clear and distinct; and his countenance came in aid of his voice, for his features were bold and lion-like, and no stranger ever passed him without mentally saying, " That is no ordinary man." It was a treat to see him in his best humour: for he was full of anecdote ; and told a story with such neatness, precision, point, and elegance of language, that it often happened, that those who came to admire his painting, went away charmed with his eloquence. By the alchymy of his genius, he distilled the essence of every topick of conversation, and gave a spirit and flavour to even playfulness and trifling. Titles, wealth, and beauty, at whose shrines the world pay their devotions, had no controlling influence over him; he was too much self-concentrated and too full of "the sin for which fell the angels," to do homage to any thing but commanding talents, and these devoted to letters and the arts. He had no respect for those engaged in the ordinary business of life; I mean that respect the world pays, and ought to bestow on prudence, economy, calculation, and thrift. Nor was he very much disposed to give a great share of praise to those who became distinguished rather by industry than by superior abilities; he really did, or effected to despise all elaborate niceties and painful finishing, for he cared for none of these himself; not that he was an advocate for careless and rapid productions, but he looked for the touches of genius, and often remarked that artists of ordinary capacity mistook *work* for *study.* He thought no man should be found among the sons of the prophets, without a good share of the true spirit of inspiration; and did not hesitate, at times, when the world were running after some new artist, to say, with some little bitterness, "That man had better have continued his pursuit for his father's lost cattle, than to have come among the prophets!" His opinions, however, of the works of young men, were, in general, candid, and often kind, if the authors were modest and desirous of instruction; but upon the pert and impudent, his satire was of the keenest sort; it came in all forms, of irony, epigram, and scourge, until the dullest brain was made to understand, and the thickest hide to feel. It was seldom that he was roused to resentment; but, when he was, his invective was fierce and terrible. He was too proud to seek admiration, but well-timed compliment was not lost on him; a love of it makes up a part of the character of every great artist.

Fickleness is an ingredient that is frequently mingled with taste and refinement. Athens, in her poudest days, gave strange evidences of this truth; and the community in which Stuart spent the latter part of his days, has, with some justice, been charged with it also. But if ever, in the restlessness of caprice, any one remarked that Stuart was growing old; that his eye had lost something of its accurary, and his hand had become tremulous; or that increasing infirmities had made him testy, the people would not listen for a moment to any such remarks; they would not give up their favourite. These rumours of the decay of his faculties sometimes reached the ears of Stuart, and suddenly some great effort of his pencil would be brought out, that showed at once that the intimations were groundless, and proved that envy, caprice, or slander, had no power over his deep rooted reputation.

The errours of men of genius—for when were men of genius without errours? are generally injurious only to themselves, and should be buried with them; but their merits should be embalmed

R 2

by their epitaphs, written by kindred spirits, and engraven on monuments and columns, and transferred to the page of history, to make up a part of their country's glory. Envy and ill nature often magnify these errours, and set them down, and con them by heart, which, when rightly understood, are only the offspring of irritable nerves and delicate fibres; and should be given over by the moralist and biographer, to the consideration of the physician; for they are mostly diseases of a physical nature.

He was impatient of criticism upon his works, even from the choice spirits who surrounded him; and in the last place of his residence, he had not a few of them; and it is to be presumed that in other cities he had as many. They did not, with all their taste and talents, dare to venture farther than just hint a defect, or an omission; and that he never received very graciously, even if his good sense induced him to adopt the suggestion. But if ignorant or vain patronizing sitters began to criticise, or find fault, he perhaps parried the first attempts with a delicate sarcasm, or a sneer, half concealed by a smile; but if this did not operate as an estoppel, and the remarks were repeated, he turned upon them with that resentful and appalling directness, that either produced silence or a quarrel. He would not bear any flippant connoisseur about him. Numerous instances have been related, and many of them believed, of his having resented a hasty word from men of the first standing in society, by refusing to finish a picture, and nothing would ever induce him to touch it again. One of these pictures, on which a dandy criticism produced a quarrel, and which is unfinished still, is one of exquisite beauty; it is three views of the beautiful face of a celebrated dame, who was then just married to a foreign magnate. It is but justice, however, to say, that it was not the lady who made the offensive remarks, but her dapper husband, who found fault with the drapery. "That you can buy," said the indignant artist, "at any milliner's shop in the city." This happened while Stuart resided in Washington. He contended that no artist should ever submit to these vexations; that they should, one and all, set their faces against them. He often remarked, that Haley, who wrote a good deal of tame poetry, should be forgiven for all this, and for lavishing so much praise on Romney, for the following lines on the painter's evils:

> "For when the canvass, with the mirror's truth,
> Reflects the perfect form of age or youth,
> The fond affections of the partial mind,
> The eye of judgement with delusions blind;
> Each mother bids him brighter tints employ,
> And give more spirit to her booby boy;

> Nor can the painter, with his utmost art,
> Express the image in the lover's heart;
> Unconscious of the change the Seasons bring,
> Autumnal beauty asks the rose of Spring;
> And vain self-love, in every age the same,
> Will fondly urge some visionary claim;
> The luckless painter, destin'd to submit,
> Mourns the lost likeness, which he once had hit;
> And, doom'd to groundless censure, bears alone
> The grievous load of errours not his own."

To one who works for gain alone, these things are no evils; he cares nothing for them, but yields to every suggestion; is a kind good man, is admired, gets his fees, and thinks no more of his work, nor of its destiny, which, probably, is to hang a while in the parlour, thence to be removed to the garret, and from there pass off to oblivion by damps or rats; but to such a painter as Stuart, who fondly hoped, and firmly believed, that he was painting for unborn ages, and that his common pictures would be sought for and valued as a Rubens or a Guido, these paltry criticisms were gall and wormwood for the moment, but were never remembered afterwards, or, if they were, they were only called up, for the amusement of some of his friends, in an hour of relaxation or merriment.

The fame of Stuart is secure: no chance can destroy it. His portraits are too numerous, and are too widely scattered, to be lost by fire or flood. Some of them will remain under any circumstances; and he has painted many men of distinction, in their day and generation, whose reputation will go down to posterity with his. There is a sort of tacit contract between a great man in the literary, political, or scientifick world, and his painter, if he, too, be distinguished, to join hand and hand, and present themselves to future ages together. On Stuart's paintings, his contemporaries have given a verdict, and it is on record, "*that his likenesses are admirable;*" and other times shall pronounce them fine paintings. He has not wasted his strength on dress and drapery, which is often admired by those it was intended to please or flatter, and in the course of a generation or two, is a subject of amusement to the descendants of the stately dame they adorn or encumber. They laugh at the niceties of ruff or stomacher, which cost weeks of labour to artists. Stuart wisely brought all his talents, and all the powers of his art, to bear upon the human countenance, which, amidst all the varieties of the race of man, in every climate, and every age of the world, still wears the image of his Maker. The seal which gave assurance of a man has never been broken or effaced. It was not that Stuart wanted the art of painting most excellent drapery. In the picture of Washington, painted for the artist's native state, and which adorns their hall of legislation, the drapery, furniture, and accompaniments, are considered superiour to the figure of Washington itself, which is one of Stuart's best paintings. He was wise in one other respect. He painted with permanent colours. If they were not so beautiful at first sight, as the delicate lakes and carmines, they were put on with a full faith in their durability. He seldom or never spoke of his colours without alluding to the melancholy fact, that most of Sir Joshua's paintings had faded, and were now out of sight.

It is often asked, of what school was your great painter? He would acknowledge no master; but if what the ancients have told us of Parrhasius and Aristides be true, he had much of their manner and spirit, and no small share of the former's self-esteem. Most certainly he had nothing of the present Italian or French schools in his compositions. Himself, his works, his taste, his conversation, his tone, were all masculine; so deeply masculine, that, in but a very few instances, did he ever succeed in making a fine picture of a great beauty. The character of so great an artist deserves a minute biography; but this is not within the plan of my work. It is said that the artists are about to erect a monument to his memory. If this be done, may some learned and tasteful brother—Trumbull, Alston, or some other one who knew him well—write his epitaph, in the spirit of admiring truth; and make his biography a portrait that may bear to be placed in the Temple of Taste, along side the productions of his pencil. He died at the advanced age of seventy-four, in the full possession of his faculties.

As a miniature painter, the reputation of Edward G. Malbone, formerly of Newport, Rhode Island, stands first of all who have come forward in this line of the art. I had prepared a short memoir of the early history of his life, from the best sources in my power to command; but, on receiving some facts of his rise and progress in his profession, from a literary gentleman of Newport, which, from his character, and from the means he had of obtaining them, cannot fail to be interesting to all; for they come, as it were, from the nursery, and the school-room, and the mansion house, with the stamp of genuineness on them. But as I shall reserve this for some more ample page, I will make a few observations on an artist, who was the first that ever gave me the slightest taste for the delicate touches of the miniature painter. It has generally been considered, that miniature painting was of an order less, in the scale of genius, than portrait painting. It has been said to compare with it, as the sonnet does with the ode; but I could never see the force of the remark; why it should not require as much taste and genius to paint a picture " in little," as in great, I cannot understand. The image of the original must be as accurately caught, and as faithfully delineated; the touch must be more nice, and the tints more delicate; a susceptibility of the beautiful and the refined must be more requisite in the miniature than the portrait or historical painter; and it is necessary that he should study nature more minutely; the exquisite tints of the flower or the pebble are to be examined by him with an intensity that cannot be required in one who sweeps with his eye the rude crag and lofty mountain, and catches the bold features of romantick scenery; nor of one who paints a full sized man. It has been said to be a rule of nature, to send taste to reside with beauty, or at least to allow him to learn his first lessons where she is to be found; and the history of Malbone is in accordance with this principle; for the shores of Greece never presented more beautiful subjects for the pencil than those on which the artist first opened his eyes; and he has done honour to his birth place, for perhaps there never was an artist, certainly never one so little acquainted with the rules of art, who gave such ethereal touches to his paintings as Malbone. With the most exact likenesses, he seemed to avoid all the coarse, earthly particles in his subjects, leaving only enough of matter to express the intellectual spirit and character they contained. Malbone's mind, like a fine piece of wax, seemed first to take the impression of that which he was to transfer to the ivory; and then it was found there, coloured by nature in her loveliest manner. The early part of Malbone's education could not be considered profound or classical, but such were his habits of critical observation, and close attention to study, that he was soon distinguished for his intellectual acquirements. He perhaps dwelt too much on the refined portions of knowledge to make a robust mind; but there is more power in a delicate one than is generally imagined; as one bred in the bowers of learning, may be as lofty and commanding as one accustomed to the toils of the chase or war. He was much admired in society; for his conversation was rich and refined, and it never failed to charm, his life being as pure as his taste. He had seen too much of men to be bigoted or vain; and he polished his own by the manners of all; but copied none.

Malbone was unfortunate, at times, in his colours, although he made many chemical attempts to improve the old colouring; and it is to be deeply regretted, that in some of his finest miniatures, a winding-sheet resemblance is all that remains of her who was once as beautiful as an angel. Other paintings of his may have been more lasting than those I have seen. The touches of the finest pencil, in these fading colours, are but little better than

26

the words of the orator who gives his eloquence to Echo, and trusts
to the remembrance of that alone for immortality.   He lived before
the time had fairly come for the just appreciation of such talents.
The generation that achieved the revolution, had enough to do to
fight it out, and in repairing their fortunes after the conflict was
over ; they and their children were busy in fixing every constitutional principle, and guarding their rights by every form of law ;
and those who were not directly engaged, were pursuing commerce
and agriculture, and laying the foundation of manufactures; therefore, there were but few who could justly appreciate such a delicate
artist as Malbone.

Another artist of some celebrity in his time, was Edward Savage.
Feeling the inspiration of a painter in his native land, he procured
means and went abroad, and put himself for a while under the direction of West, and travelled into Italy.   Before he left this country he had painted the Washington family, which, as a print, is now
found in every part of this country.   Finding no person willing, or
sufficiently at leisure, to undertake the engraving of this picture, he
took up the graver himself, and made a very respectable work of it,
for that age, when there were but few good engravings published
in London.   Those who knew Savage always spoke of him as a
man of diversified talents and great industry ; but he divided his
time among so many things, that he could not do himself justice in
any one of them ; yet he did all he undertook to do much better
than could be expected of one engaged in so many matters of taste
and art.   He commenced a museum first in New-York, and then
brought it to Boston ; and it is the same which now forms a part
of that extensive collection, the New-England Museum.   He died
in retirement, having devoted his latter days to agricultural pursuits.

Col. John Trumbull, who is now living, was the contemporary
of Stuart and Johnson, an acquaintance of Copley's, and a student
with West.   His life has been more full of incident, than his brother artists', for he has been soldier, politician, and traveller, as
well as painter.   In him the love of his art was early developed.
It began in the nursery ; and before he was prepared to enter college he had painted several pictures ; and while at Cambridge, in
his leisure moments, he indulged himself in painting.   Some of
these efforts, before he had received a single lesson, were seen by
Copley, who bestowed upon them a cordial smile of approbation.
He then had but a faint expectation of making the art his main
pursuit.   After leaving college in 1773, still quite young, he went
to his father's house in Connecticut, and was there employed in
the acquirement of general knowledge, and meditating on his fu-

ture course in life. The times were then difficult. The political
storms were gathering rapidly, and the learned professions promised but little. A belief that an appeal to arms would be necessary, induced all the citizens to be active in getting a knowledge
of their use, and they turned their eyes every way for instructers
in the art of war. Trumbull, like Knox, Brooks, Hamilton, and
many other spirited young men, had turned his attention to the
study of the elements of military tacticks, and was greatly in advance of his fellow-citizens in general, in this branch of information; and on his joining a train-band, they made him an officer, and
he began his drill; and in June, 1775, he was found a Brigade
Major in the Connecticut line, at the seat of war, discharging his
duty. During that summer he was under the eye of Washington,
who promoted him, for his talents, to be his aid, the second he had
appointed; Mifflin had come on in that capacity from Pennsylvania
with him. In the fall of 1776, he was appointed adjutant-general of
the northern army. In this capacity he acted until the autumn of
1777, with great credit to himself, and advantage to the army, in bringing the raw recruits, then pouring in at the north, to a tolerable
state of discipline. While in this office, he thought himself superseded, which his pride could not brook, and he resigned his commission and returned to his native state. Still the professions held
out no alluring prospect, and he made up his mind to become an
artist.

As soon as this determination was fixed, he made his way to
England, to place himself under the guidance and instruction of his
countryman, Mr. West, then at the head of the artists in England.
Here he had sheathed his sword, and shut his ears to all political
strife, and was advancing his knowledge in the bosom of the arts;
his love of country was neither destroyed or abated, but every thing
justified, yea, required his silence; and in quiet he was going on,
when, at the close of 1780, the news reached England that Andre
was taken and executed. The ministers received the news in a
paroxysm of rage, and the first impression on their minds was revenge. They had received an intimation that the young American
gentleman, under the instruction of Mr. West, had held, in the
American army, a rank similar to that of Andre in the British.
This was enough; an order was issued to seize Col. Trumbull and
confine him to the tower, on the principle of the *lex talionis*. He
was then brought before a board of commissioners for an examination, in order to obtain all the facts in the case. The youthful officer
bore himself proudly before them; but freely stated to them the
whole course of his military life; and the causes of his leaving it;
avowed his unceasing attachment to his country, with a full belief

of her success in the struggle; and urged, yea, dared them to an immediate trial. He gave them also to understand, that his father was at that time governor of the state of Connecticut, and had several hundred prisoners under his charge; all these would be considered as hostages for his safety. This fearless course was rather troublesome to the premier; he wished to allay the publick ferment, and yet did not venture to put in jeopardy the lives of innocent men, who might be in the hands of the Americans as prisoners. No preparations were made for bringing Trumbull to trial, although he demanded it as often as he could. A considerable portion of the British nation considered his fate as sealed, and his death as certain. After a while he was removed to more comfortable quarters, but as securely confined. During his imprisonment, Fox, Burke, and the leaders of the opposition, often visited him, but gave no decided opinions on the course the ministry would pursue. At length it was agreed that Burke should have an interview with Lord North. Burke could always approach North, even in the bitterest moments of party strife. They were both gentlemen and scholars, and these characters, towards each other, they never forgot. After this interview, Trumbull was released on bail; but an order instantly followed for his departure forthwith. He went to France, and from thence returned to America. During this difficulty, West was the warm and unshaken friend of his pupil, and proved to him that his virtues were as exalted as his talents, that his heart was as true and steady as his hand. Col. Trumbull returned to England after the peace of 1783, and was most graciously received by his old friends, and patronized by them in his profession. During this visit he painted the SORTIE OF GIBRALTAR; a production which Horace Walpole pronounced the best that had ever been executed this side the Alps.

After this period, for some years, Col. Trumbull was engaged in political life; first as secretary of legation to Mr. Jay, when he made his treaty with Great Britain; and afterwards as one of the commissioners under that treaty with Mr. Gore and Pinckney, on the part of the United States. Up to this period, and afterwards, before he returned to the United States, several productions from his pencil attracted the notice of the publick, and added to his reputation as an artist, on this and on the other side of the water. But his political life, and the details of his professional career, must be left to the biographer; they are too voluminous for our lectures; but it is proper for me to notice the labours of Col. Trumbull that are now in the possession of the nation, for they are identified with our history and his fame. The first of these pictures is THE DECLARATION OF INDEPENDENCE. This as well as the other three are purely historical;

there is no fiction in their composition. The canvass is large, and the group numerous, forty-seven in number. It was a difficult subject for the pencil. It was, in a measure, a still life scene, solemn and quiet—minds intent upon a great subject, but it was the same to nearly all; for it was no triumph of party, but the determination and decision of nearly the whole group. Those who doubted were equally anxious as patriots; but only questioned the expediency of the measure at that moment. Decision is marked in every countenance, and high-souled resolve is delineated in every feature. The demeanour of the whole is unique, and the subsequent events have given it the cast of political consequence it has now assumed. It was only a bold and noble act then; it is now a god-like one. In this picture most of the likenesses were from life, and of course a great many of the portraits of that august body have been preserved, which could not otherwise have been effected; for no one had enthusiasm sufficient to set about making a gallery of them at that time. Most of them, yea, all of them, with only one exception, have gone down to join the congregation of the dead since that period; and he stands majestick in the lonely waste of ages. This picture has been often criticised; but, like the rest of them, the more it is examined the more it has been admired.

The surrender of the army under the command of Lieutenant General Burgoyne, has a martial air. It was intended by the painter to have such an effect. The *pomp, pride*, and *circumstance of war*, were thrown into it, for it was an eventful day to the colonies. The solemn, suppressed elevation of the spirits of the conquerors, the steadfast gaze of "*young eyed wonder;*" for there were in that army but few who had seen service before, and none perhaps who had seen the surrender of an army, particularly a British army; certainly none who had seen so important a one. The autumnal sky, the *sear and yellow leaf*, is exhibited as it should be, in this painting. The likenesses of these heroes are faithful; so very true, that an old soldier, examining this picture, in the winter of eighteen hundred and twenty-seven, pointed out eleven faces which he knew, most of whom he had not seen since that period, a lapse of nearly half a century. This speaks a volume in favour of the truth of the picture. The number of figures in the foreground is less than in the picture of signing the declaration of independence, being only twenty-seven in number; but in the distant view the troops of either army is seen, and this gives great relief to the whole. The crest-fallen countenance of Burgoyne is very conspicuous. The group is not crowded, and there seems space enough for all that was transacted at this important crisis.

THE TAKING OF CORNWALLIS is of a similar character, but is

S

managed by the painter so as to appear quite unlike. This picture is more easily read than the other, and there is no point about it that can be mistaken, without the slightest reference to the explanatory account, excepting a few of the names of the French, and a few of the American officers, whose countenances were not sufficiently known to be readily named. The discipline of the American troops, which surprised and astonished the English general, is admirably seen in this picture. Many of the American army were then veterans in war, and they showed Earl Cornwallis that against such troops it would be in vain for the king his master to contend any longer. There are thirty-four large figures in this picture, and a fine background, exhibiting the British forces marching between two lines of the victorious army to lay down their arms. A greater number of that noble animal, the horse, were introduced than in the picture of the taking of Burgoyne, which to many gives it more of a military air. Many of the likenesses in this picture are also admirable. This was the closing scene of the revolutionary war.

WASHINGTON RESIGNING HIS COMMISSION TO CONGRESS, is the last of the four great pictures the property of the United States, and is, perhaps, to most spectators, the most interesting of the whole, rather, however, from its moral than natural sublimity. A warrior in the prime of manhood, on whom the glow of manly beauty was still to be seen; who had accepted the command of an undisciplined army, in every way unprepared for war, which had nothing but the justice of their cause, and an indomitable courage to support it; and who, after enduring with them every hardship and privation, had now hastened to resign his commission, without rewards or stipulations of honours from his countrymen, was a scene unparalleled in the history of nations. This scene exhibited the greatness of the patriot, free from the vulgar ambition of the military chieftain; a triumphal car, or an ovation, decreed by his country, would have diminished the effect of this solemn unostentatious ceremony, which deserves to be handed down to the latest posterity, to show how much above the level of ordinary greatness was the leader of our armies in those perilous times. It is of importance to us to retain the likenesses of some of this congress, which had then become a small and feeble body, but still contained some excellent men; but it is more important to preserve an accurate likeness of General Washington, which this is said to be, by those who knew him at that period of life. Stuart's picture of him was painted several years afterwards, when a portion of the soldier was lost in the statesman. Trumbull's was taken when Washington was unharnessing from the fight, and the chivalrous spirit of the warrior was in every word and look. This likeness should be often copied for those who wish to preserve his lineaments as a soldier.

It is to be deeply regretted that the opportunity of extending the number of the remembrances of historical events, arising out of our struggle for independence, should have been suffered to escape us. We have only a third part of those which might have been obtained and kept as rich memorials of that age. The veteran from whose pencil we have had these four pictures, was obliged to end his labours from false notions of economy arising up among our national representatives, while his eye had not lost its accuracy, nor his hand its steadiness. A youth of prudence has given him a vigorous old age. Col. Trumbull is not only at the head of the historical painters in this country, but is among our most accomplished gentlemen and scholars. A fine early education, improved by travel, and with more than half a century's intimate acquaintance with the most polished and enlightened minds in Europe and America, have enriched his understanding with vast stores of knowledge upon almost every subject, have given to his manners ease and grace, and to his style of conversation a charm and finish, that make him the delight of all circles of fashion and taste in our country. He connects the former with the present age, and is an honour to both.

New institutions, it is said, develope new talents, or awaken those which have lain dormant. The militia of the United States, which was organized soon after the adoption of the Federal Constitution, and which in some parts of the country grew up at once into a formidable body of well disciplined men, who were fond of every military appendage, and prided themselves on their standards, every company having a right to one. An emulation soon arose in the militia, for those of great splendour and taste. The custom of carrying a waving standard, made of silk or light stuff, was of eastern origin. It is said that the custom was drawn from the standard of Mahomet, which was the turban of a convert chieftain, who, on espousing the prophet's cause, fixed it, on an emergency, to the head of his lance, and unfurled it to the breeze. The standards of the christian warriors were of a different appearance. Those of the crusaders were small and square, and drawn tight over a frame. The waving ensigns were first adopted by the maritime nations of Europe, from the mussulmans', as being far more beautiful, and more easily managed, than others; and then they came into use among the military forces of the same nations. We took our colours from England; but with true characteristick ambition, we have given it a more magnificent expansion; we were not confined by the laws of any herald office. The GARTER of Arms had nothing to do

with our *northern* or *southern* ridings; we had no fees to pay for
armorial bearings, and no fears of forfeitures for trespass on another's rights, or assumption of what was not our own. The independent corps, as those who have certain privileges, have been
called with us, took great pains to appear, not only "completely
armed and equipt, as the law directs," but also to support a most
splendid uniform, and other imposing appendages. A superb ban-
ner was therefore indispensably necessary;—to effect this, they employed painters of taste, whenever they could be found, to design
and paint them. Among the first painters in this branch was Johnson, whose talents we have spoken of in a preceding part of this
lecture; but after a few years he was surpassed by Penniman. He
has brought this style of painting to very great perfection. His designs are often classical and ingenious, and frequently have an appropriate bearing upon the name of the corps, or on some circumstance of its history. The fashion has been prevalent for young
ladies to present these standards to military companies, with patriotick addresses, and eloquent prayers for the prosperity and success
of the brave defenders of the country; and if but few opportunities
have been found for the youthful soldier to fulfil his promise to the
fair—that he never would prove a recreant—not one particle of the
admiration bestowed on the beauty and elegance of the standard
was lost on the artist who painted it; he became freshly inspired
by the smile of beauty, and the publick admiration.

Engraving is a sister art to painting, and follows her in every age.
This art has grown up among us with astonishing rapidity. Thirty
years since, there were not more than half a dozen engravers in the
United States, and these of a secondary order, as their works in our
periodicals of that age will show; but since Bradford published the
Encyclopedia, the art has been cultivated with zeal in the United
States; and there are now to be found a very considerable number
of engravers, whose works are admirable, and are held in high estimation. A taste for fine engravings is extending far and wide in
our country, and patronage makes artists.

Sculpture is now attracting the attention of some of our young
men of talents, who have produced some fine specimens of the art.
They will find encouragement, for there are every day exhibited
new proofs of the partiality of the opulent in this country for this
branch of the fine arts.

LECTURE XII.

But, then, it must be remembered, that these men were bred and educated in the principles of a free government. 'Twas hence they derived
that high and manly spirit, which made them the admiration of after ages.

HARRIS'S HERMES.

'Tis LIBERTY, that is formed to nurse the sentiments of great geniuses : to
inspire them with hope, to push forward the propensity of contest, one with
another, and the generous emulation of being the first in rank.

LONGINUS.

A good orator should pierce the ear, allure the eye, and invade the mind
of his hearer.

Words are not all, nor matter is not all, nor gestures; yet together they
are. 'Tis most moving in an orator, when the soul seems to speak as well
as the tongue.

Surely, nothing decks an orator more, than a judgement, able to conceive
and utter.

The scriptures are penned in a tongue of deep expression ; wherein
almost every word hath a metaphorical sense, which does illustrate by some
allusion.

Nor is it such a fault as some make it, now and then to let a philosopher
or a poet come in and wait, and give a trencher to this banquet of eloquence.
St. Paul is a precedent for it.

I never knew a good tongue, that wanted ears to hear it.

I will honour sacred eloquence in her plain trim ; but I wish to meet her
in her graceful jewels, not that they give addition to her goodness, but that
she is more persuasive in working on the soul she meets with.

OWEN PELTHAM, on Pulpit Oratory.

EVER since the Almighty gave to man the faculty of speech, he
has been proud of using the prerogative well. In every age, to
speak well has been thought to be one of the highest human accomplishments, as well as necessary instrument, in gaining and
sustaining power and authority. It has led to the direction of the
affairs of nations, and to the establishment of creeds in philosophy
and religion. The great lawgiver of Israel felt and avowed the
want of eloquence in undertaking his divine legation.

"And Moses said unto the Lord, O my Lord, I am not eloquent,
neither heretofore, nor since thou hast spoken unto thy servant : but
I am slow of speech, and of a slow tongue.

"And the Lord said unto him, Who hath made man's mouth? or who maketh the dumb, or deaf, or the seeing, or the blind? have not I the Lord?

"Now therefore go, and I will be with thy mouth, and teach thee what thou shalt say.

"And he said, O my Lord, send, I pray thee, by the hand of him whom thou wilt send.

"And the anger of the Lord was kindled against Moses, and he said, Is not Aaron the Levite thy brother? I know that he can speak well. And also, behold, he cometh forth to meet thee, he seeth thee, he will be glad in his heart.

"And thou shalt speak unto him, and put words in his mouth: and I will be with thy mouth, and with his mouth, and will teach you what ye shall do.

"And he shall be thy spokesman unto the people: and he shall be, even he shall be to thee instead of a mouth, and thou shalt be to him instead of God."

The first efforts of poetick inspiration were those that gave immortality to eloquence. The different kinds of speakers are described by Homer with a precision and beauty that has never been surpassed; like the productions of the Grecian chisel, they remain as models to this day. All religions have been promulgated and supported by eloquence; even ours, which descended from heaven, was preached with tongues of fire, the miraculous gift of its author. Error has been propagated by eloquence; Mahomet was the most eloquent man of his race, and composed his Koran in the choicest verses of a lovely literature.

A passion for eloquence is not confined to civilized man. The sons of the forest are as fond of it as the best cultivated minds in polished life. Indian history is full of the passion for eloquence. The speech of Logan is only a common specimen of their capacity for high attainments in the noble art.

When the Winnebagoes had a deputation at the seat of government last year, the interview between them and the President of the United States was conducted with great ceremony. After sitting a while in the audience chamber, the most aged chief, then ninety years old, bald headed, with his manly arms and chest bare, arose and advanced to the president; in a few words he stated the object of his visit, and his happiness in finding the great father of his people so kind and good, but should speak but little, but leave the details and exemplifications of the mission they were sent on, to the orator of the tribe. The aged chief retired with great dignity; the signal given, the orator advanced; he was of fine size and noble proportions. He stood an almost naked bust, and extending his arm, said, that he was not a chief by birth, but was made one by the fame of his talents, and by the power of his eloquence. He was a warrior who had never committed a crime, nor sunk to any meanness, or *ever told a falsehood.* His whole demeanour was full of grave dignity, and solemn serenity. After this interview, even the aged chief, who had kept sober before, joined in a most riotous, drunken frolick, while the speaker kept himself from the errors of his brethren, and retired from the scene, to preserve the honours of a Winnebago orator.

Eloquence was the great engine by which Tecumseh rose to power. He was one of three brothers at a birth. The Indians of his native tribe, as well as those of most other tribes, have a superstitious dread of such prolifick mothers. They consider more than one at a birth as an omen of famine, and the mother with her children are banished; but by a wise direction of providence, the evil is in some degree neutralized by the impression on the savage mind, that the tribe who receive the fugitives will prosper for their kindness. The three boys were brought up together, and were most affectionate to each other; being strangers, as it were, among those with whom they lived, made them unite most closely in all their plans. One of them fell in an attack at Nashville. Tecumseh tried his powers as an orator, and succeeded most admirably; his brother had not the natural gifts for one, or it was not politick to have two orators in one tribe, still he must do something for family aggrandizement; and with a most admirable reach of thought, Tecumseh made him a prophet, and was among the first who professed to believe in his inspirations; he preached them every where, seemed to be guided by them, and keeping the prophet as much veiled as possible, promulgated, himself, the wonders of coming time; only, however, as a mouth piece. It succeeded to a charm, indeed. It was Indian eloquence that gave Indian prophecy its influence; for it has degenerated to mummery since that eloquence has ceased. By eloquence this mighty savage collected his followers and made them steadfast friends, who were ready to pour out their blood at his command. By his eloquence he made those of different tribes, naturally jealous of each other, partizans, warriors, devotees, or whatever he pleased. There was a charm about this orator of the wilderness that Demosthenes and Cicero never had; he was as brave as eloquent, as mighty in deeds as in words. The bravery of the great orators of antiquity, has been questioned, and they laid no claim to a double portion of the Winnebagoe's veracity.

Eloquence is almost as various in its character as personal appearance; yet so many of its striking points are general, that we can describe it by considering a few classes of orators. The first of these orders of eloquence, and the most charming of all of them, may be called social eloquence; that which is under the patronage of the household gods; the eloquence of the fireside, and the drawing-room; all that belongs to the charities and pleasant associations of life. The language of ordinary instruction; of joyous festivity; of gayety; of reproof, anger, and of love itself, belongs to this order. It is more practised than studied; and has more influence over the affairs of men than all the other kinds put together; but it is so unambitious in its forms, that we are not aware of its force, or elegance. There is no hour that it is not wanted, and every little domestic circumstance requires it. It sweetens the morning beverage, and spices the evening posset; it sparkles in every glass, and beams from every eye; and if it cannot turn water to wine, as in the miracle, it can give to wine, as it is poured into the cup, a Falernian ripeness, that a voyage round the world would not effect.

The next class is the lowest order of *publick speaking;* and is the most common, and, in most things of a publick nature, is indispensable. It consists in the capacity and skill of arranging one's thoughts in a fair manner; and of spreading them in good language before an audience. This grade of elocution is found in the courts of justice, the halls of legislation, and in all publick business places. It is as much as a great proportion of publick speakers aspire to, and perhaps as much as most of them could attain in the ordinary pursuits of life.

The next grade is the former, with the additional power of exciting more than an ordinary interest in the subject under discussion, by happy arrangement, earnest delivery, with the power of now and then striking a chord of the heart with a master hand, or throwing a flash of unexpected light upon every listener, and adding to all this a striking ingenuity in evading difficulties, and seizing favourable opportunities of impressing important points. A knowledge of human nature is a necessary ingredient in this order of eloquence. Men are creatures of feeling, passion, prejudice, and caprice, as well as of reason and of judgement, and must be studied to be controlled or influenced by the publick speaker. Every portion of our country is blessed by the possession of such men, who hold a commanding station in society; and particularly if they have added to this grade of eloquence, moral virtue and high intellectual acquirements; and the very possession of this talent presupposes a highly respectable advancement in the various branches of knowledge. This class of speakers take the lead in all ordinary business in the courts of justice, and in deliberative bodies. In all our state legislatures some dozen or two of these men may be seen, visit them when you will, full of matter, and one or more of them you will find engaged in the courts in every important cause of litigation. These are what our fathers used to call "*good commonwealth's men;*" for business is safe in their hands. They are too intelligent for demagogues or dupes, and are not often inordinately ambitious. The lesser men are those who run the scrub race of popularity, and jostle each other from the course, assuming much consequence, but possessing little merit.

The last and highest order of eloquence is susceptible of many subdivisions; more, perhaps, than the inferior grades; but it must contain all that is valuable in those inferior grades, with a greater grasp of thought and more ample stores of knowledge. This high and commanding power is inconsistent with petty views and absorbing selfishness. To give it all its influence, there must be something in it of the apostle's purity and the prophet's fire. It is confined to no place, nor to any class of men. It blazes in the pulpit and illumines the court room, but it is not confined to them or to the halls of legislation. The true orator wants not place to give him inspiration; wherever he moves, the oracle goes with him. A stone or stump will answer for a tripod, and to him the common air is full of Delphick incense.

There can be no lack of opportunity for acquiring and displaying eloquence in this country. There are in the United States twenty-four state legislatures, consisting of more than one hundred and fifty members to each body, on an average. These deliberative assemblies are in session for more than two months in each year, and engaged in matters of consequence to the publick; in softening the hard features of the common law, or providing for internal improvements, chartering banks, or creating other corporations for publick institutions, guided by private individuals. Many of these subjects create warm debates, for pecuniary interest is quite as wide awake as ambition, and often something of both is found in such discussions; local policy and private interest often give a piquancy and spirit to publick speaking, that no general impressions of duty can give.

Our civil and criminal tribunals are so many forums of eloquence, and much business is done in them. There are at least thirty thousand verdicts of juries returned yearly in all our courts, and many of them involve matters of deep interest, either of a publick or private nature; and when to these are added all the other opportunities in equity, arbitrations, &c., what excuse have we for not making good speakers? And these are not the only schools of eloquence, for there is not a cattle show had, or a bridge built, but affords a chance for a speech or two. Meetings for political pur-

poses are constantly convened for the selection of candidates for
state assemblies or Congress, and harangues are made on these
occasions without stint.   Charity, too, has her train of orators,
and her style of elocution, she strikes the chords of the heart with
an hundred hands, and sometimes " *creates a soul under the ribs
of death.*"

Her sister, Religion, besides her half million sermons and lectures
each revolving year, at the altar, has also her numerous associations for diffusing light and knowledge, which call forth some exquisite strains of eloquence.

It is a great mistake to judge of American eloquence, altogether,
from the speakers in Congress ; but most foreigners seem to think
that in that body is concentrated all the knowledge and eloquence
of the country.   Congress, undoubtedly, has its share of good
speakers, but no monopoly of them.

It has often been remarked in England, that the literary men
who visit the house of lords or commons but occasionally, are
disappointed in the eloquence of the speakers.   It is so with those
who, from abroad, or from various parts of our country, visit Washington to hear the debates in Congress.   This is very natural, for
they can seldom give a rational account of their anticipations; for
distance, the imposing nature of a national legislature, and the recollection of the great men who flourished in that body, and some
knowledge of the great men who are now members of it, fill the
mind with lofty but undefined impressions respecting the eloquence
of such an assembly.   But we must look at this body closely to get
at the truth; a single glance will mislead us; we must look at it in
its elements.   To take any ordinary day's business for a criterion
of talent in Congress, would be egregiously wrong.   The slovenly
and careless air of some would mislead, and the great zeal of others,
personally interested, could hardly be accounted for upon any
principle of patriotism.   There is a greater diversity of interests
than of minds in such a body, and to judge of them fairly, one
must be thoroughly acquainted with them, and also with the course
of business.   To reason correctly upon our national legislature,
we must go to the elements of which it is composed.   It has been
called the great Amphyctionick council; but the parallel runs
but a little way.   It was not modelled on it, but decidedly on the
British Parliament, and is governed by the fundamental rules of
that body.

Forty years only have elapsed since the adoption of the federal
constitution.   There were then but thirteen states to form a compact; there are now twenty-four in it.   In these forty years there
have been in both branches of the national legislature, seventeen

hundred and twenty-two members; twelve hundred and eighty-seven of them in the house of representatives, from the old states, and one hundred and seventy-nine from the new states without the limits of the old territory; two hundred and thirty-seven senators of the old states, and seventy-nine from the new ones, making, in the whole, the first mentioned number of seventeen hundred and seventy-two. Perhaps it would be gratifying to some to see the numbers belonging to the several states: Maine has had, to the close of the nineteenth Congress, fourteen representatives, and two senators; New-Hampshire fifty-eight representatives, and seventeen senators; Vermont, forty-five representatives, and fourteen senators; Massachusetts, one hundred and forty-three representatives, and nineteen senators; Rhode Island, nineteen representatives, and seventeen senators; Connecticut, fifty-five representatives, and fourteen senators; New-York, two hundred and fifty-five representatives, and twenty-one senators; New-Jersey, fifty-four representatives, and nineteen senators; Pennsylvania, one hundred and seventy-five representatives, and fifteen senators; Delaware, fifteen representatives, and seventeen senators; Maryland, eighty-five representatives, and seventeen senators; Virginia, one hundred and forty-six representatives, and twenty-two senators; North Carolina, one hundred and two representatives, and twelve senators; South Carolina, seventy-six representatives, and thirteen senators; Georgia, forty-five representatives, and twenty senators; Kentucky, sixty representatives, and twenty senators; Tennessee, thirty-eight representatives, and eighteen senators; Ohio, thirty-six representatives, and thirteen senators; Louisiana, six representatives, and nine senators; Illinois, five representatives, and four senators; Mississippi, seven representatives, and five senators; Missouri, five representatives, and two senators; Indiana, nine representatives, and four senators; Alabama, four representatives, and five senators. There have been nine delegates from the several territories. Some few have been counted twice in the foregoing estimation, when they had come to Congress the second time, after an interval of years. These, probably, are not so many as there were new ones returned for the twentieth Congress. All these have had a hand in making our code of laws, which has grown up within the last forty years. This body has contained, in the worst of times, a very considerable number of men of talents and integrity, who have laboured for their country's weal. But a small portion of the names of the whole number, however, will go down to posterity as orators and statesmen.

The constant changes in these legislative bodies, and the very considerable number of persons in them, though certainly not very

large, diminishes individual responsibility, and is one of the causes
of those agitations which arise in every Congress. Old members
are desirous of keeping up their hard-earned distinction, and new
men are fierce to become conspicuous; the latter let off their
arrows, to show the nation with what vigour they can bend the
bow; but it frequently happens, that after a few ineffectual efforts,
many of them are heard of no more.

The subjects before congress are not often of great importance,
but merely matters of our own domestic relations, for we have but
little legislating on foreign relations. Local questions, on which
some little sectional interest or opinion turns, often excite more
attention than those of great magnitude to the nation. It is such
questions as these that call up the fire, and not unfrequently cause
to flow all the venom of party. Many young members think they
must send their constituents a speech now and then, for a two-fold
reason, to show them that they are of some consequence at Washington, and to secure their next election; and it will not be denied
by any man of honesty, sagacity, and experience, that much of the
time of Congress is taken up in effecting this object.

A high standard of eloquence is expected of this body; but there
are many reasons operating against making or finding a great many
first rate speakers in Congress. In the first place, the hall of representatives is too large for easy, natural speaking. The sweetest
and richest tones of the human voice are often those of small compass and volume. In such an immense space as is contained within the walls of that hall, delicate voices are but faintly heard, or
entirely drowned; and when the voice is not distinctly heard, the
audience, whether spectators or members, after a few painful struggles to hear, give it up; and probably by locomotion or by conversation, prevent those from hearing who might have caught something of the argument, if a profound silence among the audience
had reigned in the room. The bold and full mouth speakers, by
putting forth all their strength of lungs, may, sometimes, be heard
by most of the members; but then these vociferating and stentorian
efforts seem to be giving only a wordy energy to the subject, and
magnifying trifles by the power of sound. Emphasis, which should
be used only as discriminating one part of a sentence from another,
is, in this hall, used merely to be heard. There is, to an enlightened
mind, something almost ludicrous in hearing a man detailing common place matters, and pronouncing plain maxims, in a voice of
thunder. The voice raised to the highest pitch, has no proper in-
flexions, cadences, or euphony, and often not any measure, but goes
on in that monotonous, screamy manner, so offensive to all who
have cultivated ears. The house of commons bears no propor-

tion in point of size to this hall; yet it is made to accommodate six hundred and fifty-eight members, and here there are but two hundred and sixteen, all told.

So much for the house; but it must be confessed that the business of Congress affords but few of those displays of eloquence we have heard of in deliberative assemblies. The general business of legislation is dull, and requires only attention; for these occasions the members make no preparation, and of course produce but little effect. A spectator in the gallery hears the broken echoes of the voice, oftener than the natural tones of it; and he soon grows tired, if not disgusted, with the subject and the speaker. By a continuance of these evils, the publick are disposed to give up their expectations of hearing speeches, on common occasions, remarkable for elegance in language, or happy in delivery. They turn to the papers for speeches, and these again deceive them; for there is not one speech out of twenty given to the publick as they are delivered. The reporter, according to custom, is bound to make the orator talk good English, at least, and say nothing absurd, if nothing very smart; while the speaker very often pays no regard to rules in the delivery. The highest grade of American elocution, therefore, is not to be looked for in the house of representatives, except upon particular occasions, and from those who do not often gratify the publick with a speech. "*The high and palmy state*" of American eloquence, was during the first ten years of the forty since the adoption of the constitution. The causes of its falling off are obvious. The time then was not wasted on trivial subjects and personal bickerings; there was business to be done, and they set about it in good earnest; and when proper opportunities occurred for eloquence, it was found of a manly, vigorous, classical order. They were well educated men, selected for their intelligence and character among their fellow citizens. Let it not be understood that we think that our present Congress is wanting in talent, or in information. No; we are as well aware as any can be, that our national legislature abounds in men gifted by nature, and imbued with learning; men who, on all great occasions, come forward and show the depth of their resources, and their power of investigation, and exhibit integrity, talent, and eloquence, sufficient to redeem the reputation of any body of men, and to wipe the stain from the national escutcheon; men by the light of whose minds we have been illumined, and by whose virtuous and exalted feelings we have been warmed and enamoured. These are the hope of their country, the salt of the land; but who are aroused only on great occasions, and will not enter into all the pitiful squabbles of the day, nor contend with ignorance and vulgarity for the mastery in the race for popularity. Mighty minds are seldom profuse of effort, or hasty in

T   28

conflicts; they wait until the occasion demands, and the subject justifies an interposition.

No country on earth has ever laboured harder to make orators than our own. In addition to the fifty-three colleges, where classical educations are given, there are hundreds of minor institutions in which every rule of rhetorick is committed to memory; and every student can give you all the maxims, from Blair, Campbell, and others, necessary to make an orator; can tell you when to extend the arm, balance the body, raise the eyes, quicken the utterance, elevate the voice, and all the other golden rules to build up a Demosthenes or a Chatham. We have had most of the great dramatick actors from Europe to teach us; to those of our mother tongue we have paid great attention, from Hodgkinson to Macready. Fennel came to teach us to read, Ogilvie to speak; and teachers have swarmed upon our shores, and we have followed them, and paid them extravagant sums for years, for instruction; but our eloquence is not much benefited by all this. Our canons of criticism, no doubt, have been multiplied, and our taste grown more fastidious by all their precepts and examples; but for all this, our great orators have not increased in proportion to the number of publick speakers. It may be asked, "do you mean to infer that all these rules and criticisms are of no advantage to the youthful aspirant in elocution?" We do not say this; but we do say, that all the rules in the world will not alone make an orator. The seeds of eloquence are sown while on the maternal bosom, and are developed with the first powers of utterance. It is taught in the nursery, in the primary, secondary, as well as in the high schools. It consists in the education of the human voice, together with the human mind.

All property that comes down to us from our ancestors receives the name of patrimony, as coming from our fathers, and as acquired and maintained by them, except our language, the most noble of all things we inherit, and this is called our *mother tongue*—a just and beautiful compliment to maternal instruction. It goes to say, that the elements of our language are acquired before the father's care begins. How much more sweet and noble is this term, *our mother tongue*, than that of *vernacular language*. The origin of the latter is mean, compared with the former, notwithstanding its classical decent. A *verna* was a bondman or bond-woman among the Romans of the class of the Nothi, who were household slaves, but had certain rights, which could not be taken from them. The vernæ, from whence vernacular, were instructed in all the niceties of the Latin language, in order to teach the children the vernacular in its purity. The value of these bondmen, or nursery maids, was in proportion to their knowledge of their language, and the use of a chaste, easy, colloquial style of conversation. It was the duty of these men and women to see that the legitimate children should acquire no bad habits, while they were writing the first words of their vocabulary on their memories. If the infant has good examples in speaking, the child correct precepts in reading and speaking, and the youth is in constant habits of attention to his language, in all the common affairs of life, and with this, is careful to improve his mind, he is an orator, without, perhaps, knowing it. Connexions and associations have as much to do with the tones of the human voice as with our cast of thinking and reasoning; hence professional pronunciation, provincial accents, and many other peculiarities that vitiate the correct and elegant use of our language. We, probably, have much less of this provincialism than any other people.

Eloquence must be the voice of mind, or it is nothing. The full mind will, in excitement, find utterance, and communicate its knowledge. Mental energies will, in the end, overcome most physical defects. The voice of an empty declaimer, however mellifluous, soon becomes offensive; the impassioned soul will find a tongue, and the dictates of an enlightened understanding correct its voice.

There are some specimens of written eloquence in the annals of the first century of our country, that have come down to us, with the traditions of the manner in which they were spoken, which strictly corresponds with the spirit of the composition. Such are some of Cotton Mather's sermons, and an earlier effort of Governor Winthrop.

Eloquence was in that age confined chiefly to the pulpit, as the magistrates had not many opportunities for a display of their oratory in the desultory business of their courts; but when church was entirely separated from state, opportunities grew more frequent in the legislative assemblies, and there can be no doubt but that there was much spirited debate in the questions of state policy which were constantly occurring in the several provinces. The numerous discussions upon furnishing men and supplies for Canadian and Indian wars; the manner of managing the campaign; as well as many minor matters, were all subjects which called forth the eloquence of our ancestors; and one versed in the minute history of the early times, will often see in obituary notices, in funeral sermons, and private letters, observations and epithets which afford him much information respecting the style of eloquence in that age, and of the men who were conspicuous as speakers. Of one, it was said, that he was a *Boanerges*, and he thundered on his opposers; of another, that he was *silver-tongued*, and pleased every body; and of another, that he was *a host in himself, and if you did not wish*

to follow him, you must shut your ears when he was talking.
In truth, they were eloquent, for they were engaged in matters of
importance to themselves, had "the motive and the cue to action,"
without any poverty of words. The whole meaning of the maxim,
that free governments are favourable to eloquence, is only, that
intelligent men are found there, and dare say what they think in
strong language; and this boldness gives to all that proceeds from
their lips, point and force.

We have said something of the eloquence of those who reasoned
the mass of the people into the opposition to the mother country;
but it was said in so general a manner, that we, perhaps, may be
indulged in selecting a few of the individuals who were distinguished in those days, and since; not that these we may select are the
"*twentieth of a tithe*" of those who took a part in the debates
upon the countless questions of right, and duty, and policy of our
proceedings during the time we were growing into a nation; but a
few may be brought forward to show the style and manner of the
most conspicuous of them. Some of them have lived to the days
of the lecturer, and their manner is fresh in his recollection. Of
those he never heard, he forms his opinions upon the concurrent
testimony of good judges, who have often heard them speak, and
the reports of their speeches that have come down to us.

Patrick Henry, of Virginia, was a natural orator, as some gifted
speakers are called, whose eloquence seems spontaneous, and is
impassioned and free from the trammels of rules. It is said that
he was a self-educated man, whose manner was his own, and was
blessed with the power of utterance beyond most of those who
had been taught in the groves of the academy. He felt deeply and
made others feel. His flashes of eloquence gave an electrick shock
to the audience; and these were managed with great skill, and
repeated at his will; or by some sudden transition, he let down his
hearers to a common tone of feeling, by the most felicitous illustrations or playful similes. He was, however, more powerful in
raising apprehensions than in allaying them. His eloquence was
supported by his patriotism, and what in the warmth of debate he
said he would do, he followed up in the coolness of reflection;
and if not as powerful, was as fearless with his sword as with his
tongue. His eloquence was not elaborate, nor his speeches long. His
audience easily understood him, and his speech was ended before
any part of them were tired of hearing him. His patriotism and
his eloquence have had ample justice done them by his learned
biographer.

Another of the same state, Mr. Madison, exhibited a different
style of eloquence. He had no passion, no majesty of tone, no

vehement gestures, nothing of that war-horse spirit of his co-adjutor, Patrick Henry; his was the smooth, but manly current of thought. It was philosophy, reasoning upon rights, and explaining duties, and teaching his hearers how to prepare for exigencies. He saw all things in a clear light, without enthusiasm or agitation. His speaking resembled his writing: his lines were all straight, his letters uniformly made, his spelling accurate, and his punctuation perfect. He was never off his guard; but self-possessed, he spoke until he was satisfied that he was fully understood, and then he left his arguments to work out their proper effect, without showing any anxiety for himself or them; perhaps there was never a man who spoke so often, that spoke so much to the purpose as Mr. Madison. His eloquence was one of those deep, silent, regular flowing rivers, that has no narrows, shoals, or cataracts, but winds its way in peace and dignity to the ocean. He possessed such an equanimity of temper, that he was always ready for debate, and always acquitted himself well; and if he did not rise so high in his eloquence, at times, as those who wait for inspiration, he never, like them, was liable to disappoint his hearers by inane voices, when the spirit ceased to agitate them. Mr. Madison is still living, the Nestor among orators.

The eloquence of the patriot John Adams was altogether different from either of these men. His mind was full of classick learning, and his soul for ever animated with political prophecies, and his heart was in his mouth. He came to his subject sword in hand, and carried his purposes by storm rather than by siege. He saw his object clearly, and came to it directly. There were no Ionian blandishments in his style; no Corinthian beauties; use, durability, and strength, were the components of his elocution. When he spoke, the timid grew brave, and the cunning fled, for they knew he would cut the Gordian knot without wasting his time to show his ingenuity by untying it. His imagination was never diseased by evil forebodings; he declared that America ought, could, and would be free. To this he at all times came directly, without admitting contingencies or calculating upon misfortunes. He knew the character of the people, and he trusted in it for the result. He suggested to his native state, more than a year before the declaration of independence, the propriety of attacking the enemy in the vitals, by seizing their property on the high seas. The project was astounding even to his brave countrymen; and one of his compeers, in that dark hour when it was made known, has often told me that he never should forget the *time*, the *subject*, the *manner*, or the *man*. Adams declared that the glory of America was to be on the seas; and with more than Delphick eloquence raised his voice for wooden

T 2

walls. The naval glories of the world came up in intense visions
to his mind, and he knew, by an every day observation, that the
mariners of his country had the bone and muscle, the heart, the
skill, and the indomitable courage, to make "their home upon the
deep." Not a voice in the legislature was raised against his plans;
and every old cannon that was embedded in the clay, or secured as
a highway corner-post, started from its quietude, and was harnessed
on some frail barque for the sea-fight. Was not this eloquence De-
mosthenian? It perhaps wanted something of the Athenian polish,
but it had the true effect.

The eloquence of Alexander Hamilton differed from all the preceding orators we have named. He arose deeply impressed with
his subject; and often, in the onset, seemed a little agitated, a slight
tinge of modesty crossed his cheek, but it was only the fear of himself, the only fear a man of genius and of learning can ever have,
when master of his subject. He made as few points in his case as
possible, stated these in a clear and forcible manner, and spread
them before the assembly, court, or jury, with great perspicuity and
elegance. He never descended below the dignity of argument to
catch popular applause, nor ever suffered himself to be borne away
from the course of his reasonings by irritation or passion. There
was temperance, method, and judgement in all his speeches; and
when he closed, there was nothing to mend, and but little to add.
But the great charm of his eloquence, after all, was the conviction,
in every mind, of the speaker's sincerity; there was a window in his
breast, and all the pulses of his heart were distinctly seen, beating
in the regular movements of honour. His eloquence was fascinating as well as commanding; his person was not large, but dignified
and graceful. The compass of his voice was extensive; its tones
were not loud or vociferating, but his enunciation was so clear that he
had the advantage over many, in the largest assemblies, whose lungs
were much stronger than his. No one, whatever might be his grade
of intellect, ever heard him without delight; and no good judge,
without feeling that he had been listening to a gentleman, a scholar,
and a patriot, as well as an orator. He died in the prime of
manhood; and the tears of his friends and political enemies trickled
together on his grave, as a tribute to the mighty dead.

Gouverneur Morris was a splendid orator. His mind was prolifick,
his fancy excursive, and his information extensive. He had read
books attentively, but men more thoroughly. He was well acquainted with French literature and the academicians, and had
caught something of their animation and literary fervour. His
figures were beautiful, his sentimental touches delicate and thrilling.
No orator ever made a more successful lunge at the heart than Mor-

ris, for he pierced at will. If Hamilton was the Zenophon among our intellectual lights, as he has been called, for the neatness, purity, and perspicuity of his productions, surely his friend, Gouverneur Morris, ought to be called the Isocrates among them. He had the same splendour of imagination, and poised his sentences with the same art, that is seen in the orations of "the old man eloquent." Morris's eloquence was well suited to the deliberative assembly, and to those occasions in which the heart is deeply interested. His oration over the body of Hamilton is admirable. At that moment, when the bleeding corse was before the eyes of his countrymen, and a nation's moans were wafted on every wind, from north to south, from east to west, through the country; when almost any extravagance would have been tolerated in this paroxysm of mind; for at this event the deep lamentations of the soul were commingled with the breath of execration, and there is no wild-fire like this; yet then the pathos of the orator was subdued, chastened, and harmonized to the mild and hallowed doctrines of christianity:—such exhibitions are the triumphs of the god-like art, of controlling tempers, and of conquering hearts.

He lived in republican struggles; in the sunshine of royalty; in the uproar of popular fury; and then in the calm of personal safety and national tranquillity; and from all drew lessons of experience, and through all carried the sound discretion of a high-minded man.

Fisher Ames has been, perhaps, more celebrated as an orator than any other American, except Patrick Henry; but it is not our object to make comparisons between our distinguished men who have graced the annals of our eloquence. The person of Ames was tall, thin, and interesting; his face was not what might be called handsome, but agreeable, and full of soul. The style of his eloquence was flowing, warm, and copious, and certainly partook more of the Roman than of the Grecian orator. His manner was bland, but earnest, and his whole demeanour calculated to attract the attention of all eyes. His voice was musical, and he had the command of it from the highest to the lowest note, and in all its variations it was free from monotony or false tone; for a sweet voice, he had less of sibilation than most of our orators, an evil that foreigners complain of in our language. His imagination was creative, and at his bidding new scenes arose, new beings lived, increased as he chose, and faded away at his will. He struck his hand across the chords of the hearts of his audience, and all was harmonious to his touch; but his plaintive measures were most congenial to his mind; he had nothing dark or sullen in his constitution, but there was a soft and gentle gloom that often intermingled with the light of his mind, which gave the shade of the sanctuary to the outpourings of his heart.

He mourned to think that he could not fully impress on the minds of others what he foreboded for his country; the common fault of a sensitive patriot. The diseases of his corporal frame entered deeply into his mind; and amid troublesome times he mingled dark auguries for the nation. He saw, in his imagination, the myrmidons of France sweeping over his country with rapine, fire, and dagger, and the conflagration of cities filled his eyes, and the screams of ravished virgins his ears. His countrymen seemed to him in a state of amazing apathy, and he grew almost frantick at the thought; but he mistook their cool, brave, and persevering character, for want of discernment and feeling. His warning appeals, as he thought them, were all wasted on the winds, although every one listened to him with profound respect and admiration. His friends and neighbours flocked around him, as a being of wonderful powers and superiour sagacity; but from their habits of reasoning for themselves, they thought that all these evils might not come, and they would wait the providence of God in this as in other things; but the honour and honesty of the great man they never doubted, for he was to them an angel of light; crowded with all his gloomy thoughts for his country, he sunk to the grave; but his admirers never lost one particle of their veneration for the genius and virtues of the man.

No man has a higher claim than Samuel Phillips to that solemn eloquence which was formerly common in New-England, but is now nearly extinct; and which was a union of the dignity of the eloquence of the magistracy, and the sanctity of that usual in the ecclesiastical council. Mr. Phillips was for twenty years president of the senate of the commonwealth of Massachusetts. He was a man of sterling integrity, of scrupulous exactness, and of religious solemnity; he possessed a strong mind, had a good share of classical taste, and a thorough early education. In speaking, his enunciation was slow, but not in the least drawling; his emphasis and cadence were admirable. He never rose to speak until he had fully matured his subject, and when he did, all were attentive. Point, maxim, inference, and conclusions, followed with such order, and such strength of argument, that he never spoke without making a deep impression, and seldom was on the unsuccessful side of a question. I have no belief that there are many speeches, or even skeletons of speeches, of his in print. There are several articles from his pen in the Massachusetts state papers. Among other things, there is an address of the legislature of the commonwealth of Massachusetts to John Adams, on his return to his residence in Quincy, after the election of Mr. Jefferson to the presidency of the United States. This is an elegant production, full of both dignity and affection; and all writings that are known to be his are of a high character, as well in point of composition, as in spirit and matter.

Samuel Dexter was another of our orators, who was the great man of his day. Every epithet of praise was lavished on his eloquence. He was indeed a strong man. His frame was colossal, his features prominent and marked. There were no nice graces, no delicate finishings about him as an orator. His voice was heavy, his enunciation slow, and his manner generally cool; and even when he was disturbed, it was rather the swell of the ocean, than the dash of the torrent. Like Pinckney, he was equally distinguished at the bar and in the deliberative assembly, and was constantly engaged in one or the other. Mr. Dexter was in Congress in stormy times, and fearlessly took his course. From the Congress he was made a member of the cabinet of President Adams, continued a while with his successor, and from that office he returned again to the bar. Here it was thought by many that he was without a rival as an advocate. He never did any thing by trick or cunning. In every argument he took the lion by the mane, and brought strength to match strength, and put the mastery upon the trial of superiour power; and no one will venture to say that he had inferiour intellects to contend with. He practised in an enlightened community, and had to struggle with those who wore polished armour, and bore fearful weapons, and used them with knightly skill. Yet, if not always victorious, he was never broken down by superiour energy, but kept himself ready for the combat. It is to be regretted that of such a man there should be so little remaining— not a whole political speech, not a full argument of his, in any case, can be found in print, and probably does not exist any where, in manuscript or memory.

Pinckney was truly a great man—a lawyer, a statesman, a diplomatist, an orator, and, withal, a scholar. Feeling the fire of genius kindling up within him, he broke from the common high road of business, and sought the paths of professional learning, against the suggestions of the prudent, and the advice of the sagacious. He conquered one province after another in the regions of science and letters; and went up with the unquenchable thirst of a great mind to drink of the springs of knowledge, not satisfied with the tainted currents as they flowed onwards through the world. He gave ample proofs, if any were wanting, that the highest cultivation of taste and imagination is consistent with profound research and sound judgement; that ornament was not incompatible with strength; and that even the temple of the law might, notwithstanding its gothick structure, be susceptible of elegance and high finish.

His genius was not more lofty than versatile. It might have been said of him as of the fifth Harry:

> "Hear him debate of commonwealth affairs,
> You would say, it hath been all in all his study;
> List his discourse of war, and you shall hear
> A fearful battle rendered you in musick;
> Turn him to any course of policy,
> The.gordian knot of it he will unloose,
> Familiar as his garter; that when he speaks,
> The air, a chartered libertine, is still;
> And the mute wonder lurketh in men's ears
> To steal his sweet and honeyed sentences."

The spaces he filled at the bar, in the senate, and as a foreign minister, were all great indeed. If he sometimes found equals, he had no superiors, and his country and his clients placed their interests in his hands with the fullest confidence that he would do all the case would admit of; and who could do more? He never spared himself in any efforts required for his client's interest, and he went on day by day performing Herculean labours in the court, until nature, *not early, but untimely,* sunk under them. His eloquence was of the highest grade, but not faultless. His audible whispers and his tremendous bursts were well enough in him, for he threw intellect into every thing, even into manner; and his voice was never harsh or dissonant. This habit in his imitators is shocking; they are unequal to riding the great horse. Pinckney died at Washington, in the discharge of his duty at the bar of the supreme court of the United States. He was buried in the publick grave-yard, on the eastern branch of the Potomack, about a mile and a half from the capitol, in Washington. The lonely traveller, as he gazes on the monument, calls to his recollection how lately this heap of dust was the centre of attraction! How few days have elapsed since bevies of beauties hung enamoured on his accents, and strewed flowers in his path! They make no visits now, with returning seasons, to this spot, in honour of the shade of this once gifted orator! Some other idol, perhaps, has arisen, and the pæans they sung are forgotten; or perhaps these very votaries of fashion, whose smile of approbation was fame, have also passed away, without historian or poet. The records of fashion, notwithstanding the omnipotence of her reign, are written in fading ink, and soon become illegible. Over the spot where repose the ashes of the dead, hang the scales in which the mighty deeds of men are weighed! How eloquent is the silence of the grave.

We might go on to name a great number of men justly styled orators, who have passed from the stage of action within less than twenty years past; but our limits will not permit us to proceed; not meaning simply to include the second class of the good business speakers, but only those of unquestionable superiority; and I think no candid man will hesitate to say, that our community has been prolifick in those, compared with any other people. It has been said, by the Baron de Sainte Croix, that from the commencement of the thirteenth century to that of the third before Christ, Athens did not produce more than fifty-four distinguished orators and rhetoricians. We have had many more than that number within half a century.

LECTURE XIII.

I would I were a Poet, and could write
  The passage of this mighty world in rime,
And talke of warres, and many a valiant fight,
And how the Captaines did to honour clime!
  Of wise and faire, of gratious, virtuous, kinde,
  And of the bounty of a noble minde.

NICHOLAS BRETON.

To HAVE a fair and just view of the mind which has been active in the affairs of our country, ever since it had an existence, we must look at her military and naval characters, as well as to her literary and scientifick men: in fact they are, in our time, intimately connected. In every stage of our growth, we have had to struggle with hardships of an extraordinary nature. These exertions gave a hardihood to the people, which could not have been acquired in days of peace and prosperity. We will pass over those military characters, John Smith and Miles Standish—heroes of such prowess, that, if they had lived in some other ages of the world, would have had temples erected to their memories—and proceed to trace, with rapid hand, some of the wars in which the colonies were involved, from their infancy up to the present time. The colonies classed their wars under the following names: When the country of the Indians at war with them was without their grants, they called it a war, in the common accep-

tation of the term; but if within their grants and without their settlements, they called it an *interruption*; but if within their settlements,
they called it a *rebellion*; hence the term so often used, rebel Indians: some of their bloodiest wars were of this description.

In 1634, the Pequods, a powerful nation of Indians, killed Capts.
Stone and Norton, traders in their country; this gave the colonies
the alarm. In 1636, Lords Say and Brook erected a fort near the
head quarters of the Pequods, which so incensed them, that they continued their massacres, until the people of Connecticut found it necessary to make a war of extermination upon this tribe of Indians in
their neighbourhood. Previous to this period, the colonies of New-
England had associated for self-defence, and had made a league with
the six Narragansett sachems. The Narragansetts were not friendly to
the Pequods, and entered at first into this war with alacrity. In May,
1637, a body of seventy men, with sixty Connecticut river Indians,
with two hundred Narragansetts, and one hundred Nianticks, a settlement of the Pequods in friendship with the colonists, and twenty
men from the garrison of Say-Brook, under the command of Capt.
Mason, with their friends from Massachusetts, consisting of one
hundred and sixty-three men under Mr. Staughton, and fifty from
the old colony, in three months cut up the Pequods, destroying
about seven hundred of them, and only left about two hundred remaining, who were soon scattered among the tribes, and lost their
name and sovereignty. They were fierce and brave, but fought generally with bows and battle axes, not having as yet procured many fire
arms. The colonists lost a considerable number of men in these
engagements, and had a still greater number wounded.

In 1654, the Narragansetts made war on the Indians on Long
Island, but the confederates soon suppressed these hostilities. In
New-England there was peace from this time until 1675, when Philip,
son of Massasoit—the father had been in friendship with the whites
for fifty years—commenced hostilities upon them. He had conceived the design of exterminating the colonists at a blow. For this purpose, he covered his designs in the most artful manner by a treaty, in
1671. Philip was a savage of the first order of intellect. He saw
that his people were wasting away before the growing power of the
white men, and that if a great effort was not made to destroy them, it
would soon be too late. He had for many years, during the life time
of his father, been brooding over the fate of his country, and the visions of futurity grew strong before his eyes; he meditated upon
what he saw. and silently determined on his course. His council
probably were not apprized of the extent of his plan, which was to
form a confederacy of the tribes from the St. Lawrence to the Mississippi; and so secretly did he proceed on his journey to carry this in-

to effect, that it was not for many months after his departure that the nearest colonists to Mount Hope, this sachem's usual place of residence, knew or suspected his absence. The extent of his journey will probably never be traced; but, from the numerous tribes of Indians he soon stirred up to make common cause with him, it must have been very great. The system was one worthy of the most sagacious statesman of any age. Philip began his war himself, by killing nine whites, in June, 1675. This exploit was the signal for the commencement of hostilities from the confederates. The plan was so well digested, that it would have succeeded if Philip had not been surrounded by traitors. The colonists were apprized of the designs of the alliance by friendly Indians, and made such arrangements as enabled them, in a great measure, to cut up these foes in detail, before they could make a simultaneous movement. The elements were also against the aboriginal warrior. There was quite a Russian winter in the year 1675 and 6, and the eastern Indians were obliged to sue for peace, as they were unable to fight and procure food at the same time. This was granted them; but by the genial influence of spring, and the powerful arguments of Philip, they renewed hostilities as soon as their sufferings were over. On the 12th of August, 1676, Philip was slain by one of the friendly Indians, and this formidable alliance was soon broken and destroyed. The colonists had strained every nerve to raise troops, to make a powerful impression at the onset. Governor Winslow, the second governor of that name, had made a campaign the previous winter with one thousand colonists and five hundred friendly Indians, and killed seven hundred of the enemy, with the loss of eighty-five men, and an hundred and fifty wounded. Winslow was a judicious commander, and performed his duties with great spirit and bravery; but Col. Church, of Little Compton, was in truth the hero of this war. He was pressing hard upon Philip for some days before the chieftain was slain. Church's son wrote an account of the war in which his father was engaged; a very plain, unvarnished tale of his exploits, which has lately been republished by Dr. Drake, of Boston, with copious notes, of great research and interest. Church lived many years, and was, at the commencement of the last century, engaged in Indian warfare in his old age.

There was not a village which did not suffer by the attacks of the Indians, and many of them extremely. The assailants would often conceal themselves whole weeks in ambush, to wait for the absence of the men, and then attack defenceless women and children. Many instances of female heroism are on record, which occurred in that day, and should be carefully preserved. Among the most conspicuous was that of Mrs. Hannah Duston, of Haverhill, a pleasant village

U

situated on the left bank of the Merrimack. On the 15th of March, 1698, Mrs. Duston was made prisoner by a party of Indians. She was on this day confined to her bed by sickness, attended by her nurse, Mary Niff. Seven children, besides a female infant six days old, were with her. As soon as the alarm was given, her husband sent away the seven children towards the garrison-house; by which time the Indians were so near, that, despairing of saving the others of his family, he hastened after his children, on horseback. This course was advised by his wife. She thought it was idle for her to attempt to escape. A party of Indians followed him, but the father kept in the rear of the children, and often firing on his pursuers, he kept them back, and was enabled to reach the garrison with his children in safety. The Indians took Mrs. Duston from her bed, and carried her off, with the nurse and infant; but finding the little one becoming troublesome, they took her from her mother's arms by force, and dashing her against a tree, ended her moans, and miseries, and life together. The mother had followed the Indians until this moment with faultering steps and bitter tears, thinking on the fate of herself, her babe, and her other children. After this horrid outrage, she wept no more; the agony of nature drank the tear-drop ere it fell. She looked to heaven with a silent prayer for succour and vengeance, and followed the infernal group without a word of complaint. At this instant, the high resolve was formed in her mind, and swelled every pulse of her heart. They travelled on some distance: as she thought, one hundred and fifty miles, but, perhaps, from the course they took, about seventy-five. The river had probably been broken up but a short time, and the canoes of the Indians were above the upper falls, on the Merrimack, when they commenced their journey to attack Haverhill. Above these falls, on an island in this river, the Indians had a wigwam, and in getting their canoes in order, and by rowing ten miles up the stream, became much fatigued. When they reached the place of rest, they slept soundly. Mrs. Duston did not sleep. The nurse, and an English boy, a prisoner, were apprized of her design; but were not of much use to her in the execution of it. In the stillness of the night she arose and went out of the wigwam to test the soundness and security of savage sleep. They did not move: they were to sleep until the last day. She returned, took one of their hatchets and dispatched ten of them in a moment, each with a single blow. An Indian woman who was rising when she struck her, fled with her probable death-wound; and an Indian boy was designedly spared; for the avenger of blood was a woman, and a mother, and could not deal a death-blow upon a helpless child. She surveyed the carnage ground by the light of the fire which she stirred up after the deed was done;

and catching a few handfuls of roasted corn, she commenced her journey; but on reflecting a moment, she thought the people of Haverhill would consider her tale as the ravings of madness, when she should get home, if ever that time might come; she therefore returned, and scalped the slain; then put her nurse and English boy into the canoe, and with herself they floated down to the falls, when she landed, and took to the woods, keeping the river in sight, which she knew must direct her on the way home. After suffering incredible hardships by hunger, cold, and fatigue, she reached home, to the surprise and joy of her husband, children, and friends. The general court of Massachusetts examined her story, and being satisfied of the truth of it, took her trophies, the scalps, and gave her fifty pounds. The people of Boston made her many presents. All classes were anxious to see the heroine; and as one of the writers of that day says, who saw her, "she was a right modest woman." Has Anacharsis or Mitford, in their histories of Greece, any thing to surpass this well authenticated story? Her descendants in a right line and by the same name, are now living where she was captured.

The Indian tribes, at this period, had assistance from the French in their several attacks upon the settlements, in 1688 to 1699, and from 1703 to 1713, as well as afterwards. About the year 1717, the Indians on Kennebeck river began to show a disposition to quarrel; but hearing that the small pox was prevalent among the whites, they were deterred from any very open attacks. The small pox was, in fact, very general in 1721, but in 1722, when it had abated, Lieut. Governor Dummer, acting as commander-in-chief, sent Capt. Harmon with an hundred men, in whale boats, up the Kennebeck, and surprised the Indians at Norridgewock. Several of the Norridgewocks were killed, and with them father Ralle, a pious catholick priest. He was sacrificed at the altar, while performing mass. This required no justification in that period, but the act seems to want one now, and that I am not prepared to make; but our fathers did not require many excuses from Indian killers; and perhaps we are apt to find fault with them, without considering that if the Indians had not been exterminated, the English must have been. It was very clear to every mind, that, as they viewed each other, they could not exist together. In May, 1724, was Lovewell's fight, which has been mentioned before by us in these lectures. This event has been commemorated both in verse and prose. After the Pequod war, Connecticut had not much trouble from the Indians, but they were ever ready to assist their neighbours when called upon. There had existed from the first a readiness to assist each other, a principle which grew out of the common danger, and which now can hardly be understoood, except by those who have felt the dread of a savage foe coming in upon their wives and children with indiscriminate massacre. During these struggles of New-England for her existence, several of the other colonies were grievously annoyed.

In Virginia, the Indians had been troublesome from the first settlement, at Jamestown. In 1610, the colony of Virginia was reduced from five hundred to eighty. From 1612 they kept in peace until 1622, chiefly by the good conduct of Capt. Smith, and a few of his associates. In the year 1622, the Indians murdered three hundred and forty-seven in one day, in Virginia. Harvey's arbitrary course in encroaching upon the Indian territories, caused another insurrection in 1629, in which five hundred of the colonists were slain. While Philip's war was raging at the north, Bacon was rousing up the Indians to oppose the government of Governor Berkley, for pretty much such a course as Harvey had pursued. In 1711, the Cape Fear Indians of North Carolina, made war on that colony, and after destroying about twenty families, were quelled by troops from Virginia and South Carolina coming to their aid. The Virginians and Carolinians were never wanting in chivalry.

Up to this time, and in all the wars we have mentioned, the mother country did not help a finger to assist us in fighting our enemies. They left their dear children to shift for themselves, until it was found quite convenient to fight France on our continent, and then a deep interest was taken by the British ministry in the success of our affairs with the natives.

These wars with the Indians we have enumerated, were not the only wars in which the colonies were engaged. In 1690, Col. Phipps, as Douglass calls him, was fitted out by New-England with seven hundred and fifty men, to attack the French settlement at Acadie; and he took Port Royal, which was held until 1697, when England gave it to France. This year also, 1690, Phipps made an attack upon Canada with a considerable force; one thousand colonists and fifteen hundred Indians were to proceed to take Montreal, but did not; and the naval force met with some disasters in going and returning. They began the enterprise too late in the season, and of course any one might have expected what did happen—a total failure of obtaining the object in view, with a great loss of lives. Cotton Mather gave a great many reasons for all the evils which accrued, but a few short ones would have been more correct, viz.: the force sent and the commanders of them were unequal to the task; but there never was a braver set of men than those who accompanied Phipps in this undertaking; they were of the best blood of the land; virtuous, hardy, persevering, bold, independent, high spirited citizens, who feared God, and eschewed evil, but feared no danger by "*flood or fire.*"

This expedition was fitted out under the avowed intention of defending the colonies against the French and Indians; but the true cause of the expedition might be found in the plans of the English ministry, to do something on this continent to keep an equipoise for what might be lost in Europe; and in the vanity of Phipps, who, having performed one exploit with success, thought that he was born for a conqueror and a statesman.

In 1710 and 1711, other attempts were made on Quebeck, but in these the ministry were more liberal of means, and did not throw the burden wholly on the colonies; still, in this they were heavily taxed. By an order from the British ministry, a Congress was to be assembled at New-London, formed of the governors of the provinces north of Pennsylvania, to concert measures with Nicholson, an officer of his majesty's army, at the head of the forces from England. Two regiments from Massachusetts, Rhode Island, and New-Hampshire, were to join the British troops destined for an attack on Quebeck; while the militia from Connecticut, New-York, and the Jerseys, with the Indians of the five nations, were to attack Montreal. This expedition totally failed, with immense losses; and to finish the tale of disasters, the admiral's ship blew up on her homeward voyage. These campaigns were committed to men unacquainted with the country, and the best modes of fighting the Indians and their allies, and were managed in so open a manner, that the French were generally apprized of these intended attacks months before the forces for the execution of them arrived. The colonies could at any time have taken Canada, if they had thought it necessary for their existence; but the Canadians and English settlers on the Atlantick were not jealous of each other; nor unfriendly, until the parent country excited them to hostilities. Some of the historians of that day say, that in this enterprise there were twenty-three thousand men in arms, a greater proportion, according to the number of inhabitants, than has ever been since. In 1744, a war broke out between France and England. In January, 1744–5, the legislature of Massachusetts, by a majority of one vote only, determined to make an attempt on Louisbourg, then called the Dunkirk of America, from the strength of its fortifications. The forces raised were small for the undertaking, consisting of about 3600 volunteers from Massachusetts, New-Hampshire, and Connecticut, who effected the reduction of this strong hold with the small loss of less than two hundred men. These troops were commanded by General William Pepperell. The others of note in this expedition were Brigadier General Waldo, Cols. Moulton, Hale, Willard, Richmond, and Gorham, of the infantry, and Cols. Dwight and Gridley, of the artillery; the latter of whom fell afterwards at the battle of Bunkerhill, with Capt. Barnard, an excellent engineer, who had under his command a train of expert and hardy artificers, mostly ship-carpenters, a profession to which our country has in every exigency been much indebted. Major General Wolcott, from Connecticut, had a force of five hundred men who joined this army. The colony of Rhode Island sent their province sloop, and the government of New-York sent them several excellent cannon, which proved of incalculable service in the campaign; and several of the governments south of New-York made the forces a present of some provisions, and wished them God speed. Admiral Warren joined, with a considerable fleet; but nothing could have been achieved by naval force alone. The provincials performed in this enterprise prodigies of labour: they drew the heavy cannon over a morass, thought, by the sagacious French engineers, to have been absolutely impassable, for ordnance of any considerable weight. The provincials made sledges and placed the cannon upon them, and in the thick fog, or in the darkness of the night, dragged them to a proper distance from the walls to erect a battery. Some historians say that the men were knee deep in the mire in this work; but a veteran, who served in this campaign, once told me that he was engaged in this labour, and that he and his men used the snow-shoes which had been provided for the winter, and found that they could work well with them on the morass. The besieged, seeing this battery and other formidable preparations, capitulated on the 17th of June, 1745. This exploit has no parallel in modern history. This was glorious news in England; but the safety of the colonies was put in jeopardy by it, for the next year the French ministry, sharpened at this unexpected disaster, sent the Duke D'Anville, with a formidable force, to retrieve it, and lay waste the towns on the seaboard. The discomfiture of this armada, and the death of the admiral, and all the tales of the pious and superstitious, are written in the chronicles of that day, but are too long for my purpose. There is one fact, however, which ought never to be forgotten, which is, that seven thousand troops poured in from the country, at this alarm, to save Boston and the neighbouring seaports; a wonderful army, considering the population of the interior at that day. Elated by the success of the provincials and their fleet in taking Louisbourg, the English ministry were determined on another attack upon Canada. By an order from the duke of New-castle, the secretary of state, the governors of the North American provinces were required to raise as many companies, to consist of an hundred men each, as they could spare. Those of New-York, New-Jersey, Pennsylvania, Maryland, and Virginia, to be formed into a corps to be commanded by General Gooch, then lieut. governor of Virginia. In obedience to this order, Virginia sent two companies,

Maryland three, Pennsylvania four, Jersey five, and New-York fifteen, making twenty-nine companies. These were intended for Crown Point and Montreal. Massachusetts Bay raised twenty companies, Connecticut ten, Rhode Island three, New-Hampshire two, making thirty-five companies. These were to join the forces from England against Quebeck. From misunderstanding, mismanagements, and sickness, this mighty preparation failed. The difficulties in this expedition, as in most undertaken by the mother country to fight the French in America, principally arose from the disposition of the regular troops to put the greatest burdens on the provincials, and then to claim all the laurels for themselves. This was cause of grievous complaint at that time.

In 1748, the peace of Aix la Chapelle was made, and the fortress of Louisbourg was given up without any regard to the safety of the colonies, the avowed object of the ministry in striving to obtain it.

In 1755, while there was yet a nominal peace between France and England, hostilities were carried on in this country between the colonies, and the Indians and French, assisted by troops from England. There had been no formal declaration of war, when Dinwiddie, governor of Virginia, sent Colonel Frye and Lieutenant Colonel Washington against the French and Indians; in which enterprise the latter was so much distinguished, that when Braddock arrived to take the command of all the forces in this country, he made Washington his aid. The unfortunate battle of Monongahela, on the 9th of July, 1755, in which Braddock was mortally wounded, has so often been minutely narrated, that I will not dwell upon it in this place. Braddock's fame has suffered in the history of his country as well as in ours; because he permitted himself to be surprised. This alone ought not to tarnish his fame; for commanders, more acquainted with the savages than Braddock, have been surprised and defeated long since the lesson from his fate has been given. William Johnson, the same year, with a force raised from New-England and New-York, was sent against Crown Point, but he never reached there. Near the head of Lake George, the advance of his army was attacked by the French and Indians, under the Baron Dieskeau, and driven into the main body, which, after the fight began, had thrown up a few felled trees to protect themselves. From this ground the enemy was repulsed, and Dieskeau severely wounded. Johnson was knighted for the exploit, but truth, since discovered, must give the honours of that day to General Lyman, second in command, who fought the battle. Johnson having been wounded in the early part of the engagement, retired from the field. In this battle, in the first part of it, fell the celebrated Indian chief, Hendrick, who was in friendship with us, and was fighting for the colonies. He was one of those men made a chief by nature. He was fierce, bold, and persevering in fight, and made the best arrangements for battle. He was as politick as brave ; but his superiority was in no small degree owing to his wisdom and eloquence. Many of his remarks have come down to us, and are as pithy as any of those ascribed to the ancients. When asked if a certain number of troops were sufficient for a particular expedition, he answered, " *They are too many to be sacrificed, and too few to conquer.*"

Montcalm succeeded to Dieskeau. He was an accomplished officer, who had served with great reputation in several campaigns in Europe, and was sent to succour Canada. Offensive measures were not within his calculations ; but finding that he was not likely to be disturbed at Quebeck, or at Crown Point, he proceeded up to Lake George, and made an attack on Fort William Henry, then garrisoned by Colonel Munro with British and provincial soldiers. The fort was in a low and badly selected place, and of course fell, after an obstinate defence. Montcalm guarantied to the prisoners *a safe conduct* through the woods to the settlements on the Hudson ; but, from what cause has never been explained, this article in the terms of capitulation was totally disregarded. No sooner had the march of the provincials commenced, than the Indians fell upon these disarmed soldiers, the great objects of their hatred, with infernal ferocity, butchering without discrimination all they overtook. Driven to madness, some of the provincials were collected and stood their ground, and when the savages came upon them, they met their fire, and then rushed on their foes and struggled for their arms ; and such was the success of this desperate attempt, that arms and ammunition sufficient to check the assailants were obtained long before the close of the bloody day. This track of slaughter and horrour is now traced by the traveller as consecrated ground : often has he put himself in health and spirits for such a campaign at Saratoga Springs, whose medicinal waters had been shown by Hendrick to Johnson, several years before the chief was slain.

In 1756, Governor Shirley, of Massachusetts, who was a good lawyer and excellent civil magistrate, conceiving himself to be by nature made for a warrior, marched with a considerable force to Oswego ; but that ground had as yet been very treacherous to the fame of every military leader but Johnson, and he had barely escaped a disasterous fate. Shirley returned without all the laurels he expected. He wrote a defence of himself, which goes to prove that he was more successful than others in the same campaign.

In the summer of 1758, General Abercrombie and Lord Howe,

with ten thousand regulars and six thousand militia, marched to Lake George, and made preparation to attack Ticonderoga. They moved down the lake, which had been called Lake Sacrament, from the purity of its waters, in a thousand boats, in most magnificent style; but in this expedition, Lord Howe was killed, and nineteen hundred and thirty-five of the provincials and British soldiers fell in two hours, in the attack upon the fort, and the expedition ended in a retreat. This was wholly owing to Abercrombie's disregarding the advice of the provincial commander, General Winslow, an experienced officer. Lord Howe was a young man of high promise, and so much esteemed by the provincial troops, that Massachusetts, with the permission of the king, erected a monument to his memory in Westminster Abbey. General Winslow was a gallant officer, of commanding talents, and had seen much service; he was a descendant of the first and second governors of that name of the Plymouth colony, whose military prowess is identified with the history of the country. He was well educated, and had gained the respect and confidence of the British officers, and the affection of his own troops; the papers of that day bear testimony to his spirit in supporting the claim of his own men to distinction. In this campaign, as in the preceding and following winters, the Rangers, as a particular corps was called, performed extraordinary feats. This body of troops was provincials, under the command of Major Rodgers, an experienced officer; Generals Putnam and Stark were at this time captains in this body, and distinguished themselves for bravery and skill. The journal of Major Rodgers is in print, and is worthy the attention of the American reader, as the bravery, fortitude, and sufferings, of these rangers, have no parallels in British history. The British historians only glance at these exploits of our countrymen, and we have had but few historians ourselves to record them; in all these contests, the provincial army had to pioneer the way, and met death and sufferings with a patriotick ardour, but had none of a martyr's glory. The living provincial soldiers saw the honours wrested from him in every battle, when he had done his part, and more than his part, to serve his country and his king.

At the close of this campaign, the military reputation of England was at a low ebb. The world began to think England in her dotage. One disaster had followed another so closely that these things could hardly be considered the fortune of war only. In Europe, from Italy to Russia, the historians and pamphleteers were prophesying disasters to England, and declaring glorious omens for France. The lilies were said to grow brighter every day. The political seers looked at the great efforts of France, and at their chain of fortifications, extending from the St. Lawrence to the Mississippi, and called it the great bow of power around the Atlantick settlements. At this gloomy period, when despondency seemed to reign on this and the other side of the water, Chatham was made premier of England. This statesman had been a patriot leader for many years, and had stemmed the torrent of corruption and folly with fearlessness and energy. The disasters of his country raised him to power, and he brought all the resources of his great mind to retrieve her misfortunes; at once the war assumed a new character. He broke down the system, which had long been practised upon, of sending those abroad who were not much wanted at home, and at once selected the leaders of his armies from the most determined of his generals. Amherst and Wolfe were sent to America, and the result of the calculations of the ministry proved their wisdom. Wolfe met Montcalm, and beat him; Amherst without difficulty marched over the same ground which his predecessor had attempted and failed. Ticonderoga, Crown Point, and Montreal, yielded without a struggle, and the war was ended. In the fame of Chatham, both hemispheres claim a share. He is identified with his country's honour, not only during his administration, but for ever. He saw, and gloried in the sight, that the language, the manners, the principles of government, the laws, and the sciences and literature of England, were growing up robustly and firmly in this extended country. He saw the current of liberty and law flowing with English blood, and identified his own country with her colonies. America will never forget this great man; we rejoice in the thought that " his language is our mother tongue." He knew the character of the colonies; he appreciated their sacrifices, and did justice to their exertions; and was unwilling that they should be trampled upon, and oppressed by exactions and insults. He lifted his voice in their favour at all times, but it was not always heard, as it should have been.

From the peace of 1763 to 1775, there was a constant course of irritations and bickerings between the colonies and the mother country. The colonies had been involved in debt, in support of British wars, and had bled at every pore for her glory; there was not a place on the frontier or seaboard, where the bones of the colonists were not left to whiten; nor a family in the provinces that did not mourn some member of it cut off in these wars; but all these things were forgotten, and a revenue was to be extorted from them, against their will. The storm which had long been gathering at length burst upon their heads. The battle of Lexington opened the first scene of the drama which was to close in an eternal separation of this country from England. It was hard to burst the ties of friendship and consanguinity. The colonies loved the name of Briton, and felt connected with her name and fortunes. Her step-dame cruelty had wounded the hearts of her children, but had not extinguished their affections. The colonists had often entered complaints, and sometimes murmured a threat; but at the same time prayed that all might be well again soon. It was in vain: the divorce was necessary, and has been useful to both nations, and to the world. The mother country had wrong and contradictory impressions of us; they overrated our pecuniary means to pay taxes, and underrated the military talents which we possessed. They called our determination, obstinacy; our just indignation, a factious spirit; opposition was denominated rebellion; and no measure of indulgence could, consistently with the views of the ministry, be productive of any thing but mischief. The pride of the few in England overcame the judgement of the many; and the appeal to arms became inevitable. The colonies found this could not be averted by petitions, entreaties, or reasoning, and prepared, as well as they could, for the worst. That day was full of fate to us; and by the protecting hand of Providence, we were preserved. It should never be forgotton by us. All who live at this time, and have come up since that period, can hardly realize the solemnity and distress of this preparation for the conflict. After the battle of Lexington, all were seeking for means of attack and defence. The lead was stripped from the old fashioned diamond glass windows and melted for bullets; women gave their last flannel wrapper for the use of the artillery in making cartridges; every old firelock, whether of William and Mary or of Queen Anne, or those taken from the French at Louisbourg or Quebeck, was mended up for fight. The pulpits rang with the duties of the christian soldier, and the Bible heroes were emblazoned anew as examples for imitation. The clergy were not only tongue valiant, but many of them joined the train-bands, and were ready to fight the battles of freedom. Matrons not only assisted to gird on the swords of their husbands, but put the weapons of war into the hands of their beardless sons, and urged them to the field of danger. Who could withstand such a spirit? What foe could meet men so sent out? The whole of the existence of the colonies had been preparing them for this sad crisis, as it then seemed to all; but which, in truth, was only the forerunner to national independence and national consequence, in the eyes of those who were first among the nations of the earth. A whole people, as well as individuals, have their hours of despondency; and this was one, indeed, for our own people; but the minds of men, women, and children, were all prepared for the struggle. There was nothing of hasty impulse in their determination, nothing un-

thought of, by sire and son ; they had compared notes, and settled
the course to be pursued in any event. Another hour like this will,
perhaps, never again be found in the history of man. The English
were, as a nation, totally incapable of understanding the force of this
moral pressure upon a people so educated and so oppressed. It
was a subject worthy the attention of the philosophers of the mind,
and those who wished to analyze the laws by which nations are
governed, when oppression acts upon those " *who know their
rights, and, knowing, dare maintain them.*" This solemn determination which did not vent itself in words, but was ready to show
itself by deeds, was entirely misunderstood by those who pretended
to examine the tone of feeling, and to try the spirit of the people
they were sent to awe to silence and submission. There were a
few, indeed, who came to this country, and a few in England, who
had never been here, who clearly foresaw all that would happen,
for they were well acquainted with the nature, principles, and resources of the people of America.

The battle of Bunker Hill was important in many respects. It
was fought on something like a systematick plan. The officers
had generally been in battle; many of them were at Louisbourg,
which had been taken just thirty years before, even to a day; and
others, at a later period, had been with Abercrombie, Amherst, or
Wolfe, on the frontiers. Putnam, Prescott, Gridley, Stark, and
many of the others, even to the common soldiers, had seen much
service. The British were not aware of the manner in which the
yeomanry were officered, and thought, or affected to believe, that
the show of force was nothing more than a rabble. The battle was
commenced as a matter of amusement by the British forces; about
one half of those who were led up the hill between three and four
o'clock, had crossed from Boston to Charlestown at twelve o'clock,
and dined directly in full view of the American redoubt; they
were certain that as soon as a movement was made, the Americans
would run, and the battle-field would be their own, without danger
or bloodshed. The manner in which these troops were met was
deadly and tremendous; all the beauty of the pageant was soon
over. In this battle, at least fifteen hundred of the flower of the
English army were slain in less than two hours, and a greater proportion of their officers than usual. More than three hundred of the
corses of the slain were brought to Boston, and buried at the lower
part of the common, to hide the amount of their loss. Never was
there a more sudden and awful lesson than the British soldiers experienced on this memorable day. The provincials fought until all their
ammunition was expended, and they had seen the best and bravest
of all his Majesty's troops again and again retiring from the effect

of their fire. There were not too many of the provincials killed for the desired effect of rousing the energies of the people, and giving a solemnity to the occasion; and enough of the British to show the provincials that regular soldiers were neither invulnerable nor invincible. Had the Americans gained a victory, in all probability the ministry would have sent out twice as many soldiers for the next campaign as they did. The ministry were told this was only a smart skirmish, and would not be repeated. The British disguised, as much as possible, the effects of this battle on their numbers, and more so the effect produced on the spirits of their troops. The loss of General Warren made a great impression on the minds of our people in every part of the country. His name, as president of the provincial congress, as chairman of the committee of safety, his fame as a splendid orator, and his acknowledged patriotism and bravery, had fixed him indelibly in the hearts of his countrymen. They honoured others from duty and policy, they followed him from affection. " *The blood of the martyrs,*" it has been said, "*was the seed of the church.*" From this patriot's blood, we may say, sprang myriads of armed men. The affecting fable of the sacrifice of the Athenian virgins to the sea-born monster, rightly read, is precisely this: that the best and purest of the youthful blood of Athens was spilt to maintain their naval superiority, as their only, or their best defence, in the infancy of their existence. Our fate was similar; our youthful blood was poured out for the country. Long since the events of that memorable day, the story of the fall of Warren has been told to children as matter of example and excitement, and his name and his virtues have come down to posterity with those of Washington. Great occasions produce great men. Necessity is said to instruct her children better in self-defence than other mothers.

For a century and an half the people of this country had been educated in the school of self-defence. These lessons they were often forced to write in characters of blood. They had been so often thrown upon their resources, that they never suffered any feelings of despair to weigh them down. They had known nothing of the pageantry of war, nor its power in advancing one to wealth and honour; but they had been made acquainted with its difficulties and hardships. They had a sufficiency of those native elements which make courage a principle, and something of the experience which makes it a habit.

We have opened upon the revolution; but we cannot, at this moment, indulge in even a glimpse of the heroes of that war; their deeds, and their fame, shall be the burden of some future lecture. It is now the right time, perhaps, to write out the memoirs of that age, and of these men; for we are not so near the era of the revolution as to catch, and to incorporate the partialities and prejudices which were then abroad, into our opinions upon their merits; nor are we so far from that time, as to require the aid of fiction to fill up our picture. We have been companions, in later times, with many of the actors in those scenes; and from our childhood have heard them recount the circumstances of the revolution, most minutely, again and again. There are, thank heaven, some few of these veterans still lingering among the living; these can, yea, do assist us in giving faithful descriptions of the scenes they witnessed, and correct delineations of the characters they have known. I know that it is impossible for any one writer to do justice to all; but another may finish what one begins, and in the progress of time much may be effected. I shall attempt to sketch some of these characters hereafter, without any other pretensions than that of a sincere lover of my country's talent, wherever, or whenever it may be found. I have breathed the same air, and trod the same soil, in common with them, and that is something towards a fitnesss for my labour. I will illustrate what is difficult to describe. A gentleman from this country, several years since, visited Italy, and became familiarly acquainted with the great Praxiteles of modern times, Canova; he was often at his rooms, and one day, while the great master was giving the last touch to his statue of Washington, the keen sighted physiognomist observed by the countenance of his familiar visitor, that he was making a comparison, in his mind, between this work and an exquisite bust of Napoleon, on the table. The sensitive sculptor exclaimed, but in his own sweet language,—"*I have seen the emperor, and have breathed the air of France ; but I never crossed the Atlantick—never saw your country—never heard the voice of Washington.*"

As man is constituted, civil liberty cannot be preserved without military strength; sylvan scenes, and the golden reign of perpetual peace, exist only in the dreams of the amiable theorist; they are not in nature. Military prowess shows the muscular strength and mental energy of a people, and often is a proof of their advancement in arts and sciences; for there is not a particle of human knowledge, but may be of use in a camp or on a battle-field. The higher the science of war is carried by a nation, the more certainty there is of her being at peace. There is an eloquence in cannon which reaches a foe above all the silver-tongued instruments of art. The argument from a full mouthed battery is powerfully convincing. The spirit to *defend* may degenerate into a passion to *conquer.* This, by a people of cultivated minds, will be guarded against and prevented; sages and warriors should live together; but the disposition to quarrel is generally found to be in an inverse ratio with the ability to fight. History is full of proofs to this effect; and ancient and modern fiction furnish a thousand mirrors to reflect this truth. The Lilliputians were constantly preparing their tiny bows and arrows for an attack, and misconstrued courtesy into insult; but the giants of old seldom waged war; and when they did, it was against the gods they fought, sure of the sustaining power of their mother earth.

LECTURE XIV.

For what of thrilling sympathy,
Did e'er in human bosom vie
With that which stirs the soldier's breast,
When, high in godlike worth confest,
Some noble leader gives command,
To combat for his native land?
No; friendship's freely flowing tide,
The soul expanding; filial pride,
That hears with craving, fond desire,
The bearings of a gallant sire;
The yearnings of domestick bliss,—
E'en love itself, will yield to this.

JOANNA BAILLIE.

ON the 2d day of July, 1775, Washington arrived at Cambridge, and took command of the American army. He was not at this time much known to the officers of that army; but in addition to his having been selected by the continental Congress, a body which had the confidence of all the people, his personal appearance, his military air, his sage demeanour, his attention to every minutiæ of the camp, and his punctilious regard to religious observances, at once commanded respect and admiration. This soon ripened into that enthusiastick veneration, which had before been rather the creature of the imagination than the belief of the understanding. This adoration, for it came as near it as any thing a mortal could inspire, was never for a moment lessened by accident or reverse of fortune. Washington had the undiminished affections of New-England from that hour to the last moment of his existence. The war had commenced in good earnest; for a large army besieged the town of Boston from this time until the next spring, when it was evacuated by the British. The continental Congress soon began to think of effective measures in attack as well as in defence. In the fall of 1775, Generals Schuyler and Montgomery had been sent from New-York to attack Canada. Ticonderoga and Crown Point had been previously taken. The reasons which Congress avowed for this offensive war were, the reports that General Carleton had been stirring up the Canadians and Indians to harass our frontiers. The plan of attacking Quebeck was a most magnificent one; but of very difficult execution. A detachment were to penetrate to Canada from the Kennebeck through the wilderness. Twelve hundred men were taken from Washington's camp for this service. The commander in chief cast his eye around him, and with that power of discrimination which in him was a peculiar trait of character, he fixed on General Arnold, of the Connecticut troops, to command this daring adventure. Arnold most cheerfully undertook it. The crossing of the Alps by Hannibal was nothing to so bold an adventure as this. The hunter had not passed over the ground; nor had man, civilized or savage, ever left a track of any kind for them to follow. In the midst of famine and frost, they acted with decision and firmness. Three hundred out of the twelve, after having penetrated far into the wilderness, were sent home for want of provisions, and the others marched on. On the 31st of December, in the midst of a snow storm, an attack was made on the city of Quebeck by Montgomery's and Arnold's troops in different places. Arnold was wounded and Montgomery slain. Montgomery was a gallant officer, and had seen much service; and his death was deplored by every lover of liberty. The assailants were repulsed; but the city was besieged for several months afterwards, by General Thomas from Massachusetts, and General Sullivan from New-Hampshire; both officers of great merit. Thomas died in the campaign with the small pox. He was one of the most intelligent and experienced officers in the American army.

The summer of 1776 was spent in watching the enemy, whose forces were now large, probably not far from twenty-five thousand; and our scattered forces were unequal for any thing more than holding the enemy in check. Despair sat at this time on every face. The timid had begun to think in what manner their peace was to be made with the mother country. It was at this moment of deepest despondency that the genius of Washington developed itself. With an army of two thousand four hundred men, suffering in the blast; an inclement winter having commenced, provisions become scanty, and that distress which precedes sickness of heart, and recklessness of conduct, being depicted in every countenance, Washington determined to make a dash upon the enemy, to recover the lost tone of feeling, or perish in the attempt.

"—— Oh light and force of mind,
Next to almighty in severe extremes!"

On the 26th of December, the advanced guard of the enemy were surprised and beaten at Trenton, with a slight loss on the side of the victors. Hope again illumined our horizon. The soldier felt the life blood flowing more warmly in his veins, and even the halls of Congress resounded with the accents of eloquence, dictated by hope of ultimate success. This victory was followed up by that of Princeton, in which the gallant Mercer lost his life.

Immediately following these events, the European nations began to look with interest on the scenes taking place in this country. At the commencement of this year the chivalrous and patriotick Lafayette came to assist us in our cause. The skirmishes which were daily taking place, more often than otherwise, eventuated in favour of the continentals, and the militia of the several states.

The next important circumstance, in the military history of our country at that eventful period, was the taking of Burgoyne and his army at Saratoga, on the 17th of October, 1777. This was truly the deciding point of the conflict; all who were doubtful of the issue before were settled in opinion now; and this was the general impression, not only throughout this country, but in a large proportion of Europe. This event was so important in all its bearings on our national affairs, that I feel bound to give this portion of our history in a bolder relief than I have, or can, any other epoch in our military character and history.

General Burgoyne had, by his representations to the ministry of Great Britain, induced them to furnish him with an army of ten thousand men, with which he promised to come from Canada by the Lakes Champlain and George to the North River, and from thence to New-York city; thinking that by thus separating the south from the north-east, it would so divide and dispirit the American forces, that they would soon yield to such terms as the British were disposed to offer them. He, with a large body of regular troops, and a considerable body of Indians, came to the fort at Ticonderoga, the most formidable work in North America. It had been taken from the British by Col. Ethan Allen, early in the spring of 1775, after the battle of Lexington, and before that of Bunker Hill; and was, when Burgoyne reached it, garrisoned by a considerable army under General St. Clair, who had no apprehensions for

X 2

the safety of his fort. This fortress was an old French work of
great strength, and of gigantick dimensions, with walls from six to
ten feet in thickness, with a covert way to the waters of the lake.
When the British army arrived in the neighbourhood, all was tranquil for several days, when it was, to the surprise of the Americans,
found that a blockhouse had been erected on Mount Defiance, an
eminence which overlooks the fort, and had been heretofore considered inaccessible to human foot, holding it in entire command.
St. Clair at once determined on evacuating his strong hold, and to
make his escape in the night; this was attempted, and a few succeeded in making their escape; but a great proportion of the forces
were taken or slain on their retreat. This was a dreadful blow to
the feelings of the north and east. Ticonderoga was considered
safe. It was an important post, and was dear to us from the profusion of blood which had been shed there. The progress of the
British army became alarming; and from every quarter of New-
England and New-York they mustered without much regularity or
order, to stop its progress. Stark marched with the New-Hampshire forces under the express condition that he should not be joined
to the continental forces. He had been irritated at what he considered neglect, in the selection and promotion of officers, after
Washington formed the army at Cambridge; and on no account
would be placed under continental officers. The American army
every day increased; but this did not alarm, in the slightest degree,
the British general. His army was full of gentlemen of high rank
at home; six of them at that time were members of Parliament, and
others were of the first circles of fashion in England. They had
thought the campaign would only be a mere pastime. With this
body of troops were several elegant women, who had followed the
fortunes of their husbands across the water, and through the wilderness; among them was the Baroness of Riedesel, whose husband
commanded the German troops. She was a splendid woman;
gifted with genius, and blessed with an education of the highest
order, in the most polished courts of Europe: she was destined to be
the best and most pathetick historian of that memorable expedition.
The Baroness had a daughter born in this country, and from the
kind treatment which she received here while a prisoner of war, she
gave the child the name of the country—America. Lady Harriet
Ackland was with the army; her husband was the gallant Major
Ackland, who afterwards fell in a duel defending the American
character for bravery. Lady Balcarras, a woman of great spright-
liness, was also in the circle, besides a great number of ladies of
less note, but of high taste and accomplishments, the wives of officers less known to us than those we have mentioned.

The Americans had rapidly assembled, and the British commander moved on to Saratoga. When he reached the heights of that place, he found his opposers so numerous, and so difficult to deal with in every foraging party, that he thought it best to fortify his camp as soon as possible. This was done with great skill, for Burgoyne had been bred a soldier, and had with him also some of the most scientifick men of the British army; many who had been bred, as well as himself, in the school of Frederick the Great, who was then living, and watching the movements of this revolution with great interest.

Burgoyne had, on his entrance into the territory of New-York, published a manifesto, which did not evince that good taste for which the General had been distinguished; but probably he mistook the taste and feelings of those he came to subdue. This manifesto was answered by Washington in a very forcible manner. This answer contains satire and argument conveyed in the most elegant language. Its spirit is also fine and bold; the gasconade of the English commander is met with manly defiance, and he was worsted before the battle commenced, in a way he hardly expected. Burgoyne was said to have been a natural son of Lord Bingley; some, however, think that he had still more important relations. In 1762, he had a command in Portugal. After his return to England, he was chosen a member of Parliament, and became a privy counsellor. Gallant, gay, learned, eloquent, and in the full sunshine of patronage, he had taken the command of the northern army, and indulged the hope of a brilliant campaign. The fates were against him, and he was obliged to give up all his splendid visions of glory, and prepare to defend himself before his king and country. In this he was able; and one would think that he had offered a sufficient excuse for every thing but his ignorance of the foe he was to meet, and his staying so long on the frontiers after St. Clair's retreat; but for this also he had a plausible excuse. The British ministry were mortified and distressed at this unexpected failure; and to turn the popular indignation from themselves, they were obliged to sacrifice their favourite. They ordered him to return forthwith to America as a prisoner; but this was not insisted upon; yet, he was obliged to resign all his offices and emoluments, which were very considerable. He was still returned to Parliament, or held his seat there from a previous election, and joined in the opposition to the continuance of the war; warmly contending that America would prevail. From the peace of 1783, he lived a retired life, until the 4th of August, 1792, when he died, as it was stated in the papers of that day, by a fit of the gout in the stomach. An American royalist, who was in England, and resided within a few doors of his dwelling informed me that he fell by his own hand, a prey to disappointment and neglect. There never arose a man in Great Britain who for a time held so many important offices, and on whom so much reliance was placed, of whom the world knew so little. A mystery hung about him from the cradle to the grave, and that, too, in a country where there are but few secrets of any domestick or political nature.

The American army engaged in this enterprise, contained many fine officers. Schuyler was a man of great good sense and experience, having been an officer in the war of 1755 to 1763. He preferred to assist in saving his country, rather than to put it in jeopardy by resentment at losing the honour of commanding the army in the campaign of 1777, after he had prepared the forces for it. General Morgan, the bold and intrepid Virginian, was there, and most efficient in the discharge of his duties, as he was throughout the whole war. Arnold was also one of the most intrepid soldiers in the campaign. Lincoln was there also; he was one of the most bold and discreet of the revolutionary generals. Brooks, whose share in this event, every historian of the war has celebrated, and with whose merits the present generation have been made acquainted, lived to give us many minute circumstances of the taking of Burgoyne, which otherwise would have been lost; Dearborn and Hull had their share in the honours of that day; and many more who deserve the meed of honour from the future historians, who may arise to give to distant ages the deeds of the men who fought and bled to achieve the liberties we now enjoy.

In this year, 1777, there were fifty thousand troops composing the British army for the carrying on the American war. Twenty thousand under Sir William Howe; ten thousand under Burgoyne; four thousand under Sir Guy Carleton at Quebeck, and sixteen thousand at New-York and Nova Scotia. These troops were supported at an immense expense, and it had cost great sums to transport them to this country. Their bounty money, equipments, transportation, and support for six months, was at least an hundred pounds sterling a man. From this period, the war was not pushed by England, as it was expected to have been. They seemed to wish to exhaust the patience of the Americans, as they were satisfied that it was impossible to conquer them by constant fighting. The American and English troops often came in contact, with varied success, but the enemy soon found that this was not a war to be decided by a few battles; for when they thought the provincial troops entirely routed, these very forces were forming again in the neighbourhood, and preparing to harrass those they had not force enough to subdue. The affairs at Stoney Point were well conducted, and those at Monmouth and Guilford Court House, if not of vital importance to the American cause, or if they could not be called absolutely victorious, were, all things considered, rather encouraging than otherwise; and that at Eutaw Springs was sufficiently decisive to lead directly to those measures which terminated the war, by the taking of Lord Cornwallis and his army at Yorktown. I have not mentioned these battles with the intention of giving any sort of account of them, but only to show what energy of mind was exhibited, and what exertions were called forth at every period of the revolutionary conflict. That there were moments of depression, and instances of faint-heartedness, cannot be denied; but from the opening of the drama until the curtain fell, the acting was, in general, noble, and more or less brilliant and successful as the scenes shifted. Unity of plan, and stability of purpose, were evident from the beginning to the end.

Each state might justly be proud of the share of talents and courage it furnished for this long and bloody conflict; which diminished the population, exhausted the resources of the country, and stagnated business from Georgia to Maine. The floods of paper money which had poured forth in torrents, had become worthless as the fallen leaves of Autumn; penury and distress were the rewards of the brave and the patriotick; and many of those who had fought and bled in defence of the liberties of the people, on returning home, saw their former earnings dwindled away, and felt that it was necessary to commence the world anew with injured constitutions and a soldier's habits. A good portion of them, thank heaven, were sufficiently elastick to rise from this depression, and to join in the great work of building up our free institutions, and of laying the foundation of our national prosperity.

Those who perished on the field, and those who survived to join in the labours of civil and political life, for many succeeding years, should not be forgotten by us their descendants. It is the duty of the legislatures of every state to make the greatest exertions to do justice to her portion of these heroes. It is indeed a national subject, but each state have better means, or those more directly within their reach, to give their history to the world. Most of those who have been engaged since the days of the revolution in the affairs of the nation, or who at the close of the war retired to private life, are gone; a few only remain, and these few are now imploring the representatives of the people for some remuneration for their labours and privations endured half a century ago.

The generosity of the nation to Lafayette, has met, throughout all this republic, with universal approbation. The old soldiers were willing that the gallant general should know and acknowledge the

32

truth, that republics were not always ungrateful; yet he could not comprehend the reasons that operated in preventing his own officers from coming in for a share also.　It is but seldom that legislative bodies are induced to do generous acts; these ought not to be expected of them often; but when such acts are found in the statute-books, they should be transferred to the pages of history, and preserved as a perpetual memorial, from generation to generation.　The liberality of the United States to Lafayette, should be handed down as one; and along side of it should be placed the pension law, which relieved the wretched soldier who was wasting the last sand of his life in hopeless indigence.　The construction of this act for the relief of these war-worn veterans was narrow, cold, and cutting, but was dictated, however, by prudential motives, and perhaps, on the whole, was for the best, as parsimony might have obtained a repeal of the law which distributed the bounty that justice had attempted to secure.　Has the country gone far enough in this liberal work? Is there not a debt due to the few surviving officers of the revolution? If popularity is one object of legislation, (and why should it not be, when the people have the means of judging as well as their rulers?) what easier or more direct course can there be pointed out to find it, than by doing an act of justice to these venerable relicks of another and a former age? Who is there bold enough to say aught against the law passed for the relief of the poor soldier? No one, in any place, and at any time, has murmured aught against this deed of justice and honour.　Not even the ambitious politician, haranguing before those who had a vote to give only upon the promise of *retrenchment and reform*, ever ventured to promise that he would use his exertions to have the pension law repealed.　No; nor has the miser, when nightly visiting his hidden stores, cursing taxation for every national object, ever breathed a syllable against the pension law. The language of his heart is, demolish the capitol; sink the navy; disband the army; raze your fortifications to the ground; disperse your national legislature; secure with locks and bars your treasury; but avarice never suggested to him to wish for the repeal of the pension law.

Those who, in cases of danger, do deeds of gallantry in feats against the enemies of our country, should be properly maintained while living, and duly honoured when dead.　This course will secure a succession of brave defenders of our country in every emergency.　Not all of a nation's gratitude and bounty should be lavished on a few distinguished individuals, but only on those who discharge their duty in a manner worthy notoriety.　The first thing to be done is to see that they do not suffer for the comforts of life; the next, that when dead their names shall be recorded, for their descendants to be able to look back on their deeds and services, as a stimulus for them to do likewise when called to act in similar situations. Those worthy of more consideration for services and sacrifices, should have monuments erected to their memories in places where the citizens are most interested in their fame—among their kindred and descendants. These records, history should take in charge, and give such pages in her annals as the departed may deserve, or their country's gratitude decree. We are doing something at all these, for the old and brave defenders of their country ; but have we done enough for their merits, or our honour? Montgomery has a monumental slab to tell his merits, although his ashes reposed for forty years unmarked by even a rude stone. Some few others have been remembered also; momentary excitements have been evinced, and at times have produced honourable results. The Bunker Hill association is, of all we have seen or heard of, the best. It originated in a good spirit; a feeling of patriotism and gratitude ; and is proceeding regularly and systematically. The monument they will erect, rises slowly but will stand permanently. The stone and mortar they may put together is but a small part of the plan suggested. The society is hereafter to be the repository of all the relicks of the antiquities of our country, and will keep a perpetual vigil upon Time, that his followers, Carelessness and Oblivion, may be robbed of their power to deface his records.

The treasures of a nation consist in the virtue and knowledge they possess, and in the character of their fathers, with the institutions they left to their posterity. As a people enjoy the property, it becomes a matter of principle to preserve the memory of those from whom they inherit. Except in some rare instances, the nation at large cannot take care of the fame of individuals. In small communities, a distinguished individual is well known to every member of the body politick ; but when a country is very extensive, this is seldom the case. The reputation, then, of our worthies, in every high place in life, or in every walk of intellect, must be preserved by those of the kindred and friends, and people dwelling near the scenes of his actions, and within the atmosphere of his virtues. The smallest ecclesiastical or civil association should be impressed with this duty. Let the parishes begin ; the towns and cities, counties and states, will follow. Some record should be made of the character and services of every one who acted his part with honour, at or near his death. This obituary, made short and simple in the parish record, might be expanded in those of the town or city, and when the services had been considerable, they would of course be enlarged, from time to time, as their merits were more fully disclosed. We are now indebted for half our facts in the biography of our countrymen, particularly those of an early date, to some pious effusions of the pastor of his church, at the death of the parishioner. The wish to *know* and be *known* has been, and ever will be, one of the great springs of human action. Hence, in ancient days, the connexion between the poet and the hero was sacred; and every one who harnessed himself for the fight, knew if he fought well, that he should not be forgotten when he slept in death; for the life of his minstrel was not subject to the chances and accidents of war. These minstrels noted every incident of battle, and their productions were scattered through Greece; and were chaunted at every festival, until Homer came, and by his all-powerful grasp of genius, compressed them into one unextinguishable flame of light and glory. It has been said, that science, in ancient days, invented lamps which burned perpetually in the tombs of their heroes. This was only the metaphorical language of the heroick ages, and only meant to convey the thought that the poets and historian had bathed in perpetual light—that light which is the fire of their own genius—the worthies they chose to commemorate and immortalize. The love of fame is as ardent, and as universal now, as it was then, in every man; but the nations are not so susceptible now, as in the days of Greece and Rome, or in the ages of chivalry. The local importance of a man is not, and cannot be conveyed to the remote parts of a distant land, and not lose something of its altitude and dimensions. A political popularity is often occasional and transitory, and like a burst of smoke, is soon swept away by some countervailing current of the popular breeze; but that reputation which consists in thinking *right* and acting *well*, is often as permanent in this as in any previous age. Every day some new road is opened to the temple of Fame, and the votaries are as ardent as ever. The *ambitious* man, perhaps, reaches the fane first, but the *wise one* secures the niche in which he is to repose forever. The politician should write his deeds upon the pillars that prop the state; the man of science and letters should embalm his reputation by his works; and when the soldier shall be inquired for, the answer should be, " he rests with all his country's honours blest." Saints and philanthropists, who blush at the reputation of their own good deeds, cannot be forgotten, for Fame has them in special charge; her commands will forever be imperative.

> " Rise Muses, rise, add all your tuneful breath,
> They shall not sleep in darkness and in death."

The best of all honours that can be paid the dead, is a grateful remembrance of their services; but as we are constituted, some sensible, tangible memorial, is indispensably necessary to keep their deeds fresh in our memories; hence, in every age and nation, monuments have been erected, and inscriptions written, to perpetuate the fame of those who were distinguished among men, in their day and generation.

The character of a country is involved in the honours paid their dead. Immediately after the death of Washington, the representatives in Congress, penetrated by grief at the exit of this great man, and feeling, at the moment, a deep sense of gratitude for his long and invaluable services, passed a resolution, requesting the president of the United States to solicit Mrs. Washington, the relict of the general, to consent that his mortal remains should be at the disposal of Congress. The answer of Mrs. Washington, to this request, is delicate and dignified.

The seat of government was then at Philadelphia; but was to be removed the next year to Washington City. Only one wing of the capitol was then built; but, in the plan of the whole building, the rotunda was to be as large as it now is; and in the ground story of this was to be a tomb for the burial of the father of his country. This suggestion, perhaps, does honour to their feelings, for the moment, but is no credit to their taste and judgement. The sleeping place of the dead should be in consecrated ground, uncontaminated by party strife or unhallowed bustle.

The subject, after the first moment of grief, was suffered to die away, but the plan remained on paper; and when the dome was erected, after the wings were destroyed by fire, the foundation of it was constructed in the form of a large cemetery. The intentions of Congress were not carried into effect; the mighty shade of Washington could not be sufficiently sanctified to the living, in such a place. If the dead walk abroad in the majesty of ethereal nature, it would find no consolation here. The crypt, just over the tomb, has, until the past year, been the haunt of unclean birds, in various forms. To have placed the sacred dust of Washington in such a proximity to vice and profligacy, would have been high profanation. It is well that the country have yet the debt of erecting for him a tomb to discharge, because, a better taste has sprung up, and been cultivated; and the nation must, and will redeem her pledge, and give the illustrious hero and patriot a monument worthy his name and the ability of the country. Europe and Asia are adorned with numerous monuments of departed greatness. The classical tourist finds them at every step in ancient cities and villages in Europe, and the adventurous traveller in the east, counts the pyra-

Y

mids and temples erected to the honour of those who once shook the earth with their power and pride—or to the sons of genius, who have filled the world with their glory. Many of these monuments have been spared by time, who leaves, for the contemplation of man, only a few relicks of past ages. These are the records that the thinking and the wise are anxious to read and understand, while they pass by myriads of living men, in the same countries, without interest or notice. These monuments, covered with the hoar of ages, and enwrapt in a spell, never cease to charm the man of curiosity and taste; and, at the same time, they aid the learned in penetrating the depths of ancient lore. They are the remembrances of what have been, and the teachers of what shall be; the revelations of past ages, and the prophecies of future times.*

It has been the fate of many of our revolutionary heroes, who were of secondary rank, to sink into the grave unhonoured and unknown. They died in discharge of their duties, and were, perhaps, named in a passing remark, and then thought of no more by the great mass of the people. This was in some measure excusable, when the nation was struggling for existence, and all classes were devoting their lives and fortunes to the sacred cause of freedom. But the present generation are at ease, and in the enjoyment of the earnings of their fathers, and therefore ought to rescue any deserving name from oblivion. We are a generous people in our sympathies, and have mourned over the fate of the unfortunate Andre, who fell a victim to the laws of nations, in the prime of his life, for the very reason that his case has been presented to us in every form of prose and verse by those of his own country, and we read all they write; while one of our kindred and brethren, as young, as accomplished, and as unfortunate as Andre, has hardly been mentioned by an obituarist or historian. Nathan Hale, a martyr in the cause of liberty, is a name almost unknown to his countrymen; but it is time that we should be familiar with his reputation. He was born in Connecticut, and was graduated at Yale College, in 1773, with exalted reputation as a scholar, and a lofty, highminded man. He was contemporary with Dwight, Barlow, and Humphreys, who often mourned his untimely fate, and cherished his memory by toasts and eulogies. Some of the lines of Dwight, on the melancholy occasion of Hale's death, are still extant; they breathe the affection of a friend, and are almost too true, solemn, and pathetick, to be poetical. It was a dark and gloomy period in the history of our country; and he, with many other young men, caught the spark from their fathers, in fact, anticipated them in preparing for the great

*See Appendix, note B.

struggle that was to ensue.   At the moment the war broke out, he
obtained a commission in the Connecticut line, and took the command of a company in Col. Knowlton's regiment, and was with the
army in their memorable retreat from Long Island, in 1776.   After
Washington had succeeded in an enterprise so much favoured by
Providence, he was for a while ignorant of the movements, numbers, or disposition of the British army; and anxious to get all possible information of their movements or intentions, he applied to
Col. Knowlton for a discreet, intelligent, enterprising, and bold officer,
to penetrate the enemy's camp, and bring him the desired information.   Knowlton made known the request of the commander in
chief to Hale, who was the charm of every polished circle, and the
delight of the army, the soul of honour, and "bravest among the
brave."   At the first moment it was named to him, he shrunk at the
thought of becoming a spy; but reflecting that it was Washington
who required his services, and his country that was to be benefited,
perhaps preserved, by his accepting the arduous and perilous appointment, he gave up all scruples, and instantly prepared for the
adventure.   He passed in disguise to Long Island, examined the
British camp, and having satisfied himself on every point of his
mission, he was apprehended on attempting to return; and being
carried before Sir William Howe, and finding every thing was known
to the enemy, he boldly declared himself and his object in visiting
the British camp.   Howe, without a trial, or even the forms of a
court-martial, ordered him for execution the next morning.   He was
confined for a single night, and had only an opportunity to write a
few lines to his mother and sister.   As he had led a religious life,
he asked for a clergyman to attend him in his dying moments, but
this request was denied, and he was not permitted to have even a
Bible for a moment's consolation.   A guard of pitying soldiers, with
the provost-marshal, attended him to the fatal tree.   The provost-
marshal, the common abhorrence of the camp, excited a more than
ordinary share of disgust, by the brutal manner in which the wretch
executed his victim.   The firmness and composure of Hale did not for
an instant desert him, and he died regretting that he had but one life
to lose in the sacred cause of his country—the cause of freedom and
the rights of man.   The veteran soldiers wept like children at his
untimely fate, wondering that a rebel could die so much like a hero.
The letters that he had written were destroyed; for they were so
full of fortitude, resignation, and consciousness of duty, even in this
great sacrifice, that it was thought dangerous to let the Americans
know that they had ever had such a man.   When the news of his
execution reached the American camp, every one, from the commander in chief to the humblest soldier, looked as if some general

calamity had overtaken the army.   If his death was just, the manner
of it was execrable; and a deep and settled resentment was mingled
with their grief, which was not forgotten in the future events of the
war.   It was policy, perhaps, in the methods of reasoning in the
British army, to strike terror into the hearts of the American soldiers, and to frighten them at once to allegiance.   They knew not
the people they had to deal with; for they were not to be shaken by
threats, nor awed by terror.   They could have been won by kindness, but this was never shown them.   Lictors and the axe were
too honourable for men who had dared oppose the mandates and the
arms of the mother country; the accursed tree alone would answer.
Little did the executioners of Hale think that such an awful hour
of retribution was coming as did come.

It is valiant to fight bravely when our firesides and altars are
invaded.   He who falls in such a conflict, *sleeps with all his country's honours blest:* monuments and epitaphs are given him, and
his children find a rich inheritance in his fame.   But what is this to
staking one's life and reputation together—and staking them for
love of country; to throw off the garb of distinction, which is, and
should be, a soldier's pride, and covering one's self in disguise, for
the purpose of visiting, in secresy, an enemy's camp, to discover
his nakedness or strength, not for one's own fame or emolument,
but for the general good ? It is above the common martyr's fame;
above his glory.   It is, if it can be justified at all—and nations,
polished, wise, and noble, do justify it—the highest of all mortal re-
solves.   To die is nothing; to sleep in the bed of glory is a common
lot, often an enviable one, and should never be contemplated with
horror by a brave man who draws his sword in a good cause; but
to think of the chances of an ignominious death, a dishonoured grave,
closed without funeral knell, or muffled drum, or "*volley of solemn
soldiery;*" Oh! it is too much to think on; and can never be endured without dismay, unless the living fire of patriotism is burning
with all its fierceness and unquenchable intensity.

The execution of Hale was avenged before the war was over, by
the death of Major Andre.   Justice was stern and inexorable in his
fate; but her decrees were not disgraced by brutality.   Andre was
tried by a court-martial, and had an opportunity to defend himself.
His time was protracted beyond that usually allowed a spy; he was
treated with kindness; allowed to communicate with his friends;
to write to his kindred; to dispose of his property; to do every thing
but escape his sentence, which the laws of nations would not suffer,
and the severe law of retaliation, often a preventive of the progress
of bloody crimes, forbade.   For Andre's fame the British nation have
done every thing; reared him a monument, pensioned his mother

and sisters, transported his bones to his native land, and laid them in the tomb of royalty. It is in vain that we ask our countrymen, where sleep the ashes of Hale?

The gallant Pole must not be forgotten: Pulaski was as chivalrous as a baron of romance. He landed upon our shores an exile, and threw the energies of his character into our cause—the cause of freedom and of man. He preferred the wilds of America to the refinements of European courts, to most of which he would have been welcome. With the enthusiasm of a crusader, he drew his sword in our cause. Military glory and love of freedom were the strong passions of his soul. His ancestors were soldiers; and many of them fell, foremost in the fight, while the glow of early manhood was upon them, and slept in the bed of honour. He felt, and declared, that to be alive with a head white with the snows of age, was a stain on his family name; and he feared, in the wild and romantick valour of his soul, that a winding sheet unstained with blood would be disgraceful to him. If Pulaski saw not the close of the contest, he died as he wished, in the fury of the fight, and rests in his grave in a warrior's shroud. No solemn dirge, no peaceful requiem, soothed the hero's shade; the hasty funeral rites of the battle-field alone were his. Such honours only were suited to the genius of the dead. His monument is about to arise.

Nor shall that milder, but more pure and lasting light of bravery and virtue fade from our gaze. The youthful, patriot-warrior, Kosciusko, will forever rank high among our revolutionary worthies. He was devoted to arms from his birth: a shield was his cradle, and the instruments of war were his playthings in childhood. In the joyous days of youth, the gravity of years was on his brow. Nurtured by the great, yet he felt for the humble. Liberal in political sentiment, beyond the age in which he lived, he burst from the saloons of beauty and tne sunshine of courts, to share the fare and the fate of a republican soldiery, in a perilous and a doubtful contest. His generous bearing and high attainments secured to him the confidence and admiration of the officers and soldiers of the north and south. All loved him as a brother; and Washington carried him in his bosom, as a child of his warmest affections. At the close of the conflict, he snatched a coal from off our altar of freedom, and kindled it upon that of his own country; kindred spirits gathered around him, and freedom, for a while, smiled on their efforts; but the time, in the destiny of nations, for the emancipation of Poland, had not come. Kosciusko survived his country's second thraldom, and passed the remainder of his days in the bosom of retirement—the pride of nations, and an honour to the human race. He sleeps with the mighty dead of his people; but, as yet, no monument marks his resting place; the honour of rearing the first pillar to his name must be claimed by us; but it did not arise from a resolve of Congress, nor from a statute of a state legislature, or from the sympathy of compatriots; no—his monument sprang up from the spontaneous resolve of a generation, born long since Kosciusko left our shores; from a body of youthful patriots, devoted to the attainments of science and the practice of arms, for the future defence of their country; for the cadets, at West Point academy, this deed was reserved; their Campus Martis was his beloved retreat; here he meditated new deeds for himself, new glories for Poland.

Besides the good and great La Fayette, there are others among the French troops came to our aid, that should not be forgotten. Several never returned to their native country; one of them is the subject of the following notice. When a permanent seat of government was determined on, and that to be laid out on the banks of the Potomack, an engineer of talents and experience was sought for by Washington for this service. Pierre C. L'Enfant, an officer of the French army, who had come to our shores to assist in achieving our independence, was selected by the president to superintend the business. His views were on a most magnificent scale, and those of his great employer were, perhaps, equally expanded. The engineer began his work with the enthusiasm of a Frenchman, and identified himself with the future glory of the federal city; and why should not the man of science be remembered, as well as the patriot and politician? He knew but little of the elements of a republick. L'Enfant was held in high consideration during the life of Washington, Adams, and Jefferson. He had nothing avaricious in his nature, but only wanted honourable employment and competent means of subsistence.

While engaged in superintending the building of Fort Warburton, now Fort Washington, nine miles below the city of Washington, he was dismissed from the publick service. The scanty means of the treasury ill comported with the plan he had designed, and was then proceeding to execute. He thought that the fort defending the metropolis of this great republick, should be on a scale that imperial engineers should admire, and those of our country should imitate in all future ages of their greatness. On being dismissed, his proud heart was near breaking. His accounts were ordered to be audited and settled; but he spurned to receive the amount due him, which was said to be very considerable. The country owed him employment; he wanted no pension; he would receive no winding up settlement on being thrust out of office. The country should be every way indebted to him, was his mode of reasoning.

He lived several years after he was deprived of his employments; and still in the city he had planned. He was proud and full of his wrongs; he never could forgive the pitiful spirit that deprived him of duties to perform, and means to live. So far did he carry this feeling, that he never would lift up his eyes to look towards the fort he had been building. In these latter days he was seen in all seasons of the year, taking his long walks over the high grounds of the city, silent and alone—not even muttering his wayward fancies, but wearing the calm, solemn, dark look of wounded feeling and inflexible resentment. In the independence of his soul, he shrunk from sympathy, and turned with a sense of degradation from the offers of the generous and kind hearted. For years he wore the same thread-bare long French coat, and thin nankin pantaloons, and folded his arms on his breast, as it were to keep the citadel, the heart from growing callous, or being overcome by its own griefs and resentments. The people, in general, of Washington, thought that his brain was touched by his injuries. Those who knew him well, knew all was sound there; the disease was on his heart. His great friend, and revered general, was now dead; his ashes were reposing at Mount Vernon, and those who had come up since, knew but little of him. L'Enfant was brave, generous, and manly, to the last. When the British were in possession of the city, and most of the inhabitants had fled in every direction, he went about in every street and square, to find those females who could not fly, or had courage enough to stay; and consoled them by assurance that the enemy would not disturb them; and on this occasion seemed to wake to new life himself: and assuming a cheerful manner, he entertained them with every thing a Frenchman, a wit, and a soldier, could command, to make them tranquil and confiding. The English troops knew, from his martial air, that the old gray-haired man had once set a squadron in the field; and they had so much respect for the veteran, that he wandered where he pleased, and was listened to with attention when he spoke. He died about ten years since. There is no monument erected to his memory; no epitaph has been written to condense his history, or to evince our gratitude. There were some generous spirits in the city, who strove by every delicate courtesy to soften the hardships of his closing scenes, and in some measure succeeded. He was too sensitive to be approached directly; but true generosity never hesitates to assume almost any shape, to do good to the unfortunate, who still preserve a lofty bearing.

It is now but little more than half a century since the first settlements were made in Kentucky; and now the whole valley of the Mississippi swarms with an active and adventurous population enjoying the comforts and elegancies of life, and cultivating the arts, sciences, and letters, with zeal and success, vying with her elder sisters of the republick for the palm in improvements and taste. The man who first led the way to this fruitful land, and who built the first habitation for civilized man in the wilderness beyond the mountains, cannot be too often remembered, or too much noticed. The history of Boone, if not entirely unique, belongs to the romantick spirit of the early ages. A short sketch of him may be acceptable to many.

He was born in Maryland, in 1746; but removed to the mountains of Virginia, when only eighteen years of age. Here he led the life of a hunter, then a profession known and respected by the agriculturists and other classes of society. He loved the rifle and the flaying knife more than all the implements of peaceful, quiet industry. The dangers of such a life had no terrors for him; the risks incident to it gave a zest to existence, known, perhaps, only to the brave and enterprising hunter himself; but can in part be imagined by those acquainted with his character. In 1769, Boone extended his travels to Kentucky. If he was not the first hunter who had ventured so far, he was the first who induced his countrymen to follow him, in order to make a settlement in these remote wilds. From 1769 to 1775, he visited the country, and explored it pretty thoroughly, regardless of the hardships and deprivations he endured, and in this latter year brought his family from Virginia, with others, to plant a colony in a plain now known by the name of Boonesborough. He was made a captain under the last royal governor of Virginia, but his native elements were all in favour of freedom; and he, or some of his followers, were camped on the spot where the largest city of Kentucky now stands, when the news of the first act of the revolutionary conflict reached them. Fired by the same spirit which animated their distant Atlantick brethren, they shouted for the fight, and consecrated the spot by giving it the name of Lexington, the name of that sacred ground which drank the first blood that was shed in the war of independence. The personal conflicts, the hair-breadth escapes, the successful onsets, the repeated victories of Boone, would make a volume. These will no doubt be written; but there can be no excuse necessary for giving him a passing notice when his deeds are so directly before us. It is said by those who knew him, that there was nothing fierce or savage in his nature; no love of blood, no passion for contest in his disposition; but he loved freedom, loneliness, and enterprise. He feared no hardships, and shrunk from no dangers, when necessity or duty prompted him to act; yet was at all times the most cautious of men. He met the wiles of the Indian with still greater. At times they took him for a good, and at other times, for an evil spirit. When they thought they had him in their power, he was gone; and often when they believed he was on the other side of the hills, or over the prairies, he was upon them, to disperse or destroy them. Their arrows did not reach him, nor their balls wound him, and at last they became convinced that "he bore a charmed life."

Boone had but little acquaintance with books; his study was nature and man. He abhorred that state of society which was too much trammelled by rules, and enslaved by fashion. The forest, the river, the prairie, the buffalo, and even savage man, had more charms for him than villages or cities. It was refreshing to his soul to breathe an air untainted by other breaths. He loved room; hated all restraint, grew restless in a country where hunting grounds were turned to fertile fields; and felt half his manhood depart from him in a society where he could not level his rifle to avenge his own wrongs; yet Daniel Boone was a good neighbour, and a fast friend; discreet, charitable, hospitable, and affectionate; but he enjoyed the musings of the deep solitudes, and felt the consciousness of his own superiority in proportion as he felt the necessity of relying on his own resources.

A world of anecdotes are afloat, which show his great traits of character: his daring, his fortitude, his perseverance, and elasticity. It is a well authenticated fact, that once being pursued by the Indians, he came to a precipice, on the borders of a river; when his pursuers were close on his back, he leaped from the bank, the astounding height of fifty feet, before he reached the light and wavy top of a tree, whose lithe branches had been climbing for years to catch a glimpse of the sun, above the edge of the precipice. This springy bed received him as he spread himself out; and he let himself down from branch to limb, until he fell to the margin of the stream, with only a few scratches, and some little derangement to his moose-skin dress. He forded the stream, and then poised his rifle in defiance at his pursuers. The most fierce and adventurous of the children of the forest gazed with wonder at this feat, and set down his success to preternatural power; but Boone knew his fate if taken; the stake, the fagot, the slow-consuming fire, with every insult savage ingenuity could devise, or ferocity suggest; and he preferred the chance of the leap to the certainty which would follow capture. The leap could be only death, the capture torment and death together.

The sagacity of Boone in making his pathway in the forest was superiour to his great teachers, the Indians. In this science they frequently yielded to his superiority. The stars that lighted his path, and directed his course, seemed to shed their influence on his mind; for by them he counted the long hours of the night with more than Chaldean accuracy. This wandering life kept his mind bright and active. His recollection was so perfect, that for twenty years or more, after he had blazed a tree, or marked it with his name, he would remember where it stood, even if fallen, by its stump, and the make of the land around it; and sometimes when his opinion was disregarded, as being thought impossible that he should remember, on removing or turning the log from it, proofs of his correctness became visible.

In process of time, the very wilderness he first subdued became too populous to suit his taste and habits; and he felt himself annoyed at the whole mass of laws the progress of civilization required, and which were enacted. The disputes respecting boundaries; the quarrels about *meum* and *tuum*, gave him distress; for he remembered the time when all was *mine*, and when miles and acres were not thought of, and he could not bear to mention feet and inches. Getting involved in some of these disputes about boundaries, and finding no longer that reverence which was once paid him as a patriarch and a leader, he, in the language of a border people, *pulled up stakes*, and took up his line of march for Missouri. In Kentucky, he had seen the *wilderness blossom like the rose*, where he once strayed as the only white man ; but he did not take delight in walking in the garden, and in cultivating flowers. He preferred Diana of the chase, to Flora, Ceres, or the whole train of the divinities of civilization and taste.

Such a life, it cannot be contended, gave either refinement or grace, or letters or science, to the man; but it gave a peculiarity and an elevation to his character, that all the courts of Europe could not teach. He was not destitute of letters or numbers; indeed, he had enough of each for all his purposes ; to which he added a science which is only learnt in such a school as his, a familiarity with all the indices of nature, whether they related to the formation of the surface of the ground, the flow of the river, the growth of the forest, or the haunts and tracks of animals. He followed with more than ordinary human sagacity the fox to his den, the bear to his cavern, and the beaver to his dam. To prove to himself that he had not lost his skill with his rifle, he shot, with a single ball, the humming bird, as he sucked the opening flowers, and spread his tiny wings, and presented his exquisite colours to the sun; and brought down the soaring eagle as he poised in majesty over his head, disdaining the power of the nether world. In the ungoverned spirit of the immeasurable wilderness, he reasoned, he felt, and acted, as "the monarch of all he surveyed." To such a man, the soft allurements o ' polished society would be less attractive than the beauty of the insect's wing, or the "*slight hair bell,*" which he had trodden under foot, or those immense regions of flowers, that had for successive ages *wasted their sweetness on the desert air.* Civilized man has no standard by which he can measure the operations of such a mind; he must go back to primitive ages to find a parallel; and then strip the travels of Theseus, and the labours of Hercules, of all the monstrous fictions—and what would the remainder be in comparison with the adventures and hardships of Boone. The whole country which these demi-gods of antiquity traversed, did not extend so far as one of Boone's hunting excursions. Bordering upon eighty years of age, Boone died in the interiour of Missouri, having known but little of the decay of faculties, corporal or mental. In the language of political economy, he knew nothing of *the powers of accumulating.* He thought the whole extent of the continent to the Pacifick his territory, and intended to push on to its confines, as neighbours, within fifteen or twenty miles, began to trouble him; or until he should find a grave in which his bones might moulder with those of the buffalo he had chased to the farthest west; but his fame will not go down as the fame of the mighty lords of the forest, with whom he so often struggled; for he has left children among the reputable of the land, and connexions or friends in many places, who will cherish his memory, treasure up the incidents of his life, now living only in tradition, and give them to the historian, the novelist, the painter, and the sculptor, to transmit them to posterity in the forms of truth and fancy, and perpetuate his name as *the great pioneer of the west.*

Soon after the close of the revolutionary conflict, the militia of the several states were organized by their respective governments, with more or less attention to discipline, to be prepared for future attacks from without, or commotions within. The political atmosphere was not, as yet, serene or settled, and each state was watchful of her own security and quiet. After the adoption of the federal constitution, there was a national organization of the militia, on paper; but, in truth, it was nothing more. It answered merely as some guide in drafting men, if they should have been wanted for service, but the nation did nothing for their instruction or discipline. The sagacious mind of Washington perceived that our martial spirit would soon wane in days of peace, and the knowledge of tacticks in the country be lost; he, therefore, recommended the founding of a military school, for the instruction of the youths of our country in the science and the art of war, on an extended plan, after the military academies of the old world; but so much was to be done, to carry into effect our newly adopted government, and an

Indian war still hanging on our borders, that it was not established in his day. Mr. Adams, his successor, still urged the necessity of such a school; but the agitation in this country, from the
French revolution, delayed the execution of the plan again. It was
reserved for Mr. Jefferson, the third president of the United States,
to see a military academy commenced. It was, in him, more a
passion for science, than a love of the art of war. The beginnings
were small, and the school, for several years, although it is said it
was well managed, did not attract much publick notice; business of
all sorts was brisk in this country, and most of the enterprising young
men were engaged in mercantile or professional pursuits.

The plan fixed upon for the site for this institution, was, in all respects, the most suitable that could be found in the country. West
Point was an important station during the revolutionary war. This
point is on the right bank of the Hudson, about sixty miles from the
city of New-York As you pass up the river, its appearance has
nothing more striking in it, than many other views on this majestick and picturesque river; but, on ascending the bank, the panorama is noble; a plain, of about seventy acres, is opened before you;
the river flows on the east and north of you, and is wide and deep;
a ridge of mountains stretches from the south to the northwest, of
various heights, from five hundred to fifteen hundred feet. The
up-river view is very extensive; steam boats are clearly seen ten and
twelve miles off. The city of Newburgh, situated at the distance of
nine miles from West Point, is in full view. The impression on the
mind, as you look around you, on this point, is that of a vast theatre, peculiarly fitted for defence, safety, and that deep solitude, so
necessary to bring down the attention of youth to the severity of
profound studies. There is something classical, as well as romantick,
in the situation. The vestiges of other days are still visible there;
among which, are the ruins of an old fort, on the banks of the
river, and those of fort Putnam, about half a mile distant from the
river, on a high hill, commanding, in military language, the whole
plain below. From this rocky eminence, issues a fine stream o.
pure, cold water, which, being directed to a reservoir, is conducted
by pipes to the valley, in great abundance, for the use of all the
inhabitants. West Point is not only beautiful, and convenient for
the purpose to which it is devoted, but is one of the most healthy
places in our country. The buildings for the use of the cadets
are large and convenient, but, as yet, are not sufficiently numerous
for two hundred and eighty cadets, and their instructors; but the
good feelings of the people are with this institution, and the government will not fail to patronize it.

The cadets are now under the best of all possible regulations.

The constant occupation of their time has a most salutary effect on their habits, and intellectual as well as corporal discipline. Their temperance generally lasts through life; for they acquire, with the practice of abstemiousness, the scorn of indulgence. The Spartan severity in discipline is mental as well as corporal. The course of studies is of a high order, and well calculated to give firmness and tone to the mind, and is so perfectly absorbing, as to prevent those dreamy wanderings, so enchanting to the young in the bowers of taste and the halls of learning. The votaries of science and the art of war, have no time to court the muses or invoke their inspiration. The knowledge acquired at this institution is as useful in peace as in war. As civil engineers, the graduates of West Point are of incalculable advantage to our country; an immense territory is yet to be surveyed, and its capacities ascertained. The uses of this institution are not confined to its members; the fine examples it has set in mental and corporal education, have been extended to other institutions of instruction. It has solved the problem in the minds of fathers—how much labour will the youthful mind bear? and has taught tender mothers, that their darling sons may endure hard marches, and sleep "on the tented field," without injury to their growth or beauty; for healthier young men I never saw than the cadets of West Point; if they lose by their discipline something of the bloom and ruddiness of youth, it is more than made up in the firm step and strengthened muscle seen in the elastick movements of the corps in their military evolutions.*

The cadets are arranged on the list of honour, according to their merits. This is an admirable device; it produces emulation, breaks down the aristocracy which finds its way every where, even in our republican country, and builds up an order of intellectual merit. Genius and application make out their own patents of nobility.

The physical force of our country is incalculably great. It is science alone we want, to be irresistible to all invaders; and through the medium of this school we are to obtain it. To be convinced that it is a school of morals and manners, as well as of science, one need only reside a few days at West Point, and become acquainted with the officers of the institution. A warm and deep interest in the academy, and a high respect and friendship for the superintendent of it, united to many pleasant recollections of attentions from his officers, induced me to write out a pretty full account of it; but in looking over the hasty sketches I have made of other and older institutions, I was constrained to curtail my remarks, and to content myself with the reflection, that it will not want for faithful and able historians.

* See Note C., Appendix.

LECTURE XV.

Yesterday, while I was at the metropolis, the news of a naval victory was received. To have witnessed the effect that it had on all classes in society, would have annihilated all your old prejudices against a navy. The streets were thronged with people, walking briskly, or stopping to reciprocate congratulations; men shook hands, who never had spoken to each other before; joy sparkled in every eye; every bosom palpitated with delight; pride swelled in every vein. Every one seemed to look on his neighbour, as a braver and a better man than he had ever before thought him; every sailor, as he passed the streets, was greeted with repeated cheers. I started for home; and, as I rode through the country, every oak I saw, I said to myself, that will do for ship-timber; every pine seedling, growing up for ornament, I was anxious to see ripened into "the mast of some great ammiral." The naval actions of all ages and nations crowded on my mind—Phœnician, Greek, Dutch, French, English—even the unequalled fights of our Saxon, and Danish ancestors, with their " *Steeds of the Ocean,*" came rushing to my mind; memory seemed to give up her dead for the glory of the occasion. As I passed through Marblehead, the welkin was ringing with shouts of victory; mothers joined in the general joy, whose sons were in the fight—not knowing whether they were living or dead. The Ocean-Spartan matron had no tear to shed; there was no cowardice or disgrace in the battle; if the boy was dead, he died in the discharge of his duty. As I reached my native village, parson Makepeace was in the pulpit, ascribing glory to God for the victory. The chairman of the selectmen made a speech; I followed him; heaven only knows what I said—but the speech was applauded, until the old meeting house shook to its centre. Never tell me again, that the peaceful pursuits of life will make a hero; they are created by such moments of ecstasy as these. There is not a creature, who bears the image of man, in the whole of the United States, however tame his blood, that would not fight like a lion, if called into action at this moment. I believe, in my soul, that this naval victory has exalted the character of every man, woman, and child, in the whole country; and, if I may be allowed the expression—and what shall I not be allowed in this moment of holy enthusiasm?—it will give an impulse to unborn ages.

Jonathan's letter to his cousin Buckskin.

OUR country not only puts in her claim for her military prowess, but also for her naval feats of skill and bravery, from the early days of our existence. The colonial settlements were stretched along the seaboard, through many degrees of latitude, and fine rivers were found navigable far into the interior. The ocean was, at first, looked to for a part of their sustenance, and soon regarded as one of the means of prosperity God and nature had put into their hands, for the purpose of increasing their wealth, strength, and happiness. They coasted from one settlement to another, for trade and friendly intercourse. As early as 1635, before the stump from which the first tree was cut, had withered, our ancestors began the business of ship-building. In August, of that year, a ship was built at Marblehead, and called the *Desire*. This vessel was employed, probably, as a regular trader between this country and England; for, in 1640, March 1st, the Desire, (says Winthrop, in his journal,) a ship built at Marblehead, went from hence, (Boston,) and arrived at Graves-end, in the Thames, in twenty-three days—a proof that this vessel was a good sailer, however fortunately the winds might have blown. Soon after this period, from the abundance of timber, vessels were built in this country, by agents, for the commercial purposes of Great Britain. Models and master-builders were sent out very early; and, at no time, have the colonists been backward in learning all the wisdom of the mother country, in whatever shape it was to be found.

In 1690, when the first expedition was fitted out against Canada, the New-England states furnished a large proportion of the transports; and, long before this period, every colony had one, or more, ships of war, of considerable force. In the attack on Canada, after this, in 1710 and 1717, Massachusetts furnished the transports, for troops and provisions.

In the war of 1745, it is said, by several writers, and lately mentioned in that excellent collection of facts, Walsh's Appeal, that the colonies had four hundred privateers on the ocean. In this calculation, the writer must have included all the small boats, which went out to harrass the French commerce. In this war there were several hard fights, and many prizes taken. Capt. Rouse, of the Shirley galley, of twenty guns, in company with Capt. Cleves, brought in eight ships, prizes taken from the French, with their cargoes, "ninety thousand mud-fish," meaning what we now call bank-fish. For this exploit, Rouse was made Post-Captain in the British navy. In October, the same year, the Bomb Ketch, commanded by Capt. Spry, took a French ship of sixteen guns. These were the most conspicuous cases; but there were many captures, which history has not recorded, and which I should have been able to have obtained from the records of the Admiralty court, of Boston, the only one then in New-England, had not the records been carried off by the judge of Admiralty, in 1775, who was a tory; and most of the cases were not named in other places. At the time of taking Louisbourg, the naval force of the provincials was highly respectable. It would not, perhaps, be tedious to name it.

Ships—Massachusetts Frigate, Capt. Tyng,   -   -   **20** guns.

   Cesar, Capt. Snelling,   -   -   -   -   -   **20**

   Shirley Galley, Capt. Rouse,   -   -   -   -   **20**

Snow—Prince of Orange, Capt. Smithurst,   -   -   -   **16**

Brig—Boston Packet, Capt. Fletcher,   -   -   -   **16**

Sloops—————, Capt. Donahew,   -   -   -   **12**

   ————, Capt. Saunders,   -   -   -   -   **8**

   ————, Capt. Bosch,   -   -   -   -   **8**

Rhode Island ship, hired for the purpose, and

  commanded by Capt. Griffin,   -   -   -   -   **20**

From Connecticut, there were two armed vessels,

  the Thomson,   -   -   -   -   -   -   **16**

  and the Colony Sloop,   -   °   -   -   -   -   **16**

New-Hampshire sent her colony sloop, as did Rhode Island, which were probably of about sixteen guns each.

The fisheries were nurseries of this navy. These fisheries had been carried on to a great extent, for several years. In 1732, the town of Marblehead, alone, had one hundred and twenty fishing schooners. Many other towns on the seaboard, also, were engaged in the fisheries, as well as Marblehead, but not to the same extent. The whaling fishery was then pursued by many on Cape Cod, and soon afterward at Nantucket. These fishermen were the hardiest of all the sailors in the world. The employment, with them, was a matter of choice, not of necessity, as land was yet plenty in the market. These sons of Neptune were accustomed to all climates, from the equator to the Frozen Ocean. They feared no enemies, nor storms; and the man who had harpooned a whale, was not to be daunted at the appearance of any other foe.

In the war of 1755 to 1763, there was a great call for our sailors, not only on the ocean, but on the lakes. Privateers were making depredations on the French commerce in the West Indies, and in the mouth of the St. Lawrence. The ship carpenters and seamen, built and manned the naval force on the lakes. Besides several sloops of considerable size, there were built in two seasons on Lake George, more than a thousand boats, capable of carrying from twenty to thirty men each, besides others for the artillery, of which in the attack on Ticonderoga by Abercrombie, there was a very considerable force. These boats were built with timber much of it brought a mile or more, on the shoulders of the labourers who constructed this armament. The wrecks of some of them may now be seen at the bottom in the clear waters of that beautiful lake,

Our people lost none of their enterprise from the peace of 1763 to the commencement of hostilities in 1775; in fact these twelve years were full of exertion in extending our commerce and settling the frontiers.

After the war had begun in earnest, Washington gave commission and authority to take, and bring in, such vessels as our cruisers could capture, belonging to the British government, on the high seas. By virtue of this authority, several rich prizes were taken, some of them loaded with munitions of war, which came timely to the American army. Severals vessels being private property which had been taken by these cruisers, were promptly released. Congress sanctioned his proceedings as justifiable and proper, and at once turned their attention to a naval force. In 1776, they appointed twenty-four captains of the navy, and a few lieutentants, leaving it to the naval committee to appoint the others; and, at the same time, authorised the building of sixteen ships of war, and several smaller vessels. This, with the force which was then already in the possession of the several states, a part of which were sold to Congress soon made a respectable naval force. The work of building went bravely on, for the merchants were deeply interested in it, and readily loaned the money to government for their building, or trusted the national contractor, for materials necessary in getting this naval force into effective operation. Some of the ships were as large as thirty-two's, and from these down to four's. After this, larger vessels were built, but only one seventy-four, however, and she was never in our service. These were commanded by brave men, and there was no act of cowardice known in the American navy during the revolutionary war. There might have been a few instances of indecorum and want of discretion, but none of cowardice.

But to be a little more minute in this history, as it is important to examine our beginnings as a nation, in November, 1775, the legislature of Massachusetts passed a spirited act, by which they authorised and encouraged the fitting out of private armed vessels, to defend the sea coast of America, and at the same time created a Court of Admiralty, to try and condemn all vessels that should be found infesting the same. The preamble to this act was written by the late vice president, Mr. Gerry, and it is a bold and an ingenuous exposition of the sovereign rights of the people in such an exigency, founded on the royal charter of William and Mary, under which the affairs of the province of Massachusetts had been administered for more than eighty years. The body of the act was penned by Mr. Sullivan, late governor of Massachusetts, an early and firm patriot of the revolution. On the 16th of December of

Z 2

that year, the government of Massachusetts, resolved to fit out ten vessels to go to the West Indies for military stores. On the 29th of this month John Adams and J. Palmer, were appointed by the legislature of Massachusetts, a committee to prepare and report a plan for fitting out armed vessels. On the 8th of January following, eight thousand pounds were voted for the purpose of making a respectable marine force for the province. On the 11th of January, 1776, it was resolved in council, to build two frigates, one of thirty-six, and the other of thirty-two guns. On the 7th of February, it was resolved by the whole court to build ten sloops of war to carry sixteen guns each. Ten thousand pounds were appropriated to this purpose. Some of these vessels were built, and some others were hired, so that Massachusetts soon had quite a respectable naval force on the high seas at their disposal. At the close of the year 1775, Congress commissioned several vessels of war, six sloops, and thirteen gallies; but they were restrained to the taking of publick property. After the declaration of independence, and there was no prospect of peace for a season, or at least until Great Britain had tried the strength of the United Colonies, the marine was greatly increased, and twenty-four vessels were put in commission, and additions were made from time to time, to this respectable force. These vessels were commanded by high-spirited and intelligent men, and who were wonderfully successful; for in the course of three years they had taken more than double the number of their own guns from the enemy, besides a great number of merchant-men of value. More than eight hundred guns had been taken from the enemy during this time, by the marine which Congress had fitted out; while that of Massachusetts, and of the other states, were equally successful. The vessels taken by the publick and private armed vessels from the battle of Lexington to the 17th of March, 1776, when the British evacuated Boston, amounted to thirty-four of considerable size and value, with excellent cargoes. The tonnage of these captured vessels amounted to three thousand six hundred and forty-five tons. In 1776, the British vessels captured by the private armed vessels, alone, amounted to the great number of three hundred and forty-two, of which forty-four were retaken, eighteen released, and five burnt. In the following year, 1777, the success of our privateers was still greater. Vessels were captured to the amount of four hundred and twenty-one. The success continued without any great diminution until 1780. At this time the British merchants made so strong an appeal to their government, that they provided a convoy for every fleet of merchant vessels to every part of the globe. Out of the fleet sailing from England to the West Indies, consisting of two hundred in number, in the year

1777, one hundred and thirty-seven were taken by our privateers; and from a fleet from Ireland to the West Indies of sixty sail, thirty-five were taken. Taking the years 1775, 6, 7, 8, and 9, say for the first year, thirty-four; second, three hundred and forty-two; third, four hundred and twenty-one; and for the fourth, which has not been accurately given, I believe in any work, say, and this within bounds, two hundred; and for the fifth, the same, two hundred; and allowing but one hundred for the balance of the time during the war, will make twelve hundred and ninety-seven, without including those taken by publick vessels from 1776, to the close of the war; and this latter number, if it could be precisely given, would add greatly to the list of captures. The marine, undoubtedly, fell off towards the close of the war, from several causes; one, the difficulties in the finance of the country, and from the great exertions of the Admiralty of England in capturing our privateers. They had become alarmed from the complaints of their merchants, and the rise of insurance against capture, which reached an extent unknown before or since. The French navy after that time joined us in the war, and was in itself so powerful, that our smaller vessels were not wanted to co-operate with the land forces as before. Besides the defence of Charleston and Philadelphia, which were engagements that ought to be ranked among the most memorable events in our revolutionary contest, there were others all along the seaboard, of less note, but in themselves spirited affairs. Rhode Island, Philadelphia, and Charleston, have high claims for naval distinction, and for constant efforts on the high seas during the war.

Our naval affairs were managed by a marine committee in Congress, who were as active and efficient as their limited means would allow. They had the admiralty code of England and Holland before them, and took such parts of it as would answer the purpose of their design. The committee of Congress did wonders, considering their means and the difficulties they had to encounter. John Adams was an efficient member of this committee; and, delighted with the course pursued by the merchants of the Netherlands, in gaining their independence and raising their national character, he studied their state papers, ruminated upon their history, and found it wise to copy their policy. He was born and educated among a mercantile people, and was well acquainted with their true interest. He saw an extended seaboard, and knew it were folly to defend our harbours and seaports without a naval force. To him and his coadjutors are we indebted for the shape our infant navy took, and for the Herculean tasks she performed as it were in the cradle. It is not to be denied, however, that he had the cordial co-operation of all the efficient members in Congress in every state, whether more or less maritime; for these enlightened men saw what a mighty engine of power this force might be made in a foreign war; and they soon saw, too, how much a matter of gain it was in that day. John Adams has deservedly been considered the father of the American navy. His disposition was of that prompt, effective, and daring character, that made him delight in the naval glories of his country. He knew that Great Britain was henceforth to be separated from us, and that it was only by cherishing a desire for naval distinction, that we were ever to contend upon equal ground with her. This he declared almost as soon as he saw the conflict gathering, and the storm ready to burst, long before he had assisted the people, or their representatives, to brace themselves up for the declaration of independence. A naval force was thought by all to be necessary at that day. It was long since that period, that the establishment of this great engine of national defence was considered of questionable policy. Then the representatives of all the states concurred most heartily in doing every thing in their power to encourage the increase of our naval force. The success of the privateers gave an elasticity and spirit to the people that nothing else could have given. It gave them wealth also, through the medium of enterprise and valour. The seaports were full of the bustle of preparation for cruising and reception of prizes. Articles of merchandize were common, and of a quality the frugality and economy of our people had never permitted them to think of before. These articles were of use to citizens and soldiers, and the sale and purchase gave a specious form to business. A great part of the capital on which they were obtained, was the hardihood and daring of the people. This success inspired the army likewise; for they saw that sailors of a new creation could meet, and dared fight, the hardy sons of Neptune born in old England, and educated in the best of fleets in the world; and that these veterans were often found to yield to American sailors of but a few months discipline on the high seas.

In the bustle that privateering created, the loss of lives and limbs was forgotten, and the pride of conquest, and the joy of the possession of property won by daring, concealed the pain of many wounds, and perhaps healed a great many that a want of success might have festered and rendered immedicable. In an army, individual bravery seldom finds an opportunity for display, while in these sea-fights almost every one had an opportunity of showing his prowess. These mariners on board a privateer were sharers in the success of every enterprise, often a better, or stronger motive for brave deeds, than the sound of a name. It was often that they had an opportunity of selecting the commander under whom they would serve; and men so situated, are generally sagacious in discerning the merits of their superiours; particularly when that merit, in a good measure, consisted in overt acts, of which they were as good judges as men of higher grades of mind, and of higher rank in society. Several of these commanders of privateers were men of original and commanding talent, and deserve to be handed down to posterity, as well as the leaders of small bands in the primitive wars of the classical ages. Manly, Mugford, Jones, Waters, Young, Tucker, Talbot, Nicholson, Williams, Biddle, Hopkins, Robinson, and many others, who were either in the service of one of the state sovereignties at that time, or in the service of Congress, have been noticed by the writers of biography in times past; but there are many more who are equally worthy of notice, who have been neglected, because they were only commanders of privateers. It ought however to be considered, that our vessels of war were small, and did not in general carry more guns or men than some of our privateers at that time; and the commanders of both classes of vessels, those of the United States, and those of private citizens, were educated and trained alike, and had equal sagacity, skill, and success. Scarcely a day passed, from the summer of 1775 to 1780, that the people were not animated with the news of some sea-fight, and generally victory was on our side; for these privateers were built for quick sailing, and when they thought the fight would be at odds against them, they out-sailed the enemy, and escaped to annoy them in some other quarter. These commanders, in general, were men of standing, honour, and principle, and never suffered themselves to sink into petty tyrants, or lawless buccaneers, in their manners or feelings. Instances of the most magnanimous conduct among them might be given. In several cases of capture, when they understood the owners were friendly to the cause of America, the vessels and crews were suffered to depart without losing a particle of property. In the vessels taken by these privateers, as in the publick armed ships, the officers were never deprived of their baggage, and often were allowed their *adventures,* if their owners had allowed them such privileges, and they had any on board. Some few of these commanders of privateers have lived down to our time.

John Lee, one of the race of men almost *sui generis,* was well known to the lecturer several years ago, and his reputation stood among his fellows as *the bravest of the brave.* He was born in Marblehead, a place renowned in the annals of our country, for producing a succession of mariners of the boldest, hardiest, and most muscular, and above all, the most humane that any country or age could boast. That place had the honour of building the first ship of any considerable size, that was constructed in our country, the one mentioned in the first part of this lecture; and of encouraging the

cod-fishery in the early days of our history, when the business was
hardly known, except in the vicinity of that place. Lee was bred a
sailor, and from his talents and connexions, soon came to the command of a vessel. He was engaged, at the commencement of the war,
for his connexions, the Traceys, merchants of great distinction at
that time, as a captain of one of their private armed vessels. He first
sailed in a vessel carrying six iron guns, with several wooden ones
for a show; and during this cruise he took a heavy armed merchantman, which he saw just before night, but his vessel was so low in the
water that she was not discovered by the merchantman. Lee came
near his enemy when it was dark, with indistinct lights extending beyond the bowsprit and from the stern of his vessel, which gave
her the appearance of great length. The English captain, thinking
it were idle to contend with such force, as he thought her from this
stratagem, struck his colours, and as his men came on board of Lee's
small vessel by boat loads, they were secured; but when the English
captain came on board, and saw how he had been deceived, he attempted to kill himself, but was prevented by Lee, who by gentle
treatment soothed his wounded feelings. Lee had in his composition the pure elements of a sailor; a fine constitution, great activity,
and a fearlessness that was the admiration of all. He was as generous as brave, and shared his honours with all who acted with him,
and his wealth with every one who sought him. At one time, Lee
was a prisoner in a murky dungeon, for what was called insolence
after being captured; at another time, flushed with victory, over foes
of twice his power, he was active in showing his kindness to the captured. On one day he was found rolling in riches, and on another
with clothes hardly sufficient to keep off the blast: thus he passed
through the revolutionary conflict; but there was never a moment
when his genius cowered, or his spirits were broken. If ever he
changed at all, it was that his pride increased as his fortunes were
unpropitious; and he grew more forbearing when in the flow of
prosperity. For many years he poised himself on his honesty and
good intentions, and swore away all religious thoughts; but in the
latter part of his days, he became an enthusiast in religion; and his
zeal in praising God equalled his fury in the fight; but time, religion, and reflection, gave a new form to his cast of character; and
the once boisterous captain, whose oaths were louder than the northern blast, became so meek, so mild, so patient, so exemplary, that it
was a study and a delight to see and hear him. When the most cruel
fit of the gout was upon him, and nature was sinking with her agonies,
he had the sweet serenity of the saint; and the eyes which once
flashed the fire of indignant and indomitable pride, were now beam-

ing with the radiance of heaven inspired hope: such changes there are in the lives and in the characters of men.

Wingate Newman, was another of these gallant souls, who inspired the world with confidence. He often said that he could obtain a crew in one hour for a twenty gun ship, if there were men sufficient for the purpose in the port. His character was that of amenity and distance, united to great personal strength, and with that princely generosity which attracts and secures the confidence of inferiour minds. "He was made for an admiral," was the common saying of his crew, and they relied on his judgement without thinking that he could possibly do wrong. In times of peril, genius finds his natural altitude. A thousand years of peace would never bring a hero from the crowd. If the British navy had not existed, Nelson might have been a curate of forty pounds a year.

To show the men we possessed, and the versatility of their talents, I will name another of the active spirits of that day. Michael Titcomb was a person of a colossal size, and of wonderful strength. He served as soldier and sailor with equal facility. At one time, he was an officer in Washington's guards, and received a letter of commendation for his daring and officer-like conduct in the discharge of a dangerous and important duty. At another, he was found a lieutenant on board of an armed ship, performing prodigies of valour. At the peace of 1783, he took the command of a merchant vessel; but when our navy was equipped, in 1798, he was again called into the service, and proved that he had lost nothing of his native fire and personal strength. Every sailor in the navy had some wonderful tale of his feats of strength. He had considerably passed the prime of life when I first knew him; but his constitution was firm, and his physical energies but slightly impaired; but with this great strength, he was one of the most quiet and peaceable of men, and constantly acted in fear of the effects of his own corporal powers, when insulted or assailed; the only thing he could fear. If so disposed, we might go on for many a page with such instances of worthy men, who served their country in the perilous conflict which gave us national existence: and who shall say that they ought not to be remembered? But my purpose is now only to give the characteristicks of the age, and not the biography of those men who made up our strength and glory at that day. The naval exploits of Arnold on Lake Champlain, in 1776, ought not to be passed over in silence. The subsequent conduct of this ill-starred commander ought not to keep out of sight what he, and those under him, did, when he was true to his country, and fought in her cause. He was not able, it is true, to meet and conquer his foe on the lake, but he made a noble defence with what force he had. Some of those under him on the lake were both soldiers and sailors.

Colonel Wigglesworth had been educated a scholar, was afterwards a sea captain, factor, and merchant, and had then taken the command of a regiment. He had made naval and military tacticks a study; and perhaps no man then in the country, was more accomplished in all the offices he had held, than Col. Wigglesworth. In this victory, if victory it may be called, of Carlton on the lake, there was nothing for the enemy to boast of, and nothing for this country to regret, except the fact that our fleet was not equal to that of the enemy. The genius of the place only waited for a coming age, to bind the laurel on the brow of the young republick. The lake-god saw the treason in the man, and reserved his water-greens and his corals for the brow of one who was as virtuous and patriotick as brave.

In 1785, all the vessels of this country were sold off, and we remained without a navy for nearly ten years: still the people were not less maritime. They waited for an opportunity to commence anew on a better plan. Numerous small vessels were not wanted, but a few efficient ships were indispensable, for national defence and national dignity.

Commercial enterprise is the mother and the nurse of naval greatness. No sooner had our country formed a government, and established a code of marine laws, than our daring navigators explored every sea. They had before been acquainted with the bays and harbours to a high northern latitude, having visited them for whales and furs; but they now entered the Baltick, pushed farther up the Mediterranean, swept round the Cape of Good Hope, visited China, the English East Indies, and all the straits and islands of those seas. This was not all; they followed the path of Cook and Vancouver; visited all parts of the Pacifick, and began a profitable trade on the North West coast. The whalers followed them; and supplied our own, and other countries, with oil of a better quality than had been before used. In these voyages were bred the best of seamen; inured to every climate, and accustomed to all varieties of savage men, they feared nothing in human shape. The best of sailors were at hand, as soon as they were wanted to man our ships of war. They required no drilling for naval service, every man could throw a harpoon, manage a great gun, or take any post he was appointed to fill. The protection afforded our seamen, is one reason that they are so energetick. They are, indeed, a privileged class; for, while every able bodied citizen of a certain age, is liable in time of war to be drafted for military duty, the law does not allow of a press or a draft for sailors. They ship by their own free will and accord, under which commander they choose, either in a merchantman, private armed vessel, or publick ship of war. They feel as freemen and act as such. There is no doubt but that feature in our navy can be preserved, as the population of the country will keep pace with the increase of our navy; and commerce and the fisheries will still continue the nurseries for seamen.

In 1794, a proposition was brought forward for creating a navy, and after a sharp debate, a bill was passed by a majority of two only, in the house of representatives, for building four forty-four's and two thirty-six's. The most experienced and skilful ship-builders in the country were sought for, and employed, and the work began in earnest. Humphries and Hacket, master builders and modellers, did themselves great credit by the specimens they produced. In 1798, and 1799, this country had built up a considerable navy; six forty-four's, three thirty-six's, seven thirty-two's, and from fifteen to twenty, or more, smaller vessels of war. This sudden creation of a naval force showed the maritime world, what the resources and energies of our nation were, whenever they should be pushed to develop them. In 1798, the nation were in a state of agitation, and the secretary of war, who was then charged with superintending the concerns of the navy, addressed a letter to the Hon. Samuel Sewall, *chairman of the committee of the house of representatives for the protection of commerce, and the defence of the country*, containing his views of the necessary preparation for the exigencies of the times, to protect our *territory*, *property*, and *sovereignty*. All our naval forces were soon put in requisition. An act was passed in May, 1798, which authorised "the president to direct our cruisers to *seize, take, and bring into any port of the United States*, any vessel sailing under the authority of the French Republick, hovering on our coast for the purpose of committing depredations on vessels belonging to our citizens," &c. In conformity to this act, Captain Dale, in the Ganges, who had been fitted out with limited instructions, received those of a broader nature, but still limited to come strictly within the act of the 28th of May. During the summer, others were ordered out, and our commerce in the West India seas was well protected. Until this period, we had no regular and systematick arrangement in this department; but at this period the cost of building and equipping the navies of other nations were examined, and rules for our own were readily to be found in them, if in many items, they were considerably different. The strongest arguments were used to show the propriety of efficient measures, and were generally convincing and satisfactory. In this *quasi* war, as it was called by Mr. Adams at that time, the American navy took from the French Republick, from

2 A

1798 to 1801, between eighty and ninety armed vessels, and re-captured many American vessels, which the French cruisers had taken from the citizens of the United States. The most conspicuous of the engagements in this naval contest, was that of the Constellation Captain Truxton, and the Insurgent, of forty guns, and four hundred and nine men, in which the latter was taken; and that of the same American ship and commander, with the Vengeance, a fifty-four gun ship, which escaped after she had several times struck her flag. The next in point of size was the Berceau, of twenty-four guns, and two hundred and twenty men, taken by the Boston, Captain Little. Captain John Shaw, in the Enterprize, of twelve guns, captured six armed French vessels, and re-captured eleven American vessels, in a cruise of eight months. In these engagements, in one of which he contended with superiour force, he took forty-seven guns and three hundred and seventy-nine men, and in all of them together, the enemy had thirty-one killed and sixty-six wounded. Although there were a few mistakes in the naval affairs of that period, yet, the whole course together, reflected the highest honour on our country, and gave evidence not only to France, but to the other nations, that we were fitted for a naval power, and should soon take our rank with the nations of Europe, on the high seas. Many young officers distinguished themselves, and gave early promise of the high character which they have since sustained. The whole cost of the creation and support of this navy was short of ten millions of dollars; not equal to the revenue of our nation for one year of this war.

Under the act of the third of March, 1801, all the ships and vessels, belonging to the navy of the United States, were sold, excepting thirteen, and these, mostly frigates; they brought in the market but a small proportion of their original cost. This sacrifice was a matter of no importance, in comparison with the glory we had gained; aye, something more than fame was gained. The success of our naval forces taught, not only others, but ourselves, that it did not require the pressure of a revolutionary struggle, to make us a maritime nation, in the true naval sense of the word; a nation who could make the greatest exertions to protect and extend a lawful commerce, upon the broadest basis. Avarice might have wished us to have risked nothing; and to have purchased our mercantile privileges, by debasement and sycophancy to other nations; and timidity preached to us a long homily upon the mighty powers of these nations, and entered into deep calculations upon the folly of risking any thing, when we were so weak and defenceless; but, thanks to heaven, the proud spirit of our fathers prevailed, and the honour of the nation was not compromised by parsimony or cowardice. It seemed a dream to all the world, that a navy could rise upon the bosom of the ocean, by the power of an infant nation, in so sudden a manner. The fabled pines of Mount Ida were not formed into ships, for the fugitive Trojans, more rapidly, than the oaks of our pasture-grounds and forests were thrown into naval batteries, for the protection of commerce, and our national dignity. Scarcely had it been published in the English and continental gazettes, that our navy was sold off, and that we were destitute of a ship of war, before the seas were whitened with the canvass of a navy from our ports, that fled from no equal, and were caught by no superiour force.

Scarcely had our differences with France been adjusted, before we were called to contend with a new foe; and then the diminution of our naval force was sorely felt. During our existence, as colonies, our trade had been protected in the Mediterranean, by the naval power of the mother country; but after the peace of 1783, the protection, of course, ceased, and we were obliged to purchase an immunity from capture and slavery, from the sovereignties of Morocco and Algiers. This tribute was galling to a free people, but nothing else could be done to save a valuable commerce, and we consoled ourselves that the most powerful christian nations have done the same, and some of them were still doing the same; and in fact, all of them in some way or other were still tributaries. In the year 1800, an indignity was offered our flag by the dey of Algiers. The ship which was sent to carry our tribute was forcibly sent on a mission from the dey to his master the Grand Seignior, and although it was managed in such a manner as to produce in the mind of the master of the petty tyrant, a respect for the people of the new world, by the address of the American commander, still the insult was deeply felt in every part of our country. These powers on the coast of Africa were a terrour to every mariner; for he, who feared no storms, dreaded captivity in these countries more than death itself. The Barbary powers, Algiers, Tunis, Morocco, and Tripoli, had been the scourge of christendom for ages. They had been pirates for a thousand years; from the time the Greeks had been driven from these shores to the present day, they had plundered the merchants trafficking in the Mediterranean, and made all persons they could get into their possession slaves; and these unfortunate beings they either ransomed at a great price, or cruelly devoted to labour and insults of the worst character. Spain, France, England, Portugal, Denmark, and Sweden, had suffered immeasurably from the corsairs of these piratical governments, whenever they refused to pay a tribute for their safety. These corsairs were adventurous and skilful seamen, and lived and thrived on the depredations made on all "christian dogs," as they insultingly called their foe. They often swept the Adriatick,

depredated on the coast of Spain, and Italy, and France, and infested
all the seas of that region; and sometimes ventured on the Atlantick
in search of prey. At different periods of history immense efforts
had been made to subdue them. In the time of Ferdinand of Spain,
he drove them from the seaboard, and for several years kept them
in fear and dread of him; but in 1615, Barbarossa, a Turk, and one
who had been a corsair, got possession of Algiers, and by every
species of cruelty and intrigue, extended his influence and power
along the coast for some distance. He fell, as most tyrants have
done, in violence and blood, and his brother became, for the security
of himself and friends, a tributary to the Grand Seignior. The formidable works erected by the Spaniards while they had possession
of the country were destroyed; and with thirty thousand christian
slaves, then unransomed, he built the wall and other works which
now defend the city. Spain and Italy, and all true christians, were
in tortures at the treatment of their countrymen and fellow christians;
and Charles V. of Spain, in 1641, made a bold effort to extirpate this
nest of pirates at once. With one hundred and twenty ships,
twenty gallies, and thirty thousand men and gentlemen, who had
entered into it from religious views, as it was considered a holy war,
he commenced his campaign. In this fickle climate the elements
warred against him, and all this tremendous host were either destroyed by the tempests, or killed by the foe, or returned disheartened,
notwithstanding the bull of the pope, and the blessing of the cardi-
nals and priests upon the holy expedition. France once in later
years, in a fit of resentment, made a spirited attack upon them, but
did not follow it up with any permanent efforts. It seems mysterious,
but so it was, that the United States should be the first power in
modern times who could, or who did, keep in check the corsairs of
those seas; and who dared to blow the castles round the heads of
those who sought protection in them.

In 1800, the bashaw of Tripoli was anxious to have tribute paid
him also, and made his demand in a bold insulting manner. The
Bey of Tunis also raised his voice for tribute. On the 15th of May,
1801, the bashaw of Tripoli declared war against the United States.
This was precisely the act our naval commanders were desirous of;
but the horrours of slavery made a great impression upon the minds
of some of our citizens, who clamoured to have every sacrifice made,
that we might be kept in security; fortunately this was not the general feeling. Before this declaration of war had been made, the President of the United States had sent Commodore Dale with a squadron
of observation, consisting of three frigates and a schooner. His instructions were full of caution, yet not wanting in decision. On the
6th of August, 1801, Lieutenant Sterret, in the Enterprise of twelve

guns, took the first Tripolitan ship of war, or the first of any of these Barbary powers which ever struck to our flag. The prize mounted fourteen guns; she had twenty killed and thirty wounded in the action, but there was not an American injured.

This fight fully showed our superiority in naval tacticks and gunnery over any thing these pirates could produce. Early in 1802, a relief squadron was sent out to the Mediterranean; Captain R. V. Morris was in command of it. The squadron was one of more efficiency than that of Commodore Dale's. It was well appointed, and provision made for ample supplies. In May, 1803, the bashaw of Tripoli proposed a peace; his *sine qua non* was two hundred thousand dollars and the expenses of the war. The negociation was instantly given up, and these terms considered inadmissible. He had become, however, quite tired of being blockaded in his own port. In June, Captain Morris was suspended, for it became apparent that he did not act with sufficient energy; nothing brilliant had been done under his command. The trade it is true had been protected, and probably he thought this the chief end of his duties. The secretary of the navy was not satisfied with this, and he appointed Commodore Preble to take the command of the squadron. This was a fortunate appointment; Preble was a man of sterling talents, and well acquainted with his duty; of the most cool and determined bravery, and was panting for some occasion for distinction. He had with him some noble spirits, Bainbridge, Decatur, and others, cast in the same mould, and animated by the same soul with himself. The squadron had not only to blockade Tripoli, but to watch the movements of Algiers, Morocco, and Tunis; but on the dey of Algiers seeming in better nature than usual, and the emperor of Morocco coming to terms, Preble made up his mind to attack Tripoli with what force he had, and a few gun-boats he had hired at Naples. On the 3d of August, 1804, he made the first attack. These gun-boats gave our men an opportunity of showing their personal strength, science, and bravery, in attack and defence; for the combatants came, as in ancient times, hand to hand and breast to breast. The minute details of this and the other attacks on this city, would furnish a story of as much prowess and chivalrous gallantry as any of the wars in the Holy Land. The deeds of the lover-knights were then sung by the minstrel, and for ages after were breathed in bower and hall, and are not yet forgotten, but still enamour the brave and the fair in this cool age of philosophy;—shall our heroes want an historian? After the second attack, which was made on the 5th of the same month, the bashaw lowered his terms for peace, offering to take five hundred dollars for each prisoner, and require no stipulation for peace hereafter. This also was not ad-

missible. On the 28th, another attack was made; and the next on
the 3d of September. The fickleness of the seas in winter would
not admit of any further attacks this season. The next summer
they were to be renewed with a vigorous determination to carry
fire and sword into the palace of the bashaw. On the 10th of September, Preble surrendered his command to Commodore Barron.
The secretary said that this was a matter of necessity. The secretary was an honourable man. Enough was done to induce the
bashaw to make peace on the 3d of June, 1805, on favourable terms,
or rather on just terms. Thus ended a war which surprised the
nations of Europe. They had often smiled to think the United
States, a new-born nation, should be so presumptuous as to suppose
that she could put down these predatory hordes, which had exacted
tribute from all the commercial world, from time immemorial; but
it was done, and the lookers on were astonished at the events as
they transpired. The Pope, who had ever been deeply interested
in all these pagan wars, or rather, all these wars against pagan
powers, declared that this infant nation had done more in a
few years, in checking the insolence of these infidels, than all the
nations of Europe for ages. The thunders of the Vatican had passed
harmlessly over these pirates' heads, through more than ten successors of St. Peter, until the United States had brought these infidels
to terms by the absolute force of naval power. The head of the
church saw that the people of a free nation had felt the degradation of
paying tribute, and were determined to do so no longer than they could
concentrate their energies, and direct them to bear upon the general
foe of christendom. The whole was indeed a wonder, that a nation
that scarcely had risen into the great family of independent powers,
should be able to grapple with, and in a measure subdue, these barbarians, who had been for so long a time the scourge of mankind.
We had not taken one power alone, but all from the Atlantick to
the Red Sea. The Doge, who had been wedded to the Adriatick,
and promised for the dower of his bride, the dominion of the seas
from the Delta of Egypt to the straits of Gibraltar, had never in the
pride of aristocratick strength, claimed the honour of humbling the
"insolent Turk" to the extent that the United States had done in a
few years. The arm of liberty, when properly directed, was always
deadly to despotism. These exertions gave our flag a rank among
the nations of Europe, in these classical seas, in which so great a
proportion of all the sea-fights in the annals of man had taken place,
from the early ages of fable and romance to modern times. The
corsair, who had been the terror of the world, was now found a
furious, but not unconquerable foe; and the barbarians, whose tremendous fierceness had been the tale of wonder in every age, seemed,

in our mode of warfare, less dangerous than the aboriginals we had been contending with from the cradle of our nation. We have sworn to pay no tribute in this region, but this were vain; shall not the mighty dead demand the tribute of a tear? And shall this be denied? Shall not the lover of his country shed one sacred dew drop of nature to the memory of Somers, Wadsworth, and Israel?* Shall we repeat the glories of Salamis and of the Nile, and forget our own heroes who devoted themselves to destruction for our honour? Oh! no; such actions are rare on the page of history and shall not be forgotten; the dullest of the sons of men shall acknowledge that there does exist, in the soul of the brave, a romantick love of country and of fame, when reminded of the deeds and fate of these victims; and shall we be wanting in these reminiscences? No; generous spirits! you shall be brought forth on all proper occasions, and your country's historians charged with handing down to the latest posterity your noble sacrifice—that of self-immolation on your country's altar. Your business was to die, and you have finished it up; be it ours to take in charge your fame, and transmit it to future times.

Here I shall stop as to the history of our navy, for all the incidents on which future history is to be founded, are fully blazoned in the newspapers of the day, and so generally spread upon the pages of our literary and historical journals, that it would be premature, perhaps, to attempt to condense, connect, and correct them for history; the laurels of our navy are too green and dewy at this hour to be fit to garner up for preservation; but suffice it now to say, that we are contented with the present size of our navy, and are proud of its fame in every stage of its growth. A navy should always be in proportion to the number, the wealth, the commerce, and the spirit of a people. It should grow no faster than its duties are required, and never over represent the strength of a nation. Its growth should be so gradual that no ignorance of nautical subjects should ever be seen in the crew of a ship, and still new sailors should be instructed in every cruise. The greatest possible science and efficiency in the smallest possible compass, should be the standing maxim of those who love a navy. It is not the creation of a navy, that we are now, as a nation, to think of it is only the management and increase of that navy, that should be brought forward as subjects of consideration; and for this increase we can have no particular anxiety. Skilful artizans to build a navy have never been wanting in this country since its earliest days; they abound now, and are possessed of all the improvements of the art of shipbuilding; and these are not a few. On our part of this continent we

---

* See Appendix, Note D.

have timber enough for all the navies of the world; our forests and
pastures, produce it faster than it can be used; and science has
taught us to make as much again as we used to, of what we have.
In addition to these great stores, the providence of a late secretary
of the navy, with the assistance of Congress, has secured an abundance of the best of live oak, by reserving for the use of the government, an immense forest of this growth in Florida. This cost the
nation but little more than the sagacious efforts of a man of political
forecast; the worth of a statesman is seldom known until he
passes away; and those who do the most good, often share the
fate that the ignorant and time-serving deserve, or a worse one.
We can never want for sailors, as long as our cod and whale
fishery are pursued, and our foreign commerce is protected.

Our mariners have amounted to one hundred and eight thousand,
and over; a fourth part of these can, on an emergency, be spared
for the navy, and these, with a small proportion of fresh recruits,
would instantly make up a most formidable force for naval operations. The iron and hemp, or its substitute cotton, can easily be
found here, and will be supplied as fast as wanted. The only ma-
teriel we were ever charged to be wanting in, was scientifick navigators, not hardy seaman, and these we are every day schooling
for our requisitions. The two hundred and fifty lieutenants, and
the four hundred and sixteen midshipmen, will supply the place of
those who in the course of nature pass away, and the list of our
veteran naval officers is rapidly diminishing. Those who come up
will not naturally be greater men than their predecessors; but it will
not be denied that their advantages for obtaining knowledge will
be much greater.   Bravery remains as it has been—and how
could it be exceeded?—nautical science is advancing with us as in
other countries. There is not a discovery in agriculture, the arts, or
in manufacturing, that has not a bearing upon our navy, directly
or indirectly. The cost of building, supporting, and educating a
navy, is now nearly reduced to a standing certainty. The people
can at once make calculations for themselves; there is no mystery
about the matter; for they can at a glance estimate the expenses
of this branch of power. One man from every hundred persons,
in our community, and two days labour every year for those persons
in our country capable of labour, will support a navy far superiour
to whatever the most ambitious statesman will ever ask of the
country. And to whom is this paid? All, to ourselves: *millions for
defence, but not a cent for tribute*, was the maxim of our infancy
as a nation. This will be perpetual; but a wiser one will be, never
to ask, or seek for that power, that will make other nations tributary to us, except, through the medium of a liberal reciprocity in

commerce. That nation is hated, however much it may be feared, who domineers over another from the mere consciousness of power; and that nation despised, that succumbs, while it can maintain its existence and independence by any sacrifices whatever. We must not be too impatient for greatness; we are indeed apt to be so, for we have witnessed what no other nation has before seen, a people grow as rapidly into wealth and power as an enterprising individual ever did. Other nations have waited for centuries, for what we have experienced in the course of half a human life, a fourfold increase. The growth of the navy of our mother country, has been slow, compared with ours,* but in truth no comparison exists. They made their navy for self-existence, and for an extension of power; ours grew out of a spirit of independence, and will we trust be maintained for the same glorious principle. But if all the ships we now own, were sunk in the ocean, and every navy officer with them, gallant, skilful, and intelligent as they are, the American navy would not be destroyed. The navy exists in the hearts and wills of the people; and in the event of its destruction, it would be recreated as certain as the existence of the nation; all prejudices against a navy have been overcome and destroyed forever; and this is sufficient. The permanence of our navy depends on publick opinion, and this is made up irrevocably. The decree of this republick is gone forth; and none but the God of battles can reverse it, and that decree is, *the United States must and shall be a naval power, and her flag shall be respected in every quarter of the globe.* This decree rests on no contingency, no change of party, no particular administration of government; it is incorporated with our *habits*, it is a good share of our *feelings*, and it is, also, a part of our *fame*. A mighty, a growing people, whose impulses are "*thought-executing fires*," and whose settled determination is fate, have lifted their voice, and it must be obeyed.

POSTSCRIPT.

ONE word at parting with my readers, by way of explanation and farewell. It has been said by those who are jealous of our rising greatness, that we dwell on the future, and endeavour to show what we shall be in a century or two to come; forgetting the present and the past;—they will not, I trust, charge me with taking this course; for mine certainly has been a different one. The past, almost exclusively, has occupied my attention in these pages, offered to my

---

* See Appendix, Note E.

countrymen. Among the poets, I have mentioned only two living ones, except by some slight allusion to those who are around me, when it could not fairly be avoided, and these two I have named belong to another age. Among the orators, I remember only one of the living of whom I have given an account, and the same remark would apply to him; and if I have slightly trespassed on this rule, in regard to writers of history and matters of taste, it was only to direct the youthful mind to such works as I thought proper sources of information. Among the painters, I have noticed but one among the living, and for doing this I will not ask forgiveness until the reader has considered that subject; not now; but what a galaxy of distinguished painters, who are in active life, and "buying golden opinions of all sorts of men," are now before me, my countrymen, and some of them my personal friends, that I might have named, and found it delightful to have exhibited, to borrow a phrase from the art itself, in the best lights I was master of. The engravers too, who, with us, have lately sprung up, but whose works are of a high order of genius, would have filled many a page, if justice had been done them, but have scarcely been mentioned in gross; although for them too I was prepared to say something in particular. On our living orators, and I have, perhaps, heard as many of them speak as any one of their admirers, volumes might be written; all these things, and many more, which make up our national mental affluence, I have passed over at present, in order to say, as much as I had leisure to say, of the past—that past which should be dear to us all, not merely because it is the past, but because it was filled up with many great men, and some good things. I have said that I cherished the hope of seeing my book, in some not far distant day, in the hands of school children, in a cheap and proper edition for their use. If my book has errours —and what book is without them?—and particularly one that in this way treats of historical events—What better place can there be to correct these errours, than under the eye of a shrewd instructor, who detects them.

It may be said that all school books should be written with the utmost simplicity, and no words, but such as are strictly household, should be found in them. This may hold good for books intended for very young children; but most certainly, the upper classes of our common schools are capable of understanding any historical subject, in whatever style it may be written. The study of etymology should keep pace with other studies; and words, for whose definitions we resort to the dictionary in the school-room, are remembered with more certainty and accuracy, (for the truth of this remark, I appeal to the experience of every scholar,) than those we occasionally make ourselves acquainted with in a later period of life.

A habit of correct spelling is never learnt, unless it be a matter of memory from elementary instruction; and it is in some measure true as to the signification of words. *It is a great errour in education to underrate the capacities of youth.* It is not many years ago that algebra was thought to be too severe a study for minds not arrived at a good degree of maturity; and now males and females at fourteen, are often well versed in the science.

I cannot quit this subject, without insisting most strenuously on the propriety of introducing the history of our country, in every proper shape and form, into our publick schools. It may be sometimes in a condensed form, at others, in an extended one; and so often diversified that facts and principles should be lastingly impressed on the minds of the rising generations. It is essentially wrong to commence the history of our own country after we have finished that of other countries; we may then with profit and pride review our history, but it should be read first of all. Would not a mother think the instructor beside himself, who would advise her to teach her child the ancient, or foreign languages, before he began to lisp his vernacular? And is it not equally wrong for him to study the geography and history of all the rest of the world, before he begins to think of his own? An intelligent Englishman once remarked to the writer, that he was astonished to find so many persons in the United States, so well acquainted with British history; and yet, so entirely unable to give an extended, or a minute account of their own. I find but few, (said he) that are not quite at home in our history up to the Saxon heptarchy, but I can get but little out of them respecting your affairs, no further back than the revolution; and this, (he added) I have considered as pretty good evidence that in every thing but political feeling, which is most truly sufficiently opposed to us, you are colonies still; and is not the inference a fair one? When your children and full grown scholars know more of our king and nobility, and our speeches in parliament, than they do about your own politicians, savans and literati? The answer to this was, if we know much of you, we know more of distant countries and ancient history, and would not your reasoning make us colonies of Egypt, Greece, or Rome, as well as of England? If the inference was wrong, the satire was not the less biting, for the facts on which it was founded were nevertheless fairly stated. This errour, however, is not one that originated with us, we have it by direct inheritance; our fathers brought it with them, and it has continued with us ever since. Many a learned Englishman, both now and in former times, could give a better description of every inch of classical ground, than he could of the mountains of Scotland and Wales, and tell you more about the caverns at Delphos than of the

mines of Cornwall, or turn more readily to a page of Strabo than of
Guthrie : but it is of little consequence from whence this errour in
education arose, if it is only acknowledged to be one ; for then it
will not take long to correct it.   It is not to narrow the circle of
information that I strive to induce my countrymen to make our
own affairs the centre of that circle ; do this, and then extend them
as far as you please ; to embrace all countries, and ages, and all
forms of human knowledge.   A youth bred at home, becomes familiar with all in his village, and the country around ; his heart
and memory never forget a single circumstance of his boyhood ;
his fishing, skating, and even his truant frolicks, all become en-
deared to him in after life from the charm of retrospection.   His
early associations are forever fresh ; the farther he is off, the dearer
his early associations ; his heart, untravelled, fondly turns to the
scenes of his childhood ; and he contemplates them when he wishes
to forget other scenes and many unpleasant events ; but had he
been educated abroad from his infancy, passed the bloom of his
youth in Greece and Italy, had then travelled into Asia, and had in
manhood come back to the abodes of his forefathers, would not the
gable ends, the Lutheran windows, and the low rooms of the paternal mansion, seem tasteless and almost vulgar ?   What aunt would he
think of ?   What cousin or her blooming children would he inquire for ?
He would hardly ask how long his grandfather had been dead, or if the
parish church stood in the same place it did when he went away ?
And I ask if the same process, on a larger scale, is not going on in the
mind of the youth, as it regards our country and her history, if he be
permitted to begin his education by looking to remote antiquity for
instruction and pleasure, and if not there, to those countries whose
institutions are of early date, and whose fame is the growth of a
thousand years ?   What to the boy are the tame and common place
things of life after he has become familiar with the romance of
early history, if his heart had not been previously secured by
the sweet affections of the domestick circle ?   Rivet his soul to them
first, and, true as the needle to the pole, his yearnings will be for
home, even in the palaces of the Cæsars ; and while viewing the
dome of St. Peters, on a grand festival, he will think of the village
church, where he commingled the love of his dear mother with
reverence for his God ; and perhaps there the beatings of his heart,
as a susceptible and an enamoured being, were first made known to
himself.   Secure the morning vow of the votary for his country,
and every prayer, and vigil, and oath, and sacrifice, will be hers
during his life.

APPENDIX.

Note A.

In 1731, the British merchants sent to the governors of all the provinces for a statement of their commerce, manufactures, &c. &c. Several of the governors answered the merchants to the best of their information upon the subject; but in the New-England states the business of manufacturing many useful articles had been so far extended as to excite the jealousy of the mother country, and a full development of their progress, most evidently, was not made. This famous report of the British merchants was signed by Paul Dockminique, and dated February 15th, 1731—2, and contains no small quantity of information. His report states that Virginia and Maryland together exported annually to Britain, sixty thousand hogsheads of tobacco, weighing six hundred pounds each; besides furs, skins, and some few other articles. Pennsylvania had a most flourishing commerce in provisions, and New-York had nearly the whole command of the fur trade. New-Jersey had considerable commerce at this time, and great expectations were raised on the copper mines. New-England had then a great trade, for then she was the carrier of the other provinces as well as of her own goods. Ship-building was brisk, and the French and Spaniards were ready purchasers. She had then more than forty thousand tons of shipping actually employed. The lumber trade was extensive—the masts, spars, &c. of the British navy were found in this country, as one of our poets, soon after this time, has said, in speaking of England—

> "The stately mast that bears their flag on high,
> Grew in our soil, and ripened in our sky."

At this period, Massachusetts had six furnaces and nineteen forges for making hollow ware, and for casting small cannon, bombs, shot, &c. for the supply of the demands of the militia and naval force

2 B   37

in privateers, &c.   Nails were made in considerable quantities, particularly those of a large kind.   The fisheries of New-England were very great at this time.   In the year 1732, the town of Marblehead alone had one hundred and twenty schooners engaged in the cod fishery, and made a hundred and twenty thousand quintals. This was a fortunate year, for there was a profound peace in Europe that year, or no war that extended to the Atlantick.   For several years afterwards the business fell off; and, in fact, all commerce suffered a long time, insomuch that I presume the account given by Douglass, twenty years afterwards, of the entrances and clearances, will fall short of the amount at the close of the first century—say 1731, for this was about a century from the time they got well fixed in their residences in Salem, Boston, and a few other places in the province of Massachusetts Bay.   At the close of the first century, the whale fishing had reached a considerable magnitude, and the fame of our harpooners was known in England.   The adventurous whalemen went off in small vessels for their game; and a single whale they killed often weighed more tons than their schooner measured.

The shipping of New-Hampshire, from December 25, 1747, to December 25, 1748, including only vessels engaged in foreign voyages, was as follows:—cleared out, one hundred and twenty-one; entered, seventy-three.   In addition to these, there were about two hundred coasting sloops and schooners engaged in the lumber trade to Boston and elsewhere along the coast.

The entrances and clearances from Newport, from the 25th of March, 1748, to 25th of March, 1749, were, entered seventy-five vessels of different sizes—cleared out, one hundred and sixty.   They had grown rich by privateering and driving the West India trade.

At the same period, Connecticut had less commerce; thirty-seven vessels were entered at the custom-house, and sixty-two cleared.

The commerce of New-York, from the 29th of September, 1749, to 29th of September, 1750, was entered two hundred and thirty-three vessels, including coasters—cleared out, two hundred and eighty, of the same description.   That of Massachusetts was much larger.   From the two custom-houses in Massachusetts, from December 28, 1747, to December 28, 1748, there were five hundred and forty vessels cleared out, and four hundred and thirty entered.   The commerce of New-Jersey was, at this period, considerable; from June 24, 1750, to June 24, 1751, at the custom-house at Perth Amboy, there were forty-one vessels entered, and thirty-eight cleared out. At this period Pennsylvania was, although a much younger settlement than those around her, in a most flourishing condition; from March 2, 1748-9, to Christmas of the same year, there were three hundred and three entries of vessels of considerable size, and two hundred and ninety-one clearances, and there were then thirty-nine vessels of considerable size in the harbour of Philadelphia, nineteen of which were ships.

These particulars might be extended, with a little research, but I have not the leisure to do it.

Note B.

I have often repeated, that as a nation we have done but little for the illustrious dead of our country. The extent of our territory is one great cause of our neglect in this subject; we cannot have a Westminster Abbey for statesmen, heroes, and poets, or historians; these men die too far apart to be gathered in the same cemetery; but what the nation has done, however small it may be, should be mentioned. In the plan of the city of Washington, the government appropriated about ten acres of land to a national burying ground, on the eastern branch of the Potomack, or rather went into partnership with the owners of the soil for this purpose; for there the private and publick dead rest in republican simplicity together. It is a good site for tombs; on the north-east corner are to be found the graves of the publick characters who have died at Washington since 1800. There are about twenty-two or three members of Congress, two vice-presidents, and several officers of the army and navy buried there. The monuments of the members of Congress, are plinths of about five feet square on the ground; on this rests what is properly the monumental stone, about three feet high; on this is placed a pediment coming bluntly to an apex. A very simple inscription, giving but little more than the birth, death, and, perhaps, dates of service of the deceased, is all that is found on them, or all that stay the traveller; (and every traveller is a visiter of a grave-yard by immemorial usage.) Some of these sleeping politicians were men of mind, of eloquence, of patriotism, of learning, and should be remembered; but the space any single individual ordinarily occupies in society is soon filled up after he is gone, particularly in a republican government. This is right.

These tomb-stones of the deceased members of Congress, are shaped like the cinerary urns of the ancients, which were generally placed in the niches in the walls of the sepulchral chambers of those wonderful edifices, which in early ages were erected for the resting place of the dead.

Two vice-presidents of the United States are tenants of this burial ground in Washington: George Clinton and Elbridge Gerry: they

died in office in the city. The monument of Gerry was erected by
Congress, and if the critical artist finds some fault with it, as a subject of classical taste, still he must acknowledge that, as a whole, it
is equal to any thing of the kind in our country. It is about six
and a half feet square at the base, and about fifteen feet in height;
the die diminishes as it rises, and is empannelled; on the die rests
a truncated pyramid, and on this is a multipod, intended for an ancient tripod, and this is surmounted by a sepulchral lamp. The
whole appearance is good, and the finishings are beautiful. The
epitaph is composed of a few dates, and a pithy sentence from some
of his works. The monument erected to the memory of Clinton,
is in a more severe style of the art. The shape and size of the
monument is nearly the same, except that the die does not diminish
as it rises, and the pyramid is brought to a regular point; this is
crowned with an iron hour-glass, which is in bad taste. it was a
wide stretch of the imagination, to take the lamp from the sepulchre
and place it on the apex of the mausoleum, but this was somewhat
disguised in marble; but when the conceit of time's giving up to
eternity, is shown in naked iron, in the form of a broken hour-glass,
the effect is not good. The epitaph on this monument is something
longer than on Mr. Gerry's; but it is not remarkable for any thing
but modesty. The ornaments of the work are a basso-relievo head
of Mr. Clinton, and not an indifferent likeness; the Roman fasces,
the caduceus, and the cross-swords; emblems of civil, political, and
military functions. Both of these men were patriots of the revolution, and filled a wide space in the eyes of their countrymen.
Near these are other monuments, erected to the memory of the
officers of the navy and army, in good taste. Major General Brown
lies in a small enclosure, with a very small head-stone, with this
inscription, *"Major General Brown."* Near him, a very neat
monument erected by order of the king of Prussia, to his deceased
minister, Frederick Grehum, who died in this country, in 1823.
Among the most striking of this monumental cluster, is one erected
to the memory of a Choctaw chief, *Push-ma-ta-ha.* It holds a sort
of middle space between the monuments of the vice-presidents and
the members of Congress. The inscription is worthy of note.

"PUSH-MA-TA-HA,

a

Choctaw Chief,

lies here.

This monument to his memory is erected

by his brother chiefs,

who were associated with him

in a
Delegation
from their nation,
in the year 1824, to the
general government
of the
United States."

On the reverse is the following:

"Push-ma-ta-ha was a warrior
of great distinction.
He was wise in council,
eloquent in an extraordinary degree;
and on all occasions,
and under all circumstances,
the white man's friend.
He died in Washington,
on the 24th of December, 1824,
of the cramp, in the
60th year of his age."

Amongst his last words
were the following:
"When I am gone, let the big guns
be fired over me."

This son of the forest had caught something of civilization. His nation were among the first to cultivate the ground on an extensive scale. They knew something of the value of letters, and began to see that there were surer methods of gaining immortality than by trusting to a misshapen mound, or a short-lived tradition. Push-ma-ta-ha fearlessly departed, and the big guns were fired as a farewell to the shade of *the warrior and the white man's friend.*

While my mind was on this subject of doing honour to the dead, I came across the following elegant description of a tomb, which I copy because the work from which it is taken is rare, and will not probably ever be common. It is from *Lieutenant Colonel Forrest's Picturesque Tour up the Jumna and Ganges, and through various parts of India.* Not that I ask of my countrymen to build such a one even for Washington; but I quote it to show how much others have done to venerate the dead, and to provide a sepulchre for themselves.

"The object which now calls our attention is the last in order, but

2 B 2

of the highest beauty and interest of any structure yet raised and perfected by man in any region of the earth. It is only a tomb, it is true, and contains the mouldering remains of what was noble, powerful, and beautiful; all these have passed away; but their names, their fame, their deeds remain; and these works promise to hand down to distant ages their well-earned renown.

This tomb, the mausoleum of the emperor, Shah Jehan and his favourite queen, Moomtaz ul Zemani, (or Wonder of the Age,) still exists, and in all its pristine beauty and perfection. Time, with his efforts for a period of two hundred years, has as yet scarcely cast one sullying stain on its pure and lovely mass.

The first approach to this wonderful work by no means gives an idea of the splendid scene which is to be encountered; the road is impeded and the eye bewildered by the ruins of old brick and stone buildings, said to have once been a *serai*, or place for the accommodation of travellers, or more probably pilgrims who came to visit this monument.

The main gateway is seen after passing these ruins; it faces nearly south, and is constructed with the red stone, but ornamented in pannels of rich Mosaick in various parts. It is a massive and lofty pile, and has apartments in its upper part, which can be ascended by a staircase, and from whence is a fine view of the tomb. This building is an octagon, and after passing under its grand portal, a scene bursts at once upon the eye, which dazzles the senses, and wraps every other feeling in that of astonishment. The Taje appears embosomed in a mass of foliage of a deep green at the further extremity of a large and handsome garden, with its lofty and elegant minarets, and its dome of extreme beauty and airy lightness; the whole of the purest white marble, richly inlaid in patterns of the semiprecious stones, as cornelian, jasper, onyx, and a variety of others of all hues.

A noble causeway of stone, raised considerably above the level of the garden, leads up to the main building, in the centre of which is a range of fountains, fifty in number; and midway a large basin, in which five other *jets-d'eau* of much greater height are thrown up.

The garden is filled with trees of almost every kind common to India; some bearing fruits, others perfuming the air with the odoriferous scents of their blossoms.

The Taje stands on two terraces; the lower and largest of an oblong shape, is composed wholly of red stone; this is ascended by a flight of steps, and on reaching the summit, a large mosque is perceived at each end of it, which in any other situation than so close to their lovely companion, would be considered as noble and splendid edifices. These may be ascended, and from their upper apartments command good views of the main building.

To the second or upper terrace, which has a height of about fifteen feet, you ascend by a flight of white marble steps; of these the upper slab, or landing place, is one piece of pure white marble, nine feet square. This upper terrace is floored with a chequered pavement of white and red. Upon this stands the tomb, surrounded by a marble balustrade; at each angle of which rises a graceful minaret of three stories, in sweet proportions. At each story is a door, which opens on a balustraded balcony surrounding it. That summit is finished by a light pavilion, with a small golden ornament on its top.

All that now presents itself to the eye of the spectator is pure, unsullied, white marble, variously ornamented. The entrance to the building is on the side opposite to the grand gateway. It is a lofty portico, with an arch partaking of the form of the gothick order, but differing in its proportions. Round the upper part of this are inscriptions in Arabick, done in black marble on the white ground.

Previous to viewing the grand chamber, where the cenotaphs of the emperor and his queen are placed, it is usual to descend by a trap-door, situated in the entrance, into a gradually sloping passage, which conducts to the graves of the royal dead. The vault is lined with marble, and the pavement is of the same material. In the centre is the grave of the queen, for whom this mausoleum was solely intended; and the emperor's design was to have erected a similar edifice on the opposite bank of the Jumna, which river washes the foot of the Taje Mahal, and has a breadth of five or six hundred yards. The magnificent monarch did not mean to rest here; he meditated the joining of the two mausoleums by a marble bridge, ornamented in the same splendid manner. Civil wars, caused by the rebellion of his four sons, suspended and finally put an end to these magnificent projects; and after a variety of sufferings, this unfortunate prince died in his prison, in the fort of Agra, where he was held captive for seven years, by his son Aurungzebe, then reigning emperor of Hindoostan.

Returning to the light of day, we entered the centre chamber. Description must here fail, nor can imagination figure any thing so solemnly grand, so stilly beautiful, as the scene thus suddenly presented to the view. Every tongue is mute, every sense lost in admiration. There are no gaudy, glaring decorations to arrest the vulgar eye; no glittering gold or silver to mark the riches of India's monarch. There is an awe, a feeling of deep reverence for the sacred spot on which we tread; an involuntary pause, a breathless suspension, and a recollection of, and recurrence to, events long passed, which this scene conjures up in the breast of all who witness it for the first time.

Imagine a vaulted dome, of considerable height, of the most elegant and light Gothick architecture, all composed of the finest and the whitest marble; its form octagonal. In the centre stands a screen of the same, wrought into the most lovely patterns in fret work, showing a freedom of design and extreme minuteness of execution, unequalled in this or perhaps any other country. The form of this screen corresponds with that of the apartment, an octagon with four larger and four lesser faces. At each angle are two pilasters, on which the most beautiful running patterns of various flowers, true to nature, rise from the base of this screen, while a broad and rich border of the same surrounds the upper part. There are two arched doorways in this screen, opposite to each other, and over the top of which is a rich pattern of a stone perfectly resembling the purest matt gold. An entablature of the richest pattern surrounds the upper part of the screen; and in a border of pomegranate flowers, which runs the whole length of it, every full-blown flower contains no less than sixty-one pieces of various coloured stones, according to the different shades required, and joined with such exactness and extreme nicety, that with a sharp pointed penknife no seam can be distinguished. Within this screen are the two cenotaphs, on which the sculptor and Mosaick artist have lavished all their skill. These are blocks of marble, and apparently one stone, ten feet in length by six broad. Below and above this are larger slabs, forming the pediment and cornice. A rich and large pattern is on the four faces of the cenotaphs, the two differing from each other; and the upper tablet on the queen's tomb has a cluster of flowers, arranged in the most elegant and free style of design; while that of the emperor is surrounded by the *kullum daun*, the distinguishing sign for a man, the woman not having this ornament. This screen had gates of silver in open filigree work, which were carried off by some of the invaders of India. This tomb is not altogether the work or design of artists of Hindoostan. I have seen a list of the names of all the master masons, sculptors, and artisans; the greater part are from Persia, Cabul, and some even from Constantinople, or Turkey, called by the Indians *Roum*.

Some traces of similar inlaying and Mosaick are met with at Delhi and in the palace at Agra; but the art is now lost, if it ever existed, among the Hindoostanees; and this tends to confirm the idea that it was the work of foreign artists.

The main part of this splendid edifice has fortunately been respected by all the invaders of Hindoostan, its great beauty being probably its protection. It is as pure and perfect as the day it was finished; and with common care, in the equal climate in which it is situated, it may last for centuries.

"With the description of this wonder of the world, the tour of the author closes. He is well aware that some errours may possibly be found in it; but these are almost inseparable from a work written, as this was, while moving rapidly through a country in which the subjects worthy of notice are so numerous and so widely scattered, that some, too many indeed, must be unavoidably passed unnoticed and unseen. As to the views, they are faithful copies from nature, in which no alterations have been made."

NOTE C.

TABLE *of the Number of Cadets who have entered and left the Military Academy, from its Organization to September 2, 1828.*

	Number Admitted.	Number Commissioned.	Resigned.	Discharged.	Died.	Remaining.
Maine	20	3	6	2		9
New-Hampshire	30	17	6	2		9
Massachusetts	91	53	32	3	2	12
Connecticut	39	27	9	1		8
Rhode-Island	14	5	4	2		4
Vermont	48	38	8	3	2	4
New-York	218	107	69	29	3	32
New-Jersey	30	14	10	3		7
Pennsylvania	110	42	43	17	2	26
Delaware	18	6	7	2		4
Maryland	75	31	29	11	1	12
Virginia	140	49	63	24	1	20
North Carolina	62	18	30	7	1	13
South Carolina	50	21	27	3		7
Georgia	31	8	13	2	2	9
Kentucky	59	16	22	11		17
Tennessee	39	10	15	7	3	8
Ohio	44	15	13	7	1	14
Indiana	14	5	6	2		4
Louisiana	11	4	4	2		3
Alabama	8	2	2	3		3
Mississippi	9	4	4			2
Illinois	7	2	1	2		3
Missouri	14	8	5	2		1
Michigan	6	3	2			2
Arkansas	2		1	1		1
England	1	1				
Florida	3		1			
District of Columbia	61	24	27	5	2	5
Not designated	35	1	18	9		
	1,289	540	477	162	20	239

NOTE D.

On the entrance to the navy-yard there is a monument erected to the memory of Wadsworth, Israel, Decatur, and others, who fell before Tripoli, while fighting our naval battles, and earning immortality for our navy. This monument is worthy of description. It stands within a curb-stone circle, about twenty-five feet in diameter; the plinth is about fifteen feet square; on this is a pile of dark granite, about four and a half feet high; on this, as a base, is a marble sub-plinth, and on that a die of three and a half feet square, and on this a column of ten feet high, surmounted by the national eagle. The column is enriched by emblematick designs that are full of classical history, but rather difficult to be read at a glance. On the south side is a representation of the fleet before Tripoli. On the opposite side there are appropriate records of the feats of the American navy at this period. On the four corners of the granite mass, stands four antique lamps in full blaze. The lamp is the most classical of the utensils of modern use; their antiquity is beyond all record. In the early ages they were classed as follows: *sacred, publick, domestick*, and *sepulchral*. The latter now burns only in marble, while taste and fashion have taken possession of all kinds of them, and rededicated them to the household gods, and added to them the hydrostatick and the astral. The lamp has a glorious origin; it was forged by Vulcan, supplied with oil by Minerva, and lighted up by Prometheus, as described in the beautiful fables of Greece. It is in vain to question ancient taste; the homage of the present age is constantly paid to the taste and genius of the ancients; for in spite of all the boast of modern invention, there is not a single trace of all these tributes to the dead that belongs to modern times.

On the corners of the first marble floor of this monument, stands emblematical figures; on the north-east corner is Mercury with his rod; on the south-east is Neptune—commonly taken for the genius of our country; but then it must be remembered, that other nations have claims to the same genius;—he wears a sea-weed crown, and points to an emblem of history, who is quietly on the other corner with her sketch book. The whole work is light and airy; and when carefully read is full of poetry; and if not of an epick cast, most certainly it has much in it of a beautiful dirge. The marble of this monument is fine, and some of the chiselling is exquisite. It was executed in Italy, and by some of the first masters. There is in this, and some other monuments brought from Italy, a mixture of pure classical taste, and of modern design, that makes it difficult to read them correctly; and if we do get at a right construction, they must sometimes be as incongruous as the labours of the artist, who, in a full length figure of Napoleon, gave him a cocked hat with Roman sandals. This union presents a thousand difficult points of taste. Even Chantry did not venture to make Washington a Roman consul; but shaped a modern military cloak into a consular robe. This has been ably defended; and, as Sir Roger de Coverly says, much may be said on both sides. Give us good specimens of execution, for design is more a matter of imagination; these are easily corrected.

NOTE E.

NAVY OF THE UNITED STATES, 1828.

Ships of the Line.—7.	GUNS.		Sloops of War.—12.	GUNS.	
Independence	74	In ordinary.	Hornet	18	In commission.
Franklin	do	do	Erie	do	do
Washington	do	do	Ontario	do	do
Columbus	do	do	Peacock	do	do
Ohio	do	do	Boston	do	do
North Carolina	do	do	Lexington	do	do
Delaware	do	Commiss'n.	Vincennes	do	do
			Warren	do	do
Frigates, 1st Class.—6.			Natchez	do	do
United States	44	Ordinary.	Fairfield	do	do
Constitution	do	do	Vandalia	do	do
Guerriere	do	Commiss'n.	St. Louis	do	do
Java	do	do			
Potomack	do	Ordinary.	Schooners.—7.		
Brandywine	do	Commiss'n.	Dolphin	12	Commiss'n.
			Grampus	do	do
2d Class.—4.			Porpoise	do	do
Congress	36	Ordinary.	Shark	do	do
Constellation	do	do	Fox	3	Ordinary.
Macedonian	do	Commiss'n.	Alert (store ship)		do
Fulton (steam)	do	Ordinary.	Sea Gull (galliot)		do
Corvettes, 3d Class—2.					
John Adams	24	do			
Cyane	do	do			

NOTE. We have five ships of the line on the stocks, and several smaller ones. The Hudson frigate, a 44, has been purchased, and since put in commission.

Rise of the British Navy. Henry VII. 1485.—Built the Great Harry, cost £14,000. This was, properly speaking, the first ship of the royal navy. Burnt by accident, 1554.

Henry VIII. 1509.—The Regent, the largest ship in the navy, was of 1000 tons. Burnt in fight, August, 1512. This king fixed the wages of seamen at 5s. per month. Queen Elizabeth raised them to 10s.

In 1521, the navy consisted of 45 ships. In 1545, it contained 100 ships. Laws made for planting and preserving timber. Dock yards founded at Deptford, Woolwich, and Portsmouth; also the Trinity House. At the king's death, in 1547, tonnage of the whole navy, 12,445.

	Year.	Vessels.	Tonnage.	Guns.	Men.
Edward VI.	1548	53	11,268		
Mary	1553	24	7,110		
Elizabeth, 1558,	1565	29	10,506		6,570
	1588	34	12,590		6,279
	1599	42			
	1602	42	17,055		8,346

The expense of the navy, about £30,000 per annum.

James	1607	36	14,710		8,174

Expense £50,000 per annum, exclusive of timber from the royal forests, £36,000 per annum.

	1618	39	15,100		
	1624	33	19,400		
Charles I.	1633	50	23,695	1434	9,470
Commonwealth	1652	102			
	1658	157		4390	21,910
Charles II.	1660	154	54,463		

Expenses per annum, £500,000.

	1675	151	70,587		
	1678	148	69,004	5350	30,260
	1685	179	103,558		
James II.	1688	173	101,892	6930	42,003
William and Mary	1697	323			
	1698	266			
Anne	1706	277			
	1711	313			
	1714	247	167,219		
George I.	1724	233	170,862		
George II.	1742	271			
	1753	291	234,924		
	1756	320			
George III.	1760	412	321,104		
	1783	617	500,781		
	1801	864			
	1805	949			

A SELECTIVE INDEX

So "interspersed with free and particular remarks" (p. 34) is the superstructure of these Lectures that it is not always visible through the sometimes unrelated minutiae. Some of Knapp's remarks were so "free" that it was not possible to arrive at a certain identification of a last name (occasionally misspelled) or a vague misquoted title. An effort has been made, however, to identify the significant items and to give them in correct form in this index.

Knapp's detailed table of contents, pages 5 through 8, which provides a good indication of the scope of Knapp's work, is not indexed here. Items included fall into four categories: (1) all American names; (2) all American literary works which it was possible to identify; (3) the names of British men whose activities or writings have strongly influenced American life; (4) certain subjects and areas which seem to be closely related to the author's purpose. When it was needed and available, certain pertinent information such as publication dates and identification remarks are given in parentheses after an item.